THE AUTOBIOGRAPHY

OF

JOHANN WOLFGANG VON GOETHE

Translated by

John Oxenford

And with an Introduction by

Karl J. Weintraub

VOLUME ONE

The University of Chicago Press
Chicago and London

When first published, Goethe's autobiography carried the title *Aus meinem Leben: Dichtung und Wahrheit*. As pointed out in the Introduction to the present edition, however, the work has commonly been known by the subtitle alone, *Dichtung und Wahrheit*.

The University of Chicago Press, Chicago 60637
The University of Chicago Press, Ltd., London

Phoenix edition published 1974
Printed in the United States of America
88 87 86 85 84 83 82 81   2 3 4 5 6

ISBN: 0-226-30057-9 (vol. 1), 0-226-30058-7 (vol. 2)
Library of Congress Catalog Card Number: 74-10339

CONTENTS

v

PART TWO
Was man in der Jugend wünscht,
hat man im Alter die Fülle.
What youth desires,
old age brings it in abundance.—GOETHE

INTRODUCTION

Karl J. Weintraub

Great books may have strange fates. The book in the reader's hand is possibly the finest autobiography ever written. It is the work of one of the very great writers of the Western world. For anyone in the German-speaking part of that world it is a readily available classic, both loved and revered. But for anyone in the English-speaking world it has become a strangely unknown text, most difficult to obtain. One can gather a fabulous library of the world's classic books in economically printed editions; if anyone wants to read this autobiography in English, he must borrow the book or spend more than twenty dollars—if indeed he finds it in print at all. Assigning the book in courses has meant lately that students have to beg the use of the text from, what one hopes are, the proud possessors who took the course in years past. Yet this is not a difficult, esoteric book; it is not a product of an alien Teutonic mind from which Anglo-Saxon sanity may turn with indifference. It is not a culturally encapsulated book, open only to those within that culture. As the history of earlier editions testifies, it once was much more readily available in the English-speaking world. It is not even such an untranslatable classic as Dante's *Divine Comedy*. While Goethe's poetry is indeed difficult to capture in English, the wise humanity embedded in his writing is not lost in prose translation even if the refined verbal artistry is damaged. This still very readable translation by John Oxenford has existed since 1848. It is, in its way, a witness to an earlier interest in Goethe throughout the English-speaking world;

an interest to which Carlyle's enthusiasm, the essays by Emerson, Bancroft, Matthew Arnold, and the once very influential biography by George Henry Lewes (George Eliot's companion), also testify.

The Oxenford translation of *Dichtung und Wahrheit* is now made available in this paperback edition.* Why indeed should a publisher assume this task? It is easy to argue that publishers have a cultural obligation for keeping the classical works of world literature in print. But beyond this there are some special reasons for placing this particular book in more hands.

Autobiography has become a particularly significant form of expression for us moderns. The sheer volume of autobiographic writing since roughly 1800 attests to this significance. The reasons for such interest lie deep in our culture. Through millennia of complex developments Western man has come to place an exceptionally high premium on the ideal of the autonomous personality and on self-fulfillment as a life task. At the same time, and by reason of other, equally complex developments, this commitment to the high value of personal life stands in everlasting tension with other such valued elements of our culture as the orderliness of reason, the rational dictates of science, the "purpose-rationality" of industrial capitalism, bureaucratic efficiency, expert professionalism, and national egalitarian solidarity. The more these leveling forces press upon us, the more we cling to the ideal of personality as a countervailing power. Autobiography is the genre best suited for accounting to oneself and to the world for the development of the personality. The autobiographic genre came into its own as Western man began to feel a conscious need to justify himself as that specific type of

* The present edition differs from earlier editions in a few minor particulars. Two pieces of Goethe's composition which Oxenford omitted have been restored, in translations prepared especially for this edition. These are the answer to the fictitious letter from a friend which is usually included as a preface to German editions of *Dichtung und Wahrheit* and the brief preface to part 4. Along with the latter, Oxenford also omitted, curiously enough, the heading to part 4 and its Latin epigraph. These too have been restored.

personality we call individuality—that belief in the value of each unique existence as an irreplaceable human form, a one-time-only way of being human, a human specification so highly differentiated that its justification lies exactly in its uniqueness. The more man saw his essential quality in his ineffable individuality, and his life task in being true to such a self, the less he could express himself by adhering to the great didactic models of humanity. It became his felt need to tell his very own story. Autobiography was now a cultural necessity.

Goethe's *Dichtung und Wahrheit* is a particularly important document in this twofold history of the emergence of individuality and of the autobiographic genre. It is, of course, a book with many dimensions, worthy of being read for many reasons. It is superb artistry. It is a wise book in which a man speaks to men in most comforting tones. It is a highly informative history for understanding the making of Germany. Like Dante's *Vita Nuova* it is a book for poets and writers desiring to know how a poet works and how he was formed. But while it possesses all such dimensions, it is first of all an autobiographic account of the formation of a personality, the story of an individual finding and unfolding his individuality. It is *Bildungsgeschichte*, rendering the formative processes of a historical personality—and as such the real-life parallel to Goethe's great *Bildungsroman*, the *Wilhelm Meister*, depicting the very same processes in a fictional setting. Since Goethe saw both the wonder that lay in individuality and the horror that came from following this ideal to excess, he also set the confines in *Dichtung und Wahrheit* within which this particular ideal of self must be contained for modern man.

A few reflections, therefore, on the nature of the autobiographic genre and its innate relation to our self-conception as individuality may serve as the advised introduction to this rich book.

The term *autobiography* says only that the life being written is the writer's own. It is a word of fairly recent coinage, being no older than the late eighteenth century. Used in this broad sense, the word causes confusion. Most lyric poetry has strong autobiographic elements but rarely is autobiography. Goethe knew this when he referred to all his writings, especially his poetry, as "fragments of a great confession." The lyric moment has too little scope for capturing a life. And all the lyric moments strung together still remain momentary fragments. Nor does the day's reflective precipitate that forms the diary escape the limitation of its purpose and inception. A diary, however rich, can be autobiography as little as chronicle can be history. Goethe kept his *Tagebücher* in an entirely different spirit from that in which he wrote *Dichtung und Wahrheit*. He knew that the "incoherent realia of life," entrusted moment by moment to diary entries, lacked the connective tissue demanded by autobiography. Nor is autobiography to be equated with a record of "things done," the classical testimonial of public acts for which the emperor Augustus set the model in his *Res gestae*. Closely related to this is the very widespread genre of the memoir, the record either of the actors in noteworthy events or of the intelligent observers of interesting motions of the external world. Goethe left us such memoirs in his record of the campaign against France in 1792 (*Die Kampagne in Frankreich*) and the siege of Mainz, having accompanied his prince, Karl August of Saxe-Weimar, on these ventures. Memoir separates itself from true autobiography when interest in the events of the world has overcome interest in the inner experience. This line is subtle; it does not always hold, and memoir and autobiography may at times be inseparably intertwined. The difference is validated ultimately in the stance taken by the writer: Is the mind's eye focused on the events for what they are as events? Or is it focused on the meaning of the inward coherence of experience? Autobiography depends to an extraordinary degree on the urge to reflect on this inward realm of experience; it needs a human type for whom this inwardness is important. It approaches its generic potential the more its center is "character," "personality," "self-conception," all those matters which determine the inward coherence of the meaning of a life. Self-consciousness is its connective tissue; interrelated experience is the fine stuff from which it is made. And autobiography differs from biography in that it understands this inward coherence from within, whereas the biographer is put to the task of concluding something from an aggregate of external manifestations about the inner state of the subject. Autobiography proceeds from the invaluable congruence of accumulated experience and interpreted experience, the congruence of writer and subject.

If then genuine autobiography can be separated from the other autobiographic genres, its true subject matter is the formation of a specific personality. How did this man become this very man, and what does it mean to be this man? The task that lies in this is intimately related to the conception of personality to which an individual adheres. When men hold to the great models of being human—and through most of history, and in most civilizations, men have done so—their model furnishes them with the essential script for life. The great ideal personality types—expressed in the Homeric hero, the Stoic wiseman, Aristotle's *aner megalopsychos* (the man with the great soul), the ideal knight, the ideal monk, or, most startling of all, the ideal of the *Imitatio Christi*—are prescriptive ideals upon which men have sought to model their own existence; when a person does so, his autobiography becomes the account of his striving to fulfill the demands of his model. There are given lines along which the plot of a life unfolds, even if there is room for idiosyncrasy; there are given norms by which to assess the success of life; and as lives display similarities to their model, so autobiographies resemble one another also. Only as Western man gradually attaches himself consciously to the belief that every life has its very own meaning, that no lives are interchangeable, that there is indeed no model for man when each person faces the task of fulfilling only his very own specific human potential, only then does autobiography

come truly into its own. For then it suddenly appears that
there is no way to account for the individual life by holding it
against a model; there is no given script into which to fit the
details of experience. Man faces his individuality as a value
to be consciously cultivated. Only by telling his unique story
can he account for himself. When this coincides, as it must,
with losing belief in the divine or the natural assignment of a
given human task, when man wonders whether life has
indeed a predetermined meaning or only the meaning men
give it when they assign meaning to their individual lives,
then the ground is prepared in which autobiography as "a
meaning-interpreting function" can thrive.

Such preconditions existed during the first decade of the
nineteenth century, when Goethe first undertook the autobiographic task. Born in 1749, he was then approaching his
sixtieth year. A rich literary production lay behind him; he
was the revered literary figure of Germany even if the
younger generation of romantic writers began to rebel
against the dominance he represented simply by being there
at Weimar forever active in new work. A new edition of his
"collected works" was in the offing and suggestions were
made that it should be accompanied by a life of the poet so
that understanding of the works might be enriched by insights into the circumstances of their genesis. In many respects Goethe was opposed to the idea; he thought it perverse
to expect a poet to explain what he had already said in the
highest form open to him. Yet he also knew himself to be a
poet whose best work was the elevation of very specific
moments of experience to that "second level of life" which is
its poetic reformulation; an account of their circumstances
might indeed enrich understanding. That same decade had
also broken many of the ties to his past, for death had taken
his mother (1808), the old grandduchess of Weimar, Anna
Amalia (1807), the irreplaceable literary confidant Schiller
(1805), and the slightly estranged older mentor Herder
(1803). A highly significant portion of life lay back there in
greater detachment, whereas many of the new tendencies

with which Goethe felt out of tune, and the convulsions of the revolutionary and Napoleonic ages, strengthened his sense that this eighteenth-century world in which he had been formed could and should be assessed for its value. Occasional biographic tasks, especially the work on the great art historian Winckelmann and the lesser painter Philipp Hackert, underlined Goethie's belief that it was important for the youths of the day to learn about the value of their forefathers' world. The work on Hackert, moreover, evoked memories of the times they had spent together in Italy, and the moment came when Goethe asked himself why, indeed, he should work on such a figure when he himself had so much to tell about that very same world. Shortly before her death, his mother had confided many childhood stories of her boy to the eager listener Bettina von Arnim, the wife of the poet Achim von Arnim. After Bettina had given these stories to Goethe, he began to take delight in regaling his household and table guests with more and more of his own recollections. By 1810 what had seemed a less pleasant chore of having to fill a publisher's request had indeed turned into a challenge in which Goethe took ever more delight and interest. And for the next few years he became absorbed in writing of his former life.

But how was this to be done? Throughout the preparatory phase Goethe made occasional observations, either to his amanuensis Riemer or by recording them directly, suggesting careful consideration of the peculiar demands of such a genre.

Historical work as such had its peculiar problems for Goethe. Although he read a great deal of history, he rarely had much good to say about historians or about their conception of their task. The reader of *Dichtung und Wahrheit* will note numerous passages revealing Goethe's strong feelings for the presence of the past in his own life; one of the most extraordinary scenes, in this regard, being the visit to Jabach's house in Cologne, described on pages 258–60 of volume 2 in this edition. (One of the peculiarities of Oxenford's translation is that he turns this name into *Jappach*.)

Goethe there gives expression to man's most fundamental awareness of "the historical": "a sense of the past and present together in one,—a phenomenon which brought something spectral [*etwas Gespenstermässiges*] into the present." This sense of mystery concerning the uncanny contact with past reality he valued highly; but it had value only insofar as it was a living part of an individual experience. Whenever this point of live contact was not strong, Goethe abhorred the sepulchral miasma clinging to history. He thus deemed it the historian's task to re-enliven, in the context of a concrete human life, that of the past which had been alive in the lived experience. The biographical was to be the true historical center where human worlds come together in the lived experience of concrete men; the histories of "forces" or "mere events" lacked meaning. Goethe, as historian, was thus by conviction and sentiment predisposed to biography. A good part of the work into which he had been drawn in his sixth decade was of a historical nature: the work on Winckelmann, on Hackert, and, above all, the historical part of his extensive book on the theory of color. The focus was always on the experience and thought of human beings.

Goethe came to his autobiographic work by having reflected on the nature of biography. There is a clear reminder of this in his answer to the fictitious letter of the preface. In this answer Goethe defined the biographical task as though it were the task of writing his own life. "For the principal task of biography, I believe, is to present a man in the conditions of his time, and to show to what extent those conditions, taken as a whole, thwart him or favor him, how he forms from it all a view of the world and of man, and how, if he is an artist, a poet, or a writer, he then takes that view and projects it back into the world." Admittedly, this was an unattainable ideal, requiring that an individual understand not only himself but also his age, forever changing and leaving him thus with the clear awareness that being born ten years earlier or later would have made a quite different person of him.

This high biographic ideal protected Goethe against certain aberrations of the autobiographic genre that he disliked in others. As will be seen, it also protected him against fundamental aberrations in the notion of individuality. He was well acquainted with autobiographic literature. He spoke very little of Augustine's *Confessions* and the medieval writers, but his interest was livelier when he came to the Renaissance writers and the moderns. In his earlier period he read Hutten and Goetz von Berlichingen. Montaigne he knew well. Cardano he read intensively for his work on the theory of colors; the very beginning of *Dichtung und Wahrheit*, the concern with the horoscope of his birth, he may well have borrowed outright from Cardano. Cellini's great autobiography, not printed until the first quarter of the eighteenth century, fascinated Goethe so much that he translated it into German between 1796 and 1803. He knew the autobiographies of Alfieri, Jung-Stilling, and later on Johannes Müller and Jean Paul Richter. He was most deeply troubled by Karl Philipp Moritz's autobiographic work *Anton Reiser* (he knew Moritz personally) and by the great precursor, Jean-Jacques Rousseau's *Confessions*. After reading Rousseau, Goethe, imitating many contemporaries, made his pilgrimage to Jean-Jacques's happy isle of Saint Peter in Lake Biel (depicted in the twelfth book of the *Confessions*). But in the end, Goethe took an autobiographic stance very different from both that of Moritz and that of Rousseau.

None of these autobiographic works could serve Goethe as a model. He was too little the Christian to confess his life as a hymn of praise to its creator and guiding hand, as Augustine had done. Goethe lacked Cellini's driving impulse for aggrandizing himself in an autobiographic monument; he was too conscious of his individuality to equal Cellini's naïve (that is, unreflective) rendering of his own. The intensive search for the nature of the self, which motivated both Cardano and Montaigne, was irrelevant to Goethe; he knew what and who he was. He had no need of the autobiographic activity to find himself and to orient himself toward the future. He was too much a part of a cultural development bringing to the fore history and the genetic view of life to be satisfied with more static self-portraiture. He had too thoroughly come to doubt the value of intense self-examination, which so completely absorbed the pietist, ever to believe, what so many of the young romantics seemed to believe, that introspection was the royal road to self-knowledge. Moritz's *Reiser* was the very warning, if any were needed, that constant preoccupation with the inner self was both intensely pathological and extremely disabling. Man knows himself as a living part of his world; in individual isolation he is blind to himself. To Goethe Rousseau exemplified all that was wrong with the confessional mood: it predisposes a man to dwell on his weakness and makes his writing lachrymose. (Goethe's relative lack of acquaintance with Augustine must be responsible, one assumes, for this equation of confession with *confessio peccati* and not with the Augustinian mood of *confessio laudis*.) He was too much a man of propriety and tact to see any virtue in undressing his character in public; what value was there anyway in promising to say all when all was not worth saying? Most important of all: unlike Rousseau, Goethe did not carry on a bitter quarrel with his world. He did not seek to recover a vision of pure man in an unspoiled Eden. He had a high consciousness of himself as the product of an age that he himself had helped to transform. He thought it good for the young men of the nineteenth century to be informed of the world of their fathers; the didactic task remained important to him. Despite all initial misgivings, he saw value in illuminating the contexts within which the poet had created. The exaggerated cult of the personality which he and others of the *Sturm und Drang* had helped to evoke, and which now seemed rampant among so many young romantics, he meant to oppose by a portrayal of a self which had found its saving grace in limitations. So, all in all, he meant to write his autobiography less for his own needs than for the enjoyment of others. With modesty and pride both, he held the autobiographer to be the most polite of men.

The very acts of conceiving and writing his own biography involved Goethe in the recognition that past life is dominated by present vision. Like any historical writing, autobiography stands under the imperative of a specific point of view, literally the standpoint from which the writer does his viewing. As an interpretative act autobiography is possible only because a turn of time, prior to the writer's vantage point, has opened inner lines of sight upon a life which could not be seen prior to such a turn. This is, of course, clearest in autobiographies built on a "conversion" at a distinct point in time: Augustine and the garden scene of August 386, Descartes in the night of 10–11 November 1619 "dans une poêle," Rousseau on an October afternoon in 1749 on the road to Vincennes, or Gibbon on the steps of the Capitoline hill on 15 October 1764. At such times lives took decisive turns. The subsequent reflection on the meaning of such transforming moments reorders the vision of the life prior to them. Interconnected patterns of meaning become illuminated which seemed opaque before. Not all lives have such dramatic turning points—Goethe's had none—but every full autobiography bears the mark of the moment of inception when interpreted meaning begins to lie before the writer, either as the result of dramatic illumination or as the result of a gradual process of focusing by means of a series of significant experiences. The once concretely lived events of a life are now placed in interconnected relationships dominated by the meaning now seen to be in that life. Autobiography, like any work of history, is a process of ordering and of foreshortening. The insight of the present is imposed on the past; the completed fact is superimposed on the fact in the making. The bewildering complexity of the concretely lived life becomes an ordered vision. The meaning of experience now understood turns the mere annals of life into interpreted history—if you will, into "philosophical" history. Single events derive a highly symptomatic value from the newly seen meaning of a whole life pattern. Autobiography has thus the connective tissue of patterned meaning which the diary cannot have in the same fashion.

Goethe respected the autobiographic problem of such retrospective interpretation when he set to work. If by nothing else, he made this very clear by his chosen title. When the work appeared it carried the title: *Aus meinem Leben: Dichtung und Wahrheit*. The first part of this title is essential, but has mostly been forgotten by generations of readers. The choice of the phrase *Aus meinem Leben* at once alerted the reader to the author's intention of giving but parts out of a whole life; there was no promise of a complete *vita*. When Goethe began the book in 1810–11, it was by no means clear where the account would leave off. The crude factual and chronological *schemata* he made for himself carried events down to the return of his son August from studies at the University of Heidelberg on 26 September 1809. Early indications suggest that the autobiography would also cover the years at Weimar instead of breaking off with the decision in 1775 to accept the Weimar post, as the work now does. The decision to end the book with this 1775 turn to Weimar— which now seems a very "logical" and artistically valid one— evolved only gradually. Books 1–5 were published late in 1811; books 6–10 were ready for printing a year later; books 11–15 were ready for the publisher in May 1814; books 16–19 were being drafted between 1813 and 1816, but books 16–20 were not completed until Goethe's very last year (1831– 32) and were published posthumously. As this last part IV is so heavily centered on his love for Lili Schönemann, Goethe became less willing to work on it while she was still alive. Very similar reasons inhibited him from working out the life of the Weimar period when so many who were a part of that close-knit court society were still alive. And yet, Goethe's autobiographic intent carried him into his life after 1775. For when the account of his Italian experience from September 1786 to June 1788 appeared in 1816 as that marvelous book *The Italian Journey*, it had the title *Aus meinem Leben*, Zweite Abteilung: *Italienische Reise*, with the motto "Auch ich in Arkadien." The link to *Dichtung und Wahrheit* was clear, and so was the obvious intention of

giving segments "out of his life." This was once more underlined in 1822 with the appearance of the campaign memoirs
of 1792: *Aus meinem Leben*, Zweiter Abteilung Fünfter Teil:
Kampagne in Frankreich und Belagerung von Mainz. The
correspondence with Schiller was also meant to be a part of
this larger autobiographic conception. With Goethe's habit of
protracting work and with the vicissitudes of the writer's
career he never succeeded in giving fuller coherence to this
larger conception; the fragments out of his life remained
fragments; and only *Aus meinem Leben*, Erste Abteilung:
Dichtung und Wahrheit has the full coherence of genuine
autobiography.

Goethe had no wish to reveal every aspect of his past. He
had not the slightest intention of satisfying the hunger of a
philistine German public for full revelation, fare to which it
always felt entitled and, like a cheated lover, complained of
never receiving. But he also knew the deeper reason in
choosing the modest title *Aus meinem Leben*, for he meant to
give his young life under *one* dominant aspect: the formation
of the personality of the poet. The life remembered had been
chaotically full and diversified; the life to be interpreted was
a select ordering and not the fullness of life lived.

All the varied insights into the complex demands of the
autobiographic task Goethe compressed in that magnificent
subtitle *Dichtung und Wahrheit*, which now has come to
displace the title *Aus meinem Leben*. Poetry and Truth, or
Fiction and Truth—even if *Dichtung* could be properly
translated, it is the conjunction of the terms which contains
the never exhausted puzzle and wisdom. By coupling the
terms, Goethe informs the reader that he may find here truth
and something else: poetic invention? poetry? something
other than "mere" truth? On the simplest level this seems to
say that the writer has striven to give the truth as well as he
could manage and has supplemented it beyond this by the
free play of his imagination. The reader who goes one step
further and reflects analytically upon the order of the words
—concluding that he will be given poetic imagination first,

supplemented secondly by truth—lands himself, through his
logical cleverness, in a trap. For the earliest hint at the
subtitle was *Wahrheit und Dichtung;* Goethe, ever the poet
hearing the sounds of words, inverted this simply because the
double-*d* sound displeased him. But this is a minor point—
though a nice warning. The true problem remains: What is
being joined together thus?

Goethe had no doubt whatever about the autobiographer's
absolute obligation to be truthful in recounting his life. He
was most diligent in collecting the data for his autobiography.
He read all he could find on the history of Frankfurt and on
the history of literary and philosophical movements of the
time; he reread the literature of his youth, including most of
Voltaire's correspondence. The physical description of Frankfurt in book 1 reflects a map of the city he used; the coronation proceedings of book 5 rest on detailed study of the official
documents. At one point Goethe asked his Frankfurt friend
Schlosser for an example of the kind of glove his grandfather
Textor used to receive as highest official of the town; at
another time he requested the transmittal of a big chest of
old household accounts and receipts. For many details he
had to rely, as any autobiographer must, on his memory; it
sometimes misled him. But, although lapses of memory can
be shown to have been responsible for certain factual errors,
largely chronological ones, it has proved much more difficult
to show consciously worked falsification of any part of
Dichtung und Wahrheit. Stating the truth was the self-evident
objective of its author.

But what is autobiographic truth? That question opens up
one of the most fascinating aspects of this literary-historical
genre, an aspect so complex that it can only be touched upon
here. Truly, a fact is a fact is a fact—but, as Goethe said
later on to his secretary Eckermann, a fact only counts when
it means something in our life. The autobiographer's view of
facts is guided by his quest for the meaning of the facts. But a
fact of the year 1760 may derive its meaning only from its
relationship to a fact of the year 1770, or 1800, when it is

placed in such a relationship. By placing it in relation to a later fact it is, to some extent, being wrenched from the context of facts in which it was embedded in 1760—which is another way of saying that the subsequent recognition of significance modifies the vision of the original historical constellation of which it was a part. Insights into the power of the classical heritage, maturing in Goethe after his Italian experience of 1786–88, inevitably made him deal differently with earlier formative experiences—such as, say, the encounter with Oeser at Leipzig, and through him, indirectly, with Winckelmann—than he would have treated these in 1770. And when the autobiographer, interpreting and assigning meaning, fashions the narrative, he begins to place incidents of experience in relation to the accumulated experience, shifting their account into the context of meaning to which they are now seen to belong. The succession of the moments actually lived are being compressed into differently ordered chains of developmental topics. The retrospective view over a sequence of time affects the view of each individual moment of time. But this is not comparable to poetic invention (*erdichten*, fictional creation); if done honestly, nothing is added to the life that does not belong to the life. It is a process of compressing a myriad of experiences into a coherent form of accumulated and interpreted experience— and in this it shares in the action (*dichten*) of the poet who elevates the fleeting moment to a different level of existence. There is no lack of truthfulness in this, for, when done conscientiously, it states the truth seen from the autobiographer's vantage point. *Dichtung* thus does not stand in opposition to *Wahrheit;* they complement each other, and in joining both, a different (and for Goethe, higher) form of truth emerges. In choosing his fortunate subtitle, Goethe compressed his insight into the immensely rich problem of all autobiographic work; he also stated therein one of the fundamental verities of all historical labor.

Goethe, the autobiographer, never forgot that the life of the young man was being written by the mature man of sixty, for whom accumulated experience had taken on a new pattern of meaning. He meant to give "results" of his life. However much he desired to be truthful to the world of the child and the young man, he knew that he could not recapture that world in its unmodified pristine naïveté. His autobiographic program differed essentially from Rousseau's. The genius who wrote the *Confessions* had wanted to relive the great moments of his life; he saw the real unity of his life, and of its account, in the unchanged persistence of the "chain of sentiments" which assured the much troubled outcast of the abiding continuity of his original moral sensibility, the persistence of the good man under all the perversities of civilized deceit. Goethe fundamentally distrusted such "memory of sentiment", as he says in the autobiography: "The thoughts we have had, the pictures [*better*, the images] we have seen, can be again called up before the mind and the imagination: but the heart is not so complaisant; it will not repeat its agreeable emotions. And least of all are we able to recall [*better*, make present to us—*vergegenwärtigen*] moments of enthusiasm . . ." (vol. 2, pp. 257–58). Layers of subsequent experience lay between the autobiographic moment and the lived moment in the past. How could and why should these be eliminated? The repeated reflection from the past was always different.

When Goethe came to tell of his great love for Frederike Brion at Sesenheim, he in a way of course "recalled" the charm of that moment. But he knew that there already existed a truthful reflection of those experiences in the poetry he wrote under the immediate impact of those moments; no later words could improve on their reflective function. From the distant view of the autobiographer, however, the entire wonderful and also deeply painful love affair had taken on symbolic meaning in the whole context of the Strasbourg years, when the young man, at the very border of France and Germany, had adopted his stance toward his own German culture over against the dominant French civilization, guided by Herder and the English writers, gaining a fresh view of nature, and finding a new reverence for the Gothic of the Strasbourg cathedral. From this differently refracted vision of the experience he fashioned the wonderful novelistic idyll, or idyllic novella, of the Sesenheim affair in *Dichtung und Wahrheit*, weaving the memory and the literary artifice of the *Vicar of Wakefield* into a fresh, in no way lesser, truth of the experience. And this artistic recreation of his past so stirred some to visit this fabled scene on the Rhine that the young philologist August Ferdinand Näke sent Goethe in 1822 an enthusiastic report of such a visit stimulated by the account in *Dichtung und Wahrheit.* Goethe thus could view reflection upon reflection upon reflection of his original experience, "entoptic colors" differently reflected in a series of mirrors (*Wiederholte Spiegelungen*).

Another example of the autobiographer's retrospective treatment of the great events of his life the reader will find in the Wetzlar episode involving his love for Charlotte Buff (books 12 and 13). Of this love Goethe tells very little. The painful tension of this experience he sublimated in his *Werther;* but he tells very little about the *Werther.* Instead he concentrates on the condition of the author of the *Werther* and even more on the effect of the book on its public and the reactions it occasioned. The central underlying experience is thus totally subsumed in its "results."

And as a last example of the interweaving of *Dichtung* and *Wahrheit* into truth of a special kind, attention may be drawn to an insertion that, at first glance, seems sheerest fabrication: the youthful fairy tale "The New Paris" in book 2. At that point of his account Goethe wants to give a hint of his awakening imaginative prowess by retelling a fairy tale with which the young boy regaled his attentive peers. But not even the most gifted boy could tell a story in that accomplished form. Yet, all the structural elements have a boyish involution. Detailed research has shown the incontrovertible presence of elements from Goethe's youth: images used were found on the wallpaper the French lieutenant had ordered

to be painted for his Provençal house when he was billeted in
the Goethe home; among Goethe's earliest reading were
Homeric tales simplistically retold for boys; a letter of 1773
(that is, almost forty years before the writing down of the
autobiographic scene) independently reports many elements
of the story as one he remembered telling. As soon as one
pays attention, however, to separate themes and motifs and
figures, it is clear that the later consciousness of the poet has
intervened: the young Paris reaching for the beauty of
Alerte suffers exactly the same fate as Faust reaching for
Helena—they are both struck down in the same fashion; the
play on the different colored ropes was taken from Goethe's
later preoccupation with the *Arabian Nights;* the Achilles
motifs occur again in his great epic fragment *Achilleis.* The
central content revolves, of course, around an intensely
classical theme. Therefore, as soon as one asks questions
about what Goethe wanted to state concerning a young
German boy's relation to the world of classical antiquity in
the 1750s, the richest interpretative possibilities open up: the
world of the "ancients" came to the boy in rococo forms; only
by divesting himself of this rococo encumbrance could access
to the naked Greek be found; Oriental-Christian elements
served as a guide which had to be left behind at the inner
sanctum; the true Greek element has marked plastic round-
ness—when you break it in parts, it reconstitutes itself in its
healthy fullness (in 1827 Goethe told Eckermann; Homer's
heroes are like those in Valhalla: in the morning they cut
themselves in pieces, and at noon they sit down to feast
restored to wholeness); everything is held to the miniature
befitting the child; the symbolism of the nut trees (nature),
the stone tablet (literature) and the fountain niche (art)
points to the insight that true access to that world will only
be found when all these elements are seen in their true proportionate relation. That great theme of Goethe's entire life,
the right relation to the classical inheritance, is thus most
appropriately woven into the boyishly clumsy tale, told with
all the sophistication of language and the symbolic treatment

of the sixty-year-old poet. What here is *Dichtung?* What is *Wahrheit?* And how much does one care when the interplay of *Dichtung* and *Wahrheit* delivers the truth of this dimension?

The autobiographer thus told his life by only partially reinvolving himself in his past life. The life lived had become subsumed in the ordered consciousness of the man who knew himself to have been formed in that life. The poet in him lifted this once more to yet another level of existence, the one eternalized on the pages of his book. The autobiographic stance was one of superb "detachment." Goethe had aimed at "irony in the highest sense," and he accomplished it.

The grand objective of *Dichtung und Wahrheit* was *Bildungsgeschichte,* the account of the formation of a man who also was a poet—the history of an education (if one takes this word in the broad sense that *Bildung* has). From the outset, the very conception of the task placed the highest premium on a rendering of development; Goethe faced a historical task. The more static autobiographic form of self-portraiture—as it can be found in Petrarch, Cardano, or, above all, in Montaigne—could not serve Goethe's purpose. He was neither interested in presenting the world a composite view of the poet at age sixty, nor was he drawn to the intensive processes of self-analysis which motivated those earlier autobiographic works; more than that, he was profoundly opposed to such modes of self-dissection. He several times confessed to his suspicion that the old classical exhortation "Know thyself" was an attempt by a conspiring priesthood to detract men from active living by steering them to ultimately destructive self-analytical modes of self-preoccupation! Any new reader of *Dichtung und Wahrheit* will, like all previous readers, be struck that the central "hero" of this book—so often referred to only as "he" or "the boy" or "the young man"—is so rarely in the limelight and that there are no extensive passages of self-analysis. The autobiographic Goethe is never shown in atmospheric isolation facing his soul and his self; he always stands fully in a

contextual world—his world—and in that sense he does
stand in the center of attention. The reflections in the men
and women, the books, the art, the landscape, the events,
are focused back on him and thus he is seen. Just as we see
light only because it is reflected by objects, we see ourselves
in the reflections of our circumstances. Goethe, the man, had
learned early that discovery of self was discovery of oneself in
one's world; Goethe, the autobiographer, meant to depict
that process. More important still: the growth of a self was
a never-ceasing interplay with a developing world. It was
the very insight in which the profound view of the historical
dimension of all existence rests.

Only now, and on those grounds, could autobiography
assume its full historical dimension. Goethe and the slightly
older Gibbon were the first to write their lives fully as the
history of their persons. They were—and Goethe more so
than Gibbon—part of that great "revolution" of the late
eighteenth century wherein Western man took the turn to a
historicized view of life and of the world. The "Great Chain
of Being" became temporalized; the world of fixed creation
became an evolving one; life of self and of peoples became
meaningful as a process of continuous formation and trans-
formation. The older forms of autobiography partook very
little of such a historical outlook. Christian autobiography—
as part of a world view which ultimately contributed much
to the development of Western man's historical-mindedness
—was, of course, strongly marked by a developmental pattern of the personality; but the "history" of the individual
Christian was moved more by the hand of a transcendent
Deity than by his historical interaction with his specific
historical world. In the less Christian early modern autobiographies the developmental dimension was often very
weak; despite the ever-bustling adventure of Cellini's life,
what development of the personality is there indeed in his
vita? Cardinal de Retz came closer to showing the fate of
self in the fate of events, but he forever encumbered the
view by his never-satiated need of justifying the actor as the

shaper of the events of his memoirs. Vico, by hindsight so seminal in helping create the later "historicist revolution," rendered his own life—and a fascinating work it is—by concentrating intently on the process of evolving the coherent thought which made him the author of the *New Science*. Rousseau, so grandiose in teaching men to view childhood as childhood, adolescence as adolescence, was yet incapable of giving the truly historical view of himself because his deep quarrel with his world led him to seek the true meaning of self in the persistence of an uncorrupted abiding ahistorical self. In the introductory letter to the German edition of *Dichtung und Wahrheit*, mentioned above, Goethe makes the statement that "each one, in regard to his own formation (*Bildung*) and his effect on circumstances, would have become someone quite different had he but been born ten years earlier or later." This remark, to us so innocent and self-evident, emphasizes the difference in world view separating us from the generations who lived before the latter part of the eighteenth century. No earlier autobiography has such a statement as a part of the author's consciousness of self.

Goethe thus knew that his self-explanation could be given only in the history of his self-formation. The account could not be made simply in the course of describing the unfolding of this person according to an inner law or predestined final form; there was no way of predicting that this acorn would become this kind of oak. "Something" very specific, with the inner law of its own specificity—if you will, something resembling an Aristotelean entelechy—was indeed given, at a very specific moment and in a very specific place. The first sentence of *Dichtung und Wahrheit* marks the temporal-spatial coordinate point, and the playful speculation that follows underlines immediately the importance of the constellation of which a man becomes a part from this very first moment. The coexistence of a very specifically constellated human world and a very specifically cast human being were thus given. In ceaseless interaction a self is being formed by making its world truly its own; as it makes selected parts of

its world part of itself, it also begins to act back upon its
world, thereby helping to transform it in turn. Self and world
evolve unpredictably together. That interplay opens in book
1 with the narrow world of the child's family home and ends
in book 20 with the young man's sense of coexistence with an
entire universe and the discussion of its "Demoniac" forces.
Between these two points the world's horizon grows ever
wider for the young Goethe: home opens up into the city of
Frankfurt; Frankfurt is seen as affected by the wider European world; Leipzig comes as the "modern" contrast to the
old traditions of Frankfurt; the problem of Germany appears
in the problem of German literature; the conflicts emerging
in Strasbourg point up both the wide diversity of human
cultures and man's position within nature; a growing awareness of simple social obligation imposes limits upon the
cult of the titanic personality. Although this widening and
adjusting of a man's world is a part of the structure of the
work, the reader will note that the centrally important formative elements are present from book 1 onward. After a while
one notes that the same decisive matters and questions recur:
the effect of men and women on the development of the person, the relation to books and works of art, the relation to
the surrounding landscape and buildings, the central moral
questions and the central religious questions, the growing
awareness of creative powers as artist and even more so as
poet, the eternal questions about a literate public and the
state of literature itself. The formation of the person is
constantly seen in relation to the most important strains of
the tradition: to the classical inheritance, to the Jewish-
Christian inheritance, to the German folk tradition, and to
the other European styles of civilization as well. With immense artistry the story of certain developments is dropped
at certain points, to be woven back into the narrative in
subsequent books. Every one of the four parts has a dominant
love. The Mephisto prototype, the nay-saying spirit who
ever questions creative action and yet stirs the creative person to creation, appears in many repetitions: the little

Derones, Behrisch, Herder, Merck. More and more one feels oneself being taken over the same ground, involved in the same questions, observing the same processes in the forming of the personality. The movement of the book is markedly spiral: the same ground is passed over but always on a higher plane of Goethe's development, every time freshened in its specifics and deepened in its human wisdom. Goethe added to this the steadily growing sense that he himself was affecting the world around him; for he wrote his life from the perspective of an old man who knew that he and his generation had profoundly affected their world by transforming and creating a German culture where there was, as yet, no German nation.

This intensely historical fashion of viewing and re-creating his self-formation as the continuous interplay of I-and-the-World went hand in hand with Goethe's conception of individuality. The realization of that personality ideal—belief in the full differentiation of man into ineffable, unique individualities, and the conscious acceptance of such individuality as a good, and its conscious cultivation as a life task—this is, after all, the result of the selfsame set of historical factors which gave Western man his specific historical mentality. A true sense of individuality is an expression of historicalmindedness. It rests in the belief that every existence is marked by the temporal-spatial coordinate point at which it occurs. Only one life can occupy any such intersection and every such intersection is unique and unrepeatable. I-and-my-circumstances is an ever-evolving coexistent reality and insofar as it becomes a part of successive consciousness it is an ever more integrated and expanding part of such reality. The self evolves as I and World interact; the self acts back upon the world and alters it and creates new circumstances. And so on, and so on . . . But that is simply another way of saying that self-consciousness is the consciousness of the history of the world of which the self partakes. Autobiography, as the expression of a sense of individuality, as the unique history of each life, is thus but one aspect of man's growing sense of the historical dimension of all life.

For us moderns who have committed so much of ourselves to cultivating the ideal of the autonomous personality, there may be special gratification in following Goethe's tracing out of his own development as a self-conscious individuality. The markers for this he left clearly in the text. But as we have become so readily inclined to falsify this ideal of individuality by exaggerating its uniqueness and by perceiving it in contrast to our world, a threatening, hostile world, we could derive a special benefit from observing Goethe's sense of individuality's limitations.

Goethe saw his individuality as part of his world and as a product of growing along with that world. Common elements were individually reworked and in their individual refashioning returned to the world with the chance of becoming new common elements. The distinct self was at most a harmonious blend of common building blocks, uniquely marked by a personal style. In a way, Goethe's most succinct description of the characteristics of individuality is in his brief description of the Strasbourg cathedral. The sense of individual style preserves all that is of value in the notion of individuality and yet leaves it altogether a part of a commonly shared world. Love of the ineffable self then goes hand in hand with love of, reverence for, and acceptance of the common humanity; cultivation of the self is at one and the same time loving cultivation of its world. In Goethe's reverent acceptance of the task of selfhood as an expression of one's loving concern for one's world—or, which is the same thing, building one's world as an expression of one's loving concern for selfhood—in this would seem to lie many of the healing virtues which this book has to offer us.

Introductions can try to do many different things; this one clearly has neglected to do some of the obvious things. It might have given the reader more background for understanding numerous details—but the value of this book does not depend on proper identification of all the figures and literary movements. More might have been given of the history of the time to which this book belongs—but the book is itself an excellent source for that history. Much more could have been said about the astonishing artistry by which such immense material was fashioned into a work of art—but this would seem to be the very task with which to leave each individual reader. The option instead was an attempt at drawing the reader into this book by inducing certain reflections on the nature and the task of autobiography. If this was for some the wrong option, the error in choice can be borne comfortably in the assurance that the enjoyment of this great book is in no way affected by any sort of introduction.

Part One

᾽Ο μὴ δαρεὶς ἄνθρωπος οὐ παιδεύεται.
Man does not learn unless he is thrashed. — MENANDER

PREFACE

By way of preface to the present work, which, perhaps, is in greater need of one than most works, let me quote the letter from a friend which prompted so hazardous a venture.

"We now have the twelve volumes of your collected writings to hand, dear friend, and we find, as we go through them, much that is familiar to us and much that is unfamiliar; indeed, much that had been forgotten is brought back to mind by this collection. One cannot help seeing these volumes—presented thus in a unified format—as a whole, and one wishes that one might gain from it an image of the author and his art. It cannot be denied, in view of the briskness with which that author began his literary career and the time that has elapsed since those beginnings, that a dozen volumes seem too few. When perusing the individual works, moreover, one cannot avoid the impression that they find their origins, for the most part, in specific experiences and reflect definite external objects as well as distinct inward stages of development, and that they contain certain moral and aesthetic maxims and convictions held only temporarily. As a whole these works remain unconnected; indeed, it is often hard to believe that they are from the same hand.

"Your friends have nevertheless not abandoned their quest and, being more familiar with your style of life and way of thinking, are trying to find the answer to many a riddle and the key to many a problem, aided by old affection and a long-standing relationship, they even find a certain challenge in the difficulties confronting them. But a little help here and

2a

there would not be unwelcome—a friendly request that you surely cannot refuse.

"The first thing we ask of you, then, is that you set your literary works—which in the new edition have been arranged according to certain inner relationships—in chronological order, and that you bring together in their interdependence both the circumstances of life and the states of mind which furnished the subject matter, as well as the influences which worked upon you and—no less important—the theoretical principles you followed. If you direct this effort to a rather narrow circle, something may come of it that could be both useful and pleasing to a wider one. Even in his most advanced years, a writer should not deny himself the privilege of conversing, at a distance if need be, with those who are fond of him; and if it is not granted to every author later in life to produce new, powerful, creative works, it should still be an entertaining and invigorating exercise, at that very time when understanding is fuller and consciousness clearer, to take what has already been created and to use it as subject matter a second time, reworking it as a final composition that may serve once again to educate those who earlier formed themselves under the artist's influence and in his company."

This request, so amiably presented, stirred in me an immediate desire to respond. For though in our youth we zealously go our own way, impatiently rejecting the claims of others to our attention for fear of being diverted, these are most beneficial to us in our later years when a generous expression of interest may quicken us and stir us to new activity. I therefore immediately set about to mark all the works in the twelve volumes, both the larger ones and the smaller ones, and to rearrange them according to the years in which they were written. In this I sought to evoke the times and the circumstances in which I produced them. But the task soon grew more burdensome, as detailed notes and explanations were needed to fill gaps in what had already been published. To begin with, all my earliest efforts were missing; much that had barely been begun or that had never been

completed was missing; much that had been completed had
lost its original outward form, having later been totally reworked and cast in another form. In addition, I had to recall
what I had undertaken in the natural sciences and in other
disciplines, and what I had accomplished in such apparently
unfamiliar areas, both alone and in collaboration with
friends, either for myself or for publication.

I wanted to include all of this in order to satisfy my well-
wishers, but these very efforts and observations led me ever
farther afield. In my attempt to respond to the reasonable
demands that had been made of me and in my striving to
present, in the order in which they occurred, the inner
promptings, the outward influences, and the stages I passed
through both in theory and in practice, I was driven from my
circumscribed private life into the world outside. A hundred
significant persons who had had a greater or lesser influence
upon me came to mind; the portentous motions of the world's
political course, which had had such an immense impact on
me as well as on the great mass of my contemporaries, demanded major attention. For the principal task of biography,
I believe, is to present a man in the conditions of his time, and
to show to what extent those conditions, taken as a whole,
thwart him or favor him, how he forms from it all a view of
the world and of man, and how, if he is an artist, a poet, or a
writer, he then takes that view and projects it back into the
world. It is, however, an almost impossible task, for what is
demanded is that the individual know both himself and his
century—himself insofar as he has remained the same in all
circumstances, the century inasmuch as it sweeps both the
willing and the unwilling along with it, determining and
forming them, so that it can truthfully be said that any man,
had he been born a mere ten years earlier or later, might, as
far as his own formation and his outward achievements are
concerned, have become an entirely different person.

In this manner, from such observations and probings, from
memories and reflections, the present narrative was born,
and it is from this view of its origins that it can best be en-

joyed and used and most reasonably be judged. Whatever
else might be said, especially with respect to the half-poetic,
half-historical treatment employed, can well be left to the
text that follows.

FIRST BOOK.

On the 28th of August, 1749, at midday, as the clock struck twelve, I came into the world, at Frankfort-on-the-Main. My horoscope was propitious: the sun stood in the sign of the Virgin, and had culminated for the day; Jupiter and Venus looked on him with a friendly eye, and Mercury not adversely; while Saturn and Mars kept themselves indifferent; the moon alone, just full, exerted the power of her reflection all the more, as she had then reached her planetary hour. She opposed herself, therefore, to my birth, which could not be accomplished until this hour was passed.

These good aspects, which the astrologers managed subsequently to reckon very auspicious for me, may have been the causes of my preservation; for, through the unskilfulness of the midwife, I came into the world as dead; and only after various efforts was I enabled to see the light. This event, which had put our household into sore straits, turned to the advantage of my fellow citizens, inasmuch as my grandfather, the *Schultheiss*,[1] John Wolfgang Textor, took occasion from

---

[1] A chief judge or magistrate of the town.

3

it to have an *accoucheur* appointed, and to introduce, or revive, the tuition of midwives, which may have done some good to those who were born after me.

When we desire to recall what happened to us in the earliest period of youth, it often happens that we confound what we have heard from others with that which we really possess from our own direct experience. Without, therefore, instituting a very close investigation into the point, which, after all, could lead to nothing, I am conscious that we lived in an old house, which, in fact, consisted of two adjoining houses, that had been opened into each other. A winding staircase led to rooms on different levels, and the unevenness of the stories was remedied by steps. For us children, — a younger sister and myself, — the favourite resort was a spacious floor below, near the door of which was a large wooden lattice that allowed us direct communication with the street and open air. A bird-cage of this sort, with which many houses were provided, was called a frame (*Geräms*). The women sat in it to sew and knit; the cook picked her salad there; female neighbours chatted with each other; and the streets consequently, in the fine season, wore a southern aspect. One felt at ease while in communication with the public. We children, too, by means of these frames, were brought into contact with our neighbours, of whom three brothers Von Ochsenstein, the surviving sons of the deceased *Schultheiss*, living on the other side of the way, won my love, and occupied and diverted themselves with me in many ways.

Our family liked to tell of all sorts of waggeries to which I was enticed by these otherwise grave and solitary men. Let one of these pranks suffice for all. A crockery-fair had just been held, from which not only our kitchen had been supplied for awhile with articles for a long time to come, but a great deal of small gear of the same ware had been purchased as playthings for us children. One fine afternoon, when everything was quiet in the house, I whiled away the time with my pots and dishes in the frame, and, finding that nothing more was to be got out of them, hurled one of them into the street. The Von Ochsensteins, who saw me so delighted at the fine smash it made, that I clapped my hands for joy, cried out, "Another." I was not long in flinging out a pot; and, as they made no end to their calls for more, by degrees the whole collection, platters, pipkins, mugs and all, were dashed upon the pavement. My neighbours continued to express their approbation, and I was highly delighted to give them pleasure. But my stock was exhausted; and still they shouted, "More." I ran, therefore, straight to the kitchen, and brought the earthenware, which produced a still livelier spectacle in breaking; and thus I kept running backwards and forwards, fetching one plate after another, as I could reach it from where they stood in rows on the shelf. But, as that did not satisfy my audience, I devoted all the ware that I could drag out to similar destruction. It was not till afterward that any one appeared to hinder and forbid. The mischief was done; and, in place of so much broken crockery, there was at least a ludicrous story, in which the roguish authors took special delight to the end of their days.

My father's mother, for it was her house in which we dwelt, lived in a large back room directly on the ground floor; and we were accustomed to carry on our sports even up to her chair, and, when she was ill, up to her bedside. I remember her, as it were, a spirit, — a handsome, thin woman, always neatly dressed in white. Mild, gentle, and kind, she has ever remained in my memory.

The street in which our house was situated passed by the name of the Stag-Ditch; but, as neither stags nor ditches were to be seen, we wished to have the term explained. They told us that our house stood on a spot that was once outside the city, and that, where the street now was, there had formerly been a ditch, in which a number of stags were kept. These stags were preserved and fed here because the senate, every year, according to an ancient custom, feasted publicly on a stag, which was therefore always at hand in the ditch for such a festival, in case princes or knights interfered with the city's right of chase outside, or the walls were encompassed or besieged by an enemy. This pleased us much, and we wished that such a lair for tame animals could have been seen in our times.

The back of the house, from the second story particularly, commanded a very pleasant prospect over an almost immeasurable extent of neighbouring gardens, stretching to the very walls of the city. But, alas! in transforming what were once public grounds into private gardens, our house, and some others lying toward the corner of the street, had been much stinted; since the houses toward the horse-market had appropriated spacious out-houses and large gardens to themselves, while a tolerably high wall shut us out from these adjacent paradises.

On the second floor was a room which was called the garden-room, because they had there endeavoured to supply the want of a garden by means of a few plants placed before the window. As I grew older, it was there that I made my favourite, not melancholy, but somewhat sentimental, retreat. Over these gardens, beyond the city's walls and ramparts, might be seen a beautiful and fertile plain, the same which stretches toward Höchst. In the summer season I commonly learned my lessons there, and watched the thunderstorms, but could never look my fill at the setting sun, which went down directly opposite my windows. And when, at the same time, I saw the neighbours wandering through their gardens, taking care of their flowers, the children playing, parties of friends enjoying themselves, and could hear the bowls rolling and the ninepins dropping, it early excited within me a feeling of solitude, and a sense of vague longing resulting from it, which, conspiring with the seriousness and awe implanted in me by nature, exerted its influence at an early age, and showed itself more distinctly in after-years.

The old, many-cornered, and gloomy arrangement of the house was, moreover, adapted to awaken dread and terror in childish minds. Unfortunately, too, the principle of discipline, that young persons should be early deprived of all fear for the awful and invisible, and accustomed to the terrible, still prevailed. We children, therefore, were compelled to sleep alone ; and when we found this impossible, and softly slipped from our beds, to seek the society of the servants and maids, our father, with his dressing-gown turned inside out, which disguised him sufficiently for the purpose, placed himself in the way, and frightened us back to our resting-places. The evil effect of this any one may imagine. How is he who is encompassed with a double terror to be emancipated from fear? My mother, always cheerful and gay, and willing to render others so, discovered a much better pedagogical expedient. She managed to gain her end by rewards. It was the season for peaches, the plentiful enjoyment of which she promised us every morning if we overcame our fears during the night. In this way she succeeded, and both parties were satisfied.

In the interior of the house my eyes were chiefly attracted by a series of Roman views, with which my father had ornamented an anteroom. They were engravings by some of the accomplished predecessors of Piranesi, who well understood perspective and architecture, and whose touches were clear and excellent.

There I saw every day the Piazza del Popolo, the
Colosseum, the Piazza of St. Peter's, and St. Peter's
Church, within and without, the castle of St. Angelo,
and many other places. These images impressed
themselves deeply upon me, and my otherwise very
laconic father was often so kind as to furnish descriptions of the objects. His partiality for the Italian
language, and for everything pertaining to Italy, was
very decided. A small collection of marbles and natural curiosities, which he had brought with him thence,
he often showed to us; and he devoted a great part of
his time to a description of his travels, written in
Italian, the copying and correction of which he slowly
and accurately completed, in several parcels, with his
own hand. A lively old teacher of Italian, called
Giovinazzi, was of service to him in this work.
The old man, moreover, did not sing badly, and my
mother every day must needs accompany him and herself upon the clavichord; and thus I speedily learned
the "Solitario bosco ombroso," so as to know it by
heart before I understood it.

My father was altogether of a didactic turn, and in
his retirement from business liked to communicate
to others what he knew or was able to do. Thus,
during the first years of their marriage, he had kept
my mother busily engaged in writing, playing the
clavichord, and singing, by which means she had been
laid under the necessity of acquiring some knowledge
and a slight readiness in the Italian tongue.

Generally we passed all our leisure hours with my
grandmother, in whose spacious apartment we found
plenty of room for our sports. She contrived to engage us with various trifles, and to regale us with all
sorts of nice morsels. But, one Christmas evening,
she crowned all her kind deeds by having a puppet-
show exhibited before us, and thus unfolding a new
world in the old house. This unexpected drama

attracted our young minds with great force; upon the boy particularly it made a very strong impression, which continued to vibrate with a great and lasting effect.

The little stage, with its speechless personages, which at the outset had only been exhibited to us, but was afterward given over for our own use and dramatic vivification, was prized more highly by us children, as it was the last bequest of our good grandmother, whom encroaching disease first withdrew from our sight, and death next tore away from our hearts for ever. Her departure was of still more importance to our family, as it drew after it a complete change in our condition.

As long as my grandmother lived, my father had refrained from changing or renovating the house, even in the slightest particular; though it was known that he had pretty large plans of building, which were now immediately begun. In Frankfort, as in many other old towns, when anybody put up a wooden structure, he ventured, for the sake of space, to make, not only the first, but each successive, story project over the lower one, by which means narrow streets especially were rendered somewhat dark and confined. At last a law was passed, that every one putting up a new house from the ground, should confine his projections to the first upper story, and carry the others up perpendicularly. My father, that he might not lose the projecting space in the second story, caring little for outward architectural appearance, and anxious only for the good and convenient arrangement of the interior, resorted to the expedient which others had employed before him, of propping the upper part of the house, until one part after another had been removed from the bottom upwards, and a new house, as it were, inserted in its place. Thus, while comparatively none of the old structure remained, the new one merely passed for a repair. Now, as the tearing-down and building up was done gradually, my father determined not to quit the house, that he might better direct and give his orders; as he possessed a good knowledge of the technicalities of building. At the same time, he would not suffer his family to leave him. This new epoch was very surprising and strange for the children. To see the rooms in which they had so often been confined and pestered with wearisome tasks and studies, the passages they had played in, the walls which had always been kept so carefully clean, all falling before the mason's hatchet and the carpenter's axe, — and that from the bottom upward; to float as it were in the air, propped up by beams, being, at the same time, constantly confined to a certain lesson or definite task, — all this produced a commotion in our young heads that was not easily settled. But the young people felt the inconvenience less, because they had somewhat more space for play than before, and had many opportunities of swinging on beams, and playing at seesaw with the boards.

At first my father obstinately persisted in carrying out his plan; but when at last even the roof was partly removed, and the rain reached our beds, in spite of the carpets that had been taken up, converted into tarpaulin, and stretched over as a defence, he determined, though reluctantly, that the children should be entrusted for a time to some kind friends, who had already offered their services, and sent to a public school.

This transition was rather unpleasant; for, when the children, who had all along been kept at home in a secluded, pure, refined, yet strict manner, were thrown among a rude mass of young creatures, they were compelled unexpectedly to suffer everything from the vulgar, bad, and even base, since they lacked both weapons and skill to protect themselves.

It was properly about this period that I first became
acquainted with my native city, which I strolled over
with more and more freedom, in every direction, sometimes alone, and sometimes in the company of lively
companions. To convey to others in any degree the
impression made upon me by these grave and revered
spots, I must here introduce a description of my birth-
place, as in its different parts it was gradually unfolded
to me. What I liked more than anything was, to
promenade on the great bridge spanning the Main.
Its length, its firmness, and its fine appearance, rendered it a notable structure; and it was, besides,
almost the only memorial left from ancient times of
the precautions due from the civil government to its
citizens. The beautiful stream above and below bridge
attracted my eye; and, when the gilt weathercock on
the bridge-cross glittered in the sunshine, I always
had a pleasant feeling. Generally I extended my
walk through Sachsenhausen, and for a *Kreutzer* was
ferried comfortably across the river. I was now again
on this side of the stream, stole along to the wine-
market, and admired the mechanism of the cranes
when goods were unloaded. But it was particularly
entertaining to watch the arrival of the market-boats,
from which so many and such extraordinary figures
were seen to disembark. On entering the city, the
Saalhof, which at least stood on the spot where the
castle of Emperor Charlemagne and his successors was
reported to have been, was greeted every time with
profound reverence. One liked to lose one's self in the
old trading-town, particularly on market-days, among
the crowd collected about the church of St. Bartholomew. From the earliest times, throngs of buyers and
sellers had gathered there; and the place being thus
occupied, it was not easy in later days to bring about
a more roomy and cheerful arrangement. The booths
of the so-called *Pfarreisen* were very important places

for us children, and we carried many a *Batzen* to them
in order to purchase sheets of coloured paper stamped
with gold animals; though one could but seldom make
his way through the narrow, crowded, and dirty market-place. I call to mind, also, that I always flew past
the adjoining meat-stalls, narrow and disgusting as
they were, in perfect horror. On the other hand, the
Roman Hill (*Römerberg*) was a most delightful place
for walking. The way to the New-Town, along by
the new shops, was always cheering and pleasant; yet
we regretted that a street did not lead into the Zeil by
the Church of Our Lady, and that we always had
to go a roundabout way by the *Hasengasse* or the
Catherine Gate. But what chiefly attracted the child's
attention, were the many little towns within the town,
the fortresses within the fortress; viz., the walled mon-
astic enclosures, and several other precincts, remaining
from earlier times, and more or less like castles, — as
the Nuremberg Court, the Compostella, the Braunfels,
the ancestral house of the family of Stallburg, and several strongholds, in later days transformed into dwellings and warehouses. No architecture of an elevating
kind was then to be seen in Frankfort; and everything
pointed to a period long past and unquiet, both for
town and district. Gates and towers, which defined
the bounds of the old city, — then, farther on again,
gates, towers, walls, bridges, ramparts, moats, with
which the new city was encompassed, — all showed,
but too plainly, that a necessity for guarding the
common weal in disastrous times had induced these
arrangements, that all the squares and streets, even
the newest, broadest, and best laid out, owed their
origin to chance and caprice, and not to any regulating mind. A certain liking for the antique was thus
implanted in the boy, and was specially nourished and
promoted by old chronicles and woodcuts, as, for instance, those of Grave relating to the siege of Frank-

fort. At the same time a different taste was developed in him for observing the conditions of mankind in their manifold variety and naturalness, without regard to their importance or beauty. It was, therefore, one of our favourite walks, which we endeavoured to take now and then in the course of a year, to follow the circuit of the path inside the city-walls. Gardens, courts, and back buildings extend to the *Zwinger;* and we saw many thousand people amid their little domestic and secluded circumstances. From the ornamental and show gardens of the rich, to the orchards of the citizen, anxious about his necessities; from thence to the factories, bleaching-grounds, and similar establishments, even to the burying-grounds, — for a little world lay within the limits of the city, — we passed a varied, strange spectacle, which changed at every step, and with the enjoyment of which our childish curiosity was never satisfied. In fact, the celebrated Devil-upon-two-sticks, when he lifted the roofs of Madrid at night, scarcely did more for his friend than was here done for us in the bright sunshine and open air. The keys that were to be made use of in this journey, to gain us a passage through many a tower, stair, and postern, were in the hands of the authorities, whose subordinates we never failed to coax into good humour.

But a more important, and in one sense more fruitful, place for us, was the city hall, named from the Romans. In its lower vault-like rooms we liked but too well to lose ourselves. We obtained an entrance, too, into the large and very simple session-room of the council. The walls as well as the arched ceiling were white, though wainscoted to a certain height; and the whole was without a trace of painting, or any kind of carved work; only, high up on the middle wall, might be read this brief inscription:

"One man's word is no man's word:
Justice needs that both be heard."

After the most ancient fashion, benches were ranged around the wainscoting, and raised one step above the floor for the accommodation of the members of the assembly. This readily suggested to us why the order of rank in our senate was distributed by benches. To the left of the door, on the opposite corner, sat the *Schöffen;* in the corner itself the *Schultheiss*, who alone had a small table before him; those of the second bench sat in the space to his left as far as to the wall where the windows were; while along the windows ran the third bench, occupied by the craftsmen. In the midst of the hall stood a table for the registrar (*Protoculführer*).

Once within the *Römer*, we even mingled with the crowd at the audiences of the burgomasters. But whatever related to the election and coronation of the emperors possessed a greater charm. We managed to gain the favour of the keepers, so as to be allowed to mount the new gay imperial staircase, which was painted in fresco, and on other occasions closed with a grating. The election-chamber, with its purple hangings and admirably fringed gold borders, filled us with awe. The representations of animals, on which little children or genii, clothed in the imperial ornaments and laden with the insignia of the empire, made a curious figure, were observed by us with great attention; and we even hoped that we might live to see, sometime or other, a coronation with our own eyes. They had great difficulty to get us out of the great imperial hall, when we had been once fortunate enough to steal in; and we reckoned him our truest friend, who, while we looked at the half-lengths of all the emperors painted around at a certain height, would tell us something of their deeds.

We listened to many a legend of Charlemagne. But that which was historically interesting for us began with Rudolph of Hapsburg, who by his courage put an end to such violent commotions. Charles the Fourth also attracted our notice. We had already heard of the Golden Bull, and of the statutes for the administration of criminal justice. We knew, too, that he had not made the Frankforters suffer for their adhesion to his noble rival, Emperor Gunther of Schwarzburg. We heard Maximilian praised, both as a friend to mankind, and to the townsmen, his subjects, and were also told that it had been prophesied of him he would be the last emperor of a German house, which unhappily came to pass, as after his death the choice wavered only between the King of Spain (*afterward*), Charles V., and the King of France, Francis I. With some anxiety it was added, that a similar prophecy, or rather intimation, was once more in circulation; for it was obvious that there was room left for the portrait of only one more emperor, — a circumstance which, though seemingly accidental, filled the patriotic with concern.

Having once entered upon this circuit, we did not fail to repair to the cathedral, and there visit the grave of that brave Gunther, so much prized both by friend and foe. The famous stone which formerly covered it is set up in the choir. The door close by, leading into the conclave, remained long shut against us, until we at last managed, through the higher authorities, to gain access to this celebrated place. But we should have done better had we continued as before to picture it merely in our imagination; for we found this room, which is so remarkable in German history, where the most powerful princes were accustomed to meet for an act so momentous, in no respect worthily adorned, and even disfigured with beams, poles, scaffolding, and similar lumber, which people had wanted to put out of the way. The imagination, for that very reason, was the more excited and the heart elevated, when we soon after received permission to be present in the city hall, at the exhibition of the Golden Bull to some distinguished strangers.

The boy then heard, with much curiosity, what his own family, as well as other older relations and acquaintances, liked to tell and repeat; viz., the histories of the two last coronations, which had followed close upon each other; for there was no Frankforter of a certain age who would not have regarded these two events, and their attendant circumstances, as the crowning glory of his whole life. Splendid as had been the coronation of Charles Seventh, during which particularly the French ambassador had given magnificent feasts at great cost and with distinguished taste, the results were all the more afflicting to the good emperor, who could not preserve his capital Munich, and was compelled in some degree to implore the hospitality of his imperial towns.

Although the coronation of Francis First was not so strikingly splendid as the former one, it was dignified by the presence of the Empress Maria Theresa, whose beauty appears to have created as much impression on the men as the earnest and noble form and the blue eyes of Charles Seventh on the women. At any rate, both sexes vied with each other in giving to the attentive boy a highly favourable opinion of both these personages. All these descriptions and narratives were given in a serene and quiet state of mind; for the peace of Aix-la-Chapelle had, for the moment, put an end to all feuds: and they spoke at their ease of past contests, as well as of their former festivities, — the battle of Dettingen for instance, and other remarkable events of bygone years; and all that was important or dangerous seemed, as generally happens when a peace has been concluded, to have occurred only to afford entertainment to prosperous and unconcerned people.

Half a year had scarcely passed away in this narrow patriotism before the fairs began, which always produced an incredible ferment in the heads of all children. The erection, in so short a time, of so many booths, creating a new town within the old one; the roll and crush, the unloading and unpacking of wares, — excited from the very first dawn of consciousness an insatiable active curiosity, and a boundless desire for childish property, which the boy with increasing years endeavoured to gratify, in one way or another, as far as his little purse permitted. At the same time, he obtained a notion of what the world produces, what it wants, and what the inhabitants of its different parts exchange with each other.

These great epochs, which came round regularly in spring and autumn, were announced by curious solemnities, which seemed the more dignified because they vividly brought before us the old time, and what had come down from it to ourselves. On Escort Day, the whole population were on their legs, thronging to the *Fahrgasse*, to the bridge, and beyond Sachsenhausen; all the windows were occupied, though nothing unusual took place on that day; the crowd seeming to be there only for the sake of jostling each other, and the spectators merely to look at one another: for the real occasion of their coming did not begin till nightfall, and was then rather taken upon trust than seen with the eyes.

The affair was thus: in those old, unquiet times, when every one did wrong according to his pleasure, or helped the right as his liking led him, traders on their way to the fairs were so wilfully beset and harassed by waylayers, both of noble and ignoble birth, the princes and other persons of power caused their people to be accompanied to Frankfort by an armed escort. Now, the burghers of the imperial city would yield no rights pertaining to themselves or their district: they went out to meet the advancing party; and thus contests often arose as to how far the escort should advance, or whether it had a right to enter the city at all. But as this took place, not only in regard to matters of trade and fairs, but also when high personages came, in times of peace or war, and especially on the days of election; and as the affair often came to blows when a train which was not to be endured in the city strove to make its way in along with its lord, — many negotiations had from time to time been resorted to, and many temporary arrangements concluded, though always with reservations of rights on both sides. The hope had not been relinquished of composing once for all a quarrel that had already lasted for centuries, inasmuch as the whole institution, on account of which it had been so long and often so hotly contested, might be looked upon as nearly useless, or at least as superfluous.

Meanwhile, on those days, the city cavalry in several divisions, each having a commander in front, rode forth from different gates, and found on a certain spot some troopers or hussars of the persons entitled to an escort, who, with their leaders, were well received and entertained. They stayed till toward evening, and then rode back to the city, scarcely visible to the expectant crowd, many a city knight not being in a condition to manage his horse, or keep himself in the saddle. The most important bands returned by the bridge-gate, where the pressure was consequently the strongest. Last of all, just as night fell, the Nuremberg post-coach arrived, escorted in the same way, and always containing, as the people fancied, in pursuance of custom, an old woman. Its arrival, therefore, was a signal for all the urchins to break out into an ear-splitting shout, though it was utterly impossible to distinguish any one of the passengers within. The throng that pressed after the coach through the bridge-gate was quite incredible, and perfectly bewildering to the senses. The houses nearest the bridge were those, therefore, most in demand among spectators.

Another more singular ceremony, by which the people were excited in broad daylight, was the Piper's Court (*Pfeifergericht*). It commemorated those early times when important larger trading-towns endeavoured, if not to abolish tolls altogether, at least to bring about a reduction of them, as they increased in proportion with trade and industry. They were allowed this privilege by the emperor, who needed their aid, when it was in his power to grant it, but commonly only for one year; so that it had to be annually renewed. This was effected by means of symbolical gifts, which were presented before the opening of St. Bartholomew's Fair to the imperial magistrate (*Schultheiss*), who might have sometimes been the chief toll-gatherer; and, for the sake of a more imposing show, the gifts were offered when he was sitting in full court with the *Schöffen*. But when the chief magistrate afterward came to be no longer appointed by the emperor, and was elected by the city itself, he still retained these privileges; and thus both the immunities of the cities from toll, and the ceremonies by which the representatives from Worms, Nuremberg, and old Bamberg, once acknowledged the ancient favour, had come down to our times. The day before Lady Day, an open court was proclaimed. In an enclosed space in the great Imperial Hall, the *Schöffen* took their elevated seats; a step higher, sat the *Schultheiss* in the midst of them; while below, on the right hand, were the procurators of both parties invested with plenipotentiary powers. The *Actuarius* begins to read aloud the weighty judgments reserved for this day: the lawyers demand copies, appeal, or do whatever else seems necessary. All at once a singular sort of music announces, if we may so speak, the advent of former centuries. It proceeds from three pipers, one of whom plays an old *shawm*, another a *sackbut*, and the third a *pommer*, or oboe. They wear blue mantles trimmed with gold, having the notes made fast to their sleeves, and their heads covered. Having thus left their inn at ten o'clock, followed by the deputies and their attendants, and stared at by all, natives and strangers, they enter the hall. The law proceedings are stayed, the pipers and their train halt before the railing, the deputy steps in and stations himself in front of the *Schultheiss*. The emblematic presents, which were required to be precisely the same as in the old precedents, consisted commonly of the staple wares of the city offering them. Pepper passed, as it were, for everything else; and, even on this occasion, the deputy brought a handsomely turned wooden goblet filled with pepper. Upon it lay a pair of gloves, curiously slashed, stitched, and tasselled with silk, — a token of a favour granted and received, — such as the emperor himself made use of in certain cases. Along with this was a white staff, which in former times could not easily be dispensed with in judicial proceedings. Some small pieces of silver money were added: and the city of Worms brought an old felt hat, which was always redeemed again; so that the same one had been a witness of these ceremonies for many years.

After the deputy had made his address, handed over his present, and received from the *Schultheiss* assurance of continued favour, he quitted the enclosed circle, the pipers blew, the train departed as it had come, the court pursued its business, until the second and at last the third deputy had been introduced. For each came some time after the other, partly that the pleasure of the public might thus be prolonged, and partly because they were always the same antiquated *virtuosi* whom Nuremberg, for itself and its co-cities, had undertaken to maintain, and produce annually at the appointed place.

We children were particularly interested in this festival, because we were not a little flattered to see our grandfather in a place of so much honour; and because commonly, on the self-same day, we used to visit him, quite modestly, in order that we might, when my grandmother had emptied the pepper into her spice-box, lay hold of a cup or small rod, a pair of gloves, or an old *Räder Albus*.[1] These symbolical ceremonies, restoring antiquity as if by magic, could not be explained to us without leading us back into past times, and informing us of the manners, customs, and feelings of those early ancestors who were so strangely made present to us by pipers and deputies seemingly risen from the dead, and by tangible gifts which might be possessed by ourselves.

These venerable solemnities were followed, in the fine season, by many festivals, delightful for us children, which took place in the open air, outside the city. On the right shore of the Main, going down, about half an hour's walk from the gate, there rises a sulphur spring, neatly enclosed, and surrounded by aged lindens. Not far from it stands the *Good-People's-Court*, formerly a hospital erected for the sake of the waters. On the commons around, the herds of cattle from the neighbourhood were collected on a certain day of the year; and the herdsmen, together with their sweethearts, celebrated a rural festival with dancing and singing, with all sorts of pleasure and clownishness. On the other side of the city lay a similar but larger common, likewise graced with a spring and still finer lindens. Thither, at Whitsuntide, the flocks of sheep were driven: and, at the same time, the poor, pale orphan children were allowed to come out of their walls into the open air; for the thought had not yet occurred that these destitute creatures, who must some time or other help

[1] An old silver coin.

themselves through the world, ought soon to be brought in contact with it; that, instead of being kept in dreary confinement, they should rather be accustomed to serve and to endure; and that there was every reason to strengthen them physically and morally from their infancy. The nurses and maids, always ready to take a walk, never failed to carry or conduct us to such places, even in our first years; so that these rural festivals belong to the earliest impressions that I can recall.

Meanwhile, our house had been finished, and that too in tolerably short time; because everything had been judiciously planned and prepared, and the needful money provided. We now found ourselves all together again, and felt comfortable; for, when a well-considered plan is once carried out, we forget the various inconveniences of the means that were necessary to its accomplishment. The building, for a private residence, was roomy enough, light and cheerful throughout, with broad staircases, agreeable parlours, and a prospect of the gardens that could be enjoyed easily from several of the windows. The internal completion, and what pertained to mere ornament and finish, was gradually accomplished, and served at the same time for occupation and amusement.

The first thing brought into order was my father's collection of books, the best of which, in calf and half-calf binding, were to ornament the walls of his office and study. He possessed the beautiful Dutch editions of the Latin classics, which, for the sake of outward uniformity, he had endeavoured to procure all in quarto; and also many other works relating to Roman antiquities and the more elegant jurisprudence. The most eminent Italian poets were not wanting, and for Tasso he showed a great predilection. There were also the best and most recent Travels, and he took great delight in correcting and completing Keyssler

and Nemeiz from them. Nor had he omitted to surround himself with all needful aids to learning, such
as dictionaries of various languages, and encyclopædias
of science and art, which, with much else adapted
to profit and amusement, might be consulted at
will.

The other half of this collection, in neat parchment
bindings, with very beautifully written titles, was
placed in a separate attic. The acquisition of new
books, as well as their binding and arrangement, he
pursued with great composure and love of order; and
he was much influenced in his opinion by the critical
notices that ascribed particular merit to any work.
His collection of juridical treatises was annually increased by some volumes.

Next, the pictures, which in the old house had hung
about promiscuously, were now collected, and sym-
metrically hung on the walls of a cheerful room near
the study, all in black frames set off with gilt mould-
ings. It was my father's principle, to which he gave
frequent and even passionate utterance, that one ought
to employ the living masters, and to spend less upon
the departed, in the estimation of whom prejudice
greatly concurred. He had the notion that it was precisely the same with pictures as with Rhenish wines,
which, though age may impart to them a higher value,
can be produced in any coming year of just as excellent quality as in years past. After the lapse of some
time, the new wine also becomes old, quite as valuable
and perhaps more delicious. This opinion he chiefly
confirmed by the observation that many old pictures
seemed to derive their chief value for lovers of art
from the fact that they had become darker and
browner, and that the harmony of tone in such pictures was often vaunted. My father, on the other
hand, protested that he had no fear that the new pictures would not also turn black in time; though

whether they were likely to gain anything by this he was not so positive.

In pursuance of these principles, he employed for many years the whole of the Frankfort artists, — the painter Hirt, who excelled in animating oak and beech woods, and other so-called rural scenes, with cattle; Trautmann, who had adopted Rembrandt as his model, and had attained great perfection in enclosed lights and reflections, as well as in effective conflagrations, so that he was once ordered to paint a companion-piece to a Rembrandt; Schütz, who diligently elaborated landscapes of the Rhine country, in the manner of Sachtlebens; and Junker, who executed with great purity flower and fruit pieces, still life, and figures quietly employed, after the models of the Dutch. But now, by the new arrangement, by more convenient room, and still more by the acquaintance of a skilful artist, our love of art was again quickened and animated. This artist was Seekatz, a pupil of Brinkmann, court painter at Darmstadt, whose talent and character will be more minutely unfolded in the sequel.

In this way the remaining rooms were finished, according to their several purposes. Cleanliness and order prevailed throughout. Above all, the large panes of plate glass contributed toward a perfect lightness, which had been wanting in the old house for many causes, but chiefly on account of the panes, which were for the most part round. My father was cheerful on account of the success of his undertaking; and if his good humour had not been often interrupted because the diligence and exactness of the mechanics did not come up to his wishes, a happier life than ours could not have been conceived, since much good partly arose in the family itself, and partly flowed from without.

But an extraordinary event deeply disturbed the

boy's peace of mind for the first time. On the 1st of November, 1755, the earthquake at Lisbon took place, and spread a prodigious alarm over the world, long accustomed to peace and quiet. A great and magnificent capital, which was at the same time a trading and mercantile city, is smitten without warning by a most fearful calamity. The earth trembles and totters; the sea foams; ships dash together; houses fall in, and over them churches and towers; the royal palace is in part swallowed by the waters; the bursting land seems to vomit flames, since smoke and fire are seen everywhere amid the ruins. Sixty thousand persons, a moment before in ease and comfort, fall together; and he is to be deemed most fortunate who is no longer capable of a thought or feeling about the disaster. The flames rage on; and with them rage a troop of desperadoes, before concealed, or set at large by the event. The wretched survivors are exposed to pillage, massacre, and every outrage; and thus on all sides Nature asserts her boundless capriciousness.

Intimations of this event had spread over wide regions more quickly than the authentic reports: slight shocks had been left in many places; in many springs, particularly those of a mineral nature, an unusual receding of the waters had been remarked; and so much the greater was the effect of the accounts themselves, which were rapidly circulated, at first in general terms, but finally with dreadful particulars. Hereupon the religious were neither wanting in reflections, nor the philosophic in grounds for consolation, nor the clergy in warnings. So complicated an event arrested the attention of the world for a long time; and, as additional and more detailed accounts of the extensive effects of this explosion came from every quarter, the minds already aroused by the misfortunes of strangers began to be more and more anxious about themselves and their friends. Perhaps the demon of terror had never so speedily and powerfully diffused his terrors over the earth.

The boy, who was compelled to put up with frequent repetitions of the whole matter, was not a little staggered. God, the Creator and Preserver of heaven and earth, whom the explanation of the first article of the creed declared so wise and benignant, having given both the just and the unjust a prey to the same destruction, had not manifested himself by any means in a fatherly character. In vain the young mind strove to resist these impressions. It was the more impossible, as the wise and scripture-learned could not themselves agree as to the light in which such a phenomenon should be regarded.

The next summer gave a closer opportunity of knowing directly that angry God, of whom the Old Testament records so much. A sudden hail-storm, accompanied by thunder and lightning, violently broke the new panes at the back of our house, which looked toward the west, damaged the new furniture, destroyed some valuable books and other things of worth, and was the more terrible to the children, as the whole household, quite beside themselves, dragged them into a dark passage, where, on their knees, with frightful groans and cries, they thought to conciliate the wrathful Deity. Meanwhile, my father, who was the only one self-possessed, forced open and unhinged the window-frames, by which we saved much glass, but made a broader inlet for the rain that followed the hail; so that, after we were finally quieted, we found ourselves in the rooms and on the stairs completely surrounded by floods and streams of water.

These events, startling as they were on the whole, did not greatly interrupt the course of instruction which my father himself had undertaken to give us children. He had passed his youth in the Coburg Gymnasium, which stood as one of the first among German educational institutions. He had there laid a good foundation in languages, and other matters reckoned part of a learned education, had subsequently applied himself to jurisprudence at Leipzig, and had at last taken his degree at Giessen. His dissertation, " Electa de aditione Hereditatis," which had been earnestly and carefully written, is still cited by jurists with approval.

It is a pious wish of all fathers to see what they have themselves failed to attain realised in their sons, as if in this way they could live their lives over again, and at last make a proper use of their early experience. Conscious of his acquirements, with the certainty of faithful perseverance, and distrusting the teachers of the day, my father undertook to instruct his own children, allowing them to take particular lessons from particular masters only so far as seemed absolutely necessary. A pedagogical *dilettantism* was already beginning to show itself everywhere. The pedantry and heaviness of the masters appointed in the public schools had probably given rise to this evil. Something better was sought for, but it was forgotten how defective all instruction must be which is not given by persons who are teachers by profession.

My father had prospered in his own career tolerably according to his wishes : I was to follow the same course, only more easily, and much farther. He prized my natural endowments the more, because he was himself wanting in them ; for he had acquired everything only by means of unspeakable diligence, pertinacity, and repetition. He often assured me, early and late, both in jest and earnest, that with my talents he would have deported himself very differently, and would not have turned them to such small account.

By means of a ready apprehension, practice, and a good memory, I very soon outgrew the instructions which my father and the other teachers were able to give, without being thoroughly grounded in anything.

Grammar displeased me, because I regarded it as a mere arbitrary law : the rules seemed ridiculous, inasmuch as they were invalidated by so many exceptions, which had all to be learned by themselves. And if the first Latin work had not been in rhyme, I should have got on but badly in that ; but, as it was, I hummed and sang it to myself readily enough. In the same way we had a geography in memory-verses, in which the most wretched doggerel best served to fix the recollection of that which was to be retained ; e. g., —

"Upper-Yssel has many a fen,
Which makes it hateful to all men."

The forms and inflections of language I caught with ease ; and I also quickly unravelled what lay in the conception of a thing. In rhetoric, composition, and such matters, no one excelled me ; although I was often put back for faults of grammar. Yet these were the attempts that gave my father particular pleasure, and for which he rewarded me with many presents of money, considerable for such a lad.

My father taught my sister Italian in the same room in which I had to commit Cellarius to memory. As I was soon ready with my task, and was yet obliged to sit quiet, I listened with my book before me, and very readily caught the Italian, which struck me as an agreeable softening of Latin.

Other precocities, with respect to memory and the power to combine, I possessed in common with those children who thus acquire an early reputation. For that reason, my father could scarcely wait for me to go to college. He very soon declared that I must study jurisprudence in Leipzig, for which he retained a strong predilection ; and I was afterward to visit some other university and take my degree. As for this second one he was indifferent as to which I might choose, except

that he had for some reason or other a disinclination
to Göttingen, to my disappointment, since it was precisely there that I had placed such confidence and high
hopes.

He told me further, that I was to go to Wetzlar and
Ratisbon, as well as to Vienna, and thence toward
Italy; although he repeatedly mentioned that Paris
should first be seen, because after coming out of Italy
nothing else could be pleasing.

These tales of my future youthful travels, often as
they were repeated, I listened to eagerly, the more so
as they always led to accounts of Italy, and at last to
a description of Naples. His otherwise serious and dry
manner seemed on these occasions to relax and quicken,
and thus a passionate wish awoke in us children to
participate in the paradise he described.

Private lessons, which now gradually multiplied,
were shared with the children of the neighbours. This
learning in common did not advance me: the teachers
followed their routine; and the rudeness, sometimes
the ill nature, of my companions, interrupted the brief
hours of study with tumult, vexation, and disturbance.
Chrestomathies, by which learning is made pleasant
and varied, had not yet reached us. Cornelius Nepos,
so dry to young people; the New Testament, which
was much too easy, and which by preaching and religious instructions had been rendered even commonplace; Cellarius and Pasor, — could impart no kind of
interest; on the other hand, a certain rage for rhyme
and versification, a consequence of reading the prevalent
German poets, took complete possession of us. Me it
had seized much earlier, as I had found it agreeable
to pass from the rhetorical to the poetical treatment
of subjects.

We boys held a Sunday assembly where each of us
was to produce original verses. And here I was struck
by something strange, which long caused me uneasi-

ness. My poems, whatever they might be, always seemed to me the best. But I soon remarked that my competitors, who brought forth very lame affairs, were in the same condition, and thought no less of themselves. Nay, what appeared yet more suspicious, a good lad (though in such matters altogether unskilful), whom I liked in other respects, but who had his rhymes made by his tutor, not only regarded these as the best, but was thoroughly persuaded they were his own, as he always maintained in our confidential intercourse. Now, as this illusion and error was obvious to me, the question one day forced itself upon me, whether I myself might not be in the same state, whether those poems were not really better than mine, and whether I might not justly appear to those boys as mad as they to me? This disturbed me much and long, for it was altogether impossible for me to find any external criterion of the truth : I even ceased from producing, until at length I was quieted by my own light temperament, and the feeling of my own powers, and lastly by a trial of skill, — started on the spur of the moment by our teachers and parents, who had noted our sport, — in which I came off well, and won general praise.

No libraries for children had at that time been established. The old had themselves still childish notions, and found it convenient to impart their own education to their successors. Except the "Orbis Pictus" of Amos Comenius, no book of the sort fell into our hands; but the large folio Bible, with copperplates by Merian, was diligently gone over leaf by leaf; Gottfried's "Chronicles," with plates by the same master, taught us the most notable events of universal history; the "Acerra Philologica" added thereto all sorts of fables, mythologies, and wonders; and, as I soon became familiar with Ovid's "Metamorphoses," the first books of which in particular I studied carefully, my young brain was rapidly furnished with a mass of images and events, of significant and wonderful shapes and occurrences; and I never felt time hang upon my hands, as I always occupied myself in working over, repeating, and reproducing these acquisitions.

A more salutary moral effect than that of these rude and hazardous antiquities was produced by Fénélon's "Telemachus," with which I first became acquainted in Neukirch's translation, and which, imperfectly as it was executed, had a sweet and beneficent influence on my mind. That "Robinson Crusoe" was added in due time, follows in the nature of things; and it may be imagined that the "Island of Falsenberg" was not wanting. Lord Anson's "Voyage round the Globe" combined the dignity of truth with the rich fancies of fable; and, while our thoughts accompanied this excellent seaman, we were conducted over all the world, and endeavoured to follow him with our fingers on the globe. But a still richer harvest was to spring up before me, when I lighted on a mass of writings, which, in their present state, it is true, cannot be called excellent, but the contents of which, in a harmless way, bring near to us many a meritorious action of former times.

The publication, or rather the manufacture, of those books, which have at a later day become so well known and celebrated under the name *Volkschriften, Volksbücher* (popular works or books), was carried on in Frankfort. The enormous sales they met with led to their being almost illegibly printed from stereotypes on horrible blotting-paper. We children were so fortunate as to find these precious remains of the Middle Ages every day on a little table at the door of a dealer in cheap books, and to obtain them at the cost of a couple of *Kreutzer.* "The Eulenspiegel," "The Four Sons of Haimon," "The Emperor Octavian," "The Fair Melusina," "The Beautiful Magelone," "Fortunatus," with the whole race down to "The Wandering Jew," were all at our service, as often as we preferred the relish of these works to the taste of sweet things. The greatest benefit of this was, that, when we had read through or damaged such a sheet, it could soon be reprocured, and swallowed a second time.

As a family picnic in summer is vexatiously disturbed by a sudden storm, which transforms a pleasant state of things into the very reverse: so the diseases of childhood fall unexpectedly on the most beautiful season of early life. And thus it happened with me. I had just purchased "Fortunatus with his Purse and Wishing-hat," when I was attacked by a restlessness and fever which announced the smallpox. Inoculation was still with us considered very problematical; and, although it had already been intelligibly and urgently recommended by popular writers, the German physicians hesitated to perform an operation that seemed to forestall Nature. Speculative Englishmen, therefore, had come to the Continent, and inoculated, for a considerable fee, the children of such persons as were opulent, and free from prejudices. Still, the majority were exposed to the old disease: the infection raged through families, killed and disfigured many children; and few parents dared to avail themselves of a method, the probable efficacy of which had been abundantly confirmed by the result. The evil now invaded our house, and attacked me with unusual severity. My whole body was sown over with spots, and my face covered; and for several days I lay blind and in great pain. They tried the only possible alleviation, and promised me heaps of gold if I would keep quiet, and not increase the mischief by rubbing and scratching. I controlled myself, while, according to the prevailing prejudice, they kept me as warm as possible, and thus only rendered my suffering more acute. At last, after a woful time, there fell, as it were, a mask

from my face. The blotches had left no visible mark
upon the skin, but the features were plainly altered.
I myself was satisfied merely with seeing the light of
day again, and gradually putting off my spotted skin;
but others were pitiless enough to remind me often of
my previous condition, especially a very lively aunt,
who had formerly regarded me with idolatry, but in
after-years could seldom look at me without exclaim-
ing, "The deuce, cousin, what a fright he's grown!"
Then she would tell me circumstantially how I had
once been her delight, and what attention she had
excited when she carried me about; and thus I early
learned that people very often subject us to a severe
atonement for the pleasure which we have afforded
them.

I escaped neither measles nor chicken-pox, nor any
other of the tormenting demons of childhood; and I
was assured each time that it was a great piece of good
luck that this malady was now past for ever. But alas!
another again threatened in the background, and advanced. All these things increased my propensity to
reflection; and as I had already practised myself in
fortitude, in order to remove the torture of impatience,
the virtues which I had heard praised in the stoics
appeared to me highly worthy of imitation, and the
more so, as something similar was commended by the
Christian doctrine of patience.

While on the subject of these family diseases, I will
mention a brother about three years younger than myself, who was likewise attacked by that infection, and
suffered not a little from it. He was of a tender
nature, quiet and capricious; and we were never on
the most friendly terms. Besides, he scarcely survived
the years of childhood. Among several other children
born afterward, who, like him, did not live long, I only
remember a very pretty and agreeable girl, who also
soon passed away; so that, after the lapse of some

years, my sister and I remained alone, and were therefore the more deeply and affectionately attached to each other.

These maladies, and other unpleasant interruptions, were in their consequences doubly grievous; for my father, who seemed to have laid down for himself a certain calendar of education and instruction, was resolved immediately to repair every delay, and imposed double lessons upon the young convalescent. These were not hard for me to accomplish, but were so far troublesome, that they hindered, and, to a certain extent, repressed, my inward development, which had taken a decided direction.

From these didactic and pedagogic oppressions, we commonly fled to my grandfather and grandmother. Their house stood in the Friedberg Street, and appeared to have been formerly a fortress; for, on approaching it, nothing was seen but a large gate with battlements, which were joined on either side to the two neighbouring houses. On entering through a narrow passage, we reached at last a tolerably wide court, surrounded by irregular buildings, which were now all united into one dwelling. We usually hastened at once into the garden, which extended to a considerable length and breadth behind the buildings, and was very well kept. The walks were mostly skirted by vine-trellises: one part of the space was used for vegetables, and another devoted to flowers, which from spring till autumn adorned in rich succession the borders as well as the beds. The long wall, erected toward the south, was used for some well-trained espalier peach-trees, the forbidden fruit of which ripened temptingly before us through the summer. Yet we rather avoided this side, because we here could not satisfy our dainty appetites; and we turned to the side opposite, where an interminable row of currant and gooseberry bushes furnished our voracity with a succession of harvests till autumn. Not less important to us was an old, high, wide-spreading mulberry-tree, both on account of its fruits, and because we were told that the silkworms fed upon its leaves. In this peaceful region my grandfather was found every evening, tending with genial care, and with his own hand, the finer growths of fruits and flowers; while a gardener managed the drudgery. He was never vexed by the various toils which were necessary to preserve and increase a fine show of pinks. The branches of the peach-trees were carefully tied to the espaliers with his own hands, in a fan-shape, in order to bring about a full and easy growth of the fruit. The sorting of the bulbs of tulips, hyacinths, and plants of a similar nature, as well as the care of their preservation, he entrusted to none; and I still with pleasure recall to my mind how diligently he occupied himself in inoculating the different varieties of roses. That he might protect himself from the thorns, he put on a pair of those ancient leather gloves, of which three pair were given him annually at the Piper's Court; so that there was no dearth of the article. He wore also a loose dressing-gown, and a folded black velvet cap upon his head; so that he might have passed for an intermediate person between Alcinous and Laertes.

All this work in the garden he pursued as regularly and with as much precision as his official business; for, before he came down, he always arranged the list of cases for the next day, and read the legal papers. In the morning he proceeded to the city hall, dined after his return, then took a nap in his easy-chair, and so went through the same routine every day. He conversed little, never exhibited any vehemence; and I do not remember ever to have seen him angry. All that surrounded him was in the fashion of the olden time. I never perceived any alteration in his wainscoted room. His library contained, besides law-works, only the earliest books of travels, sea-voyages, and discoveries of countries. Altogether I can call to mind no situation more adapted than his to awaken the feeling of uninterrupted peace and eternal duration.

But the reverence we entertained for this venerable old man was raised to the highest degree by a conviction that he possessed the gift of prophecy, especially in matters that pertained to himself and his destiny. It is true he revealed himself to no one distinctly and minutely, except to my grandmother; yet we were all aware that he was informed of what was going to happen by significant dreams. He assured his wife, for instance, at a time when he was still a junior councillor, that, on the first vacancy, he would obtain the place left open on the bench of the *Schöffen;* and soon afterward, when one of those officers actually died of apoplexy, my grandfather gave orders that his house should be quietly got ready prepared on the day of electing and balloting, to receive his guests and congratulators. Sure enough, the decisive gold ball was drawn in his favour. The simple dream by which he had learned this, he confided to his wife as follows: He had seen himself in the ordinary full assembly of councilmen, where all went on just as usual. Suddenly the late *Schöff* rose from his seat, descended the steps, pressed him in the most complimentary manner to take the vacant place, and then departed by the door.

Something similar occurred on the death of the *Schultheiss.* They make no delay in supplying this place; as they always have to fear that the emperor will, at some time, resume his ancient right of nominating the officer. On this occasion, the messenger of the court came at midnight to summon an extraordinary session for the next morning; and, as the light in his lantern was about to expire, he asked for a candle's end to help him on his way. "Give him a whole one," said my grandfather to the ladies: "he takes the trouble all on my account." This expression anticipated the result, — he was made *Schultheiss*. And what rendered the circumstance particularly remarkable was, that, although his representative was the third and last to draw at the ballot, the two silver balls first came out, leaving the golden ball at the bottom of the bag for him.

Perfectly prosaic, simple, and without a trace of the fantastic or miraculous, were the other dreams, of which we were informed. Moreover, I remember that once, as a boy, I was turning over his books and memoranda, and found, among some other remarks which related to gardening, such sentences as these: "To-night N. N. came to me, and said," — the name and revelation being written in cipher; or, "This night I saw," — all the rest being again in cipher, except the conjunctions and similar words, from which nothing could be learned.

It is worthy of note also, that persons who showed no signs of prophetic insight at other times, acquired, for the moment, while in his presence, and that by means of some sensible evidence, presentiments of diseases or deaths which were then occurring in distant places. But no such gift has been transmitted to any of his children or grandchildren, who, for the most part, have been hearty people, enjoying life, and never going beyond the actual.

While on this subject, I remember with gratitude many kindnesses I received from them in my youth. Thus, for example, we were employed and entertained in many ways when we visited the second daughter, married to the druggist Melber, whose house and shop stood near the market, in the midst of the liveliest and most crowded part of the town. There we could look down from the windows pleasantly enough upon the hurly-burly, in which we feared to lose ourselves; and though at first, of all the goods in the shop, nothing had much interest for us but the licorice, and the little brown stamped cakes made from it, we became in time better acquainted with the multitude of articles bought and sold in that business. This aunt was the most vivacious of all the family. Whilst my mother, in her early years, took pleasure in being neatly dressed, working at some domestic occupation, or reading a book, the other, on the contrary, ran about the neighbourhood to pick up neglected children, take care of them, comb then, and carry them about in the way she had done with me for a good while. At a time of public festivities, such as coronations, it was impossible to keep her at home. When a little child, she had already scrambled for the money scattered on such occasions; and it was related of her, that once when she had got a good many together, and was looking at them with great delight in the palm of her hand, it was struck by somebody, and all her well-earned booty vanished at a blow. There was another incident of which she was very proud. Once, while standing on a post as the Emperor Charles VII. was passing, at a moment when all the people were silent, she shouted a vigorous " Vivat ! " into the coach, which made him take off his hat to her, and thank her quite graciously for her bold salutation.

Everything in her house was stirring, lively, and cheerful; and we children owed her many a gay hour.

In a more quiet situation, which was, however, suited to her character, was a second aunt, married to the Pastor Stark, incumbent of St. Catherine's Church. He lived much alone, in accordance with his temperament and vocation, and possessed a fine library. Here I first became acquainted with Homer, in a prose translation, which may be found in the seventh part of Herr von Loen's new collection of the most remarkable travels, under the title, " Homer's Description of the

Conquest of the Kingdom of Troy," ornamented with copperplates in the theatrical French taste. These pictures perverted my imagination to such a degree, that, for a long time, I could conceive the Homeric heroes only under such forms. The incidents themselves gave me unspeakable delight; though I found great fault with the work for affording us no account of the capture of Troy, and breaking off so abruptly with the death of Hector. My uncle, to whom I mentioned this defect, referred me to Virgil, who perfectly satisfied my demands.

It will be taken for granted, that we children had among our other lessons a continued and progressive instruction in religion. But the Church-Protestantism imparted to us was, properly speaking, nothing but a kind of dry morality: ingenious exposition was not thought of, and the doctrine appealed neither to the understanding nor to the heart. For that reason, there were various secessions from the Established Church. Separatists, Pietists, Herrnhuter (Moravians), Quiet-in-the-Land, and others differently named and characterised, sprang up, all of whom are animated by the same purpose of approaching the Deity, especially through Christ, more closely than seemed to them possible under the forms of the established religion.

The boy heard these opinions and sentiments constantly spoken of, for the clergy as well as the laity divided themselves into *pro* and *con*. The minority were composed of those who dissented more or less broadly; but their modes of thinking attracted by originality, heartiness, perseverance, and independence. All sorts of stories were told of their virtues, and of the way in which they were manifested. The reply of a pious master-tinman was especially noted, who, when one of his craft attempted to shame him by asking, " Who is really your confessor ? " answered with great cheerfulness, and confidence in the goodness of his cause, "I have a famous one, — no less than the confessor of King David."

Things of this sort naturally made an impression on the boy, and led him into similar states of mind. In fact, he came to the thought that he might immediately approach the great God of nature, the Creator and Preserver of heaven and earth, whose earlier manifestations of wrath had been long forgotten in the beauty of the world, and the manifold blessings in which we participate while upon it. The way he took to accomplish this was very curious.

The boy had chiefly kept to the first article of belief. The God who stands in immediate connection with nature, and owns and loves it as his work, seemed to him the proper God, who might be brought into closer relationship with man, as with everything else, and who would take care of him, as of the motion of the stars, the days and seasons, the animals and plants. There were texts of the Gospels which explicitly stated this. The boy could ascribe no form to this Being: he therefore sought him in his works, and would, in the good Old-Testament fashion, build him an altar. Natural productions were set forth as images of the world, over which a flame was to burn, signifying the aspirations of man's heart toward his Maker. He brought out of the collection of natural objects which he possessed, and which had been increased as chance directed, the best ores and other specimens. But the next difficulty was, as to how they should be arranged and raised into a pile. His father possessed a beautiful red-lacquered music-stand, ornamented with gilt flowers, in the form of a four-sided pyramid, with different elevations, which had been found convenient for quartets, but lately was not much in use. The boy laid hands on this, and built up his representatives of nature one above the other in steps; so that it all looked quite pretty and at the same time sufficiently

significant. On an early sunrise his first worship of
God was to be celebrated, but the young priest had
not yet settled how to produce a flame which should
at the same time emit an agreeable odour. At last it
occurred to him to combine the two, as he possessed
a few fumigating pastils, which diffused a pleasant
fragrance with a glimmer, if not with a flame. Nay,
this soft burning and exhalation seemed a better representation of what passes in the heart, than an open
flame. The sun had already risen for a long time, but
the neighbouring houses concealed the east. At last
it glittered above the roofs: a burning-glass was at
once taken up and applied to the pastils, which were
fixed on the summit in a fine porcelain saucer. Everything succeeded according to the wish, and the devotion was perfect. The altar remained as a peculiar
ornament of the room which had been assigned him
in the new house. Every one regarded it only as a
well-arranged collection of natural curiosities. The
boy knew better, but concealed his knowledge. He
longed for a repetition of the solemnity. But unfortunately, just as the most opportune sun arose, the
porcelain cup was not at hand: he placed the pastils
immediately on the upper surface of the stand; they
were kindled; and so great was the devotion of the
priest, that he did not observe, until it was too late,
the mischief his sacrifice was doing. The pastils had
burned mercilessly into the red lacquer and beautiful
gold flowers, and, as if some evil spirit had disappeared,
had left their black, ineffaceable footprints. By this
the young priest was thrown into the most extreme
perplexity. The mischief could be covered up, it was
true, with the larger pieces of his show materials; but
the spirit for new offerings was gone, and the accident
might almost be considered a hint and warning of the
danger there always is in wishing to approach the
Deity in such a way.

SECOND BOOK.

ALL that has been hitherto recorded indicates that happy and easy condition in which nations exist during a long peace. But nowhere probably is such a beautiful time enjoyed in greater comfort than in cities living under their own laws, and large enough to include a considerable number of citizens, and so situated as to enrich them by trade and commerce. Strangers find it to their advantage to come and go, and are under a necessity of bringing profit in order to acquire profit. Even if such cities rule but a small territory, they are the better qualified to advance their internal prosperity; as their external relations expose them to no costly undertakings or alliances.

Thus the Frankforters passed a series of prosperous years during my childhood; but scarcely, on the 28th of August, 1756, had I completed my seventh year, than that world-renowned war broke out which was also to exert great influence upon the next seven years of my life. Frederick the second, King of Prussia, had fallen upon Saxony with sixty thousand men; and, instead of announcing his invasion by a declaration of war, he followed it up with a manifesto, composed by himself as it was said, which explained the causes that had moved and justified him in so monstrous a step. The world, which saw itself appealed to, not merely as spectator, but as judge, immediately split into two parties; and our family was an image of the great whole.

42

My grandfather, who, as *Schöff* of Frankfort, had carried the coronation canopy over Francis the First, and had received from the empress a heavy gold chain with her likeness, took the Austrian side, along with some of his sons-in-law and daughters. My father having been nominated to the imperial council by Charles the Seventh, and sympathising sincerely in the fate of that unhappy monarch, leaned toward Prussia, with the other and smaller half of the family. Our meetings, which had been held on Sundays for many years uninterruptedly, were very soon disturbed. The misunderstandings so common among persons related by marriage found only now a form in which they could be expressed. Contention, discord, silence, and separation ensued. My grandfather, generally a cheerful, quiet man, and fond of ease, became impatient. The women vainly endeavoured to smother the flames; and, after some unpleasant scenes, my father was the first to quit the society. At home we now rejoiced undisturbed at the Prussian victories, which were commonly announced with great glee by our vivacious aunt. Every other interest had to give way to this, and we passed the rest of the year in perpetual agitation. The occupation of Dresden, the moderation of the king at the outset, his slow but secure advances, the victory at Lowositz, the capture of the Saxons, were so many triumphs for our party. Everything that could be alleged for the advantage of our opponents was denied or depreciated; and, as the members of the family on the other side did the same, they could not meet in the streets without disputes arising, as in "Romeo and Juliet."

Thus I also was then a Prussian in my views, or, to speak more correctly, a Fritzian; since what cared we for Prussia? It was the personal character of the great king that worked upon all hearts. I rejoiced with my father in our conquests, readily copied the songs of triumph, and almost more willingly the lampoons directed against the other party, poor as the rhymes might be.

Being their eldest grandson and godchild, I had dined every Sunday since my infancy with my grandfather and grandmother; and the hours so spent had been the most delightful of the whole week. But now I relished not a morsel, because I was compelled to hear the most horrible slanders of my hero. Here blew another wind, here sounded another tone, than at home. My liking and even my respect for my grandfather and grandmother fell off. I could mention nothing of this to my parents, but avoided the matter, both on account of my own feelings, and because I had been warned by my mother. In this way I was thrown back upon myself; and as in my sixth year, after the earthquake at Lisbon, the goodness of God had become to me in some measure suspicious: so I began now, on account of Frederick the Second, to doubt the justice of the public. My heart was naturally inclined to reverence, and it required a great shock to stagger my faith in anything that was venerable. But alas! they had commended good manners and a becoming deportment to us, not for their own sake, but for the sake of the people. What will people say? was always the cry; and I thought that the people must be right good people, and would know how to judge of anything and everything. But my experience went just to the contrary. The greatest and most signal services were defamed and attacked; the noblest deeds, if not denied, were at least misrepresented and diminished; and this base injustice was done to the only man who was manifestly elevated above all his contemporaries, and who daily proved what he was able to do, — and that, not by the populace, but by distinguished men, as I took my grandfather and uncles to be. That parties existed, and that he himself belonged to a party, had never entered into the conceptions of the boy. He, therefore, believed himself all the more right, and dared hold his own opinion for the better one; since he and those of like mind appreciated the beauty and other good qualities of Maria Theresa, and even did not grudge the Emperor Francis his love of jewelry and money. That Count Daun was often called an old dozer, they thought justifiable.

But, now that I look more closely into the matter, I here trace the germ of that disregard and even disdain of the public, which clung to me for a whole period of my life, and only in later days was brought within the bounds by insight and cultivation. Suffice it to say, that the perception of the injustice of parties had even then a very unpleasant, nay, an injurious, effect upon the boy; as it accustomed him to separate himself from beloved and highly valued persons. The quick succession of battles and events left the parties neither quiet nor rest. We ever found a malicious delight in reviving and resharpening those imaginary evils and capricious disputes; and thus we continued to tease each other, until the occupation of Frankfort by the French some years afterward brought real inconvenience into our homes.

Although to most of us the important events occurring in distant parts served only for topics of hot controversy, there were others who perceived the seriousness of the times, and feared that the sympathy of France might open a scene of war in our own vicinity. They kept us children at home more than before, and strove in many ways to occupy and amuse us. With this view, the puppet-show bequeathed by our grandmother was again brought forth, and arranged in such a way that the spectators sat in my gable room; while the persons managing and performing, as well as the theatre itself as far as the proscenium, found a place in the room adjoining. We were allowed, as a special favour, to invite first one and then another of the neighbours' children as spectators; and thus at the outset I gained many friends, but the restlessness inherent in children did not suffer them to remain long a patient audience. They interrupted the play; and we were compelled to seek a younger public, which could at any rate be kept in order by the nurses and maids. The original drama, to which the puppets had been specially adapted, we had learned by heart; and in the beginning this was exclusively performed. Soon growing weary of it, however, we changed the dresses and decorations, and attempted various other pieces, which were indeed on too grand a scale for so narrow a stage. Although this presumption spoiled and finally quite destroyed what we performed, such childish pleasures and employments nevertheless exercised and advanced in many ways my power of invention and representation, my fancy, and a certain technical skill, to a degree which in any other way could not perhaps have been secured in so short a time, in so confined a space, and at so little expense.

I had early learned to use compasses and ruler, because all the instructions they gave me in geometry were forthwith put into practice; and I occupied myself greatly with pasteboard work. I did not stop at geometrical figures, little boxes, and such things, but invented pretty pleasure-houses adorned with pilasters, steps, and flat roofs. However, but little of this was completed.

Far more persevering was I, on the other hand, in arranging, with the help of our domestic (a tailor by trade), an armory for the service of our plays and tragedies, which we ourselves performed with delight when we had outgrown the puppets. My playfellows, too, prepared for themselves such armories, which they considered to be quite as fine and good as mine; but I had made provision, not for the wants of one person only, and could furnish several of the little band with every requisite, and thus made myself more and more indispensable to our little circle. That such games tended to factions, quarrels, and blows, and commonly came to a sad end in tumult and vexation, may easily be supposed. In such cases certain of my companions generally took part with me, while others sided against me; though many changes of party occurred. One single boy, whom I will call Pylades, urged by the others, once only left my party, but could scarcely for a moment maintain his hostile position. We were reconciled amid many tears, and for a long time afterward kept faithfully together.

To him, as well as other well-wishers, I could render myself very agreeable by telling tales, which they most delighted to hear when I was the hero of my own story. It greatly rejoiced them to know that such wonderful things could befall one of their own playfellows; nor was it any harm that they did not understand how I could find time and space for such adventures, as they must have been pretty well aware of all my comings and goings, and how I was occupied the entire day. Not the less necessary was it for me to select the localities of these occurrences, if not in another world, at least in another spot; and yet all was told as having taken place only to-day or yesterday. They therefore had to form for themselves greater illusions than I could have palmed off upon them. If I had not gradually learned, in accordance with the instincts of my nature, to work up these visions and conceits into artistic forms, such vainglorious beginnings could not have gone on without producing evil consequences for myself in the end.

Considering this impulse more closely, we may see in it that presumption with which the poet authoritatively utters the greatest improbabilities, and requires every one to recognise as real whatever may in any way seem to him, the inventor, as true.

But what is here told only in general terms, and by way of reflection, will perhaps become more apparent and interesting by means of an example. I subjoin, therefore, one of these tales, which, as I often had to repeat it to my comrades, still hovers entire in my imagination and memory.

THE NEW PARIS.

A BOY'S LEGEND.

On the night before Whitsunday, not long since, I dreamed that I stood before a mirror engaged with the new summer clothes which my dear parents had given me for the holiday. The dress consisted, as you know, of shoes of polished leather, with large silver buckles, fine cotton stockings, black nether garments of serge, and a coat of green baracan with gold buttons. The waistcoat of gold cloth was cut out of my father's bridal waistcoat. My hair had been frizzled and powdered, and my curls stuck out from my head like little wings; but I could not finish dressing myself, because I kept confusing the different articles, the first always falling off as soon as I was about to put on the next. In this dilemma, a young and handsome man came to me, and greeted me in the friendliest manner. " Oh! you are welcome," said I: " I am very glad to see you here." — " Do you know me, then?" replied he, smiling. " Why not?" was my no less smiling answer. " You are Mercury — I have often enough seen you represented in pictures." — " I am, indeed," replied he, " and am sent to you by the gods on an important errand. Do you see these three apples?" He stretched forth his hand and showed me three apples, which it could hardly hold, and which were as wonderfully beautiful as they were large, the one of a red, the other of a yellow, the third of a green, colour. One could not help thinking they were precious stones made into the form of fruit. I would have snatched them; but he drew back, and said, "You must know, in the first place, that they are not for you. You must give them to the three handsomest youths of the city, who then, each according to his lot, will find wives to the utmost of their wishes. Take them, and success to you!" said he, as he departed, leaving the apples in my open hands. They appeared to me to have become still larger. I held them up at once against the light, and found them quite transparent; but soon they expanded upward, and became three beautiful little ladies about as large as middle-sized dolls, whose clothes were of the colours of the apples. They glided gently up my fingers: and when I was about to catch them, to make sure of one at least, they had already soared high and far; and I had to put up with the disappointment. I stood there all amazed and petrified, holding up my hands, and staring at my fingers as if there were still something on them to see. Suddenly I saw a most lovely girl dance upon the very tips. She was smaller, but pretty and lively; and as she did not fly away like the others, but remained dancing, now on one finger-point, now on another, I regarded her for a long while with admiration. And, as she pleased me so much, I thought in the end I could catch her, and made, as I fancied, a very adroit grasp. But at the moment I felt such a blow on my head that I fell down stunned, and did not awake from my stupor till it was time to dress myself and go to church.

During the service I often called those images to mind, and also when I was eating dinner at my grandfather's table. In the afternoon I wished to visit some friends, partly to show myself in my new dress, with my hat under my arm and my sword by my side, and partly to return their visits. I found no one at home; and, as I heard that they were gone to the gardens, I resolved to follow them, and pass the evening pleasantly. My way led toward the intrenchments; and I came to the spot which is rightly called the Bad Wall, for it is never quite safe from ghosts there. I walked slowly, and thought of my three goddesses, but especially of the little nymph, and often held up my fingers in hopes she might be kind enough to balance herself there again. With such thoughts I was proceeding, when I saw in the wall on my left hand a little gate which I did not remember to have ever noticed before. It looked low, but its pointed arch would have allowed the tallest man to enter. Arch and wall had been chiselled in the handsomest way, both by mason and sculptor; but it was the door itself which first properly attracted my attention. The old brown wood, though slightly ornamented, was crossed with broad bands of brass wrought both in relief and intaglio. The foliage on these, with the most natural birds sitting in it, I could not sufficiently admire. But, what seemed most remarkable, no keyhole could be seen, no latch, no knocker; and from this I conjectured that the door could be opened only from within. I was not in error; for, when I went nearer in order to touch the ornaments, it opened inwards; and there appeared a man whose dress was somewhat long, wide, and singular. A venerable beard enveloped his chin, so that I was inclined to think him a Jew. But he, as if he had divined my thoughts, made the sign of the holy cross, by which he gave me to understand that he was a good Catholic Christian. "Young gentleman, how came you here, and what are you doing?" he said to me, with a friendly voice and manner. "I am admiring," I replied, "the workmanship of this door; for I have never seen anything like it, except in some small pieces in the

collections of amateurs." "I am glad," he answered,
"that you like such works. The door is much more
beautiful inside. Come in, if you like." My heart, in
some degree, failed me. The mysterious dress of the
porter, the seclusion, and a something, I know not
what, that seemed to be in the air, oppressed me. I
paused, therefore, under the pretext of examining the
outside still longer; and at the same time I cast stolen
glances into the garden, for a garden it was which had
opened before me. Just inside the door I saw a space.
Old linden-trees, standing at regular distances from each
other, entirely covered it with their thickly interwoven
branches; so that the most numerous parties, during
the hottest of the day, might have refreshed themselves
in the shade. Already I had stepped upon the threshold, and the old man contrived gradually to allure me
on. Properly speaking, I did not resist; for I had
always heard that a prince or sultan in such a case
must never ask whether there be danger at hand. I
had my sword by my side too; and could I not soon
have finished with the old man, in case of hostile demonstrations? I therefore entered perfectly reassured: the
keeper closed the door, which bolted so softly that I
scarcely heard it. He now showed me the workmanship on the inside, which in truth was still more artistic than the outside, explained it to me, and at the
same time manifested particular good-will. Being thus
entirely at my ease, I let myself be guided in the
shaded space by the wall, that formed a circle, where I
found much to admire. Niches tastefully adorned with
shells, corals, and pieces of ore, poured a profusion of
water from the mouths of Tritons into marble basins.
Between them were aviaries and other latticework, in
which squirrels frisked about, guinea-pigs ran hither
and thither, with as many other pretty little creatures
as one could wish to see. The birds called and sang
to us as we advanced: the starlings, particularly, chat-

tered the silliest stuff. One always cried, " Paris, Paris ! " and the other, " Narcissus, Narcissus ! " as plainly as a schoolboy can say them. The old man seemed to continue looking at me earnestly while the birds called out thus; but I feigned not to notice it, and had in truth no time to attend to him, for I could easily perceive that we went round and round, and that this shaded space was in fact a great circle, which enclosed another much more important. Indeed, we had actually reached the small door again, and it seemed as though the old man would let me out. But my eyes remained directed toward a golden railing, which seemed to hedge round the middle of this wonderful garden, and which I had found means enough of observing in our walk; although the old man managed to keep me always close to the wall, and therefore pretty far from the centre. And now, just as he was going to the door, I said to him, with a bow, " You have been so extremely kind to me that I would fain venture to make one more request before I part from you. Might I not look more closely at that golden railing, which appears to enclose in a very wide circle the interior of the garden ? " " Very willing," replied he, " but in that case you must submit to some conditions." " In what do they consist ? " I asked hastily. " You must leave here your hat and sword, and must not let go my hand while I accompany you." " Most willingly," I replied ; and laid my hat and sword on the nearest stone bench. Immediately he grasped my left hand with his right, held it fast, and led me with some force straight forward. When we reached the railing, my wonder changed into amazement. On a high socle of marble stood innumerable spears and partisans, ranged beneath each other, joined by their strangely ornamented points, and forming a complete circle. I looked through the intervals, and saw just behind a gently flowing piece of water, bounded on both sides by marble, and displaying in its clear depths a multitude of gold and silver fish, which moved about now slowly and now swiftly, now alone and now in shoals. I would also fain have looked beyond the canal, to see what there was in the heart of the garden. But I found, to my great sorrow, that the other side of the water was bordered by a similar railing, and with so much art, that to each interval on this side exactly fitted a spear or partisan on the other. These, and the other ornaments, rendered it impossible for one to see through, stand as he would. Besides, the old man, who still held me fast, prevented me from moving freely. My curiosity, meanwhile, after all I had seen, increased more and more; and I took heart to ask the old man whether one could not pass over. " Why not ?" returned he, " but on new conditions." When I asked him what these were, he gave me to understand that I must put on other clothes. I was satisfied to do so: he led me back toward the wall into a small, neat room, on the sides of which hung many kinds of garments, all of which seemed to approach the Oriental costume. I soon changed my dress. He confined my powdered hair under a many coloured net, after having to my horror violently dusted it out. Now, standing before a great mirror, I found myself quite handsome in my disguise, and pleased myself better than in my formal Sunday clothes. I made gestures, and leaped, as I had seen the dancers do at the fair-theatres. In the midst of this I looked in the glass, and saw by chance the image of a niche which was behind me. On its white ground hung three green cords, each of them twisted up in a way which from the distance I could not clearly discern. I therefore turned round rather hastily, and asked the old man about the niche as well as the cords. He very courteously took a cord down, and showed it to me. It was a band of green silk of moderate thickness, the ends of which, joined by green leather with two holes in it, gave it the appearance of an instrument for no very desirable purpose. The thing struck me as suspicious, and I asked the old man the meaning. He answered me very quietly and kindly, " This is for those who abuse the confidence which is here readily shown them." He hung the cord again in its place, and immediately desired me to follow him ; for this time he did not hold me, and so I walked freely beside him.

My chief curiosity now was, to discover where the gate and bridge, for passing through the railing and over the canal, might be ; since as yet I had not been able to find anything of the kind. I therefore watched the golden fence very narrowly as we hastened toward it. But in a moment my sight failed : lances, spears, halberds, and partisans began unexpectedly to rattle and quiver ; and the strange movement ended in all the points sinking toward each other just as if two ancient hosts, armed with pikes, were about to charge. The confusion to the eyes, the clatter to the ears, was hardly to be borne ; but infinitely surprising was the sight, when, falling perfectly level, they covered the circle of the canal, and formed the most glorious bridge that one can imagine. For now a most variegated garden parterre met my sight. It was laid out in curvilinear beds, which, looked at together, formed a labyrinth of ornaments ; all with green borders of a low, woolly plant, which I had never seen before ; all with flowers, each division of different colours, which, being likewise low and close to the ground, allowed the plan to be easily traced. This delicious sight, which I enjoyed in the full sunshine, quite riveted my eyes. But I hardly knew where I was to set my foot ; for the serpentine paths were most delicately laid with blue sand, which seemed to form upon the earth a darker sky, or a sky seen in the water : and so I walked for awhile beside my conductor, with my eyes fixed upon the ground, until at last I perceived, that, in the middle of this round of beds and flowers, there was a great circle of cypresses or poplar-like trees, through which one could not see, because the lowest branches seemed to spring out of the ground. My guide, without taking me exactly the shortest way, led me nevertheless immediately toward that centre; and how was I astonished, when, on entering the circle of high trees, I saw before me the peristyle of a magnificent garden-house, which seemed to have similar prospects and entrances on the other sides! The heavenly music which streamed from the building transported me still more than this model of architecture. I fancied that I heard now a lute, now a harp, now a guitar, and now something tinkling which did not belong to any of these instruments. The door for which we made opened soon on being lightly touched by the old man. But how was I amazed when the porteress who came out perfectly resembled the delicate girl who had danced upon my fingers in the dream! She greeted me as if we were already acquainted, and invited me to walk in. The old man stayed behind; and I went with her through a short passage, arched and finely ornamented, to the middle hall, the splendid, dome-like ceiling of which attracted my gaze on my entrance, and filled me with astonishment. Yet my eye could not dwell on this long, being allured down by a more charming spectacle. On a carpet, directly under the middle of the cupola, sat three women in a triangle, clad in three different colours, — one red, the other yellow, the third green. The seats were gilt, and the carpet was a perfect flower-bed. In their arms lay the three instruments which I had been able to distinguish from without; for, being disturbed by my arrival, they had stopped their playing. " Welcome ! " said the middle one, who sat with her face to the door, in a red dress, and with the harp. " Sit down by Alerte, and listen, if you are a lover of music."

Now only I remarked that there was a rather long bench placed obliquely before them, on which lay a mandolin. The pretty girl took it up, sat down, and drew me to her side. Now also I looked at the second lady on my right. She wore the yellow dress, and had the guitar in her hand; and if the harp-player was dignified in form, grand in features, and majestic in her deportment, one might remark in the guitar-player an easy grace and cheerfulness. She was a slender blonde, while the other was adorned by dark brown hair. The variety and accordance of their music could not prevent me from remarking the third beauty, in the green dress, whose lute-playing was for me at once touching and striking. She was the one who seemed to notice me the most, and to direct her music to me: only I could not make up my mind about her; for she appeared to me now tender, now whimsical, now frank, now self-willed, according as she changed her mien and mode of playing. Sometimes she seemed to wish to excite my emotions, sometimes to tease me; but, do what she would, she got little out of me; for my little neighbour, by whom I sat elbow to elbow, had gained me entirely to herself: and while I clearly saw in those three ladies the sylphides of my dream, and recognised the colours of the apples, I conceived that I had no cause to detain them. I should have liked better to lay hold of the pretty little maiden if I had not but too well remembered the blow she had given me in my dream. Hitherto she had remained quite quiet with her mandolin; but, when her mistresses had ceased, they commanded her to perform some pleasant little piece. Scarcely had she jingled off some dance-tune, in a most exciting manner, than she sprang up: I did the same. She played and danced; I was hurried on to accompany her steps; and we executed a kind of little ballet, with which the ladies seemed satisfied; for, as soon as we had done, they commanded the little girl to refresh me with something nice till supper should come in. I had indeed forgotten that there was anything in the world beyond this paradise. Alerte led me back immediately into the passage by which I had entered. On one side of it she had two well-arranged rooms. In that in which she lived she set before me oranges, figs, peaches, and grapes; and I enjoyed with great gusto both the fruits of foreign lands and those of our own not yet in season. Confectionery there was in profusion: she filled, too, a goblet of polished crystal with foaming wine; but I had no need to drink, as I had refreshed myself with the fruits. " Now we will play," said she, and led me into the other room. Here all looked like a Christmas fair, but such costly and exquisite things were never seen in a Christmas booth. There were all kinds of dolls, dolls' clothes, and dolls' furniture; kitchens, parlours, and shops, and single toys innumerable. She led me round to all the glass cases in which these ingenious works were preserved. But she soon closed again the first cases, and said, " That is nothing for you, I know well enough. Here," she said, " we could find building-materials, walls and towers, houses, palaces, churches, to put together a great city. But this does not entertain me. We will take something else, which will be amusing to both of us." Then she brought out some boxes, in which I saw an army of little soldiers piled one upon the other, of which I must needs confess that I had never seen anything so beautiful. She did not leave me time to examine them in detail, but took one box under her arm, while I seized the other. " We will go," she said, " to the golden bridge. There one plays best with soldiers: the lances give at once the direction in which the armies are to be opposed to each other." We had now reached the golden, trembling floor; and below me I could hear the waters gurgle and the fishes splash, while I knelt down to range my columns. All, as I now saw, were cavalry. She boasted that she had the queen of the Amazons as leader of her female host. I, on the contrary, found Achilles and a very stately Grecian cavalry. The armies stood facing each other, and nothing could have been seen more beautiful. They were not flat, leaden horsemen like ours; but man and horse were round and solid, and most finely wrought: nor could one conceive how they kept their balance; for they stood of themselves, without a support for their feet.

Both of us had inspected our hosts with much self-complacency, when she announced the onset. We had found ordnance in our chests; viz., little boxes full of well-polished agate balls. With these we were to fight against each other from a certain distance; while, however, it was an express condition that we should not throw with more force than was necessary to upset the figures, as none of them were to be injured. Now the cannonade began on both sides, and at first it succeeded to the satisfaction of us both. But when my adversary observed that I aimed better than she, and might in the end win the victory, which depended on the majority of pieces remaining upright, she came nearer, and her girlish way of throwing had then the desired result. She prostrated a multitude of my best troops, and the more I protested the more eagerly did she throw. This at last vexed me, and I declared that I would do the same. In fact, I not only went nearer, but in my rage threw with much more violence; so that it was not long before a pair of her little centauresses flew in pieces. In her eagerness she did not instantly notice it, but I stood petrified when the broken figures joined together again of themselves: Amazon and horse became again one, and also perfectly close, set up a gallop from the golden bridge under the lime-trees, and, running swiftly backwards and forwards, were lost in their career, I know not

how, in the direction of the wall. My fair opponent
had hardly perceived this, when she broke out into
loud weeping and lamentation, and exclaimed that I
had caused her an irreparable loss, which was far
greater than could be expressed. But I, by this time
provoked, was glad to annoy her, and blindly flung a
couple of the remaining agate balls with force into the
midst of her army. Unhappily I hit the queen, who
had hitherto, during our regular game, been excepted.
She flew in pieces, and her nearest officers were also
shivered. But they swiftly set themselves up again,
and started off like the others, galloping very merrily
about under the lime-trees, and disappearing against
the wall. My opponent scolded and abused me; but,
being now in full play, I stooped to pick up some
agate balls which rolled about upon the golden lances.
It was my fierce desire to destroy her whole army.
She, on the other hand, not idle, sprang at me, and
gave me a box on the ear, which made my head ring.
Having always heard that a hearty kiss was the proper
response to a girl's box of the ear, I took her by the
ears, and kissed her repeatedly. But she uttered such
a piercing scream as frightened even me. I let her
go; and it was fortunate that I did so, for in a moment I knew not what was happening to me. The
ground beneath me began to shake and rattle. I
soon remarked that the railings again set themselves
in motion; but I had no time to consider, nor could I
get a footing so as to fly. I feared every instant to be
pierced; for the partisans and lances, which had lifted
themselves up, were already slitting my clothes. It is
sufficient to say, that, I know not how it was, hearing
and sight failed me; and I recovered from my swoon
and terror at the foot of a lime-tree, against which the
pikes in springing up had thrown me. As I awoke,
my anger awakened also, and violently increased when
I heard from the other side the gibes and laughter of

my opponent, who had probably reached the earth somewhat more softly than I. Therefore I jumped up, and as I saw the little host with its leader Achilles scattered around me, having been driven over with me by the rising of the rails, I seized the hero first and threw him against a tree. His resuscitation and flight now pleased me doubly, a malicious pleasure combining with the prettiest sight in the world; and I was on the point of sending all the other Greeks after him, when suddenly hissing waters spurted at me on all sides, from stones and wall, from ground and branches, and, wherever I turned, dashed against me crossways.

In a short time my light garment was wet through. It was already rent, and I did not hesitate to tear it entirely off my body. I cast away my slippers, and one covering after another. Nay, at last I found it very agreeable to let such a shower-bath play over me in the warm day. Now, being quite naked, I walked gravely along between these welcome waters, where I thought to enjoy myself for some time. My anger cooled, and I wished for nothing more than a reconciliation with my little adversary. But, in a twinkling, the water stopped; and I stood drenched upon the saturated ground. The presence of the old man, who appeared before me unexpectedly, was by no means welcome. I could have wished, if not to hide, at least to clothe, myself. The shame, the shivering, the effort to cover myself in some degree, made me cut a most piteous figure. The old man employed the moment in venting the severest reproaches against me. " What hinders me," he exclaimed, " from taking one of the green cords, and fitting it, if not to your neck, to your back ? " This threat I took in very ill part. " Refrain," I cried, " from such words, even from such thoughts; for otherwise you and your mistresses will be lost." — " Who, then, are you," he asked in defiance,

" who dare speak thus ? " — " A favourite of the gods,"
I said, " on whom it depends whether those ladies shall
find worthy husbands and pass a happy life, or be left
to pine and wither in their magic cell." The old man
stepped some paces back. " Who has revealed that to
you ? " he inquired, with astonishment and concern.
" Three apples," I said, " three jewels." — " And what
reward do you require ? " he exclaimed. " Before all
things, the little creature," I replied, " who has brought
me into this accursed state." The old man cast himself down before me, without shrinking from the wet
and miry soil : then he rose without being wetted,
took me kindly by the hand, led me into the hall, clad
me again quickly ; and I was soon once more decked
out and frizzled in my Sunday fashion as before. The
porter did not speak another word ; but, before he let
me pass the entrance, he stopped me, and showed me
some objects on the wall over the way, while, at the
same time, he pointed backwards to the door. I
understood him ; he wished to imprint the objects on
my mind, that I might the more certainly find the
door, which had unexpectedly closed behind me. I
now took good notice of what was opposite me.
Above a high wall rose the boughs of extremely old
nut-trees, and partly covered the cornice at the top.
The branches reached down to a stone tablet, the
ornamented border of which I could perfectly recognise, though I could not read the inscription. It
rested on the top-stone of a niche, in which a finely
wrought fountain poured water from cup to cup into a
great basin, that formed, as it were, a little pond, and
disappeared in the earth. Fountain, inscription, nut-
trees, all stood perpendicularly, one above another : I
would paint it as I saw it.

Now, it may well be conceived how I passed this
evening, and many following days, and how often I
repeated to myself this story, which even I could

hardly believe. As soon as it was in any degree possible, I went again to the Bad Wall, at least to refresh my remembrance of these signs, and to look at the precious door. But, to my great amazement, I found all changed. Nut-trees, indeed, overtopped the wall; but they did not stand immediately in contact. A tablet also was inserted in the wall, but far to the right of the trees, without ornament, and with a legible inscription. A niche with a fountain was found far to the left, but with no resemblance whatever to that which I had seen; so that I almost believed that the second adventure was, like the first, a dream, for of the door there is not the slightest trace. The only thing that consoles me is the observation, that these three objects seem always to change their places. For, in repeated visits to the spot, I think I have noticed that the nut-trees have moved somewhat nearer together, and that the tablet and the fountain seem likewise to approach each other. Probably, when all is brought together again, the door, too, will once more be visible; and I will do my best to take up the thread of the adventure. Whether I shall be able to tell you what further happens, or whether I shall be expressly forbidden to do so, I cannot say.

This tale, of the truth of which my playfellows vehemently strove to convince themselves, received great applause. Each of them visited alone the places described, without confiding it to me or the others, and discovered the nut-trees, the tablet, and the spring, though always at a distance from each other; as they at last confessed to me afterward, because it is not easy to conceal a secret at that early age. But here the contest first arose. One asserted that the objects did not stir from the spot, and always maintained the same distance; a second averred that they did move, and that, too, away from each other; a third agreed with the latter as to the first point of their moving, though it seemed to him that the nut-trees, tablet, and fountain rather drew near together; while a fourth had something still more wonderful to announce, which was, that the nut-trees were in the middle, but that the tablet and the fountain were on sides opposite to those which I had stated. With respect to the traces of the little door, they also varied. And thus they furnished me an early instance of the contradictory views men can hold and maintain in regard to matters quite simple and easily cleared up. As I obstinately refused the continuation of my tale, a repetition of the first part was˙ often desired. I took good care not to change the circumstances much; and, by the uniformity of the narrative, I converted the fable into truth in the minds of my hearers.

Yet I was averse to falsehood and dissimulation, and altogether by no means frivolous. Rather, on the contrary, the inward earnestness, with which I had early begun to consider myself and the world, was seen, even in my exterior; and I was frequently called to account, often in a friendly way, and often in raillery, for a certain dignity which I had assumed. For, although good and chosen friends were certainly not wanting to me, we were always a minority against those who found pleasure in assailing us with wanton rudeness, and who indeed often awoke us in no gentle fashion from that legendary and self-complacent dreaming in which we — I by inventing, and my companions by sympathising — were too readily absorbed. Thus we learned once more, that, instead of sinking into effeminacy and fantastic delights, there was reason rather for hardening ourselves, in order either to bear or to counteract inevitable evils.

Among the stoical exercises which I cultivated, as earnestly as it was possible for a lad, was even the endurance of bodily pain. Our teachers often treated us very unkindly and unskilfully, with blows and cuffs, against which we hardened ourselves all the more as obstinacy was forbidden under the severest penalties. A great many of the sports of youth depend on a rivalry in such endurances; as, for instance, when they strike each other alternately with two fingers or the whole fist, till the limbs are numb; or when they bear the penalty of blows incurred in certain games, with more or less firmness; when, in wrestling or scuffling, they do not let themselves be perplexed by the pinches of a half-conquered opponent; or, finally, when they suppress the pain inflicted for the sake of teasing, and even treat with indifference the nips and ticklings with which young persons are so active toward each other. Thus we gain a great advantage, of which others cannot speedily deprive us.

But, as I made a sort of boast of this impassiveness, the importunity of the others was increased; and, since rude barbarity knows no limits, it managed to force me beyond my bounds. Let one case suffice for several. It happened once that the teacher did not come for the usual hour of instruction. As long as we children were all together, we entertained ourselves quite agreeably; but when my adherents, after waiting long enough, had left, and I remained alone with three of my enemies, these took it into their heads to torment me, to shame me, and to drive me away. Having left me an instant in the room, they came back with switches, which they had made by quickly cutting up a broom. I noted their design; and, as I supposed the end of the hour near, I at once resolved not to resist them till the clock struck. They began, therefore, without remorse, to lash my legs and calves in the cruellest fashion. I did not stir, but soon felt that I had miscalculated, and that such pain greatly lengthened the minutes. My wrath grew with my endurance; and, at the first stroke of the hour, I grasped the

one who least expected it by the hair behind, hurled
him to the earth in an instant, pressing my knee upon
his back; the second, a younger and weaker one, who
attacked me from behind, I drew by the head under
my arm, and almost throttled him with the pressure.
The last, and not the weakest, still remained; and my
left hand only was left for my defence. But I seized
him by the clothes; and, with a dexterous twist on my
part and an over-precipitate one on his, I brought him
down and struck his face on the ground. They were
not wanting in bites, pinches, and kicks; but I had
nothing but revenge in my limbs as well as in my
heart. With the advantage which I had acquired, I
repeatedly knocked their heads together. At last they
raised a dreadful shout of murder, and we were soon
surrounded by all the inmates of the house. The
switches scattered around, and my legs, which I had
bared of the stockings, soon bore witness for me.
They put off the punishment, and let me leave the
house; but I declared, that in future, on the slightest
offence, I would scratch out the eyes, tear off the ears,
of any one of them, if not throttle him.

Though, as usually happens in childish affairs, this
event was soon forgotten, and even laughed at, it was
the cause that these joint instructions became fewer,
and at last entirely ceased. I was thus again, as
formerly, kept more at home; where I found my sister
Cornelia, who was only one year younger than myself,
a companion always growing more agreeable.

Still, I will not leave this topic without telling some
more stories of the many vexations caused me by my
playfellows; for this is the instructive part of such
moral communications, that a man may learn how it
has gone with others, and what he also has to expect
from life; and that, whatever comes to pass, he may
consider that it happens to him as a man, and not as
one specially fortunate or unfortunate. If such knowl-

edge is of little use for avoiding evils, it is very serviceable so far as it qualifies us to understand our condition, and bear or even to overcome it.

And general remark will not be out of place here, which is, that, as the children of the cultivated classes grow up, a great contradiction appears. I refer to the fact, that they are urged and trained by parents and teachers to deport themselves moderately, intelligently, and even wisely ; to give pain to no one from petulance or arrogance ; and to suppress all the evil impulses which may be developed in them ; but yet, on the other hand, while the young creatures are engaged in this discipline, they have to suffer from others that which in them is reprimanded and punished. In this way the poor things are brought into a sad strait between the natural and civilised states, and, after restraining themselves for awhile, break out, according to their characters, into cunning or violence.

Force may be warded off by force; but a well-disposed child, inclined to love and sympathy, has little to oppose to scorn and ill-will. Though I managed pretty well to keep off the assaults of my companions, I was by no means equal to them in sarcasm and abuse ; because he who merely defends himself in such cases is always a loser. Attacks of this sort consequently, when they went so far as to excite anger, were repelled with physical force, or at least excited strange reflections in me which could not be without results. Among other advantages which my ill-wishers saw with envy, was the pleasure I took in the relations that accrued to the family from my grandfather's position of *Schultheiss ;* since, as he was the first of his class, this had no small effect on those belonging to him. Once when, after the holding of the Piper's Court, I appeared to pride myself on having seen my grandfather in the midst of the council, one step higher than the rest, enthroned, as it were, under the portrait of the emperor, one of the boys said to me in derision, that, like the peacock contemplating his feet, I should cast my eyes back to my paternal grandfather, who had been keeper of the Willow Inn, and would never have aspired to thrones and coronets. I replied, that I was in no wise ashamed of that, as it was the glory and honour of our native city that all its citizens might consider each other equal, and every one derive profit and honour from his exertions in his own way. I was sorry only that the good man had been so long dead; for I had often yearned to know him in person, had many times gazed upon his likeness, nay, had visited his tomb, and had at least derived pleasure from the inscription on the simple monument of that past existence to which I was indebted for my own. Another ill-wisher, who was the most malicious of all, took the first aside, and whispered something in his ear; while they still looked at me scornfully. My gall already began to rise, and I challenged them to speak out. "What is more, then, if you will have it," continued the first, "this one thinks you might go looking about a long time before you could find your grandfather." I now threatened them more vehemently if they did not more clearly explain themselves. Thereupon they brought forward an old story, which they pretended to have overheard from their parents, that my father was the son of some eminent man, while that good citizen had shown himself willing to take outwardly the paternal office. They had the impudence to produce all sorts of arguments: as, for example, that our property came exclusively from our grandmother; that the other collateral relations who lived in Friedburg and other places were alike destitute of property; and other reasons of the sort, which could merely derive their weight from malice. I listened to them more composedly than they expected, for they stood ready to fly the very moment that I should make a gesture as if I would seize their hair. But I replied quite calmly, and in substance, " that even this was no great injury to me. Life was such a boon, that one might be quite indifferent as to whom one had to thank for it; since at least it must be derived from God, before whom we all were equals." As they could make nothing of it, they let the matter drop for this time: we went on playing together as before, which among children is an approved mode of reconciliation.

Still, these spiteful words inoculated me with a sort of moral disease, which crept on in secret. It would not have displeased me at all to have been the grandson of any person of consideration, even if it had not been in the most lawful way. My acuteness followed up the scent, my imagination was excited, and my sagacity put in requisition. I began to investigate the allegation, and invented or found for it new grounds of probability. I had heard little said of my grandfather, except that his likeness, together with my grandmother's, had hung in a parlour of the old house; both of which, after the building of the new one, had been kept in an upper chamber. My grandmother must have been a very handsome woman, and of the same age as her husband. I remembered also to have seen in her room the miniature of a handsome gentleman in uniform, with star and order, which after her death, and during the confusion of house-building, had disappeared, with many other small pieces of furniture. These and many other things I put together in my childish head, and exercised that modern poetical talent which contrives to obtain the sympathies of the whole cultivated world by a marvellous combination of the important events of human life.

But as I did not venture to trust such an affair to any one, or even to ask the most remote questions concerning it, I was not wanting in a secret diligence, in order to get, if possible, somewhat nearer to the matter. I had heard it explicitly maintained, that sons often bore a decided resemblance to their fathers or grandfathers. Many of our friends, especially Councillor Schneider, a friend of the family, were connected by business with all the princes and noblemen of the neighbourhood, of whom, including both the ruling and the younger branches, not a few had estates on the Rhine and Main, and in the intermediate country, and who at times honoured their faithful agents with their portraits. These, which I had often seen on the walls from my infancy, I now regarded with redoubled attention; seeking whether I could not detect some resemblance to my father or even to myself, which too often happened to lead me to any degree of certainty. For now it was the eyes of this, now the nose of that, which seemed to indicate some relationship. Thus these marks led me delusively backward and forward: and though in the end I was compelled to regard the reproach as a completely empty tale, the impression remained; and I could not from time to time refrain from privately calling up and testing all the noblemen whose images had remained very distinct in my imagination. So true is it that whatever inwardly confirms man in his self-conceit, or flatters his secret vanity, is so highly desirable to him, that he does not ask further, whether in other respects it may turn to his honour or disgrace.

But, instead of mingling here serious and even reproachful reflections, I rather turn my look away from those beautiful times; for who is able to speak worthily of the fulness of childhood? We cannot behold the little creatures which flit about before us otherwise than with delight, nay, with admiration; for they generally promise more than they perform: and it seems that Nature, among the other roguish tricks that she plays us, here also especially designs to make sport of us. The first organs she bestows upon children coming into the world are adapted to the nearest immediate condition of the creature, which, unassuming and artless, makes use of them in the readiest way for its present purposes. The child, considered in and for himself, with his equals, and in relations suited to his powers, seems so intelligent and rational, and at the same time so easy, cheerful, and clever, that one can hardly wish it further cultivation. If children grew up according to early indications, we should have nothing but geniuses; but growth is not merely development: the various organic systems which constitute one man spring one from another, follow each other, change into each other, supplant each other, and even consume each other; so that after a time scarcely a trace is to be found of many aptitudes and manifestations of ability. Even when the talents of the man have on the whole a decided direction, it will be hard for the greatest and most experienced connoisseur to declare them beforehand with confidence; although afterward it is easy to remark what has pointed to a future.

By no means, therefore, is it my design wholly to comprise the stories of my childhood in these first books; but I will rather afterward resume and continue many a thread which ran through the early years unnoticed. Here, however, I must remark what an increasing influence the incidents of the war gradually exercised upon our sentiments and mode of life.

The peaceful citizen stands in a wonderful relation to the great events of the world. They already excite and disquiet him from a distance; and, even if they do not touch him, he can scarcely refrain from an opinion and a sympathy. Soon he takes a side, as his character or external circumstances may determine. But when such grand fatalities, such important changes, draw nearer to him, then with many outward inconveniences remains that inward discomfort, which doubles and sharpens the evil, and destroys the good which is still possible. Then he has really to suffer from friends and foes, often more from the former than from the latter; and he knows not how to secure and preserve either his interests or his inclinations.

The year 1757, which still passed in perfectly civic tranquillity, kept us, nevertheless, in great uneasiness of mind. Perhaps no other was more fruitful of events than this. Conquests, achievements, misfortunes, restorations, followed one upon another, swallowed up and seemed to destroy each other; yet the image of Frederick, his name and glory, soon hovered again above all. The enthusiasm of his worshippers grew always stronger and more animated; the hatred of his enemies more bitter; and the diversity of opinion, which separated even families, contributed not a little to isolate citizens, already sundered in many ways and on other grounds. For in a city like Frankfort, where three religions divide the inhabitants into three unequal masses; where only a few men, even of the ruling faith, can attain to political power, — there must be many wealthy and educated persons who are thrown back upon themselves, and, by means of studies and tastes, form for themselves an individual and secluded existence. It will be necessary for us to speak of such men, now and hereafter, if we are to bring before us the peculiarities of a Frankfort citizen of that time.

My father, immediately after his return from his travels, had in his own way formed the design, that, to prepare himself for the service of the city, he would undertake one of the subordinate offices, and discharge its duties without emolument, if it were conferred upon him without balloting. In the consciousness of his good intentions, and according to his way of thinking and the conception he had of himself, he believed that he deserved such a distinction, which, indeed, was not conformable to law or precedent. Consequently, when his suit was rejected, he fell into ill humour and disgust, vowed that he would never accept of any place, and, in order to render it impossible, procured the title of Imperial Councillor, which the *Schultheiss* and elder *Schöffen* bear as a special honour. He had thus made himself an equal of the highest, and could not begin again at the bottom. The same impulse induced him also to woo the eldest daughter of the *Schultheiss*, so that he was excluded from the council on this side also. He was now of that number of recluses who never form themselves into a society. They are as much isolated in respect to each other as they are in regard to the whole, and the more so as in this seclusion the character becomes more and more uncouth. My father, in his travels and in the world which he had seen, might have formed some conception of a more elegant and liberal mode of life than was, perhaps, common among his fellow citizens. In this respect, however, he was not entirely without predecessors and associates.

The name of Uffenbach is well known. At that time, there was a Schöff von Uffenbach, who was generally respected. He had been in Italy; had applied himself particularly to music; sang an agreeable tenor; and, having brought home a fine collection of pieces, concerts and oratorios were performed at his house. Now, as he sang in these himself, and held musicians in great favour, it was not thought altogether suitable to his dignity; and his invited guests, as well as the other people of the country, allowed themselves many a jocose remark on the matter.

I remember, too, a Baron von Hakel, a rich nobleman, who, being married, but childless, occupied a charming house in the Antonius Street, fitted up with all the appurtenances of a dignified position in life. He also possessed good pictures, engravings, antiques, and much else which generally accumulates with collectors and lovers of art. From time to time he asked the more noted personages to dinner, and was beneficent in a careful way of his own; since he clothed the poor in his own house, but kept back their old rags, and gave them a weekly charity, on condition that they should present themselves every time clean and neat in the clothes bestowed on them. I can recall him but indistinctly, as a genial, well-made man; but more clearly his auction, which I attended from beginning to end, and, partly by command of my father, partly from my own impulse, purchased many things that are still to be found in my collections.

At an earlier date than this, — so early that I scarcely set eyes upon him, — John Michael von Loen gained considerable repute in the literary world as well as at Frankfort. Not a native of Frankfort, he settled there, and married a sister of my grandmother Textor, whose maiden name was Lindheim. Familiar with the court and political world, and rejoicing in a renewed title of nobility, he had acquired reputation by daring to take part in the various excitements which arose in Church and state. He wrote "The Count of Rivera," a didactic romance, the subject of which is made apparent by the second title, " or, The Honest Man at Court." This work was well received, because it insisted on morality, even in courts, where prudence only is generally at home; and thus his labour brought him applause and respect. A second work, for that very reason, would be accompanied by more danger. He wrote " The Only True Religion," a book designed to advance tolerance, especially between Lutherans and Calvinists. But here he got in a controversy with the theologians: one Doctor Benner of Giessen, in particular, wrote against him. Von Loen rejoined; the contest grew violent and personal, and the unpleasantness which arose from it caused him to accept the office of president at Lingen, which

Frederick II. offered him; supposing that he was an enlightened, unprejudiced man, and not averse to the new views that more extensively obtained in France. His former countrymen, whom he had left in some displeasure, averred that he was not contented there, nay, could not be so, as a place like Lingen was not to be compared with Frankfort. My father also doubted whether the president would be happy, and asserted that the good uncle would have done better not to connect himself with the king, as it was generally hazardous to get too near him, extraordinary sovereign as he undoubtedly was; for it had been seen how disgracefully the famous Voltaire had been arrested in Frankfort, at the requisition of the Prussian Resident Freitag, though he had formerly stood so high in favour, and had been regarded as the king's teacher in French poetry. There was, on such occasions, no want of reflections and examples to warn one against courts and princes' service, of which a native Frankforter could scarcely form a conception.

An excellent man, Doctor Orth, I will only mention by name; because here I have not so much to erect a monument to the deserving citizens of Frankfort, but rather refer to them only in as far as their renown or personal character had some influence upon me in my earliest years. Doctor Orth was a wealthy man, and was also of that number who never took part in the government, although perfectly qualified to do so by his knowledge and penetration. The antiquities of Germany, and more especially of Frankfort, have been much indebted to him: he published remarks on the so-called " Reformation of Frankfort," a work in which the statutes of the state are collected. The historical portions of this book I diligently read in my youth.

Von Ochsenstein, the eldest of the three brothers whom I have mentioned above as our neighbours, had not been remarkable during his lifetime, in consequence of his recluse habits, but became the more remarkable after his death, by leaving behind him a direction that common workingmen should carry him to the grave, early in the morning, in perfect silence, and without an attendant or follower. This was done; and the affair caused great excitement in the city, where they were accustomed to the most pompous funerals. All who discharged the customary offices on such occasions rose against the innovation. But the stout patrician found imitators in all classes; and, though such ceremonies were derisively called ox-burials,[1] they came into fashion, to the advantage of many of the more poorly provided families; while funeral parades were less and less in vogue. I bring forward this circumstance, because it presents one of the earlier symptoms of that tendency to humility and equality, which, in the second half of the last century, was manifested in so many ways, from above downward, and broke out in such unlooked-for effects.

Nor was there any lack of antiquarian amateurs. There were cabinets of pictures, collections of engravings; while the curiosities of our own country especially were zealously sought and hoarded. The older decrees and mandates of the imperial city, of which no collection had been prepared, were carefully searched for in print and manuscript, arranged in the order of time, and preserved with reverence, as a treasure of native laws and customs. The portraits of Frank-forters, which existed in great number, were also brought together, and formed a special department of the cabinets.

Such men my father appears generally to have taken as his models. He was wanting in none of the qualities that pertain to an upright and respectable citizen. Thus, after he had built his house, he put his property of every sort into order. An excellent collection of

----

[1] A pun upon the name of Ochsenstein.—TRANS.

maps by Schenck and other geographers at that time eminent, the aforesaid decrees and mandates, the portraits, a chest of ancient weapons, a case of remarkable Venetian glasses, cups and goblets, natural curiosities, works in ivory, bronzes, and a hundred other things, were separated and displayed; and I did not fail, whenever an auction occurred, to get some commission for the increase of his possessions.

I must still speak of one important family, of which I had heard strange things since my earliest years, and of some of whose members I myself lived to see a great deal that was wonderful, — I mean the Senkenbergs. The father, of whom I have little to say, was an opulent man. He had three sons, who, even in their youth, uniformly distinguished themselves as oddities. Such things are not well received in a limited city, where no one is suffered to render himself conspicuous, either for good or evil. Nicknames and odd stories, long kept in memory, are generally the fruit of such singularity. The father lived at the corner of Hare Street (*Hasengasse*), which took its name from a sign on the house, that represented one hare at least, if not three hares. They consequently called these three brothers only the three hares, which nickname they could not shake off for a long while. But as great endowments often announce themselves in youth in the form of singularity and awkwardness, so was it also in this case. The eldest of the brothers was the *Reichshofrath* (Imperial Councillor) von Senkenberg, afterward so celebrated. The second was admitted into the magistracy, and displayed eminent abilities, which, however, he subsequently abused in a pettifogging and even infamous way, if not to the injury of his native city, certainly to that of his colleagues. The third brother, a physician and man of great integrity, but who practised little, and that only in high families, preserved even in his old age a somewhat whimsical exterior. He was always very neatly dressed, and was never seen in the street otherwise than in shoes and stockings, with a well-powdered, curled wig, and his hat under his arm. He walked on rapidly, but with a singular sort of stagger; so that he was sometimes on one and sometimes on the other side of the way, and formed a complete zigzag as he went. The wags said that he made this irregular step to get out of the way of the departed souls, who might follow him in a straight line, and that he imitated those who are afraid of a crocodile. But all these jests and many merry sayings were transformed at last into respect for him, when he devoted his handsome dwelling-house in Eschenheimer Street, with court, garden, and all other appurtenances, to a medical establishment, where, in addition to a hospital designed exclusively for the citizens of Frankfort, a botanic garden, an anatomical theatre, a chemical laboratory, a considerable library, and a house for the director, were instituted in a way of which no university need have been ashamed.

Another eminent man, whose efficiency in the neighbourhood and whose writings, rather than his presence, had a very important influence upon me, was Charles Frederick von Moser, who was perpetually referred to in our district for his activity in business. He also had a character essentially moral, which, as the vices of human nature frequently gave him trouble, inclined him to the so-called pious. Thus, what Von Loen had tried to do in respect to court-life, he would have done for business-life; introducing into it a more conscientious mode of proceeding. The great number of small German courts gave rise to a multitude of princes and servants, the former of whom desired unconditional obedience; while the latter, for the most part, would work or serve only according to their own convictions. Thus arose an endless conflict, and rapid changes and explosions; because the effects of an unrestricted course of proceeding become much sooner noticeable and injurious on a small scale than on a large one. Many families were in debt, and Imperial Commissions of Debts were appointed; others found themselves sooner or later on the same road: while the officers either reaped an unconscionable profit, or conscientiously made themselves disagreeable and odious. Moser wished to act as a statesman and man of business; and here his hereditary talent, cultivated to a profession, gave him a decided advantage: but he at the same time wished to act as a man and a citizen, and surrender as little as possible of his moral dignity. His "Prince and Servant," his "Daniel in the Lions' Den," his "Relics," paint throughout his own condition, in which he felt himself, not indeed tortured, but always cramped. They all indicate impatience in a condition, to the bearings of which one cannot reconcile one's self, yet from which one cannot get free. With this mode of thinking and feeling, he was, indeed, often compelled to seek other employments, which, on account of his great cleverness, were never wanting. I remember him as a pleasing, active, and, at the same time, gentle man.

The name of Klopstock had already produced a great effect upon us, even at a distance. In the outset, people wondered how so excellent a man could be so strangely named; but they soon got accustomed to this, and thought no more of the meaning of the syllables. In my father's library I had hitherto found only the earlier poets, especially those who in his day had gradually appeared and acquired fame. All these had written in rhyme, and my father held rhyme as indispensable in poetical works. Canitz, Hagedorn, Drollinger, Gellert Creuz, Haller, stood in a row, in handsome calf bindings: to these were added Neukirch's "Telemachus," Koppen's "Jerusalem Delivered,"

and other translations. I had from my childhood
diligently perused the whole of these works, and committed portions of them to memory, whence I was
often called upon to amuse the company. A vexatious
era on the other hand opened upon my father, when,
through Klopstock's "Messiah," verses, which seemed
to him no verses, became an object of public admiration.[1] He had taken good care not to buy this book;
but the friend of the family, Councillor Schneider,
smuggled it in, and slipped it into the hands of my
mother and her children.

On this man of business, who read but little, "The
Messiah," as soon as it appeared, made a powerful
impression. Those pious feelings, so naturally expressed, and yet so beautifully elevated; that pleasant
diction, even if considered merely as harmonious prose,
— had so won the otherwise dry man of business, that
he regarded the first ten cantos, of which alone we are
properly speaking, as the finest book of devotion, and
once every year in Passion Week, when he managed
to escape from business, read it quietly through by
himself, and thus refreshed himself for the entire year.
In the beginning he thought to communicate his emotions to his old friend; but he was much shocked
when forced to perceive an incurable dislike cherished
against a book of such valuable substance, merely
because of what appeared to him an indifferent external form. It may readily be supposed that their
conversation often reverted to this topic; but both
parties diverged more and more widely from each
other, there were violent scenes: and the compliant
man was at last pleased to be silent on his favourite
work, that he might not lose, at the same time, a
friend of his youth, and a good Sunday meal.

It is the most natural wish of every man to make
proselytes; and how much did our friend find himself

[1] "The Messiah" is written in hexameter verse.—TRANS.

rewarded in secret, when he discovered in the rest of the family hearts so openly disposed for his saint. The copy which he used only one week during the year was given over to our edification all the remaining time. My mother kept it secret; and we children took possession of it when we could, that in leisure hours, hidden in some nook, we might learn the most striking passages by heart, and particularly might impress the most tender as well as the most violent parts on our memory as quickly as possible.

Porcia's dream we recited in a sort of rivalry, and divided between us the wild dialogue of despair between Satan and Adramelech, who have been cast into the Red Sea. The first part, as the strongest, had been assigned to me; and the second, as a little more pathetic, was undertaken by my sister. The alternate and horrible but well-sounding curses flowed only thus from our mouths, and we seized every opportunity to accost each other with these infernal phrases.

One Saturday evening in winter, — my father always had himself shaved over night, that on Sunday morning he might dress for church at his ease, — we sat on a footstool behind the stove, and muttered our customary imprecations in a tolerably low voice, while the barber was putting on the lather. But now Adramelech had to lay his iron hands on Satan: my sister seized me with violence, and recited, softly enough, but with increasing passion:

" Give me thine aid, I entreat thee : I'll worship thee if thou
    demandest,
Thee, thou reprobate monster, yes, thee, of all criminals
    blackest !
Aid me. I suffer the tortures of death, everlasting, avenging !
Once, in the times gone by, I with furious hatred could hate
    thee :
Now I can hate thee no more ! E'en this is the sharpest of
    tortures."

Thus far all went on tolerably; but loudly, with a dreadful voice, she cried the following words:

"Oh, how utterly crushed I am now!"

The good surgeon was startled, and emptied the lather-basin into my father's bosom.   There was a great uproar: and a severe investigation was held, especially with respect to the mischief which might have been done if the shaving had been actually going forward. In order to relieve ourselves of all suspicions of mischievousness, we pleaded guilty of having acted these Satanic characters; and the misfortune occasioned by the hexameters was so apparent, that they were again condemned and banished.

Thus children and common people are accustomed to transform the great and sublime into a sport, and even a farce; and how indeed could they otherwise abide and endure it?

THIRD BOOK.

AT that time the general interchange of personal good wishes made the city very lively on New-year's Day. Those who otherwise did not easily leave home, donned their best clothes, that for a moment they might be friendly and courteous to their friends and patrons. The festivities at my grandfather's house on this day were pleasures particularly desired by us children. At early dawn the grandchildren had already assembled there to hear the drums, oboes, clarinets, trumpets, and cornets played upon by the military, the city musicians, and whoever else might furnish his tones. The New-year's gifts, sealed and superscribed, were divided by us children among the humbler congratulators; and, as the day advanced, the number of those of higher rank increased. The relations and intimate friends appeared first, then the subordinate officials; even the gentlemen of the council did not fail to pay their respects to the *Schultheiss*, and a select number were entertained in the evening in rooms which were else scarcely opened throughout the year. The tarts, biscuits, marchpane, and sweet wine had the greatest charm for the children; and, besides, the *Schultheiss* and the two burgomasters annually received from some institutions some article of silver, which was then bestowed upon the grandchildren and godchildren in regular gradation. In fine, this small festival was not wanting in any of those things which usually glorify the greatest.

The New-year's Day of 1759 approached, as desirable and pleasant to us children as any preceding one, but full of import and foreboding to older persons. To the passage of the French troops people certainly had become accustomed; and they happened often, but they had been most frequent in the last days of the past year. According to the old usage of an imperial town, the warder of the chief tower sounded his trumpet whenever troops approached; and on this New-year's Day he would not leave off, which was a sign that large bodies were in motion on several sides. They actually marched through the city in greater masses on this day, and the people ran to see them pass by. We had generally been used to see them go through in small parties; but these gradually swelled, and there was neither power nor inclination to stop them. In short, on the 2d of January, after a column had come through Sachsenhausen over the bridge, through the Fahrgasse, as far as the police guard-house, it halted, overpowered the small company which escorted it, took possession of the beforementioned guard-house, marched down the Zeil, and, after a slight resistance, the main guard were also obliged to yield. In a moment the peaceful streets were turned into a scene of war. The troops remained and bivouacked there until lodgings were provided for them by regular billeting.

This unexpected, and, for many years, unheard-of, burden weighed heavily upon the comfortable citizens; and to none could it be more cumbersome than to my father, who was obliged to take foreign military inhabitants into his scarcely finished house, to open for them his well-furnished reception-rooms, which were generally closed, and to abandon to the caprices of strangers all that he had been used to arrange and keep so carefully. Siding as he did with the Prussians, he was now to find himself besieged in his own chambers by the French: it was, according to his way of thinking, the greatest misfortune that could happen to him. Had it, however, been possible for him to have taken the matter more easily, he might have saved himself and us many sad hours; since he spoke French well, and could deport himself with dignity and grace in the daily intercourse of life. For it was the king's lieutenant who was quartered on us; and he, although a military person, had only to settle civil occurrences, disputes between soldiers and citizens, and questions of debt and quarrels. This was the Count Thorane, a native of Grasse in Provence, not far from Antibes; a tall, thin, stern figure, with a face much disfigured by the smallpox; black, fiery eyes; and a dignified, reserved demeanour. His first entrance was at once favourable for the inmates of the house. They spoke of the different apartments, some of which were to be given up and others retained by the family; and, when the count heard a picture-room mentioned, he immediately requested permission, although it was already night, at least to give a hasty look at the pictures by candle-light. He took extreme pleasure in these things, behaved in the most obliging manner to my father, who accompanied him; and when he heard that the greater part of the artists were still living, and resided in Frankfort and its neighbourhood, he assured us that he desired nothing more than to know them as soon as possible, and to employ them.

But even this sympathy in respect to art could not change my father's feelings nor bend his character. He permitted what he could not prevent, but kept at a distance in inactivity; and the uncommon state of things around him was intolerable to him, even in the veriest trifle.

Count Thorane behaved himself, meanwhile, in an exemplary manner. He would not even have his maps nailed on the walls, that he might not injure the new hangings. His people were skilful, quiet, and orderly : but in truth, as, during the whole day and a part of the night there was no quiet with him, one complainant quickly following another, arrested persons being brought in and led out, and all officers and adjutants being admitted to his presence, — as, moreover, the count kept an open table every day, it made, in the moderately sized house, arranged only for a family, and with but one open staircase running from top to bottom, a movement and a buzzing like that in a beehive; although everything was managed with moderation, gravity, and severity.

As mediator between the irritable master of the house — who became daily more of a hypochondriac self-tormentor — and his well-intentioned, but stern and precise, military guest, there was a pleasant interpreter, a handsome, corpulent, lively man, who was a citizen of Frankfort, spoke French well, knew how to adapt himself to everything, and only made a jest of many little annoyances. Through him my mother had sent to the count a representation of the situation in which she was placed, owing to her husband's state of mind. He had explained the matter so skilfully, — had laid before him the new and scarcely furnished house, the natural reserve of the owner, his occupation in the education of his family, and all that could be said to the same effect, — that the count, who in his capacity took the greatest pride in the utmost justice, integrity, and honourable conduct, resolved here also to behave in an exemplary manner to those upon whom he was quartered, and, indeed, never swerved from this resolution under varying circumstances, during the several years he stayed with us.

My mother possessed some knowledge of Italian, a language not altogether unknown to any of the family : she therefore resolved to learn French immediately; for which purpose the interpreter, for whose child she had stood godmother during these stormy times, and who now, therefore, as a gossip,[1] felt a redoubled interest in our house, devoted every spare moment to his child's godmother (for he lived directly opposite); and, above all, he taught her those phrases which she would be obliged to use in her personal intercourse with the count. This succeeded admirably. The count was flattered by the pains taken by the mistress of the house at her age: and as he had a cheerful, witty vein in his character, and he liked to exhibit a certain dry gallantry, a most friendly relation arose between them; and the allied godmother and father could obtain from him whatever they wanted.

If, as I said before, it had been possible to cheer up my father, this altered state of things would have caused little inconvenience. The count practised the severest disinterestedness; he even declined receiving gifts which pertained to his situation; the most trifling thing which could have borne the appearance of bribery, he rejected angrily, and even punished. His people were most strictly forbidden to put the proprietor of the house to the least expense. We children, on the contrary, were bountifully supplied from the dessert. To give an idea of the simplicity of those times, I must take this opportunity to mention that my mother grieved us excessively one day, by throwing away the ices which had been sent us from the table, because she would not believe it possible for the stomach to bear real ice, however it might be sweetened.

Besides these dainties, which we gradually learned to enjoy and to digest with perfect ease, it was very

---

[1] The obsolete word, "gossip," has been revived as an equivalent for the German, "*Gevatter*." But it should be observed that this word not only signifies godfather, but that the person whose child has another person for godfather (or godmother) is that person's *Gevatter* or *Gevatterin* (feminine).

agreeable for us children to be in some measure released from fixed hours of study and strict discipline. My father's ill humour increased: he could not resign himself to the unavoidable. How he tormented himself, my mother, the interpreter, the councillors, and all his friends, only to rid him of the count! In vain they represented to him, that, under existing circumstances, the presence of such a man in the house was an actual benefit, and that the removal of the count would be followed by a constant succession of officers or of privates. None of these arguments had any effect. To him the present seemed so intolerable, that his indignation prevented his conceiving anything worse that could follow.

In this way his activity, which he had been used chiefly to devote to us, was crippled. The lessons he gave us were no longer required with the former exactness; and we tried to gratify our curiosity for military and other public proceedings as much as possible, not only at home, but also in the streets, which was the more easily done, as the front door, open day and night, was guarded by sentries who paid no attention to the running to and fro of restless children.

The many affairs which were settled before the tribunal of the royal lieutenant had quite a peculiar charm, from his making it a point to accompany his decisions with some witty, ingenious, or lively turn. What he decreed was strictly just, his manner of expressing it whimsical and piquant. He seemed to have taken the Duke of Ossuna as his model. Scarcely a day passed in which the interpreter did not tell some anecdote or other of this kind to amuse us and my mother. This lively man had made a little collection of such Solomonian decisions; but I only remember the general impression, and cannot recall to my mind any particular case.

By degrees we became better acquainted with the

strange character of the count. This man clearly understood his own peculiarities; and as there were times in which he was seized with a sort of dejection, hypochondria, or by whatever name we may call the evil demon, he withdrew into his room at such hours, which were often lengthened into days, saw no one but his valet, and in urgent cases could not even be prevailed upon to receive any one. But, as soon as the evil spirit had left him, he appeared as before, active, mild, and cheerful. It might be inferred from the talk of his valet, Saint Jean, a small, thin man of lively good nature, that in his earlier years he had caused a great misfortune when overcome by this temper; and that, therefore, in so important a position as his, exposed to the eyes of all the world, he had earnestly resolved to avoid similar aberrations.

During the very first days of the count's residence with us, all the Frankfort artists, as Hirt, Schütz, Trautmann, Nothnagel, and Junker, were called to him. They showed their finished pictures, and the count bought such as were for sale. My pretty, light room in the gable-end of the attic was given up to him, and immediately turned into a cabinet and studio; for he designed to keep all the artists at work for a long time, especially Seekatz of Darmstadt, whose pencil, particularly in simple and natural representations, highly pleased him. He therefore caused to be sent from Grasse, where his elder brother possessed a handsome house, the dimensions of all the rooms and cabinets; then considered, with the artists, the divisions of the walls, and fixed accordingly upon the size of the large oil-pictures, which were not to be set in frames, but to be fastened upon the walls like pieces of tapestry. And now the work went on zealously. Seekatz undertook country scenes, and succeeded extremely well in his old people and children, which were copied directly from nature. His young men did not answer so well, — they were almost all too thin; and his women failed from the opposite cause. For as he had a little, fat, good, but unpleasant-looking, wife, who would let him have no model but herself, he could produce nothing agreeable. He was also obliged to exceed the usual size of his figures. His trees had truth, but the foliage was over minute. He was a pupil of Brinkmann, whose pencil in easel pictures is not contemptible.

Schütz, the landscape painter, had perhaps the best of the matter. He was thoroughly master of the Rhine country, and of the sunny tone which animates it in the fine season. Nor was he entirely unaccustomed to work on a larger scale, and then he showed no want of execution or keeping. His paintings were of a cheerful cast.

Trautmann *Rembrandtised* some resurrection miracles out of the New Testament, and alongside of them set fire to villages and mills. One cabinet was entirely allotted to him, as I found from the designs of the rooms. Hirt painted some good oak and beech forests. His cattle were praiseworthy. Junker, accustomed to the imitation of the most elaborate Dutch, was least able to manage this tapestry-work; but he condescended to ornament many compartments with flowers and fruits for a handsome price.

As I had known all these men from my earliest youth, and had often visited them in their studios, and as the count also liked to have me with him, I was present at the suggestions, consultations, and orders, as well as at the deliveries, of the pictures, and ventured to speak my opinion freely when sketches and designs were handed in. I had already gained among amateurs, particularly at auctions, which I attended diligently, the reputation of being able to tell at once what any historical picture represented, whether taken from biblical or profane history, or from mythology;

and, even if I did not always hit upon the meaning of
allegorical pictures, there was seldom any one present
who understood it better than I. Often had I persuaded the artists to represent this or that subject, and
I now joyfully made use of these advantages. I still
remember writing a circumstantial essay, in which I
described twelve pictures which were to exhibit the
history of Joseph : some of them were executed.

After these achievements, which were certainly laudable in a boy, I will mention a little disgrace which
happened to me within this circle of artists. I was
well acquainted with all the pictures which had from
time to time been brought into that room. My youthful curiosity left nothing unseen or unexplored. I once
found a little black box behind the stove : I did not
fail to investigate what might be concealed in it, and
drew back the bolt without long deliberation. The
picture contained was certainly of a kind not usually
exposed to view ; and, although I tried to bolt it again
immediately, I was not quick enough. The count entered, and caught me. " Who allowed you to open that
box ? " he asked, with all his air of a royal lieutenant.
I had not much to say for myself, and he immediately
pronounced my sentence in a very stern manner : " For
eight days," said he, " you shall not enter this room."
I made a bow, and walked out. Even this order I
obeyed most punctually ; so that the good Seekatz,
who was then at work in the room, was very much
annoyed, for he liked to have me about him : and, out
of a little spite, I carried my obedience so far, that I
left Seekatz's coffee, which I generally brought him,
upon the threshold. He was then obliged to leave his
work and fetch it, which he took so ill, that he well
nigh began to dislike me.

It now seems necessary to state more circumstantially, and to make intelligible, how, under the circumstances, I made my way with more or less ease through

the French language, which, however, I had never learned. Here, too, my natural gift was of service to me; enabling me easily to catch the sound of a language, its movement, accent, tone, and all other outward peculiarities. I knew many words from the Latin; Italian suggested still more; and by listening to servants and soldiers, sentries and visitors, I soon picked up so much, that, if I could not join in conversation, I could at any rate manage single questions and answers. All this, however, was little compared to the profit I derived from the theatre. My grandfather had given me a free ticket, which I used daily, in spite of my father's reluctance, by dint of my mother's support. There I sat in the pit, before a foreign stage, and watched the more narrowly the movement and the expression, both of gesture and speech; as I understood little or nothing of what was said, and therefore could only derive entertainment from the action and the tone of voice. I understood least of comedy; because it was spoken rapidly, and related to the affairs of common life, of the phrases of which I knew nothing. Tragedy was not so often played; and the measured step, the rhythm of the Alexandrines, the generality of the expression, made it more intelligible to me in every way. It was not long before I took up Racine, which I found in my father's library, and declaimed the plays to myself, in the theatrical style and manner, as the organ of my ear, and the organ of speech, so nearly akin to that, had caught it, and this with considerable animation; although I could not yet understand a whole connected speech. I even learned entire passages by rote like a trained talking-bird, which was easier to me, from having previously committed to memory passages from the Bible which are generally unintelligible to a child, and accustomed myself to reciting them in the tone of the Protestant preachers. The versified

French comedy was then much in vogue: the pieces of Destouches, Marivaux, and La Chaussée were often produced; and I still remember distinctly many characteristic figures. Of those of Molière I recollect less. What made the greatest impression upon me was "The Hypermnestra" of Lemière, which, as a new piece, was brought out with care and often repeated. The "Devin du Village," "Rose et Colas," "Annette et Lubin," made each a very pleasant impression upon me. I can even now recall the youths and maidens decorated with ribbons, and their gestures. It was not long before the wish arose in me to see the interior of the theatre, for which many opportunities were offered me. For as I had not always patience to stay and listen to the entire plays, and often carried on all sorts of games with other children of my age in the corridors, and in the milder season even before the door, a handsome, lively boy joined us, who belonged to the theatre, and whom I had seen in many little parts, though only casually. He came to a better understanding with me than with the rest, as I could turn my French to account with him; and he the more attached himself to me because there was no boy of his age or his nation at the theatre, or anywhere in the neighbourhood. We also went together at other times, as well as during the play; and, even while the representations went on, he seldom left me in peace. He was a most delightful little braggart, chattered away charmingly and incessantly, and could tell so much of his adventures, quarrels, and other strange incidents, that he amused me wonderfully; and I learned from him in four weeks more of the language, and of the power of expressing myself in it, than can be imagined: so that no one knew how I had attained the foreign tongue all at once, as if by inspiration.

In the very earliest days of our acquaintance, he

took me with him upon the stage, and led me especially to the foyers, where the actors and actresses remained during the intervals of the performance, and dressed and undressed. The place was neither convenient nor agreeable; for they had squeezed the theatre into a concert-room, so that there were no separate chambers for the actors behind the stage. A tolerably large room adjoining, which had formerly served for card-parties, was now mostly used by both sexes in common, who appeared to feel as little ashamed before each other as before us children, if there was not always the strictest propriety in putting on or changing the articles of dress. I had never seen anything of the kind before; and yet from habit, after repeated visits, I soon found it quite natural.

It was not long before a very peculiar interest of my own arose. Young Derones, for so I will call the boy whose acquaintance I still kept up, was, with the exception of his boasting, a youth of good manners and very courteous demeanour. He made me acquainted with his sister, a girl who was a few years older than we were, and a very pleasant, well-grown girl, of regular form, brown complexion, black hair and eyes: her whole deportment had about it something quiet, even sad. I tried to make myself agreeable to her in every way, but I could not attract her notice. Young girls think themselves much more advanced than younger boys; and, while aspiring to young men, they assume the manner of an aunt toward the boy whose first inclination is turned toward them. With a younger brother of his, I had no acquaintance.

Sometimes, when their mother had gone to rehearsals, or was out visiting, we met at her house to play and amuse ourselves. I never went there without presenting the fair one with a flower, a fruit, or something else; which she always received very courteously, and thanked me for most politely: but I never saw her sad look brighten, and found no trace of her having given me a further thought. At last I fancied I had discovered her secret. The boy showed me a crayon-drawing of a handsome man, behind his mother's bed, which was hung with elegant silk curtains; remarking at the same time, with a sly look, that this was not papa, but just the same as papa: and as he glorified this man, and told me many things in his circumstantial and ostentatious manner, I thought I had discovered that the daughter might belong to the father, but the other two children to the intimate friend. I thus explained to myself her melancholy look, and loved her for it all the more.

My liking for this girl assisted me in bearing the braggadocio of her brother, who did not always keep within bounds. I had often to endure prolix accounts of his exploits, — how he had already often fought, without wishing to injure the other, all for the mere sake of honour. He had always contrived to disarm his adversary, and had then forgiven him; nay, he was such a good fencer, that he was once very much perplexed by striking the sword of his opponent up into a high tree, so that it was not easy to be got again.

What much facilitated my visits to the theatre was, that my free ticket, coming from the hands of the *Schultheiss*, gave me access to any of the seats, and therefore also to those in the proscenium. This was very deep, after the French style, and was bordered on both sides with seats, which, surrounded by a low rail, ascended in several rows one behind another, so that the first seats were but a little elevated above the stage. The whole was considered a place of special honour, and was generally used only by officers; although the nearness of the actors destroyed, I will not say all illusion, but, in a measure, all enjoyment. I have thus experienced and seen with my own eyes the

usage or abuse of which Voltaire so much complains.
If, when the house was very full at such time as
troops were passing through the town, officers of distinction strove for this place of honour, which was
generally occupied already, some rows of benches and
chairs were placed in the proscenium on the stage
itself, and nothing remained for the heroes and hero-
ines but to reveal their secrets in the very limited
space between the uniforms and orders. I have
even seen the "Hypermnestra" performed under such
circumstances.

The curtain did not fall between the acts: and I
must yet mention a strange custom, which I thought
quite extraordinary; as its inconsistency with art was
to me, as a good German boy, quite unendurable. The
theatre was considered the greatest sanctuary, and any
disturbance occurring there would have been instantly
resented as the highest crime against the majesty of
the public. Therefore, in all comedies, two grenadiers
stood with their arms grounded, in full view, at the
two sides of the back scene, and were witnesses of all
that occurred in the bosom of the family. Since, as I
said before, the curtain did not fall between the acts,
two others, while music struck up, relieved guard, by
coming from the wings, directly in front of the first,
who retired in the same measured manner. Now, if
such a practice was well fitted to destroy all that is
called illusion on the stage, it is the more striking,
because it was done at a time when, according to
Diderot's principles and examples, the most *natural
naturalness* was required upon the stage, and a perfect
deception was proposed as the proper aim of theatrical
art. Tragedy, however, was absolved from any such
military-police regulations; and the heroes of antiquity
had the right of guarding themselves: nevertheless,
the same grenadiers stood near enough behind the side
scenes.

I will also mention that I saw Diderot's "Father of a Family," and "The Philosophers" of Palissot, and still perfectly remember the figure of the philosopher in the latter piece going upon all fours, and biting into a raw head of lettuce.

All this theatrical variety could not, however, keep us children always in the theatre. In fine weather we played in front of it, and in the neighbourhood, and committed all manner of absurdities, which, especially on Sundays and festivals, by no means corresponded to our personal appearance; for I and my comrades then appeared dressed as I described myself in the tale, with the hat under the arm, and a little sword, the hilt of which was ornamented with a large silk knot. One day when we had long gone in this way, and Derones had joined us, he took it into his head to affirm that I had insulted him, and must give him satisfaction. I could not, in truth, conceive what was the cause of this; but I accepted his challenge, and was going to draw my sword. However, he assured me, that in such cases it was customary to go to secluded spots, in order to be able to settle the matter more conveniently. We therefore went behind some barns, and placed ourselves in the proper position. The duel took place in a somewhat theatrical style, — the blades clashed, and the thrusts followed close upon each other; but in the heat of the combat he remained with the point of his sword lodged in the knot of my hilt. This was pierced through; and he assured me that he had received the most complete satisfaction, then embraced me, also theatrically: and we went to the next coffee-house to refresh ourselves with a glass of almond-milk after our mental agitation, and to knit more closely the old bond of friendship.

On this occasion I will relate another adventure which also happened to me at the theatre, although at a later time. I was sitting very quietly in the pit with one of my playmates; and we looked with pleasure at a *pas seul*, which was executed with much skill and grace by a pretty boy about our own age, — the son of a French dancing-master, who was passing through the city. After the fashion of dancers, he was dressed in a close vest of red silk, which, ending in a short hoop-petticoat, like a runner's apron, floated above the knee. We had given our meed of applause to this young artist with the whole public, when, I know not how, it occurred to me to make a moral reflection. I said to my companion, " How handsomely this boy was dressed, and how well he looked ! Who knows in how tattered a jacket he may sleep to-night ! " All had already risen, but the crowd prevented our moving. A woman who had sat by me, and who was now standing close beside me, chanced to be the mother of the young artist, and felt much offended by my reflection. Unfortunately, she knew German enough to understand me, and spoke it just as much as was necessary to scold. She abused me violently. Who was I, she would like to know, that had a right to doubt the family and respectability of this young man ? At all events, she would be bound he was as good as I ; and his talents might probably procure him a fortune, of which I could not even venture to dream. This moral lecture she read me in the crowd, and made those about me wonder what rudeness I had committed. As I could neither excuse myself, nor escape from her, I was really embarrassed, and, when she paused for a moment, said without thinking, " Well ! why do you make such a noise about it ? — to-day red, to-morrow dead." [1] These words seemed to strike the woman dumb. She stared at me, and moved away from me as soon as it was in any degree possible. I thought no more of my words; only, some time afterward, they occurred to me, when the boy, instead of continuing to perform, became ill, and

[1] A German proverb, " Heute roth, Morgen todt."

that very dangerously. Whether he died, or not, I cannot say.

Such intimations, by an unseasonably or even improperly spoken word, were held in repute, even by the ancients; and it is very remarkable that the forms of belief and of superstition have always remained the same among all people and in all times.

From the first day of the occupation of our city, there was no lack of constant diversion, especially for children and young people. Plays and balls, parades, and marches through the town, attracted our attention in all directions. The last particularly were always increasing, and the soldiers' life seemed to us very merry and agreeable.

The residence of the king's lieutenant at our house procured us the advantage of seeing by degrees all the distinguished persons in the French army, and especially of beholding close at hand the leaders whose names had already been made known to us by reputation. Thus we looked from stairs and landing-places, as if from galleries, very conveniently upon the generals who passed by. More than all the rest do I remember the Prince Soubise as a handsome, courteous gentleman; but most distinctly, the Maréchal de Broglio, who was a younger man, not tall, but well built, lively, nimble, and abounding in keen glances, betraying a clever mind.

He repeatedly came to see the king's lieutenant, and it was easily noticed that they were conversing on weighty matters. We had scarcely become accustomed to having strangers quartered upon us in the first three months, when a rumour was obscurely circulated that the allies were on the march, and that Duke Ferdinand of Brunswick was coming to drive the French from the Main. Of these, who could not boast of any special success in war, no high opinion was held; and, after the battle of Rossbach, it was thought they might be dispersed. The greatest confidence was placed in Duke Ferdinand, and all those favourable to Prussia awaited with eagerness their delivery from the yoke hitherto borne. My father was in somewhat better spirits: my mother was apprehensive. She was wise enough to see that a small present evil might easily be exchanged for a great affliction; since it was but too plain that the French would not advance to meet the duke, but would wait an attack in the neighbourhood of the city. A defeat of the French, a flight, a defence of the city, if it were only to cover their rear and hold the bridge, a bombardment, a sack, — all these presented themselves to the excited imagination, and gave anxiety to both parties. My mother, who could bear everything but suspense, imparted her fears to the count through the interpreter. She received the answer usual in such cases: she might be quite easy, for there was nothing to fear; and should keep quiet, and mention the matter to no one.

Many troops passed through the city: we learned that they halted at Bergen. The coming and going, the riding and running, constantly increased; and our house was in an uproar day and night. At this time I often saw Marshal de Broglio, always cheerful, always the same in look and manner; and I was afterward pleased to find a man, whose form had made such a good and lasting impression upon me, so honourably mentioned in history.

Thus, after an unquiet Passion Week, the Good Friday of 1759 arrived. A profound stillness announced the approaching storm. We children were forbidden to quit the house: my father had no quiet, and went out. The battle began: I ascended to the garret, where indeed I was prevented seeing the country round, but could very well hear the thunder of cannon and the general discharge of musketry. After some hours we saw the first symptoms of the battle in a line of wagons, in which the wounded, with various sad mutilations and gestures, were slowly drawn by us, to be taken to the convent of St. Mary, now transformed into a hospital. The compassion of the citizens was instantly moved. Beer, wine, bread, and money were distributed to those who were yet able to take them. But when, some time after, wounded and captive Germans were seen in the train, the pity knew no limits; and it seemed as if everybody would strip himself of every movable that he possessed to assist his suffering countrymen.

The prisoners, however, were an evidence of a battle unfavourable to the allies. My father, whose party feelings made him quite certain that these would come off victorious, had the violent temerity to go forth to meet the expected victors, without thinking that the beaten party must pass over him in their flight. He first repaired to his garden before the Friedburg gate, where he found everything lonely and quiet; then ventured to the Bornheim heath, where he soon descried various stragglers of the army, who were scattered, and amused themselves by shooting at the boundary stones, so that the rebounding lead whizzed round the head of the inquisitive wanderer. He therefore considered it more prudent to go back, and learned on inquiry what the report of the firing might have before informed him, that all stood well for the French, and that there was no thought of retreating. Reaching home in an ill humour, the sight of his wounded and captured countrymen brought him altogether out of his usual self-command. He also caused various donations to be given to the passers-by; but only the Germans were to have them, which was not always possible, as fate had packed together both friend and foe.

My mother and we children, who had already relied on the count's word, and had therefore passed a tolerably quiet day, were highly rejoiced; and my mother doubly consoled the next day, when, having consulted the oracle of her treasure box, by the prick of a needle, she received a very comfortable answer, both for present and future. We wished our father similar faith and feelings; we flattered him as much as we could; we entreated him to take some food, from which he had abstained all day; but he repulsed our caresses and every enjoyment, and betook himself to his chamber. Our joy, however, was not interrupted; the affair was decided: the king's lieutenant, who, against his habit, had been on horseback that day, at last returned home, where his presence was more necessary than ever. We sprang to meet him, kissed his hands, and testified our delight. This seemed much to please him. "Well," said he more kindly than usual, "I am glad also for your sakes, my dear children." He immediately ordered that sweetmeats, sweet wine, and the best of everything should be given us, and went to his room, already surrounded by a crowd of the urging, demanding, supplicating.

We had now a fine collation, pitied our poor father who would not partake of it, and pressed our mother to call him in; but she, more prudent than we, well knew how distasteful such gifts would be to him. In the meantime she had prepared some supper, and would readily have sent a portion up to his room; but he never tolerated such an irregularity, even in the most extreme cases: and, after the sweet things were removed, we endeavoured to persuade him to come down into the ordinary dining-room. At last he allowed himself to be persuaded unwillingly, and we had no notion of the mischief which we were preparing for him and ourselves. The staircase ran through the whole house, along all the anterooms. My father, in coming down, had to go directly past the count's apartment. This anteroom was so full of people, that the count, to get through much at once, resolved to come out ; and this happened unfortunately at the moment when my father descended. The count met him cheerfully, greeted him, and remarked, " You will congratulate yourselves and us that this dangerous affair is so happily terminated." " By no means ! " replied my father in a rage : " would that it had driven you to the devil, even if I had gone with you ! " The count restrained himself for a moment, and then broke out with wrath, " You shall pay for this," cried he : " you shall find that you have not thus insulted the good cause and myself for nothing ! "

My father, meanwhile, came down very calmly, seated himself near us, seemed more cheerful than before, and began to eat. We were glad of this, unconscious of the dangerous method in which he had rolled the stone from his heart. Soon afterward my mother was called out, and we had great pleasure in chattering to our father about the sweet things the count had given us. Our mother did not return. At last the interpreter came in. At a hint from him we were sent to bed : it was already late, and we willingly obeyed. After a night quietly slept through, we heard of the violent commotion which had shaken the house the previous evening. The king's lieutenant had instantly ordered my father to be led to the guard-house. The subalterns well knew that he was never to be contradicted, yet they had often earned thanks by delaying the execution of his orders. The interpreter, whose presence of mind never forsook him, contrived to excite this disposition in them very strongly. The tumult, moreover, was so great, that a delay brought with it its own concealment and excuse. He had called out my mother, and put the adjutant, as it were, into her hands, that, by prayers and representations, she might gain a brief postponement of the matter. He himself hurried up to the count, who with great self-command had immediately retired into the inner room, and would rather allow the most urgent affair to stand still, than wreak on an innocent person the ill humour once excited in him, and give a decision derogatory to his dignity.

The address of the interpreter to the count, the train of the whole conversation, were often enough repeated to us by the fat interpreter, who prided himself not a little on the fortunate result, so that I can still describe it from recollection.

The interpreter had ventured to open the cabinet and enter, an act which was severely prohibited. "What do you want?" shouted the count angrily. "Out with you!—no one but St. Jean has a right to enter here."

"Well, suppose I am St. Jean for a moment," answered the interpreter.

"It would need a powerful imagination for that! Two of him would not make one such as you. Retire!"

"Count, you have received a great gift from heaven; and to that I appeal."

"You think to flatter me! Do not fancy you will succeed."

"You have the great gift, count, of listening to the opinions of others, even in moments of passion—in moments of rage."

"Well, well! the question now is just about opinions, to which I have listened too long. I know but too well that we are not liked here, and that these citizens look askance at us."

"Not all!"

"Very many. What! These towns will be imperial towns, will they? They saw their emperor elected and crowned: and when, being unjustly attacked, he is in danger of losing his dominions and surrendering to an usurper; when he fortunately finds faithful allies who pour out their blood and treasure in his behalf,—they will not put up with the slight burden that falls to their share toward humbling the enemy."

"But you have long known these sentiments, and have endured them like a wise man : they are, besides, held only by a minority. A few, dazzled by the splendid qualities of the enemy, whom you yourself prize as an extraordinary man, — a few only, as you are aware."

"Yes, indeed! I have known and suffered it too long! otherwise this man would not have presumed to utter such insults to my face, and at the most critical moment. Let them be as many as they please, they shall be punished in the person of this their audacious representative, and perceive what they have to expect."

"Only delay, count."

"In certain things one cannot act too promptly."

"Only a little delay, count."

"Neighbour, you think to mislead me into a false step : you shall not succeed."

"I would neither lead you into a false step nor restrain you from one : your resolution is just, — it becomes the Frenchman and the king's lieutenant ; but consider that you are also Count Thorane."

"He has no right to interfere here."

"But the gallant man has a right to be heard."

"What would he say, then ? "

" ' King's lieutenant,' he would begin, ' you have so long had patience with so many gloomy, untoward, bungling men, if they were not really too bad. This man has certainly been too bad : but control yourself, king's lieutenant ; and every one will praise and extol you on that account.' "

"You know I can often endure your jests, but do not abuse my good-will. These men — are they, then, completely blinded? Suppose we had lost the battle : what would have been their fate at this moment? We fight up to the gates, we shut up the city, we halt, we defend ourselves to cover our retreat over the bridge. Think you the enemy would have stood with his hands before him? He throws grenades, and what he has at hand; and they catch where they can. This householder — what would he have? Here, in these rooms, a bomb might now have burst, and another have followed it; — in these rooms, the cursed China-paper of which I have spared, incommoding myself by not nailing up my maps! They ought to have spent the whole day on their knees."

" How many would have done that ! "

" They ought to have prayed for a blessing on us, and to have gone out to meet the generals and officers with tokens of honour and joy, and the wearied soldiers with refreshments. Instead of this, the poison of party-spirit destroys the fairest and happiest moments of my life, won by so many cares and efforts."

" It is party-spirit, but you will only increase it by the punishment of this man. Those who think with him will proclaim you a tyrant and a barbarian; they will consider him a martyr, who has suffered for the good cause; and even those of the other opinion, who are now his opponents, will see in him only their fellow citizen, will pity him, and, while they confess your justice, will yet feel that you have proceeded too severely."

" I have listened to you too much already, — now, away with you ! "

" Hear only this. Remember, this is the most un-heard-of thing that could befall this man, this family. You have had no reason to be edified by the good-will of the master of the house ; but the mistress has antici-pated all your wishes, and the children have regarded you as their uncle. With this single blow, you will for ever destroy the peace and happiness of this dwell-ing. Indeed, I may say, that a bomb falling into the house would not have occasioned greater desolation. I have so often admired your self-command, count: give me this time opportunity to adore you. A warrior is worthy of honour, who considers himself a guest in the house of an enemy; but here there is no enemy, only a mistaking man. Control yourself, and you will acquire an everlasting fame."

"That would be odd," replied the count, with a smile.

"Merely natural," continued the interpreter: "I have not sent the wife and children to your feet, because I know you detest such scenes; but I will depict to you this wife and these children, how they will thank you. I will depict them to you conversing all their lives of the battle of Bergen, and of your magnanimity on this day, relating it to their children, and children's children, and inspiring even strangers with their own interest for you: an act of this kind can never perish."

"But you do not hit my weak side yet, interpreter. About posthumous fame I am not in the habit of thinking; that is for others, not for me: but to do right at the moment, not to neglect my duty, not to prejudice my honour, — that is my care. We have already had too many words; now go — and receive the thanks of the thankless, whom I spare."

The interpreter, surprised and moved by this unexpectedly favourable issue, could not restrain his tears, and would have kissed the count's hands. The count motioned him off, and said severely and seriously, "You know I cannot bear such things." And with these words he went into the anteroom to attend to his pressing affairs, and hear the claims of so many expectant persons. So the matter was disposed of; and the next morning we celebrated, with the remnants of the yesterday's sweetmeats, the passing over of an evil through the threatenings of which we had happily slept.

Whether the interpreter really spoke so wisely, or

merely so painted the scene to himself, as one is apt to do after a good and fortunate action, I will not decide; at least he never varied it in repeating it. Indeed, this day seemed to him both the most anxious and the most glorious in his life.

One little incident will show how the count in general rejected all false parade, never assumed a title which did not belong to him, and how witty he was in his more cheerful moods.

A man of the higher class, who was one of the abstruse, solitary Frankforters, thought he must complain of the quartering of the soldiers upon him. He came in person; and the interpreter proffered him his services, but the other supposed that he did not need them. He came before the count with a most becoming bow, and said, "Your excellency!" The count returned the bow, as well as the "excellency." Struck by this mark of honour, and not supposing but that the title was too humble, he stooped lower, and said, "Monseigneur." — "Sir," said the count very seriously, "we will not go farther, or else we may easily bring it to Majesty." The other gentleman was extremely confused, and had not a word to utter. The interpreter, standing at some distance, and apprised of the whole affair, was wicked enough not to move; but the count, with much cheerfulness, continued, "Well, now, for instance, sir, what is your name?" — "Spangenberg," replied the other. "And mine," said the count, "is Thorane. Spangenberg, what is your business with Thorane? Now, then, let us sit down: the affair shall at once be settled."

And thus the affair was indeed settled at once, to the great satisfaction of the person I have here named Spangenberg; and the same evening, in our family circle, the story was not only told by the waggish interpreter, but was given with all the circumstances and gestures.

After these confusions, disquietudes, and grievances, the former security and thoughtlessness soon returned, in which the young particularly live from day to day, if it be in any degree possible. My passion for the French theatre grew with every performance. I did not miss an evening; though on every occasion, when, after the play, I sat down with the family to supper, — often putting up with the remains, — I had to endure my father's constant reproaches, that theatres were useless, and would lead to nothing. In these cases I adduced all and every argument which is at hand for the apologists of the stage when they fall into a difficulty like mine. Vice in prosperity, and virtue in misfortune, are in the end set right by poetical justice. Those beautiful examples of misdeeds punished, "Miss Sarah Sampson," and "The Merchant of London," were very energetically cited on my part: but, on the other hand, I often came off worst when the "Fouberies de Scapin," and others of the sort, were in the bill; and I was forced to bear reproaches for the delight felt by the public in the deceits of intriguing servants, and the successful follies of prodigal young men. Neither party was convinced; but my father was very soon reconciled to the theatre when he saw that I advanced with incredible rapidity in the French language.

Men are so constituted that everybody would rather undertake himself what he sees done by others, whether he has aptitude for it or not. I had soon exhausted the whole range of the French stage; several plays were performed for the third and fourth times; all had passed before my eyes and mind, from the stateliest tragedy to the most frivolous afterpiece; and, as when a child I had presumed to imitate Terence, I did not fail now as a boy, on a much more inciting occasion, to copy the French forms to the best of my ability and want of ability. There were then performed some half-mythological, half-allegorical pieces in the taste of Piron : they partook somewhat of the nature of parody, and were much liked. These representations particularly attracted me: the little gold wings of a lively Mercury, the thunderbolt of a disguised Jupiter, an amorous Danaë, or by whatever name a fair one visited by the gods might be called, if indeed it were not a shepherdess or huntress to whom they descended. And as elements of this kind, from Ovid's " Metamorphoses," or the " Pantheon Mythicum " of Pomey, were humming in swarms about my head, I had soon put together in my imagination a little piece of the kind, of which I can only say that the scene was rural, and that there was no lack in it of kings' daughters, princes, or gods. Mercury, especially, made so vivid an impression on me, that I could almost be sworn that I had seen him with my own eyes.

I presented my friend Derones with a very neat copy, made by myself ; which he accepted with quite a special grace, and with a truly patronising air, glanced hastily over the manuscript, pointed out a few grammatical blunders, found some speeches too long, and at last promised to examine and judge the work more attentively when he had the requisite leisure. To my modest question, whether the piece could by any chance be performed, he assured me that it was not altogether impossible. In the theatre, he said, a great deal went by favour ; and he would support me with all his heart : only the affair must be kept private ; for he had himself once on a time surprised the directors with a piece of his own, and it would certainly have been acted if it had not been too soon detected that he was the author. I promised him all possible silence, and already saw in my mind's eye the name of my piece posted up in large letters on the corners of the streets and squares.

Light-minded as my friend generally was, the oppor-

tunity of playing the master was but too desirable. He
read the piece through with attention, and, while he
sat down with me to make some trivial alterations,
turned the whole thing, in the course of the conversation, completely topsy-turvy, so that not one stone
remained on another. He struck out, added, took
away one character, substituted another, — in short,
went on with the maddest wantonness in the world, so
that my hair stood on end. My previous persuasion
that he must surely understand the matter, allowed
him to have his way; for he had often laid before me
so much about the Three Unities of Aristotle, the
regularity of the French drama, the probability, the
harmony of the verse, and all that belongs to these,
that I was forced to regard him, not merely as informed, but thoroughly grounded. He abused the
English and scorned the Germans; in short, he laid
before me the whole dramaturgic litany which I have
so often in my life been compelled to hear.

Like the boy in the fable, I carried my mangled
offspring home, and strove in vain to bring it to life.
As, however, I would not quite abandon it, I caused a
fair copy of my first manuscript, after a few alterations, to be made by our clerk, which I presented
to my father, and thus gained so much, that, for a long
time, he let me eat my supper in quiet after the play
was over.

This unsuccessful attempt had made me reflective;
and I resolved now to learn, at the very sources, these
theories, these laws, to which every one appealed, but
which had become suspicious to me chiefly through the
unpoliteness of my arrogant master. This was not
indeed difficult, but laborious. I immediately read
Corneille's " Treatise on the Three Unities," and learned
from that how people would have it, but why they
desired it so was by no means clear to me; and, what
was worst of all, I fell at once into still greater con-

fusion when I made myself acquainted with the disputes on the " Cid," and read the prefaces in which Corneille and Racine are obliged to defend themselves against the critics and public. Here at least I plainly saw that no man knew what he wanted ; that a piece like the " Cid," which had produced the noblest effect, was to be condemned at the command of an all-powerful cardinal ; that Racine, the idol of the French living in my day, who had now also become my idol (for I had got intimately acquainted with him when Schöff Von Olenschlager made us children act " Britannicus," in which the part of Nero fell to me), — that Racine, I say, even in his own day, was not able to get on with the amateurs nor critics. Through all this I became more perplexed than ever ; and after having pestered myself a long time with this talking backwards and forwards, and theoretical quackery of the previous century, threw them to the dogs, and was the more resolute in casting all the rubbish away, the more I thought I observed that the authors themselves who had produced excellent things, when they began to speak about them, when they set forth the grounds of their treatment, when they desired to defend, justify, or excuse themselves, were not always able to hit the proper mark. I hastened back again, therefore, to the living present, attended the theatre far more zealously, read more scrupulously and connectedly, so that I had perseverance enough this time to work through the whole of Racine and Molière and a great part of Corneille.

The king's lieutenant still lived at our house. He in no respect had changed his deportment, especially toward us ; but it was observable, and the interpreter made it still more evident to us, that he no longer discharged his duties with the same cheerfulness and zeal as at the outset, though always with the same rectitude and fidelity. His character and habits, which

showed the Spaniard rather than the Frenchman ; his
caprices, which were not without their influence on his
business; his unbending will under all circumstances ;
his susceptibility as to whatever had reference to his
person or reputation, — all this together might perhaps
sometimes bring him into conflict with his superiors.
Add to this, that he had been wounded in a duel,
which had arisen in the theatre, and it was deemed
wrong that the king's lieutenant, himself chief of
police, should have committed a punishable offence.
As I have said, all this may have contributed to make
him live more retired, and here and there perhaps
to act with less energy.

Meanwhile, a considerable part of the pictures he
had ordered had been delivered. Count Thorane passed
his leisure hours in examining them; while in the
aforesaid gable-room he had them nailed up, canvas
after canvas, large and small, side by side, and, because
there was want of space, even one over another, and
then taken down and rolled up. The works were constantly inspected anew, the parts that were considered
the most successful were repeatedly enjoyed, but there
was no want of wishes that this or that had been differently done.

Hence arose a new and very singular operation. As
one painter best executed figures, another middle-
grounds and distances, a third trees, a fourth flowers,
it struck the count that these talents might perhaps
be combined in the paintings, and that in this way
perfect works might be produced. A beginning was
made at once, by having, for instance, some beautiful
cattle painted into a finished landscape. But because
there was not always adequate room for all, and a few
sheep more or less was no great matter to the cattle-
painter, the largest landscape proved in the end too
narrow. Now also the painter of figures had to introduce the shepherd and some travellers: these deprived

each other of air, as we may say; and we marvelled
that they were not all stifled, even in the most open
country. No one could anticipate what was to come
of the matter, and when it was finished it gave no
satisfaction. The painters were annoyed. They had
gained something by their first orders, but lost by these
after-labours; though the count paid for them also very
liberally. And, as the parts worked into each other
in one picture by several hands produced no good
effect after all the trouble, every one at last fancied
that his own work had been spoiled and destroyed by
that of the others; hence the artists were within a
hair's breadth of falling out, and becoming irreconcilably
hostile to each other. These alterations, or rather
additions, were made in the before-mentioned studio,
where I remained quite alone with the artists; and it
amused me to hunt out from the studies, particularly
of animals, this or that individual or group, and to
propose it for the foreground or the distance, in which
respect they many times, either from conviction or
kindness, complied with my wishes.

The partners in this affair were therefore greatly discouraged, especially Seekatz, a very hypochondriacal,
retired man, who, indeed, by his incomparable humour,
was the best of companions among friends, but who,
when he worked, desired to work alone, abstracted and
perfectly free. This man, after solving difficult problems, and finishing them with the greatest diligence
and the warmest love, of which he was always capable,
was forced to travel repeatedly from Darmstadt to
Frankfort, either to change something in his own pictures, or to touch up those of others, or even to allow,
under his superintendence, a third person to convert his
pictures into a variegated mess. His peevishness augmented, his resistance became more decided, and a great
deal of effort was necessary on our part to guide this
"gossip;" for he was one also, according to the count's

wishes. I still remember, that when the boxes were standing ready to pack up all the pictures, in the order in which the upholsterer might hang them up at once, at their place of destination, a small but indispensable bit of afterwork was demanded; but Seekatz could not be moved to come over. He had, by way of conclusion, done the best he could, having represented, in paintings to be placed over the doors, the four elements as children and boys, after life, and having expended the greatest care, not only on the figures, but on the accessories. These were delivered and paid for, and he thought he was quit of the business for ever; but now he was to come over again, that he might enlarge, by a few touches of his pencil, some figures, the size of which was too small. Another, he thought, could do it just as well; he had already set about some new work; in short, he would not come. The time for sending off the pictures was at hand; they had, moreover, to get dry; every delay was untoward; and the count, in despair, was about to have him fetched in military fashion. We all wished to see the pictures finally gone, and found at last no expedient than for the gossip interpreter to seat himself in a wagon, and fetch over the refractory subject, with his wife and child. He was kindly received by the count, well treated, and at last dismissed with liberal payment.

After the pictures had been sent away, there was great peace in the house. The gable-room in the attic was cleaned, and given up to me; and my father, when he saw the boxes go, could not refrain from wishing to send off the count after them. For much as the tastes of the count coincided with his own, much as he must have rejoiced to see his principle of patronising living artists so generously followed out by a man richer than himself, much as it may have flattered him that his collection had been the occasion of bringing so considerable a profit to a number of brave artists in a pressing time, he nevertheless felt such a repugnance to the foreigner who had intruded into his house, that he could not think well of any of his doings. One ought to employ painters, but not degrade them to paper-stainers; one ought to be satisfied with what they have done, according to their conviction and ability, even if it does not thoroughly please one, and not be perpetually carping at it. In short, in spite of all the count's own generous endeavours, there could, once for all, be no mutual understanding. My father only visited that room when the count was at table; and I can recall but one instance, when, Seekatz having excelled himself, and the wish to see these pictures having brought the whole house together, my father and the count met, and manifested a common pleasure in these works of art, which they could not take in each other.

Scarcely, therefore, had the house been cleared of the chests and boxes, than the plan for removing the count, which had formerly been begun, but was afterward interrupted, was resumed. The endeavour was made to gain justice by representations, equity by entreaties, favour by influence; and the quartermasters were prevailed upon to decide thus: the count was to change his lodgings; and our house, in consideration of the burden borne day and night for several years uninterruptedly, was to be exempt for the future from billeting. But, to furnish a plausible pretext for this, we were to take in lodgers on the first floor, which the count had occupied, and thus render a new quartering, as it were, impossible. The count, who, after the separation from his dear pictures, felt no further peculiar interest in the house, and hoped, moreover, to be soon recalled and placed elsewhere, was pleased to move without opposition to another good residence, and left us in peace and good-will. Soon afterward he quitted the city, and received different appointments in gradation, but, it was rumoured, not to his own satisfaction. Meantime, he had the pleasure of seeing the pictures which he had preserved with so much care felicitously arranged in his brother's château : he wrote sometimes, sent dimensions, and had different pieces executed by the artists so often named. At last we heard nothing further about him, except after several years we were assured that he had died as governor of one of the French colonies in the West Indies.

FOURTH BOOK.

HOWEVER much inconvenience the quartering of the French had caused us, we had become so accustomed to it, that we could not fail to miss it; nor could we children fail to feel as if the house were deserted. Moreover, it was not decreed that we should again attain perfect family unity. New lodgers were already bespoken; and after some sweeping and scouring, planing, and rubbing with beeswax, painting and varnishing, the house was completely restored again. The chancery-director Moritz, with his family, very worthy friends of my parents, moved in. He was not a native of Frankfort, but an able jurist and man of business, and managed the legal affairs of many small princes, counts, and lords. I never saw him otherwise than cheerful and pleasant, and diligent with his law-papers. His wife and children, gentle, quiet, and benevolent, did not indeed increase the sociableness of our house; for they kept to themselves: but a stillness, a peace, returned, which we had not enjoyed for a long time. I now again occupied my attic-room, in which the ghosts of the many pictures somtimes hovered before me; while I strove to frighten them away by labour and study.

The counsellor of legation, Moritz, a brother of the chancellor, came from this time often to our house. He was even more a man of the world, had a handsome figure, while his manners were easy and agreeable. He also managed the affairs of different persons of

117

rank, and on occasions of meetings of creditors and imperial commissions frequently came into contact with my father. They had a high opinion of each other, and commonly stood on the side of the creditors; though they were generally obliged to perceive, much to their vexation, that a majority of the agents on such occasions are usually gained over to the side of the debtors. The counsellor of legation readily communicated his knowledge, was fond of mathematics; and, as these did not occur in his present course of life, he made himself a pleasure by helping me on in this branch of study. I was thus enabled to finish my architectural sketches more accurately than heretofore, and to profit more by the instruction of a drawing-master, who now also occupied us an hour every day.

This good old man was indeed only half an artist. We were obliged to draw and combine strokes, from which eyes and noses, lips and ears, nay, at last, whole faces and heads, were to arise; but of natural or artistic forms there was no thought. We were tormented a long while with this *quid pro quo* of the human figure; and when the so-called Passions of Le Brun were given us to copy, it was supposed at last that we had made great progress. But even these caricatures did not improve us. Then we went off to landscapes, foliage, and all the things which in ordinary instruction are practised without consistency or method. Finally we dropped into close imitation and neatness of strokes, without troubling ourselves about the merit or taste of the original.

In these endeavours our father led the way in an exemplary manner. He had never drawn; but he was unwilling to remain behind, now that his children pursued this art, and would give, even in his old age, an example how they should proceed in their youth. He therefore copied several heads of Piazetta, from his well-known sheets in small octavo, with an English lead-pencil upon the finest Dutch paper. In these he not only observed the greatest clearness of outline, but most accurately imitated the hatching of the copper-plate with a light hand — only too slightly, as in his desire to avoid hardness he brought no keeping into his sketches. Yet they were always soft and accurate. His unrelaxing and untiring assiduity went so far, that he drew the whole considerable collection number by number; while we children jumped from one head to another, and chose only those that pleased us.

About this time the long-debated project, long under consideration, for giving us lessons in music, was carried into effect; and the last impulse to it certainly deserves mention. It was settled that we should learn the harpsichord, but there was always a dispute about the choice of a master. At last I went once accidentally into the room of one of my companions, who was just taking his lesson on the harpsichord, and found the teacher a most charming man: for each finger of the right and left hand he had a nickname, by which he indicated in the merriest way when it was to be used. The black and white keys were like-wise symbolically designated, and even the tones appeared under figurative names. Such a motley company worked most pleasantly together. Finger-ing and time seemed to become perfectly easy and obvious; and, while the scholar was put into the best humour, everything else succeeded beautifully.

Scarcely had I reached home, than I importuned my parents to set about the matter in good earnest at last, and give us this incomparable man for our master on the harpsichord. They hesitated, and made inquiries: they indeed heard nothing bad of the teacher, but, at the same time, nothing particularly good. Meanwhile, I had informed my sister of all the droll names: we could hardly wait for the lesson, and succeeded in hav-ing the man engaged.

The reading of the notes began first; but, as no jokes occurred here, we comforted ourselves with the hope, that when we went to the harpsichord, and the fingers were needed, the jocular method would commence. But neither keys nor fingering seemed to afford opportunity for any comparisons. Dry as the notes were, with their strokes on and between the five lines, the black and white keys were no less so: and not a syllable was heard, either of "thumbling," "pointerling," or "goldfinger;" while the countenance of the man remained as imperturbable during his dry teaching as it had been before during his dry jests. My sister reproached me most bitterly for having deceived her, and actually believed that it was all an invention of mine. But I was myself confounded and learned little, though the man at once went regularly enough to work; for I kept always expecting that the former jokes would make their appearance, and so consoled my sister from one day to another. They did not reappear, however; and I should never have been able to explain the riddle if another accident had not solved it for me.

One of my companions came in during a lesson, and at once all the pipes of the humourous *jet d'eau* were opened: the "thumblings" and "pointerlings," the "pickers" and "stealers," as he used to call the fingers; the "falings" and "galings," meaning "f" and "g;" the "fielings" and "gielings," meaning "f" and "g" sharp,[1] — became once more extant, and made the most wonderful manikins. My young friend could not leave off laughing, and was rejoiced that one could learn in such a merry manner. He vowed that he would give his parents no peace until they had given him such an excellent man for a teacher.

And thus the way to two arts was early enough

[1] The names of the sharp notes in German terminate in "is," and hence "f" and "g" sharp are called "fis" and "gis."

opened to me, according to the principles of a modern theory of education, merely by good luck, and without any conviction that I should be furthered therein by a native talent. My father maintained that everybody ought to learn drawing; for which reason he especially venerated the Emperor Maximilian, by whom this had been expressly commanded. He therefore held me to it more steadily than to music; which, on the other hand, he especially recommended to my sister, and even out of the hours for lessons kept her fast, during a good part of the day, at her harpsichord.

But the more I was in this way made to press on, the more I wished to press forward of myself; and my hours of leisure were employed in all sorts of curious occupations. From my earliest years I felt a love for the investigation of natural things. It is often regarded as an instinct of cruelty that children like at last to break, tear, and devour objects with which for a long time they have played, and which they have handled in various manners. Yet even in this way is manifested the curiosity, the desire of learning how such things hang together, how they look within. I remember, that, when a child, I pulled flowers to pieces to see how the leaves were inserted into the calyx, or even plucked birds to observe how the feathers were inserted into the wings. Children are not to be blamed for this, when even our naturalists believe they get their knowledge oftener by separation and division than by union and combination, — more by killing than by making alive.

An armed lodestone, very neatly sewed up in scarlet cloth, was one day destined to experience the effects of this spirit of inquiry. For the secret force of attraction which it exercised, not only on the little iron bar attached to it, but which was of such a kind that it could gain strength and could daily bear a heavier

weight, — this mysterious virtue had so excited my
admiration, that for a long time I was pleased with
merely staring at its operation.   But at last I thought
I might arrive at some nearer revelation by tearing
away the external covering.   This was done; but I
became no wiser in consequence, as the naked iron
taught me nothing further.   This also I took off; and
I held in my hand the mere stone, with which I never
grew weary of making experiments of various kinds
on filings and needles, — experiments from which my
youthful mind drew no further advantage beyond that
of a varied experience.   I could not manage to recon-
struct the whole arrangement: the parts were scattered,
and I lost the wondrous phenomenon at the same time
with the apparatus.

Nor was I more fortunate in putting together an
electrical machine.   A friend of the family, whose
youth had fallen in the time when electricity occupied all minds, often told us how, when a child, he
had desired to possess such a machine: he got together
the principal requisites, and, by the aid of an old spinning-wheel and some medicine bottles, had produced
tolerable results.   As he readily and frequently repeated the story, and imparted to us some general
information on electricity, we children found the thing
very plausible, and long tormented ourselves with an
old spinning-wheel and some medicine bottles, without
producing even the smallest result.   We nevertheless
adhered to our belief, and were much delighted, when
at the time of the fair, among other rarities, magical and
legerdemain tricks, an electrical machine performed its
marvels, which, like those of magnetism, were at that
time already very numerous.

The want of confidence in the public method of
instruction was daily increasing.   People looked about
for private tutors; and, because single families could
not afford the expense, several of them united to attain

their object. Yet the children seldom agreed; the young man had not sufficient authority; and, after frequently repeated vexations, there were only angry partings. It is not surprising, therefore, that other arrangements were thought of which should be more permanent as well as more advantageous.

The thought of establishing boarding-schools (*Pensionen*) had arisen from the necessity, which every one felt, of having the French language taught and communicated orally. My father had brought up a young person, who had been his footman, valet, secretary, and in short successively all in all. This man, whose name was Pfeil, spoke French well. After he had married, and his patrons had to think of a situation for him, they hit upon the plan of making him establish a boarding-school, which extended gradually into a small academy, in which everything necessary, and at last even Greek and Latin, were taught. The extensive connections of Frankfort caused young French and English men to be brought to this establishment, that they might learn German and acquire other accomplishments. Pfeil, who was a man in the prime of life, and of the most wonderful energy and activity, superintended the whole very laudably; and as he could never be employed enough, and was obliged to keep music-teachers for his scholars, he set about music on the occasion, and practised the harpsichord with such zeal, that, without having previously touched a note, he very soon played with perfect readiness and spirit. He seemed to have adopted my father's maxim, that nothing can more cheer and excite young people, than when at mature years one declares one's self again a learner; and at an age when new accomplishments are acquired with difficulty, one endeavours, nevertheless, by zeal and perseverance, to excel the younger, who are more favoured by nature.

By this love of playing the harpsichord, Pfeil was

led to the instruments themselves, and, while he hoped
to obtain the best, came into connection with Frederici
of Gera, whose instruments were celebrated far and
wide. He took a number of them on sale, and had
now the joy of seeing, not only one piano, but many,
set up in his residence, and of practising and being
heard upon them.

The vivacity of this man brought a great rage for
music into our house. My father remained on lasting
good terms with him up to certain points of dispute.
A large piano of Frederici was purchased also for us,
which I, adhering to my harpsichord, hardly touched;
but which so much increased my sister's troubles, as, to
duly honour the new instrument, she had to spend
some time longer every day in practice; while my
father, as overseer, and Pfeil, as a model and encouraging friend, alternately took their positions at her side.

A singular taste of my father's caused much inconvenience to us children. This was the cultivation of
silk, of the advantages of which, if it were more widely
extended, he had a high opinion. Some acquaintances
at Hanau, where the breeding of the worms was carried on with great care, gave him the immediate impulse. At the proper season, the eggs were sent to him
from that place: and, as soon as the mulberry-trees
showed sufficient leaves, they had to be stripped; and
the scarcely visible creatures were most diligently
tended. Tables and stands with boards were set up in
a garret-chamber, to afford them more room and sus-
tenance; for they grew rapidly, and, after their last
change of skin, were so voracious that it was scarcely
possible to get leaves enough to feed them, — nay, they
had to be fed day and night, as everything depends
upon there being no deficiency of nourishment when
the great and wondrous change is about to take place
in them. When the weather was favourable, this business could indeed be regarded as a pleasant amuse-

ment; but, if the cold set in so that the mulberry-trees suffered, it was exceedingly troublesome. Still more unpleasant was it when rain fell during the last epoch; for these creatures cannot at all endure moisture, and the wet leaves had to be carefully wiped and dried, which could not always be done quite perfectly: and for this, or perhaps some other reason also, various diseases came among the flock, by which the poor things were swept off in thousands. The state of corruption which ensued produced a smell really pestilential; and, because the dead and diseased had to be taken away and separated from the healthy, the business was indeed extremely wearisome and repulsive, and caused many an unhappy hour to us children.

After we had one year passed the finest weeks of the spring and summer in tending the silkworms, we were obliged to assist our father in another business, which, though simpler, was no less troublesome. The Roman views, which, bound by black rods at the top and bottom, had hung for many years on the walls of the old house, had become very yellow through the light, dust, and smoke, and not a little unsightly through the flies. If such uncleanliness was not to be tolerated in the new house, yet, on the other hand, these pictures had gained in value to my father, in consequence of his longer absence from the places represented. For at the outset such copies serve only to renew and revive the impressions received shortly before. They seem trifling in comparison, and at the best only a melancholy substitute. But, as the remembrance of the original forms fades more and more, the copies imperceptibly assume their place: they become as dear to us as those once were, and what we at first contemned now gains esteem and affection. Thus it is with all copies, and particularly with portraits. No one is easily satisfied with the counterfeit of an object still present, but how we value every silhouette of one who is absent or departed.

In short, with this feeling of his former extravagance, my father wished that these engravings might be restored as much as possible. It was well known that this could be done by bleaching: and the operation, always critical with large plates, was undertaken under rather unfavourable circumstances; for the large boards, on which the smoked engravings were moistened and exposed to the sun, stood in the gutters before the garret windows, leaning against the roof, and were therefore liable to many accidents. The chief point was, that the paper should never thoroughly dry, but must be kept constantly moist. This was the duty of my sister and myself; and the idleness, which would have been otherwise so desirable, was excessively annoying on account of the tedium and impatience, and the watchfulness which allowed of no distraction. The end, however, was attained; and the bookbinder, who fixed each sheet upon thick paper, did his best to match and repair the margins, which had been here and there torn by our inadvertence. All the sheets together were bound in a volume, and for this time preserved.

That we children might not be wanting in every variety of life and learning, a teacher of the English language had to announce himself just at this time, who pledged himself to teach anybody not entirely raw in languages, English in four weeks, and to advance him to such a degree, that, with some diligence, he could help himself farther. His price was moderate, and he was indifferent as to the number of scholars at one lesson. My father instantly determined to make the attempt, and took lessons, together with my sister and myself, of this expeditious master. The hours were faithfully kept; there was no want of repeating our lessons; other exercises were neglected rather than this during the four weeks; and the teacher parted from us, and we from him, with satisfaction. As he remained longer in the town, and found many employers, he came from time to time to look after us and to help us, grateful that we had been among the first who placed confidence in him, and proud to be able to cite us as examples to the others.

My father, in consequence of this, entertained a new anxiety, that English might neatly stand in the series of my other studies in languages. Now, I will confess that it became more and more burdensome for me to take my occasions for study now from this grammar or collection of examples, now from that; now from one author, now from another, — and thus to divert my interest in a subject every hour. It occurred to me, therefore, that I might despatch all at the same time; and I invented a romance of six or seven brothers and sisters, who, separated from each other and scattered over the world, should communicate with each other alternately as to their conditions and feelings. The eldest brother gives an account, in good German, of all the manifold objects and incidents of his journey. The sister, in a ladylike style, with short sentences and nothing but stops, much as "Siegwart" was afterward written, answers now him, now the other brothers, partly about domestic matters, and partly about affairs of the heart. One brother studies theology, and writes a very formal Latin, to which he often adds a Greek postscript. To another brother, holding the place of mercantile clerk at Hamburg, the English correspondence naturally falls; while a still younger one at Marseilles has the French. For the Italian was found a musician, on his first trip into the world; while the youngest of all, a sort of pert nestling, had applied himself to Jew-German, — the other languages having been cut off from him, — and, by means of his frightful ciphers, brought the rest of them into despair, and my parents into a hearty laugh at the good notion.

To obtain matter for filling up this singular form, I studied the geography of the countries in which my creations resided, and by inventing for those dry localities all sorts of human incidents which had some affinity with the characters and employments of my heroes. Thus my exercise-books became much more voluminous, my father was better satisfied, and I was much sooner made aware of my deficiency in both what I had acquired and possessed of my own.

Now, as such things, once begun, have no end nor limits, so it happened in the present case ; for while I strove to attain the odd Jew-German, and to write it as well as I could read it, I soon discovered that I ought to know Hebrew, from which alone the modern corrupted dialect could be derived, and handled with any certainty. I consequently explained the necessity of my learning Hebrew to my father, and earnestly besought his consent; for I had a still higher object. Everywhere I heard it said, that, to understand the Old as well as the New Testament, the original languages were requisite. The latter I could read quite easily ; because, that there might be no want of exercise, even on Sundays, the so-called Epistles and Gospels had, after church, to be recited, translated, and in some measure explained. I now purposed doing the same thing with the Old Testament, the peculiarities of which had always especially interested me.

My father, who did not like to do anything by halves, determined to request the rector of our gymnasium, one Doctor Albrecht, to give me private lessons weekly, until I should have acquired what was most essential in so simple a language ; for he hoped, that, if it would not be despatched as soon as English was learned, it could at least be managed in double the time.

Rector Albrecht was one of the most original figures in the world, — short, broad, but not fat, ill-shaped without being deformed ; in short, an Æsop in gown and wig. His more than seventy-years-old face was

completely twisted into a sarcastic smile; while his
eyes always remained large, and, though red, were
always brilliant and intelligent. He lived in the old
cloister of the barefoot friars, the seat of the gymnasium.
Even as a child, I had often visited him in company
with my parents, and had, with a kind of trembling
delight, glided through the long, dark passages, the
chapels transformed into reception-rooms, the place
broken up and full of stairs and corners. Without
making me uncomfortable, he questioned me familiarly
whenever we met, and praised and encouraged me.
One day, on the changing of the pupils' places after a
public examination, he saw me standing, as a mere
spectator, not far from his chair, while he distributed
the silver *prœmia virtutis et diligentiœ*. I was probably gazing very eagerly upon the little bag out of
which he drew the medals: he nodded to me, descended a step, and handed me one of the silver pieces.
My joy was great; although others thought that this
gift, bestowed upon a boy not belonging to the school,
was out of all order. But for this the good old man
cared but little, having always played the eccentric,
and that in a striking manner. He had a very good
reputation as a schoolmaster, and understood his business; although age no more allowed him to practise it
thoroughly. But almost more than by his own infirmities was he hindered by greater circumstances; and, as
I already knew, he was satisfied neither with the con-
sistory, the inspectors, the clergy, nor the teachers.
To his natural temperament, which inclined to satire,
and the watching for faults and defects, he allowed
free play, both in his programmes and his public
speeches; and, as Lucian was almost the only writer
whom he read and esteemed, he spiced all that he said
and wrote with biting ingredients.

Fortunately for those with whom he was dissatisfied,
he never went directly to work, but only jeered at the

he wanted to reprove, with hints, allu-
passages, and Scripture-texts. His de-
r, — he always read his discourses, —
unintelligible, and, above all, was often
a cough, but more frequently by a
paunch-convulsing laugh, with which he was
wont to announce and accompany the biting passages.
This singular man I found to be mild and obliging
when I began to take lessons of him. I now went to
his house daily at six o'clock in the evening, and
always experienced a secret pleasure when the outer
door closed behind me, and I had to thread the long,
dark cloister passage. We sat in his library, at a table
covered with oilcloth, a much-read Lucian never quit-
ting his side.

In spite of all my willingness, I did not get at the
matter without difficulty; for my teacher could not
suppress certain sarcastic remarks as to the real truth
about Hebrew. I concealed from him my designs
upon Jew-German, and spoke of a better understanding
of the original text. He smiled at this, and said I
should be satisfied if I only learned to read. This
vexed me in secret, and I concentrated all my attention when we came to the letters. I found an alphabet
something like the Greek, of which the forms were
easy, and the names, for the most part, not strange to
me. All this I had soon comprehended and retained,
and supposed we should now take up reading. That
this was done from right to left I was well aware.
But now all at once appeared a new army of little
characters and signs, of points and strokes of all sorts,
which were in fact to represent vowels. At this I
wondered the more, as there were manifestly vowels in
the larger alphabet; and the others only appeared to
be hidden under strange appellations. I was also
taught that the Jewish nation, as long as it flourished,
actually were satisfied with the former signs, and knew

no other way of writing and reading. Most willingly, then, would I have gone on along this ancient and, as it seemed to me, easier path; but my worthy declared rather sternly that we must go by the grammar as it had been approved and composed. Reading without these points and strokes, he said, was a very hard undertaking, and could be accomplished only by the learned and those who were well practised. I must, therefore, make up my mind to learn these little characters; but the matter became to me more and more confused. Now, it seemed, some of the first and larger primitive letters had no value in their places, in order that their little after-born kindred might not stand there in vain. Now they indicated a gentle breathing, now a guttural more or less rough, and now served as mere equivalents. But finally, when one fancied that he had well noted everything, some of these personages, both great and small, were rendered inoperative; so that the eyes always had very much, and the lips very little, to do.

As that of which I already knew the contents had now to be stuttered in a strange gibberish, in which a certain snuffle and gargle were not a little commended as something unattainable, I in a certain degree deviated from the matter, and diverted myself, in a childish way, with the singular names of these accumulated signs. There were " emperors," " kings," and " dukes," [1] which, as accents governing here and there, gave me not a little entertainment. But even these shallow jests soon lost their charm. Nevertheless I was indemnified, inasmuch as by reading, translating, repeating, and committing to memory, the substance of the book came out more vividly; and it was this, properly, about which I desired to be enlightened. Even before this time, the contradiction

[1] These are the technical names for classes of accents in the Hebrew grammar.—Trans.

between tradition, and the actual and possible, had appeared to me very striking; and I had often put my private tutors to a nonplus with the sun which stood still on Gibeon, and the moon in the vale of Ajalon, to say nothing of other improbabilities and incongruities. Everything of this kind was now awakened; while, in order to master the Hebrew, I occupied myself exclusively with the Old Testament, and studied it, though no longer in Luther's translation, but in the literal version of Sebastian Schmid, printed under the text, which my father had procured for me. Here, I am sorry to say, our lessons began to be defective in regard to practice in the language. Reading, interpreting, grammar, transcribing, and the repetition of words, seldom lasted a full half-hour; for I immediately began to aim at the sense of the matter, and, though we were still engaged in the first book of Moses, to utter several things suggested to me by the later books. At first the good old man tried to restrain me from such digressions, but at last they seemed to entertain him also. It was impossible for him to suppress his characteristic cough and chuckle: and, although he carefully avoided giving me any information that might have compromised himself, my importunity was not relaxed; nay, as I cared more to set forth my doubts than to learn their solution, I grew constantly more vivacious and bold, seeming justified by his deportment. Yet I could get nothing out of him, except that ever and anon he would exclaim with his peculiar, shaking laugh, "Ah! mad fellow! ah! mad boy!"

Still, my childish vivacity, which scrutinised the Bible on all sides, may have seemed to him tolerably serious and worthy of some assistance. He therefore referred me, after a time, to the large English Biblical work which stood in his library, and in which the interpretation of difficult and doubtful passages was attempted in an intelligent and judicious manner. By

the great labours of German divines the translation
had obtained advantages over the original. The different opinions were cited; and at last a kind of reconciliation was attempted, so that the dignity of the
book, the ground of religion, and the human understanding, might in some degree coexist. Now, as
often as toward the end of the lesson I came out with
my usual questions and doubts, so often did he point
to the repository. I took the volume, he let me read,
turned over his Lucian; and, when I made any remarks on the book, his ordinary laugh was the only
answer to my sagacity. In the long summer days he
let me sit as long as I could read, many times alone;
after a time he suffered me to take one volume after
another home with me.

Man may turn which way he please, and undertake
anything whatsoever, he will always return to the path
which nature has once prescribed for him. Thus it
happened also with me in the present case. The
trouble I took with the language, with the contents
of the sacred Scriptures themselves, ended at last in
producing in my imagination a livelier picture of that
beautiful and famous land, its environs and its vicini-
ties, as well as of the people and events by which that
little spot of earth was made glorious for thousands of
years.

This small space was to see the origin and growth
of the human race; thence we were to derive our first
and only accounts of primitive history; and such a
locality was to lie before our imagination, no less
simple and comprehensible than varied, and adapted
to the most wonderful migrations and settlements.
Here, between four designated rivers, a small, delightful spot was separated from the whole habitable earth,
for youthful man. Here he was to unfold his first
capacities, and here at the same time was the lot to
befall him, which was appointed for all his posterity;

namely, that of losing peace by striving after knowledge. Paradise was trifled away; men increased and grew worse; and the Elohim, not yet accustomed to the wickedness of the new race, became impatient, and utterly destroyed it. Only a few were saved from the universal deluge; and scarcely had this dreadful flood ceased, than the well-known ancestral soil lay once more before the grateful eyes of the preserved.

Two rivers out of four, the Euphrates and Tigris, still flowed in their beds. The name of the first remained: the other seemed to be pointed out by its course. Minuter traces of paradise were not to be looked for after so great a revolution. The renewed race of man went forth hence a second time: it found occasion to sustain and employ itself in all sorts of ways, but chiefly to gather around it large herds of tame animals, and to wander with them in every direction.

This mode of life, as well as the increase of the families, soon compelled the people to disperse. They could not at once resolve to let their relatives and friends go for ever: they hit upon the thought of building a lofty tower, which should show them the way back from the far distance. But this attempt, like their first endeavour, miscarried. They could not be at the same time happy and wise, numerous and united. The Elohim confounded their minds; the building remained unfinished; the men were dispersed; the world was peopled, but sundered.

But our regards, our interests, continue fixed on these regions. At last the founder of a race again goes forth from hence, and is so fortunate as to stamp a distinct character upon his descendants, and by that means to unite them for all time to come into a great nation, inseparable through all changes of place or destiny.

From the Euphrates, Abraham, not without divine guidance, wanders toward the west. The desert opposes no invincible barrier to his march. He attains the Jordan, passes over its waters, and spreads himself over the fair southern regions of Palestine. This land was already occupied, and tolerably well inhabited. Mountains, not extremely high, but rocky and barren, were severed by many watered vales favourable to cultivation. Towns, villages, and solitary settlements lay scattered over the plain, and on the slopes of the great valley, the waters of which are collected in Jordan. Thus inhabited, thus tilled, was the land: but the world was still large enough; and the men were not so circumspect, necessitous, and active, as to usurp at once the whole adjacent country. Between their possessions were extended large spaces, in which grazing herds could freely move in every direction. In one of these spaces Abraham resides; his brother Lot is near him: but they cannot long remain in such places. The very condition of a land, the population of which is now increasing, now decreasing, and the productions of which are never kept in equilibrium with the wants, produces unexpectedly a famine; and the stranger suffers alike with the native, whose own support he has rendered difficult by his accidental presence. The two Chaldean brothers move onward to Egypt; and thus is traced out for us the theatre on which, for some thousands of years, the most important events of the world were to be enacted. From the Tigris to the Euphrates, from the Euphrates to the Nile, we see the earth peopled; and this space also is traversed by a well-known, heaven-beloved man, who has already become worthy to us, moving to and fro with his goods and cattle, and, in a short time, abundantly increasing them. The brothers return; but, taught by the distress they have endured, they determine to part. Both, indeed, tarry in southern Canaan; but while Abraham remains at Hebron, near the wood of Mamre, Lot departs for the valley of Siddim, which, if our imagination is bold enough to give Jordan a subterranean outlet, so that, in place of the present

Dead Sea, we should have dry ground, can and must
appear like a second paradise, — a conjecture all the
more probable, because the residents about there, noto-
rious for effeminacy and wickedness, lead us to infer
that they led an easy and luxurious life. Lot lives
among them, but apart.

But Hebron and the wood of Mamre appear to us as
the important place where the Lord speaks with Abraham, and promises him all the land as far as his eye
can reach in four directions. From these quiet districts,
from these shepherd-tribes, who can associate with
celestials, entertain them as guests, and hold many conversations with them, we are compelled to turn our
glance once more toward the East, and to think of
the condition of the surrounding world, which, on the
whole, perhaps, may have been like that of Canaan.

Families hold together : they unite, and the mode of
life of the tribes is determined by the locality which
they have appropriated or appropriate. On the mountains which send down their waters to the Tigris, we
find warlike populations, who even thus early fore-
shadow those world-conquerors and world-rulers, and
in a campaign, prodigious for those times, give us a
prelude of future achievements. Chedor Laomer, King
of Elam, has already a mighty influence over his allies.
He reigns a long while ; for twelve years before Abraham's arrival in Canaan, he had made all the people
tributary to him as far as the Jordan. They revolted
at last, and the allies equipped for war. We find them
unawares upon a route by which, probably, Abraham
also reached Canaan. The people on the left and lower
side of the Jordan were subdued. Chedor Laomer di-
rects his march southwards toward the people of the
desert ; then, wending north, he smites the Amale-
kites ; and, when he has also overcome the Amorites,
he reaches Canaan, falls upon the kings of the valley
of Siddim, smites and scatters them, and marches with

great spoil up the Jordan, in order to extend his conquests as far as Lebanon.

Among the captives, despoiled, and dragged along with their property, is Lot, who shares the fate of the country in which he lives a guest. Abraham learns this, and here at once we behold the patriarch a warrior and hero. He hurriedly gathers his servants, divides them into troops, attacks and falls upon the luggage of booty, confuses the victors, who could not suspect another enemy in the rear, and brings back his brother and his goods, with a great deal more belonging to the conquered kings. Abraham, by means of this brief contest, acquires, as it were, the whole land. To the inhabitants he appears as a protector, saviour, and, by his disinterestedness, a king. Gratefully the kings of the valley receive him; Melchisedek, the king and priest, with blessings.

Now the prophecies of an endless posterity are renewed; nay, they take a wider and wider scope. From the waters of the Euphrates to the river of Egypt all the lands are promised him, but yet there seems a difficulty with respect to his next heirs. He is eighty years of age, and has no son. Sarai, less trusting in the heavenly powers than he, becomes impatient: she desires, after the Oriental fashion, to have a descendant, by means of her maid. But no sooner is Hagar given up to the master of the house, no sooner is there hope of a son, than dissensions arise. The wife treats her own dependent ill enough, and Hagar flies to seek a happier position among other tribes. She returns, not without a higher intimation, and Ishmael is born.

Abraham is now ninety-nine years old, and the promises of a numerous posterity are constantly repeated: so that, in the end, the pair regard them as ridiculous. And yet Sarai becomes at last pregnant, and brings forth a son, to whom the name of Isaac is given.

History, for the most part, rests upon the legitimate

propagation of the human race. The most important events of the world require to be traced to the secrets of families, and thus the marriages of the patriarchs give occasion for peculiar considerations. It is as if the Divinity, who loves to guide the destiny of mankind, wished to prefigure here connubial events of every kind. Abraham, so long united by childless marriage to a beautiful woman whom many coveted, finds himself, in his hundredth year, the husband of two women, the father of two sons; and at this moment his domestic peace is broken. Two women, and two sons by different mothers, cannot possibly agree. The party less favoured by law, usage, and opinion must yield. Abraham must sacrifice his attachment to Hagar and Ishmael. Both are dismissed; and Hagar is compelled now, against her will, to go upon a road which she once took in voluntary flight, at first, it seems, to the destruction of herself and child; but the angel of the Lord, who had before sent her back, now rescues her again, that Ishmael also may become a great people, and that the most improbable of all promises may be fulfilled beyond its limits.

Two parents in advanced years, and one son of their old age — here, at last, one might expect domestic quiet and earthly happiness. By no means. Heaven is yet preparing the heaviest trial for the patriarch. But of this we cannot speak without premising several considerations.

If a natural universal religion was to arise, and a special revealed one to be developed from it, the countries in which our imagination has hitherto lingered, the mode of life, the race of men, were the fittest for the purpose. At least, we do not find in the whole world anything equally favourable and encouraging. Even to natural religion, if we assume that it arose earlier in the human mind, there pertains much of delicacy of sentiment; for it rests upon the conviction of a universal providence, which conducts the order of the world as a whole. A particular religion, revealed by Heaven to this or that people, carries with it the belief in a special providence, which the Divine Being vouchsafes to certain favoured men, families, races, and people. This faith seems to develop itself with difficulty from man's inward nature. It requires tradition, usage, and the warrant of a primitive time.

Beautiful is it, therefore, that the Israelitish tradition represents the very first men who confide in this particular providence as heroes of faith, following all the commands of that high Being on whom they acknowledge themselves dependent, just as blindly as, undisturbed by doubts, they are unwearied in awaiting the later fulfilments of his promises.

As a particular revealed religion rests upon the idea that one man may be more favoured by Heaven than another, so it also arises preëminently from the separation of classes. The first men appeared closely allied, but their employments soon divided them. The hunter was the freest of all: from him was developed the warrior and the ruler. Those who tilled the field bound themselves to the soil, erected dwellings and barns to preserve what they had gained, and could estimate themselves pretty highly, because their condition promised durability and security. The herdsman in his position seemed to have acquired the most unbounded condition and unlimited property. The increase of herds proceeded without end, and the space which was to support them widened itself on all sides. These three classes seemed from the very first to have regarded each other with dislike and contempt; and as the herdsman was an abomination to the townsman, so did he in turn separate from the other. The hunters vanish from our sight among the hills, and reappear only as conquerors.

The patriarchs belonged to the shepherd class.

Their manner of life upon the ocean of deserts and pastures gave breadth and freedom to their minds; the vault of heaven, under which they dwelt, with all its nightly stars, elevated their feelings; and they, more than the active, skilful huntsman, or the secure, careful, householding husbandman, had need of the immovable faith that a God walked beside them, visited them, cared for them, guided and saved them.

We are compelled to make another reflection in passing to the rest of the history. Humane, beautiful, and cheering as the religion of the patriarchs appears, yet traits of savageness and cruelty run through it, out of which man may emerge, or into which he may again be sunk.

That hatred should seek to appease itself by the blood, by the death, of the conquered enemy, is natural; that men concluded a peace upon the battle-field among the ranks of the slain may easily be conceived; that they should in like manner think to give validity to a contract by slain animals, follows from the preceding. The notion also that slain creatures could attract, propitiate, and gain over the gods, whom they always looked upon as partisans, either opponents or allies, is likewise not at all surprising. But if we confine our attention to the sacrifices, and consider the way in which they were offered in that primitive time, we find a singular, and, to our notions, altogether repugnant, custom, probably derived from the usages of war; viz., that the sacrificed animals of every kind, and whatever number was devoted, had to be hewn in two halves, and laid out on two sides: so that in the space between them were those who wished to make a covenant with the Deity.

Another dreadful feature wonderfully and portentously pervades that fair world; namely, that whatever had been consecrated or vowed must die. This also was probably a usage of war transferred to peace. The inhabitants of a city which forcibly defends itself are threatened with such a vow: it is taken by storm or otherwise. Nothing is left alive; men never: and often women, children, and even cattle, share a similar fate. Such sacrifices are rashly and superstitiously and with more or less distinctness promised to the gods; and those whom the votary would willingly spare, even his nearest of kin, his own children, may thus bleed, the expiatory victims of such a delusion.

In the mild and truly patriarchal character of Abraham, such a savage kind of worship could not arise; but the Godhead,[1] which often, to tempt us, seems to put forth those qualities which man is inclined to assign to it, imposes a monstrous task upon him. He must offer up his son as a pledge of the new covenant, and, if he follows the usage, not only kill and burn him, but cut him in two, and await between the smoking entrails a new promise from the benignant Deity. Abraham, blindly and without lingering, prepares to execute the command: to Heaven the will is sufficient. Abraham's trials are now at an end, for they could not be carried farther. But Sarai dies, and this gives Abraham an opportunity for taking typical possession of the land of Canaan. He requires a grave, and this is the first time he looks out for a possession in this earth. He had before this probably sought out a twofold cave by the grove of Mamre. This he purchases, with the adjacent field; and the legal form which he observes on the occasion shows how important this possession is to him. Indeed, it was more so, perhaps, than he himself supposed: for there he, his sons and his grandsons, were to rest; and by this means the proximate title to the whole land, as well as the everlasting desire of his posterity to

[1] It should be observed, that in this Biblical narrative, when we have used the expressions, "Deity," "Godhead," or "Divinity," Goethe generally has "die Götter," or "the gods." — TRANS.

gather themselves there, was most properly grounded. From this time forth the manifold incidents of the family life become varied. Abraham still keeps strictly apart from the inhabitants; and though Ishmael, the son of an Egyptian woman, has married a daughter of that land, Isaac is obliged to wed a kinswoman of equal birth with himself.

Abraham despatches his servant to Mesopotamia, to the relatives whom he had left behind there. The prudent Eleazer arrives unknown, and, in order to take home the right bride, tries the readiness to serve of the girls at the well. He asks to be permitted to drink; and Rebecca, unasked, waters his camels also. He gives her presents, he demands her in marriage, and his suit is not rejected. He conducts her to the home of his lord, and she is wedded to Isaac. In this case, too, issue has to be long expected. Rebecca is not blessed until after some years of probation; and the same discord, which, in Abraham's double marriage, arose through two mothers, here proceeds from one. Two boys of opposite characters wrestle already in their mother's womb. They come to light, the elder lively and vigorous, the younger gentle and prudent. The former becomes the father's, the latter the mother's, favourite. The strife for precedence, which begins even at birth, is ever going on. Esau is quiet and indifferent as to the birthright which fate has given him: Jacob never forgets that his brother forced him back. Watching every opportunity of gaining the desirable privilege, he buys the birthright of his brother, and defrauds him of their father's blessing. Esau is indignant, and vows his brother's death: Jacob flees to seek his fortune in the land of his forefathers.

Now, for the first time, in so noble a family appears a member who has no scruple in attaining by prudence and cunning the advantages which nature and circumstances have denied him. It has often enough been remarked and expressed, that the Sacred Scriptures by no means intend to set up any of the patriarchs and other divinely favoured men as models of virtue. They, too, are persons of the most different characters, with many defects and failings. But there is one leading trait, in which none of these men after God's own heart can be wanting; that is, unshaken faith that God has them and their families in his special keeping.

General, natural religion, properly speaking, requires no faith; for the persuasion that a great producing, regulating, and conducting Being conceals himself, as it were, behind Nature, to make himself comprehensible to us — such a conviction forces itself upon every one. Nay, if we for a moment let drop this thread, which conducts us through life, it may be immediately and everywhere resumed. But it is different with a special religion, which announces to us that this Great Being distinctly and preëminently interests himself for one individual, one family, one people, one country. This religion is founded on faith, which must be immovable if it would not be instantly destroyed. Every doubt of such a religion is fatal to it. One may return to conviction, but not to faith. Hence the endless probation, the delay in the fulfilment of so often repeated promises, by which the capacity for faith in those ancestors is set in the clearest light.

It is in this faith also that Jacob begins his expedition; and if, by his craft and deceit, he has not gained our affections, he wins them by his lasting and inviolable love for Rachel, whom he himself woos on the instant, as Eleazer had courted Rebecca for his father. In him the promise of a countless people was first to be fully unfolded: he was to see many sons around him, but through them and their mothers was to endure manifold sorrows of heart.

Seven years he serves for his beloved, without impatience and without wavering. His father-in-law, crafty like himself, and disposed, like him, to consider legitimate this means to an end, deceives him, and so repays him for what he has done to his brother. Jacob finds in his arms a wife whom he does not love. Laban, indeed, endeavours to appease him, by giving him his beloved also after a short time, and this but on the condition of seven years of further service. Vexation arises out of vexation. The wife he does not love is fruitful: the beloved one bears no children. The latter, like Sarai, desires to become a mother through her handmaiden: the former grudges her even this advantage. She also presents her husband with a maid, but the good patriarch is now the most troubled man in the world. He has four women, children by three, and none from her he loves. Finally she also is favoured; and Joseph comes into the world, the late fruit of the most passionate attachment. Jacob's fourteen years of service are over; but Laban is unwilling to part with him, his chief and most trusty servant. They enter into a new compact, and portion the flocks between them. Laban retains the white ones, as most numerous: Jacob has to put up with the spotted ones, as the mere refuse. But he is able here, too, to secure his own advantage: and as by a paltry mess (*of pottage*) he had procured the birthright, and, by a disguise, his father's blessing, he manages by art and sympathy to appropriate to himself the best and largest part of the herds; and on this side also he becomes the truly worthy progenitor of the people of Israel, and a model for his descendants. Laban and his household remark the result, if not the stratagem. Vexation ensues: Jacob flees with his family and goods, and partly by fortune, partly by cunning, escapes the pursuit of Laban. Rachel is now about to present him another son, but dies in the travail; Benjamin, the child of sorrow, survives her; but the aged father is to experience a still greater sorrow from the apparent loss of his son Joseph.

Perhaps some one may ask why I have so circumstantially narrated histories so universally known, and so often repeated and explained. Let the inquirer be satisfied with the answer, that I could in no other way exhibit how, with my life full of diversion, and with my desultory education, I concentrated my mind and feelings in quiet action on one point; that I was able in no other way to depict the peace that prevailed about me, even when all without was so wild and strange. When an ever busy imagination, of which that tale may bear witness, led me hither and thither; when the medley of fable and history, mythology and religion, threatened to bewilder me, — I liked to take refuge in those Oriental regions, to plunge into the first books of Moses, and to find myself there, amid the scattered shepherd tribes, at the same time in the greatest solitude and the greatest society.

These family scenes, before they were to lose themselves in a history of the Jewish nation, show us now, in conclusion, a form by which the hopes and fancies of the young in particular are agreeably excited, — Joseph, the child of the most passionate wedded love. He seems to us tranquil and clear, and predicts to himself the advantages which are to elevate him above his family. Cast into misfortune by his brothers, he remains steadfast and upright in slavery, resists the most dangerous temptations, rescues himself by prophecy, and is elevated according to his deserts to high honours. He shows himself first serviceable and useful to a great kingdom, then to his own kindred. He is like his ancestor Abraham in repose and greatness, his grandfather Isaac in silence and devotedness. The talent for traffic, inherited from his father, he exercises on a large scale. It is no longer flocks which are gained for himself from a father-in-law, but nations, with all their possessions, which he knows how to purchase for a king. Extremely graceful is this natural story, only it appears too short; and one feels called upon to paint it in detail.

Such a filling-up of Biblical characters and events given only in outline, was no longer strange to the Germans. The personages of both the Old and New Testaments had received through Klopstock a tender and affectionate nature, highly pleasing to the boy, as well as to many of his contemporaries. Of Bodmer's efforts in this line, little or nothing came to him; but "Daniel in the Lions' Den," by Moser, made a great impression on the young heart. In that work, a right-minded man of business, and courtier, arrives at high honours through manifold tribulations; and the piety for which they threatened to destroy him became, early and late, his sword and buckler. It had long seemed to me desirable to work out the history of Joseph; but I could not get on with the form, particularly as I was conversant with no kind of versification which would have been adapted to such a work. But now I found a treatment of it in prose very suitable, and I applied all my strength to its execution. I now endeavoured to discriminate and paint the characters, and, by the interpolation of incidents and episodes, to make the old simple history a new and independent work. I did not consider, what, indeed, youth cannot consider, that subject-matter was necessary to such a design, and that this could only arise by the perceptions of experience. Suffice it to say, that I represented to myself all the incidents down to the minutest details, and narrated them accurately to myself in their succession.

What greatly lightened this labour was a circumstance which threatened to render this work, and my authorship in general, exceedingly voluminous. A well-gifted young man, who, however, had become imbecile from over-exertion and conceit, resided as a ward in my father's house, lived quietly with the family, and, if allowed to go on in his usual way, was contented and agreeable. He had, with great care, written out notes of his academical course, and acquired a rapid, legible hand. He liked to employ himself in writing better than in anything else, and was pleased when something was given him to copy; but still more when he was dictated to, because he then felt carried back to his happy academical years. To my father, who was not expeditious in writing, and whose German letters were small and tremulous, nothing could be more desirable; and he was consequently accustomed, in the conduct of his own and other business, to dictate for some hours a day to this young man. I found it no less convenient, during the intervals, to see all that passed through my head fixed upon paper by the hand of another; and my natural gift of feeling and imitation grew with the facility of catching up and preserving.

As yet, I had not undertaken any work so large as that Biblical prose-epic. The times were tolerably quiet, and nothing recalled my imagination from Palestine and Egypt. Thus my manuscripts swelled more and more every day, as the poem, which I recited to myself, as it were, in the air, stretched along the paper; and only a few pages from time to time needed to be rewritten.

When the work was done, — for, to my own astonishment, it really came to an end, — I reflected, that from former years many poems were extant, which did not even now appear to me utterly despicable, and which, if written together in the same size with "Joseph," would make a very neat quarto, to which the title "Miscellaneous Poems" might be given. I

was pleased with this, as it gave me an opportunity of
quietly imitating well-known and celebrated authors.
I had composed a good number of so-called Anacre-
ontic poems, which, on account of the convenience
of the metre, and the lightness of the subject, flowed
forth readily enough. But these I could not well take,
as they were not in rhyme; and my desire before
all things was to show my father something that would
please him. So much the more, therefore, did the
spiritual odes seem suitable, which I had very zealously attempted in imitation of the "Last Judgment"
of Elias Schlegel. One of these, written to celebrate
the descent of Christ into hell, received much applause
from my parents and friends, and had the good fortune
to please myself for some years afterward. The so-
called texts of the Sunday church-music, which were
always to be had printed, I studied with diligence.
They were, indeed, very weak; and I could well believe that my verses, of which I had composed many
in the prescribed manner, were equally worthy of being
set to music, and performed for the edification of
the congregation. These, and many like them, I had
for more than a year before copied with my own hand;
because through this private exercise I was released
from the copies of the writing-master. Now all were
corrected and put in order, and no great persuasion was
needed to have them neatly copied by the young man
who was so fond of writing. I hastened with them to
the bookbinder: and when, very soon after, I handed
the nice-looking volume to my father, he encouraged
me with peculiar satisfaction to furnish a similar
quarto every year; which he did with the greater
conviction, as I had produced the whole in my spare
moments alone.

Another circumstance increased my tendency to
these theological, or, rather, Biblical, studies. The
senior of the ministry, John Philip Fresenius, a mild

man, of handsome, agreeable appearance, who was respected by his congregation and the whole city as an exemplary pastor and good preacher, but who, because he stood forth against the Herrnhüters, was not in the best odour with the peculiarly pious; while, on the other hand, he had made himself famous, and almost sacred, with the multitude, by the conversion of a free-thinking general who had been mortally wounded, — this man died; and his successor, Plitt, a tall, hand-some, dignified man, who brought from his *chair* (he had been a professor in Marburg) the gift of teach-ing rather than of edifying, immediately announced a sort of religious course, to which his sermons were to be devoted in a certain methodical connection. I had already, as I was compelled to go to church, remarked the distribution of the subject, and could now and then show myself off by a pretty complete recitation of a sermon. But now, as much was said in the con-gregation, both for and against the new senior, and many placed no great confidence in his announced didactic sermons, I undertook to write them out more carefully; and I succeeded the better from having made smaller attempts in a seat very convenient for hearing, but concealed from sight. I was extremely attentive and on the alert: the moment he said Amen, I hastened from church, and spent a couple of hours in rapidly dictating what I had fixed in my memory and on paper, so that I could hand in the written sermon before dinner. My father was very proud of this suc-cess; and the good friend of the family, who had just come in to dinner, also shared in the joy. Indeed, this friend was very well disposed toward me, because I had made his "Messiah" so much my own, that in my repeated visits, paid to him with a view of getting impressions of seals for my collection of coats-of-arms, I could recite long passages from it till the tears stood in his eyes.

The next Sunday I prosecuted the work with equal zeal; and, as the mechanical part of it mainly interested me, I did not reflect upon what I wrote and preserved. During the first quarter these efforts may have continued pretty much the same; but as I fancied at last, in my self-conceit, that I found no particular enlightenment as to the Bible, nor clearer insight into dogmas, the small vanity which was thus gratified seemed to me too dearly purchased for me to pursue the matter with the same zeal. The sermons, once so many-leaved, grew more and more lean: and before long I should have relinquished this labour altogether, if my father, who was a fast friend to completeness, had not, by words and promises, induced me to persevere till the last Sunday in Trinity; though, at the conclusion, scarcely more than the text, the statement, and the divisions were scribbled on little pieces of paper.

My father was particularly pertinacious on this point of completeness. What was once undertaken had to be finished, even if the inconvenience, tedium, vexation, nay, uselessness, of the thing begun were plainly manifested in the meantime. It seemed as if he regarded completeness as the only end, and perseverance as the only virtue. If in our family circle, in the long winter evenings, we had begun to read a book aloud, we were compelled to finish, though we were all in despair about it, and my father himself was the first to yawn. I still remember such a winter, when we had thus to work our way through Bower's " History of the Popes." It was a terrible time, as little or nothing that occurs in ecclesiastical affairs can interest children and young people. Still, with all my inattention and repugnance, so much of that reading remained in my mind that I was able, in after times, to take up many threads of the narrative.

Amid all these heterogeneous occupations and

labours, which followed each other so rapidly that one could hardly reflect whether they were permissible and useful, my father did not lose sight of the main object. He endeavoured to direct my memory and my talent for apprehending and combining to objects of jurisprudence, and therefore gave me a small book by Hopp, in the shape of a catechism, and worked up according to the form and substance of the institutions. I soon learned questions and answers by heart, and could represent the catechist as well as the catechumen : and, as in religious instruction at that time, one of the chief exercises was to find passages in the Bible as readily as possible ; so here a similar acquaintance with the " Corpus Juris " was found necessary, in which, also, I soon became completely versed. My father wished me to go on, and the little " Struve " was taken in hand ; but here affairs did not proceed so rapidly. The form of the work was not so favourable for beginners, that they could help themselves on ; nor was my father's method of illustration so liberal as greatly to interest me.

Not only by the warlike state in which we lived for some years, but also by civil life itself, and the perusal of history and romances, was it made clear to me that there were many cases in which the laws are silent, and give no help to the individual, who must then see how to get out of the difficulty by himself. We had now reached the period when, according to the old routine, we were to learn, besides other things, fencing and riding, that we might guard our skins upon occasion, and present no pedantic appearance on horseback. As to the first, the practice was very agreeable to us ; for we had already, long ago, contrived to make broadswords out of hazel sticks, with basket-hilts neatly woven of willow, to protect the hands. Now we might get real steel blades, and the clash we made with them was very merry.

There were two fencing-masters in the city: an old, earnest German, who went to work in a severe and solid style; and a Frenchman, who sought to gain his advantage by advancing and retreating, and by light, fugitive thrusts, which he always accompanied by cries. Opinions varied as to whose manner was the best. The little company with which I was to take lessons sided with the Frenchman; and we speedily accustomed ourselves to move backwards and forwards, make passes and recover, always breaking out into the usual exclamations. But several of our acquaintance had gone to the German teacher, and practised precisely the opposite. These distinct modes of treating so important an exercise, the conviction of each that his master was the best, really caused a dissension among the young people, who were of about the same age: and the fencing-schools occasioned serious battles, for there was almost as much fighting with words as with swords; and, to decide the matter in the end, a trial of skill between the two teachers was arranged, the consequences of which I need not circumstantially describe. The German stood in his position like a wall, watched his opportunity, and contrived to disarm his opponent over and over again with his cut and thrust. The latter maintained that this mattered not, and proceeded to exhaust the other's wind by his agility. He fetched the German several lunges too, which, however, if they had been in earnest, would have sent him into the next world.

On the whole, nothing was decided or improved, except that some went over to our countryman, of whom I was one. But I had already acquired too much from the first master; and hence a considerable time elapsed before the new one could break me of it, who was altogether less satisfied with us renegades than with his original pupils.

With riding I fared still worse. It happened that

they sent me to the course in the autumn, so that I commenced in the cool and damp season. The pedantic treatment of this noble art was highly repugnant to me. From first to last, the whole talk was about sitting the horse: and yet no one could say in what a proper sitting consisted, though all depended on that; for they went to and fro on the horse without stirrups. Moreover, the instruction seemed contrived only for cheating and degrading the scholars. If one forgot to hook or loosen the curb-chain, or let his switch fall down, or even his hat, — every delay, every misfortune, had to be atoned for by money; and one was laughed at into the bargain. This put me in the worst of humours, particularly as I found the place of exercise itself quite intolerable. The wide, nasty space, either wet or dusty, the cold, the mouldy smell, all together was in the highest degree repugnant to me; and since the stable-master always gave the others the best and me the worst horses to ride, —perhaps because they bribed him by breakfasts and other gifts, or even by their own cleverness; since he kept me waiting, and, as it seemed, slighted me, — I spent the most disagreeable hours in an employment that ought to have been the most pleasant in the world. Nay, the impression of that time and of these circumstances has remained with me so vividly, that although I afterward became a passionate and daring rider, and for days and weeks together scarcely got off my horse, I carefully shunned covered riding-courses, and at least passed only a few moments in them. The case often happens, that, when the elements of an exclusive art are taught us, this is done in a painful and revolting manner. The conviction that this is both wearisome and injurious has given rise, in later times, to the educational maxim, that the young must be taught everything in an easy, cheerful, and agreeable way: from which, however, other evils and disadvantages have proceeded.

With the approach of spring, times became again more quiet with us; and if in earlier days I had endeavoured to obtain a sight of the city, its ecclesiastical, civil, public, and private structures, and especially found great delight in the still prevailing antiquities, I afterward endeavoured, by means of "Lersner's Chronicle," and other Frankfortian books and pamphlets belonging to my father, to revive the persons of past times. This seemed to me to be well attained by great attention to the peculiarities of times and manners and of distinguished individuals.

Among the ancient remains, that which, from my childhood, had been remarkable to me, was the skull of a state criminal, fastened up on the tower of the bridge, who, out of three or four, as the naked iron spikes showed, had, since 1616, been preserved in spite of the encroachments of time and weather. Whenever one returned from Sachsenhausen to Frankfort, one had this tower before one; and the skull was directly in view. As a boy, I liked to hear related the history of these rebels, — Fettmilch and his confederates, — how they had become dissatisfied with the government of the city, had risen up against it, plotted a mutiny, plundered the Jews' quarter, and excited a fearful riot, but were at last captured, and condemned to death by a deputy of the emperor. Afterward I felt anxious to know the most minute circumstance, and to hear what sort of people they were. When from an old contemporary book, ornamented with woodcuts, I learned, that, while these men had indeed been condemned to death, many councillors had at the same time been deposed, because various kinds of disorder and very much that was unwarrantable was then going on; when I heard the nearer particulars how all took place, — I pitied the unfortunate persons who might be regarded as sacrifices made for a future better constitution. For from that time was dated the regulation which allows the noble old house of Limpurg, the Frauenstein-house, sprung from a club, besides lawyers, trades-people, and artisans, to take part in a government, which, completed by a system of ballot, complicated in the Venetian fashion, and restricted by the civil colleges, was called to do right, without acquiring any special privilege to do wrong.

Among the things which excited the misgivings of the boy, and even of the youth, was especially the state of the Jewish quarter of the city (*Judenstadt*), properly called the Jew Street (*Judengasse*); as it consisted of little more than a single street, which in early times may have been hemmed in between the walls and trenches of the town, as in a prison (*Zwinger*). The closeness, the filth, the crowd, the accent of an unpleasant language, altogether made a most disagreeable impression, even if one only looked in as one passed the gate. It was long before I ventured in alone; and I did not return there readily, when I had once escaped the importunities of so many men unwearied in demanding and offering to traffic. At the same time, the old legends of the cruelty of the Jews toward Christian children, which we had seen hideously illustrated in " Gottfried's Chronicle," hovered gloomily before my young mind. And although they were thought better of in modern times, the large caricature, still to be seen, to their disgrace, on an arched wall under the bridge-tower, bore extraordinary witness against them; for it had been made, not through private ill-will, but by public order.

However, they still remained the chosen people of God, and passed, no matter how it came about, as a memorial of the most ancient times. Besides, they also were men, active and obliging; and, even to the tenacity with which they clung to their peculiar customs, one could not refuse one's respect. The girls, moreover, were pretty, and were far from displeased when a Christian lad, meeting them on the Sabbath in the Fischerfeld, showed himself kindly and attentive. I was consequently extremely curious to become acquainted with their ceremonies. I did not desist until I had frequently visited their school, had assisted at a circumcision and a wedding, and formed a notion of the Feast of the Tabernacles. Everywhere I was well received, pleasantly entertained, and invited to come again; for it was through persons of influence that I had been either introduced or recommended.

Thus, as a young resident in a large city, I was thrown about from one object to another; and horrible scenes were not wanting in the midst of the municipal quiet and security. Sometimes a more or less remote fire aroused us from our domestic peace: sometimes the discovery of a great crime, with its investigation and punishment, set the whole city in an uproar for many weeks. We were forced to be witnesses of different executions; and it is worth remembering, that I was also once present at the burning of a book. The publication was a French comic romance, which indeed spared the state, but not religion and manners. There was really something dreadful in seeing punishment inflicted on a lifeless thing. The packages burst asunder in the fire, and were raked apart by an oven-fork, to be brought in closer contact with the flames. It was not long before the kindled sheets were wafted about in the air, and the crowd caught at them with eagerness. Nor could we rest until we had hunted up a copy, while not a few managed likewise to procure the forbidden pleasure. Nay, if it had been done to give the author publicity, he could not himself have made a more effectual provision.

But there were also more peaceable inducements which took me about in every part of the city. My father had early accustomed me to manage for him his little affairs of business. He charged me particularly to stir up the labourers whom he set to work, as they commonly kept him waiting longer than was proper; because he wished everything done accurately, and was used in the end to lower the price for a prompt payment. In this way, I gained access to all the workshops: and as it was natural to me to enter into the condition of others, to feel every species of human existence, and sympathise in it with pleasure, these commissions were to me the occasion of many most delightful hours; and I learned to know every one's method of proceeding, and what joy and sorrow, what advantages and hardships, were incident to the indispensable conditions of this or that mode of life. I was thus brought nearer to that active class which connects the lower and upper classes. For if on the one side stand those who are employed in the simple and rude products, and on the other those who desire to enjoy something that has been already worked up, the manufacturer, with his skill and hand, is the mediator through whom the other two receive something from each other: each is enabled to gratify his wishes in his own way. The household economy of many crafts, which took its form and colour from the occupation, was likewise an object of my quiet attention; and thus was developed and strengthened in me the feeling of the equality, if not of all men, yet of all human conditions, — the mere fact of existence seeming to me the main point, and all the rest indifferent and accidental.

As my father did not readily permit himself an expense which would be consumed at once in some momentary enjoyment, — as I can scarcely call to mind that we ever took a walk together, and spent anything in a place of amusement, — he was, on the other hand, not niggardly in procuring such things as had a good external appearance in addition to inward value. No one could desire peace more than he, although he had not felt the smallest inconvenience during the last days of the war. With this feeling, he had promised my mother a gold snuff-box, set with diamonds, which she was to receive as soon as peace should be publicly declared. In the expectation of the happy event, they had laboured now for some years on this present. The box, which was tolerably large, had been executed in Hanau; for my father was on good terms with the gold-workers there, as well as with the heads of the silk establishments. Many designs were made for it: the cover was adorned by a basket of flowers, over which hovered a dove with the olive branch. A vacant space was left for the jewels, which were to be set partly in the dove and partly on the spot where the box is usually opened. The jeweller, to whom the execution and the requisite stones were entrusted, was named Lautensak, and was a brisk, skilful man, who, like many artists, seldom did what was necessary, but usually works of caprice, which gave him pleasure. The jewels were very soon set, in the shape in which they were to be put upon the box, on some black wax, and looked very well; but they would not come off to be transferred to the gold. In the outset, my father let the matter rest: but as the hope of peace became livelier, and finally when the stipulations, — particularly the elevation of the Archduke Joseph to the Roman throne, — seemed more precisely known, he grew more and more impatient; and I had to go several times a week, nay, at last, almost daily, to visit the tardy artist. Owing to my unremitted teasing and exhortation, the work went on, though slowly enough; for, as it was of that kind which can be taken in hand or laid aside at will, there was always something by which it was thrust out of the way, and put aside.

The chief cause of this conduct, however, was a task which the artist had undertaken on his own account. Everybody knew that the Emperor Francis cherished a strong liking for jewels, and especially for coloured stones. Lautensak had expended a considerable sum, and, as it afterward turned out, larger than his means, on such gems, out of which he had begun to shape a nosegay, in which every stone was to be tastefully disposed, according to its shape and colour, and the whole form a work of art worthy to stand in the treasure vaults of an emperor. He had, in his desultory way, laboured at it for many years, and now hastened — because after the hoped-for peace the arrival of the emperor, for the coronation of his son, was expected in Frankfort — to complete it and finally to put it together. My desire to become acquainted with such things he used very dexterously to divert my attention by sending me forth as his dun, and to turn me away from my intention. He strove to impart a knowledge of these stones to me, and made me attentive to their properties and value; so that in the end I knew his whole bouquet by heart, and quite as well as he could have demonstrated its virtues to a customer. It is even now present to my mind; and I have since seen more costly, but not more graceful, specimens of show and magnificence in this sort. He possessed, moreover, a pretty collection of engravings, and other works of art, with which he liked to amuse himself; and I passed many hours with him, not without profit. Finally, when the Congress of Hubertsburg was finally fixed, he did for my sake more than was due; and the dove and flowers actually reached my mother's hands on the festival in celebration of the peace.

I then received also many similar commissions to urge on painters with respect to pictures which had been ordered. My father had confirmed himself in the notion — and few men were free from it — that a picture painted on wood was greatly to be preferred to one that was merely put on canvas. It was therefore his great care to possess good oak boards, of every shape; because he knew well that just on this important point the more careless artists trusted to the joiners. The oldest planks were hunted up, the joiners were obliged to go accurately to work with gluing, painting, and arranging; and they were then kept for years in an upper room, where they could be sufficiently dried. A precious board of this kind was entrusted to the painter Junker, who was to represent on it an ornamental flower-pot, with the most important flowers drawn after nature in his artistic and elegant manner. It was just about the springtime; and I did not fail to take him several times a week the most beautiful flowers that fell in my way, which he immediately put in, and by degrees composed the whole out of these elements with the utmost care and fidelity. On one occasion I had caught a mouse, which I took to him, and which he desired to copy as a very pretty animal; nay, really represented it, as accurately as possible, gnawing an ear of corn at the foot of the flower-pot. Many such inoffensive natural objects, such as butterflies and chafers, were brought in and represented; so that finally, as far as imitation and execution were concerned, a highly valuable picture was put together.

Hence I was not a little astonished when the good man formally declared one day, when the work was just about to be delivered, that the picture no longer pleased him, — since, while it had turned out quite well in its details, it was not well composed as a whole, because it had been produced in this gradual manner; and he had committed a blunder at the outset, in not at least devising a general plan for light and shade, as well as for colour, according to which the single flowers might have been arranged. He scrutinised, in my presence, the minutest parts of the picture, which had arisen before my eyes during six months, and had pleased me in many respects, and, much to my regret, managed to thoroughly convince me. Even the copy of the mouse he regarded as a mistake; for many persons, he said, have a sort of horror of such animals: and they should not be introduced where the object is to excite pleasure. As it commonly happens with those who are cured of a prejudice, and think themselves much more knowing than they were before, I now had a real contempt for this work of art, and agreed perfectly with the artist when he caused to be prepared another tablet of the same size, on which, according to his taste, he painted a better-formed vessel and a more artistically arranged nosegay, and also managed to select and distribute the little living accessories in an ornamental and agreeable way. This tablet also he painted with the greatest care, though altogether after the former copied one, or from memory, which, through a very long and assiduous practice, came to his aid. Both paintings were now ready; and we were thoroughly delighted with the last, which was certainly the more artistic and striking of the two. My father was surprised with two pictures instead of one, and to him the choice was left. He approved of our opinion, and of the reasons for it, and especially of our good will and activity; but, after considering both pictures some days, decided in favour of the first, without saying much about the motives of his choice. The artist, in an ill humour, took back his second well-meant picture, and could not refrain from the remark that the good oaken tablet on which the first was painted had certainly had its effect on my father's decision.

Now that I am again speaking of painting, I am reminded of a large establishment, where I passed much time, because both it and its managers especially attracted me. It was the great oilcloth factory which the painter Nothnagel had erected, — an expert artist, but one who by his mode of thought inclined more to manufacture than to art. In a very large space of courts and gardens, all sorts of oilcloths were made, from the coarsest, that are spread with a trowel, and used for baggage-wagons and similar purposes, and the carpets impressed with figures, to the finer and the finest, on which sometimes Chinese and grotesque, sometimes natural flowers, sometimes figures, sometimes landscapes, were represented by the pencils of accomplished workmen. This multiplicity, to which there was no end, amused me vastly. The occupation of so many men, from the commonest labour to that in which a certain artistic worth could not be denied, was to me extremely attractive. I made the acquaintance of this multitude of younger and older men, working in several rooms one behind the other, and occasionally lent a hand myself. The sale of these commodities was extraordinarily brisk. Whoever at that time was building or furnishing a house, wished to provide for his lifetime ; and this oilcloth carpeting was certainly quite indestructible. Nothnagel had enough to do in managing the whole, and sat in his office surrounded by factors and clerks. The remainder of his time he employed in his collection of works of art, consisting chiefly of engravings, in which, as well as in the pictures he possessed, he traded occasionally. At the same time he had acquired a taste for etching : he etched a variety of plates, and prosecuted this branch of art even into his latest years.

As his dwelling lay near the Eschenheim gate, my way when I had visited him led me out of the city to some pieces of ground which my father owned beyond the gates. One was a large orchard, the soil of which was used as a meadow, and in which my father carefully attended the transplanting of trees, and whatever else pertained to their preservation ; though the ground itself was leased. Still more occupation was furnished by a very well-preserved vineyard beyond the Friedburg gate, where, between the rows of vines, rows of asparagus were planted and tended with great care. Scarcely a day passed in the fine season in which my father did not go there; and as on these occasions we might generally accompany him, we were provided with joy and delight from the earliest productions of spring to the last of autumn. We now also acquired a knowledge of gardening matters, which, as they were repeated every year, became in the end perfectly known and familiar to us. But, after the manifold fruits of summer and autumn, the vintage at last was the most lively and the most desirable; nay, there is no question, that as wine gives a freer character to the very places and districts where it is grown and drunk, so also do these vintage-days, while they close summer and at the same time open the winter, diffuse an incredible cheerfulness. Joy and jubilation pervade a whole district. In the daytime, huzzas and shoutings are heard from every end and corner; and at night rockets and fire-balls, now here, now there, announce that the people, everywhere awake and lively, would willingly make this festival last as long as possible. The subsequent labour at the wine-press, and during the fermentation in the cellar, gave us also a cheerful employment at home; and thus we ordinarily reached winter without being properly aware of it.

These rural possessions delighted us so much the more in the spring of 1763, as the 15th of February in that year was celebrated as a festival day, on account of the conclusion of the Hubertsburg peace, under the happy results of which the greater part of my life was to flow away. But, before I go farther, I think I am bound to mention some men who exerted an important influence on my youth.

Von Olenschlager, a member of the Frauenstein family, a *Schöff*, and son-in-law of the above-mentioned Doctor Orth, a handsome, comfortable, sanguine man. In his official holiday costume he could well have personated the most important French prelate. After his academical course, he had employed himself in political and state affairs, and directed even his travels to that end. He greatly esteemed me, and often conversed with me on matters which chiefly interested him. I was with him when he wrote his "Illustration of the Golden Bull," when he managed to explain to me very clearly the worth and dignity of that document. My imagination was led back by it to those wild and unquiet times; so that I could not forbear representing what he related historically, as if it were present, by pictures of characters and circumstances, and often by mimicry. In this he took great delight, and by his applause excited me to repetition.

I had from childhood the singular habit of always learning by heart the beginnings of books, and the divisions of a work, first of the five books of Moses, and then of the "Æneid" and Ovid's "Metamorphoses." I now did the same thing with the "Golden Bull," and often provoked my patron to a smile, when I quite seriously and unexpectedly exclaimed, "*Omne regnum in se divisum desolabitur; nam principes ejus facti sunt socii furum.*" [1] The knowing man shook his head, smiling, and said doubtingly, "What times those must have been, when, at a grand diet, the emperor had such words published in the face of his princes!"

There was a great charm in Von Olenschlager's society. He received little company, but was strongly inclined to intellectual amusement, and induced us young people from time to time to perform a play; for such exercises were deemed particularly useful to the young. We acted "Canute" by Schlegel, in which the part of the king was assigned to me, Elfrida to my sister, and Ulfo to the younger son of the family. We

[1] Every kingdom divided against itself shall be brought to desolation, for the princes thereof have become the associates of robbers. — TRANS.

then ventured on the " Britannicus ; " [1] for, besides our dramatic talents, we were to bring the language into practice. I took Nero, my sister Agrippina, and the younger son Britannicus. We were more praised than we deserved, and fancied we had done it even beyond the amount of praise. Thus I stood on the best terms with this family, and have been indebted to them for many pleasures and a speedier development.

Von Reineck, of an old patrician family, able, honest, but stubborn, a meagre, swarthy man, whom I never saw smile. The misfortune befell him that his only daughter was carried off by a friend of the family. He pursued his son-in-law with the most vehement prosecution : and because the tribunals, with their formality, were neither speedy nor sharp enough to gratify his desire of vengeance, he fell out with them ; and there arose quarrel after quarrel, suit after suit. He retired completely into his own house and its adjacent garden, lived in a spacious but melancholy lower room, into which for many years no brush of a whitewasher, and perhaps scarcely the broom of a maid-servant, had found its way. He was very fond of me, and had especially commended to me his younger son. He many times asked his oldest friends, who knew how to humour him, his men of business and agents, to dine with him, and on these occasions never omitted inviting me. There was good eating and better drinking at his house. But a large stove, that let out the smoke from many cracks, caused his guests the greatest pain. One of the most intimate of these once ventured to remark upon this, by asking the host whether he could put up with such an inconvenience all the winter. He answered, like a second Timon or Heautontimoroumenos, " Would to God this was the greatest evil of those which torment me ! " It was long before he allowed himself to be persuaded to see his

[1] Racine's tragedy. — TRANS.

daughter and grandson. The son-in-law never again dared to come into his presence.

On this excellent but unfortunate man my visits had a very favourable effect; for while he liked to converse with me, and particularly instructed me on world and state affairs, he seemed to feel himself relieved and cheered. The few old friends who still gathered round him, often, therefore, made use of me when they wished to soften his peevish humour, and persuade him to any diversion. He now really rode out with us many times, and again contemplated the country, on which he had not cast an eye for so many years. He called to mind the old landowners, and told stories of their characters and actions, in which he showed himself always severe, but often cheerful and witty. We now tried also to bring him again among other men, which, however, nearly turned out badly.

About the same age, if indeed not older, was one Herr von Malapert, a rich man, who possessed a very handsome house by the horse-market, and derived a good income from salt-pits. He also lived quite secluded; but in summer he was a great deal in his garden, near the Bockenheim gate, where he watched and tended a very fine plot of pinks.

Von Reineck was likewise an amateur of pinks: the season of flowering had come, and suggestions were made as to whether these two could not visit each other. We introduced the matter, and persisted in it; till at last Von Reineck resolved to go out with us one Sunday afternoon. The greeting of the two old gentlemen was very laconic, indeed almost pantomimic; and they walked up and down by the long pink frames with true diplomatic strides. The display was really extraordinarily beautiful: and the particular forms and colours of the different flowers, the advantages of one over the other, and their rarity, gave at last occasion to a sort of conversation which appeared to get quite friendly; at which we others rejoiced the more because we saw the most precious old Rhine wine in cut decanters, fine fruits, and other good things spread upon a table in a neighbouring bower. But these, alas! we were not to enjoy. For Von Reineck unfortunately saw a very fine pink with its head somewhat hanging down : he therefore took the stalk near the calyx very cautiously between his fore and middle fingers, and lifted the flower so that he could well inspect it. But even this gentle handling vexed the owner. Von Malapert courteously, indeed, but stiffly enough, and somewhat self-complacently, reminded him of the *Oculis, non manibus*.[1] Von Reineck had already let go the flower, but at once took fire at the words, and said in his usual dry, serious manner, that it was quite consistent with an amateur to touch and examine them in such a manner. Whereupon he repeated the act, and took the flower again between his fingers. The friends of both parties — for Von Malapert also had one present — were now in the greatest perplexity. They set one hare to catch another (that was our proverbial expression, when a conversation was to be interrupted, and turned to another subject), but it would not do ; the old gentleman had become quite silent; and we feared every moment that Von Reineck would repeat the act, when it would be all over with us. The two friends kept their principals apart by occupying them, now here, now there, and at last we found it most expedient to make preparation for departure. Thus, alas! we were forced to turn our backs on the inviting sideboard, yet unenjoyed.

Hofrath Huesgen, not born in Frankfort, of the Reformed[2] religion, and therefore incapable of public office, including the profession of advocate, which, how-

---

[1] Eyes, not hands.—TRANS.
[2] That is to say, he was a Calvinist, as distinguished from a Lutheran.—TRANS.

ever, because much confidence was placed in him as an
excellent jurist, he managed to exercise quietly, both
in the Frankfort and the imperial courts, under assumed signatures, was already sixty years old when I
took writing-lessons with his son, and so came into his
house. His figure was tall without being thin, and
broad without corpulency. You could not look, for the
first time, on his face, which was not only disfigured
by smallpox, but deprived of an eye, without apprehension. He always wore on his bald head a perfectly
white bell-shaped cap, tied at the top with a ribbon.
His morning-gowns, of calamanco or damask, were
always very clean. He dwelt in a very cheerful suite
of rooms on the ground-floor by the *Allée*, and the
neatness of everything about him corresponded with
this cheerfulness. The perfect arrangement of his
papers, books, and maps produced a favourable impression. His son, Heinrich Sebastian, afterward known
by various writings on art, gave little promise in his
youth. Good-natured but dull, not rude but blunt, and
without any special liking for instruction, he rather
sought to avoid the presence of his father, as he could
get all he wanted from his mother. I, on the other
hand, grew more and more intimate with the old man,
the more I knew of him. As he attended only to important cases, he had time enough to occupy and amuse
himself in another manner. I had not long frequented
his house, and heard his doctrines, before I could well
perceive that he stood in opposition to God and the
world. One of his favourite books was "Agrippa
de Vanitate Scientiarum," which he especially commended to me, and so set my young brains in a considerable whirl for a long time. In the happiness of
youth I was inclined to a sort of optimism, and had
again pretty well reconciled myself with God or the
gods; for the experience of a series of years had taught
me that there was much to counterbalance evil, that

one can well recover from misfortune, and that one may be saved from dangers and need not always break one's neck. I looked with tolerance, too, on what men did and pursued, and found many things worthy of praise which my old gentleman could not by any means abide. Indeed, once when he had sketched the world to me, rather from the distorted side, I observed from his appearance that he meant to close the game with an important trump-card. He shut tight his blind left eye, as he was wont to do in such cases, looked sharp out of the other, and said in a nasal voice, " Even in God I discover defects."

My Timonic mentor was also a mathematician ; but his practical turn drove him to mechanics, though he did not work himself. A clock, wonderful indeed in those days, which indicated, not only the days and hours, but the motions of the sun and moon, he caused to be made according to his own plan. On Sunday, about ten o'clock in the morning, he always wound it up himself; which he could do the more regularly, as he never went to church. I never saw company nor guests at his house; and only twice in ten years do I remember to have seen him dressed, and walking out of doors.

My various conversations with these men were not insignificant, and each of them influenced me in his own way. From every one, I had as much attention as his own children, if not more; and each strove to increase his delight in me as in a beloved son, while he aspired to mould me into his moral counterpart. Olenschlager would have made me a courtier, Von Reineck a diplomatic man of business: both, the latter particularly, sought to disgust me with poetry and authorship. Huesgen wished me to be a Timon after his fashion, but, at the same time, an able jurisconsult, — a necessary profession, as he thought, with which one could, in a regular manner, defend one's self and

friends against the rabble of mankind, succour the oppressed, and, above all, pay off a rogue; though the
last is neither especially practicable nor advisable.

But if I liked to be at the side of these men to profit
by their counsels and directions, younger persons, only
a little older than myself, roused me to immediate
emulation. I name here, before all others, the brothers
Schlosser and Griesbach. But as, subsequently, there
arose between us greater intimacy, which lasted for
many years uninterruptedly, I will only say, for the
present, that they were then praised as being distinguished in languages, and other studies which opened
the academical course, and held up as models, and that
everybody cherished the certain expectation that they
would once do something uncommon in Church and
state.

With respect to myself, I also had it in my mind to
produce something extraordinary; but in what it was
to consist was not clear. But as we are apt to look
rather to the reward which may be received than to
the merit which is to be acquired; so, I do not deny,
that if I thought of a desirable piece of good fortune, it
appeared to me most fascinating in the shape of that
laurel garland which is woven to adorn the poet.

FIFTH BOOK.

Every bird has its decoy, and every man is led and misled in a way peculiar to himself. Nature, education, circumstances, and habit kept me apart from all that was rude; and though I often came into contact with the lower classes of people, particularly mechanics, no close connection grew out of it. I had indeed boldness enough to undertake something uncommon and perhaps dangerous, and many times felt disposed to do so; but I was without the handle by which to grasp and hold it.

Meanwhile I was quite unexpectedly involved in an affair which brought me near to a great hazard, and at least for a long time into perplexity and distress. The good terms on which I before stood with the boy whom I have already named Pylades was maintained up to the time of my youth. We indeed saw each other less often, because our parents did not stand on the best footing with each other; but, when we did meet, the old raptures of friendship broke out immediately. Once we met in the alleys which offer a very agreeable walk between the outer and inner gate of Saint Gallus. We had scarcely returned greetings when he said to me, " I hold to the same opinion as ever about your verses. Those which you recently communicated to me, I read aloud to some pleasant companions; and not one of them will believe that you have made them." " Let it pass," I answered: " we will make and enjoy them, and the others may think and say of them what they please."

"There comes the unbeliever now," added my friend. "We will not speak of it," I replied: "what is the use of it? one cannot convert them." "By no means," said my friend: "I cannot let the affair pass off in this way."

After a short, insignificant conversation, my young comrade, who was but too well disposed toward me, could not suffer the matter to drop, without saying to the other, with some resentment, "Here is my friend who made those pretty verses, for which you will not give him credit!" "He will certainly not take it amiss," answered the other; "for we do him an honour when we suppose that more learning is required to make such verses than one of his years can possess." I replied with something indifferent; but my friend continued, "It will not cost much labour to convince you. Give him any theme, and he will make you a poem on the spot." I assented; we were agreed; and the other asked me whether I would venture to compose a pretty love-letter in rhyme, which a modest young woman might be supposed to write to a young man, to declare her inclination. "Nothing is easier than that," I answered, "if I only had writing materials." He pulled out his pocket almanac, in which there were a great many blank leaves; and I sat down upon a bench to write. They walked about in the meanwhile, but always kept me in sight. I immediately brought the required situation before my mind, and thought how agreeable it must be if some pretty girl were really attached to me, and would reveal her sentiments to me, either in prose or verse. I therefore began my declaration with delight, and in a little while executed it in a flowing measure, between doggerel and madrigal, with the greatest possible *naïveté*, and in such a way that the skeptic was overcome with admiration, and my friend with delight. The request of the former to possess the poem I could the less refuse, as it was written in his almanac; and I liked to see the documentary evidence of my capabilities in his hands. He departed with many assurances of admiration and respect, and wished for nothing more than that we should often meet; so we settled soon to go together into the country.

Our excursion actually took place, and was joined by several more young people of the same rank. They were men of the middle, or, if you please, of the lower, class, who were not wanting in brains, and who, moreover, as they had gone through school, were possessed of various knowledge and a certain degree of culture. In a large, rich city, there are many modes of gaining a livelihood. These eked out a living by copying for the lawyers, and by advancing the children of the lower order more than is usual in common schools. With grown-up children, who were about to be confirmed, they went through the religious courses; then, again, they assisted factors and merchants in some way, and were thus enabled to enjoy themselves frugally in the evenings, and particularly on Sundays and festivals.

On the way there, while they highly extolled my love-letter, they confessed to me that they had made a very merry use of it; viz., that it had been copied in a feigned hand, and, with a few pertinent allusions, had been sent to a conceited young man, who was now firmly persuaded that a lady to whom he had paid distant court was excessively enamoured of him, and sought an opportunity for closer acquaintance. They at the same time told me in confidence, that he desired nothing more now than to be able to answer her in verse; but that neither he nor they were skilful enough, so that they earnestly solicited me to compose the much-desired reply.

Mystifications are and will continue to be an amusement for idle people, whether more or less ingenious.

A venial wickedness, a self-complacent malice, is an enjoyment for those who have neither resources in themselves nor a wholesome external activity. No age is quite exempt from such pruriences. We had often tricked each other in our childish years: many sports turn upon mystification and trick. The present jest did not seem to me to go farther: I gave my consent. They imparted to me many particulars which the letter ought to contain, and we brought it home already finished.

A little while afterward I was urgently invited, through my friend, to take part in one of the evening feasts of that society. The lover, he said, was willing to bear the expense on this occasion, and desired expressly to thank the friend who had shown himself so excellent a poetical secretary.

We came together late enough, the meal was most frugal, the wine drinkable; while, as for the conversation, it turned almost entirely on jokes upon the young man, who was present, and certainly not very bright, and who, after repeated readings of the letter, almost believed that he had written it himself.

My natural good nature would not allow me to take much pleasure in such a malicious deception, and the repetition of the same subject soon disgusted me. I should certainly have passed a tedious evening, if an unexpected apparition had not revived me. On our arrival we found the table already neatly and orderly set, and sufficient wine served on it: we sat down and remained alone, without requiring further service. As there was, however, a scarcity of wine at last, one of them called for the maid; but, instead of the maid, there came in a girl of uncommon, and, when one saw her with all around her, of incredible, beauty. "What do you desire?" she asked, after having cordially wished us a good evening: "the maid is ill in bed. Can I serve you?" "The wine is out," said one: "if you would fetch us a few bottles, it would be very kind." "Do it, Gretchen,"[1] said another: "it is but a cat's leap from here." "Why not?" she answered; and, taking a few empty bottles from the table, she hastened out. Her form, as seen from behind, was almost more elegant. The little cap sat so neatly upon her little head, which a slender throat united very gracefully to her neck and shoulders. Everything about her seemed choice; and one could survey her whole form the more at ease, as one's attention was no more exclusively attracted and fettered by the quiet, honest eyes and lovely mouth. I reproved my comrades for sending the girl out alone at night, but they only laughed at me; and I was soon consoled by her return, as the publican lived only just across the way. "Sit down with us, in return," said one. She did so; but, alas! she did not come near me. She drank a glass to our health, and speedily departed, advising us not to stay very long together, and not to be so noisy, as her mother was just going to bed. It was not, however, her own mother, but the mother of our hosts.

The form of that girl followed me from that moment on every path; it was the first durable impression which a female being had made upon me: and as I could find no pretext to see her at home, and would not seek one, I went to church for love of her, and had soon traced out where she sat. Thus, during the long Protestant service, I gazed my fill at her. When the congregation left the church, I did not venture to accost her, much less to accompany her, and was perfectly delighted if she seemed to have remarked me and to have returned my greeting with a nod. Yet I was not long denied the happiness of approaching her. They had persuaded the lover, whose poetical secretary I had been, that the letter written in his name had been actually despatched to the lady, and had strained

---

[1] The diminutive of Margaret. — TRANS.

to the utmost his expectations that an answer must come soon. This, also, I was to write; and the waggish company entreated me earnestly, through Pylades, to exert all my wit and employ all my art, in order that this piece might be quite elegant and perfect.

In the hope of again seeing my beauty, I immediately set to work, and thought of everything that would be in the highest degree pleasing if Gretchen were writing it to me. I thought I had composed everything so completely according' to her form, her nature, her manner, and her mind, that I could not refrain from wishing that it were so in reality, and lost myself in rapture at the mere thought that something similar could be sent from her to me. Thus I mystified myself, while I intended to impose upon another; and much joy and much trouble was yet to arise out of the affair. When I was once more summoned, I had finished, promised to come, and did not fail at the appointed hour. There was only one of the young people at home; Gretchen sat at the window spinning: the mother was going to and fro. The young man desired that I should read it over to him: I did so, and read, not without emotion, as I glanced over the paper at the beautiful girl; and when I fancied that I remarked a certain uneasiness in her deportment, and a gentle flush on her cheeks, I uttered better and with more animation that which I wished to hear from herself. The lover, who had often interrupted me with commendations, at last entreated me to make some alterations. These affected some passages which indeed were rather suited to the condition of Gretchen than to that of the lady, who was of a good family, wealthy, and known and respected in the city. After the young man had designated the desired changes, and had brought me an inkstand, but had taken leave for a short time on account of some business, I remained sitting on the bench against the wall, behind

the large table, and essayed the alterations that were
to be made, on the large slate, which almost covered
the whole table, with a pencil that always lay in the
window; because upon this slate reckonings were often
made, and various memoranda noted down, and those
coming in or going out even communicated with each
other.

I had for awhile written different things and rubbed
them out again, when I exclaimed impatiently, "It
will not do!" "So much the better," said the dear
girl in a grave tone: "I wished that it might not do!
You should not meddle in such matters." She arose
from the distaff, and, stepping toward the table, gave
me a severe lecture, with a great deal of good sense
and kindliness. "The thing seems an innocent jest:
it is a jest, but it is not innocent. I have already
lived to see several cases, in which our young people,
for the sake of such mere mischief, have brought themselves into great difficulty." "But what shall I do?"
I asked: "the letter is written, and they rely upon me
to alter it." "Trust me," she replied, "and do not
alter it; nay, take it back, put it in your pocket, go
away, and try to make the matter straight through
your friend. I will also put in a word; for look you,
though I am a poor girl, and dependent upon these
relations,— who indeed do nothing bad, though they
often, for the sake of sport or profit, undertake a good
deal that is rash,—I have resisted them, and would
not copy the first letter, as they requested. They
transcribed it in a feigned hand; and, if it is not otherwise, so may they also do with this. And you, a
young man of good family, rich, independent, why will
you allow yourself to be used as a tool in a business
which can certainly bring no good to you, and may
possibly bring much that is unpleasant?" It made
me very happy to hear her speak thus continuously,
for generally she introduced but few words into con-

versation. My liking for her grew incredibly. I was
not master of myself, and replied, "I am not so independent as you suppose; and of what use is wealth to
me, when the most precious thing I can desire is
wanting?"

She had drawn my sketch of the poetic epistle
toward her, and read it half aloud in a sweet and
graceful manner.

"That is very pretty," said she, stopping at a sort of
naïve point; "but it is a pity that it is not destined
for a real purpose." "That were indeed very desirable," I cried; "and, oh! how happy must he be, who
receives from a girl he infinitely loves, such an assurance of her affection." "There is much required for
that," she answered, "and yet many things are possible." "For example," I continued, "if any one who
knew, prized, honoured, and adored you, laid such a
paper before you, what would you do?" I pushed the
paper nearer to her, which she had previously pushed
back to me. She smiled, reflected for a moment, took
the pen, and subscribed her name. I was beside myself with rapture, jumped up, and was going to embrace
her. "No kissing!" said she, "that is so vulgar; but
let us love if we can." I had taken up the paper, and
thrust it into my pocket. "No one shall ever get it,"
said I: "the affair is closed. You have saved me."
"Now complete the salvation," she exclaimed, "and
hurry off, before the others arrive, and you fall into
trouble and embarrassment!" I could not tear myself
away from her; but she asked me in so kindly a manner, while she took my right hand in both of hers, and
lovingly pressed it! The tears stood in my eyes: I
thought hers looked moist. I pressed my face upon
her hands, and hastened away. Never in my life had
I found myself in such perplexity.

The first propensities to love in an uncorrupted
youth take altogether a spiritual direction. Nature

seems to desire that one sex may by the senses perceive goodness and beauty in the other. And thus to
me, by the sight of this girl, — by my strong inclination for her, — a new world of the beautiful and the
excellent had arisen. I perused my poetical epistle a
hundred times, gazed at the signature, kissed it, pressed
it to my heart, and rejoiced in this amiable confession.
But the more my transports increased, the more did it
pain me not to be able to visit her immediately, and to
see and converse with her again; for I dreaded the
reproofs and importunities of her cousins. The good
Pylades, who might have arranged the affair, I could
not contrive to meet. The next Sunday, therefore, I
set out for Niederrad, where these associates generally
used to go, and actually found them there. I was,
however, greatly surprised, when, instead of behaving
in a cross, distant manner, they came up to me with
joyful countenances. The youngest particularly was
very kind, took me by the hand, and said, " You have
lately played us a sorry trick, and we were very angry
with you; but your absconding and taking away the
poetical epistle has suggested a good thought to us,
which otherwise might never have occurred. By way
of atonement, you may treat us to-day; and you shall
learn at the same time the notion we have, which
will certainly give you pleasure." This harangue
caused me no small embarrassment, for I had about
me only money enough to regale myself and a friend:
but to treat a whole company, and especially one which
did not always stop at the right time, I was by no
means prepared; nay, the proposal astonished me the
more, as they had always insisted, in the most honourable manner, that each one should pay only his own
share. They smiled at my distress; and the youngest
proceeded, " Let us first take a seat in the bower, and
then you shall learn more." We sat down; and he
said, " When you had taken the love-letter with you,

we talked the whole affair over again, and came to
a conclusion that we had gratuitously misused your
talent to the vexation of others and our own danger,
for the sake of a mere paltry love of mischief, when
we could have employed it to the advantage of all of
us. See, I have here an order for a wedding-poem, as
well as for a dirge. The second must be ready immediately, the other can wait a week. Now, if you
make these, which is easy for you, you will treat us
twice; and we shall long remain your debtors." This
proposal pleased me in every respect; for I had already
in my childhood looked with a certain envy on the
occasional poems,[1] — of which then several circulated
every week, and at respectable marriages especially
came to light by the dozen, — because I thought I
could make such things as well, nay, better than
others. Now an opportunity was offered me to show
myself, and especially to see myself in print. I did
not appear disinclined. They acquainted me with the
personal particulars and the position of the family: I
went somewhat aside, made my plan, and produced
some stanzas. However, when I returned to the company, and the wine was not spared, the poem began to
halt; and I could not deliver it that evening. "There
is still time till to-morrow evening," they said; "and we
will confess to you that the fee which we receive for
the dirge is enough to get us another pleasant evening
to-morrow. Come to us; for it is but fair that
Gretchen, too, should sup with us, as it was she properly who gave us the notion." My joy was unspeakable. On my way home I had only the remaining
stanzas in my head, wrote down the whole before I
went to sleep, and the next morning made a very neat,
fair copy. The day seemed infinitely long to me; and

[1]That is to say, a poem written for a certain occasion, as a
wedding, funeral, etc. The German word is "*Gelegenheitsge-
dicht.*" — TRANS.

scarcely was it dusk, than I found myself again
in the narrow little dwelling beside the dearest of
girls.

The young people, with whom in this way I formed
a closer and closer connection, were not exactly of a
low, but of an ordinary, type. Their activity was com-
mendable, and I listened to them with pleasure when
they spoke of the manifold ways and means by which
one could gain a living: above all, they loved to tell
of people, now very rich, who had begun with nothing.
Others to whom they referred had, as poor clerks, rendered themselves indispensable to their employers, and
had finally risen to be their sons-in-law; while others
had so enlarged and improved a little trade in matches
and the like, that they were now prosperous merchants
and tradesmen. But above all, to young men who
were active on their feet, the trade of agent and factor,
and the undertaking of all sorts of commissions and
charges for helpless rich men was, they said, a most
profitable means of gaining a livelihood. We all liked
to hear this; and each one fancied himself somebody,
when he imagined, at the moment, that there was
enough in him, not only to get on in the world, but to
acquire an extraordinary fortune. But no one seemed
to carry on this conversation more earnestly than
Pylades, who at last confessed that he had an extraordinary passion for a girl, and was actually engaged to
her. The circumstances of his parents would not
allow him to go to universities; but he had endeavoured to acquire a fine handwriting, a knowledge of
accounts and the modern languages, and would now
do his best in hopes of attaining that domestic felicity.
His fellows praised him for this, although they did not
approve of a premature engagement; and they added,
that while forced to acknowledge him to be a fine, good
fellow, they did not consider him active or enterprising
enough to do anything extraordinary. While he, in

vindication of himself, circumstantially set forth what he thought himself fit for, and how he was going to begin, the others were also incited; and each one began to tell what he was now able to do, doing, or carrying on, what he had already accomplished, and what he saw immediately before him. The turn at last came to me. I was to set forth my course of life and prospects; and, while I was considering, Pylades said, " I make this one proviso, lest we be at too great a disadvantage, that he does not bring into the account the external advantages of his position. He should rather tell us a tale how he would proceed if at this moment he were thrown entirely upon his own resources, as we are."

Gretchen, who till this moment had kept on spinning, rose, and seated herself as usual at the end of the table. We had already emptied some bottles, and I began to relate the hypothetical history of my life in the best humour. "First of all, then, I commend myself to you," said I, "that you may continue the custom you have begun to bestow on me. If you gradually procure me the profit of all the occasional poems, and we do not consume them in mere feasting, I shall soon come to something. But then, you must not take it ill if I dabble also in your handicraft." Upon this, I told them what I had observed in their occupations, and for which I held myself fit at any rate. Each one had previously rated his services in money, and I asked them to assist me also in completing my establishment. Gretchen had listened to all hitherto very attentively, and that in a position which well suited her, whether she chose to hear or to speak. With both hands she clasped her folded arms, and rested them on the edge of the table. Thus she could sit a long while without moving anything but her head, which was never done without some occasion or meaning. She had several times put in a word, and helped us on over this and that, when we halted in our projects, and then was again still and quiet as usual. I kept her in my eye, and it may readily be supposed that I had not devised and uttered my plan without reference to her. My passion for her gave to what I said such an air of truth and probability, that, for a moment, I deceived myself, imagined myself as lonely and helpless as my story supposed, and felt extremely happy in the prospect of possessing her. Pylades had closed his confession with marriage; and the question arose among the rest of us, whether our plans went as far as that. "I have not the least doubt on that score," said I; "for properly a wife is necessary to every one of us, in order to preserve at home, and enable us to enjoy as a whole, what we rake together abroad in such an odd way." I then made a sketch of a wife, such as I wished; and it must have turned out strangely if she had not been a perfect counterpart of Gretchen.

The dirge was consumed; the epithalamium now stood beneficially at hand: I overcame all fear and care, and contrived, as I had many acquaintances, to conceal my actual evening entertainments from my family. To see and to be near the dear girl was soon an indispensable condition of my being. The friends had grown just as accustomed to me, and we were almost daily together, as if it could not be otherwise. Pylades had, in the meantime, introduced his fair one into the house; and this pair passed many an evening with us. They, as bride and bridegroom, though still very much in the bud, did not conceal their tenderness: Gretchen's deportment toward me was only suited to keep me at a distance. She gave her hand to no one, not even to me; she allowed no touch: yet she many times seated herself near me, particularly when I wrote, or read aloud, and then, laying her arm familiarly upon my shoulder, she looked over the book or paper. If, however, I ventured to take on a similar liberty with her, she withdrew, and did not return very soon. This position she often repeated; and, indeed, all her attitudes and motions were very uniform, but always equally becoming, beautiful, and charming. But such a familiarity I never saw her practise toward anybody else.

One of the most innocent, and, at the same time, amusing, parties of pleasure in which I engaged with different companies of young people, was this, — that we seated ourselves in the Höchst market-ship, observed the strange passengers packed away in it, and bantered and teased, now this one, now that, as pleasure or caprice prompted. At Höchst we got out at the time when the market-boat from Mainz arrived. At a hotel there was a well-spread table, where the better sort of travellers, coming and going, ate with each other, and then proceeded, each on his way, as both ships returned. Every time, after dining, we sailed up to Frankfort, having, with a very large company, made the cheapest water-excursion that was possible. Once I had undertaken this journey with Gretchen's cousins, when a young man joined us at table in Höchst, who might be a little older than we were. They knew him, and he got himself introduced to me. He had something very pleasing in his manner, though he was not otherwise distinguished. Coming from Mainz, he now went back with us to Frankfort, and conversed with me of everything that related to the internal arrangements of the city, and the public offices and places, on which he seemed to me to be very well informed. When we separated, he bade me farewell, and added, that he wished I might think well of him, as he hoped on occasion to avail himself of my recommendation. I did not know what he meant by this, but the cousins enlightened me some days after. They spoke well of him, and asked me to intercede with my grandfather, as a moderate appointment was just now vacant, which this friend would like to obtain. I at first wished to be excused, as I had never meddled in such affairs; but they went on urging me until I resolved to do it. I had already many times remarked, that in these grants of offices, which unfortunately were regarded as matters of favour, the mediation of my grandmother or an aunt had not been without effect. I was now so advanced as to arrogate some influence to myself. For that reason, to gratify my friends, who declared themselves under every sort of obligation for such a kindness, I overcame the timidity of a grandchild, and undertook to deliver a written application that was handed in to me.

One Sunday, after dinner, while my grandfather was busy in his garden, all the more because autumn was approaching, and I tried to assist him on every side, I came forward with my request and the petition, after some hesitation. He looked at it, and asked me whether I knew the young man. I told him in general terms what was to be said, and he let the matter rest there. "If he has merit, and, moreover, good testimonials, I will favour him for your sake and his own." He said no more, and for a long while I heard nothing of the matter.

For some time I had observed that Gretchen was no longer spinning, but instead was employed in sewing, and that, too, on very fine work, which surprised me the more, as the days were already shortening, and winter was coming on. I thought no further about it; only it troubled me that several times I had not found her at home in the morning as formerly, and could not learn, without importunity, whither she had gone. Yet I was destined one day to be surprised in a very odd manner. My sister, who was getting herself ready for a ball, asked me to fetch her some so-called Italian flowers, at a fashionable milliner's. They were made in convents, and were small and pretty: myrtles especially, dwarf-roses, and the like, came out quite beautifully and naturally. I did her the favour, and went to the shop where I had been with her often already. Hardly had I entered, and greeted the proprietress, than I saw sitting in the window a lady, who, in a lace cap, looked very young and pretty, and in a silk mantilla seemed very well shaped. I could easily recognise that she was an assistant, for she was occupied in fastening a ribbon and feathers upon a hat. The milliner showed me the long box with single flowers of various sorts. I looked them over, and, as I made my choice, glanced again toward the lady in the window; but how great was my astonishment when I perceived an incredible similarity to Gretchen, nay, was forced to be convinced at last that it was Gretchen herself. Nor could I doubt any longer, when she winked with her eyes, and gave me a sign that I must not betray our acquaintance. I now, with my choosing and rejecting, drove the milliner into despair more than even a lady could have done. I had, in fact, no choice; for I was excessively confused, and at the same time liked to linger, because it kept me near the girl, whose disguise annoyed me, though in that disguise she appeared to me more enchanting than ever. Finally the milliner seemed to lose all patience, and with her own hands selected for me a whole bandbox full of flowers, which I was to place before my sister, and let her choose for herself. Thus I was, as it were, driven out of the shop, she sending the box in advance by one of her girls.

Scarcely had I reached home than my father caused me to be called, and communicated to me that it was now quite certain that the Archduke Joseph would be elected and crowned King of Rome. An event so

highly important was not to be expected without preparation, nor allowed to pass with mere gaping and
staring. He wished, therefore, he said, to go through
with me the election and coronation diaries of the two
last coronations, as well as through the last capitula-
tions of election, in order to remark what new conditions might be added in the present instance. The
diaries were opened, and we occupied ourselves with
them the whole day till far into the night; while the
pretty girl, sometimes in her old house-dress, sometimes in her new costume, ever hovered before me,
backwards and forwards among the most august objects of the Holy Roman Empire. This evening it
was impossible to see her, and I lay awake through
a very restless night. The study of yesterday was the
next day zealously resumed; and it was not till toward
evening that I found it possible to visit my fair one,
whom I met again in her usual house-dress. She
smiled when she saw me, but I did not venture to
mention anything before the others. When the whole
company sat quietly together again, she began, and
said, " It is unfair that you do not confide to our friend
what we have lately resolved upon." She then continued to relate, that after our late conversation, in
which the discussion was how any one could get on
in the world, something was also said of the way in
which a woman could enhance the value of her talent
and labour, and advantageously employ her time. The
cousin had consequently proposed that she should
make an experiment at a milliner's, who was just then
in want of an assistant. They had, she said, arranged
with the woman: she went there so many hours a day,
and was well paid; but she would there be obliged, for
propriety's sake, to conform to a certain dress, which,
however, she left behind her every time, as it did not
at all suit her other modes of life and employment. I
was indeed set at rest by this declaration; but it did

not quite please me to know that the pretty girl was in a public shop, and at a place where the fashionable world found a convenient resort. But I betrayed nothing, and strove to work off my jealous care in silence. For this the younger cousin did not allow me a long time, as he once more came forward with a proposal for an occasional poem, told me all the personalities, and at once desired me to prepare myself for the invention and disposition of the work. He had spoken with me several times already concerning the proper treatment of such a theme; and, as I was voluble in these cases, he readily asked me to explain to him, circumstantially, what is rhetorical in these things, to give him a notion of the matter, and to make use of my own and others' labours in this kind for examples. The young man had some brains, but not a trace of a poetical vein; and now he went so much into particulars, and wished to have such an account of everything, that I gave utterance to the remark, "It seems as if you wanted to encroach upon my trade, and take away my customers!" "I will not deny it," said he, smiling, "as I shall do you no harm by it. This will only continue to the time when you go to the university, and till then you must allow me still to profit something by your society." "Most cordially," I replied; and I encouraged him to draw out a plan, to choose a metre according to the character of his subject, and to do whatever else might seem necessary. He went to work in earnest, but did not succeed. I was in the end compelled to rewrite so much of it, that I could more easily and better have written it all from the beginning myself. Yet this teaching and learning, this mutual labour, afforded us good entertainment. Gretchen took part in it, and had many a pretty notion; so that we were all pleased, we may, indeed, say happy. During the day she worked at the milliner's: in the evenings we generally met together, and

our contentment was not even disturbed when at last
the commissions for occasional poems began to leave
off. Still we felt hurt once, when one of them came
back under protest, because it did not suit the party
who ordered it. We consoled ourselves, however, as
we considered it our very best work, and could, therefore, declare the other a bad judge. The cousin, who
was determined to learn something at any rate, resorted
to the expedient of inventing problems, in the solution
of which we always found amusement enough; but, as
they brought in nothing, our little banquets had to be
much more frugally managed.

That great political object, the election and coronation of a King of Rome, was pursued with more and
more earnestness. The assembling of the electoral
college, originally appointed to take place at Augsburg
in the October of 1763, was now transferred to Frankfort; and both at the end of this year and in the beginning of the next, preparations went forward which
should usher in this important business. The beginning was made by a parade never yet seen by us.
One of our chancery officials on horseback, escorted
by four trumpeters likewise mounted, and surrounded
by a guard of infantry, read in a loud, clear voice at
all the corners of the city, a prolix edict, which announced the forthcoming proceedings, and exhorted the
citizens to a becoming deportment suitable to the circumstances. The council was occupied with weighty
considerations; and it was not long before the imperial
quartermaster, despatched by the hereditary grand
marshal, made his appearance, in order to arrange and
designate the residences of the ambassadors and their
suites, according to the old custom. Our house lay in
the Palatine district, and we had to provide for a new
but agreeable billeting. The middle story, which
Count Thorane had formerly occupied, was given up
to a cavalier of the Palatinate; and as Baron von

Königsthal, the Nuremberg *chargé-d'affaires*, occupied the upper floor, we were still more crowded than in the time of the French. This served me as a new pretext for being out of doors, and to pass the greater part of the day in the streets, that I might see all that was open to public view.

After the preliminary alteration and arrangement of the rooms in the town-house had seemed to us worth seeing; after the arrival of the ambassadors one after another, and their first solemn ascent in a body, on the 6th of February, had taken place, — we admired the coming in of the imperial commissioners, and their ascent also to the Römer, which was made with great pomp. The dignified person of the Prince of Lichtenstein made a good impression; yet connoisseurs maintained that the showy liveries had already been used on another occasion, and that this election and coronation would hardly equal in brilliancy that of Charles the Seventh. We younger folks were content with what was before our eyes: all seemed to us very fine, and much of it perfectly astonishing.

The electoral congress was fixed at last for the 3d of March. New formalities again set the city in motion, and the alternate visits of ceremony on the part of the ambassadors kept us always on our legs. We were, moreover, compelled to watch closely; as we were not only to gape about, but to note everything well, in order to give a proper report at home, and even to make out many little memoirs, on which my father and Herr von Königsthal had deliberated, partly for our exercise and ·partly for their own information. And certainly this was of peculiar advantage to me; as I was enabled very tolerably to keep a living election and coronation diary, as far as regarded externals.

The person who first of all made a durable impression upon me was the chief ambassador from the elect-

orate of Mainz, Baron von Erthal, afterward elector.
Without having anything striking in his figure, he was
always highly pleasing to me in his black gown
trimmed with lace. The second ambassador, Baron
von Groschlag, was a well-formed man of the world,
easy in his exterior, but conducting himself with great
decorum. He everywhere produced a very agreeable
impression. Prince Esterhazy, the Bohemian envoy,
was not tall, though well formed, lively, and at the
same time eminently decorous, without pride or coldness. I had a special liking for him, because he reminded me of Marshal de Broglio. Yet the form and
dignity of these excellent persons vanished, in a certain degree, before the prejudice that was entertained
in favour of Baron von Plotho, the Brandenburg ambassador. This man, who was distinguished by a certain
parsimony, both in his own clothes and in his liveries
and equipages, had been greatly renowned, from the
time of the Seven Years' War, as a diplomatic hero.
At Ratisbon, when the notary April thought, in the
presence of witnesses, to serve him with the declaration of outlawry which had been issued against his
king, he had, with the laconic exclamation, "What!
you serve?" thrown him, or caused him to be thrown,
down-stairs. We believed the first, because it pleased
us best; and we could readily believe it of the little
compact man, with his black, fiery eyes glancing here
and there. All eyes were directed toward him, particularly when he alighted. There arose every time a
sort of joyous whispering; and but little was wanting
to a regular explosion, or a shout of "Vivat! Bravo!"
So high did the king, and all who were devoted to him,
body and soul, stand in favour with the crowd, among
whom, besides the Frankforters, were Germans from
all parts.

On the one hand these things gave me much pleasure; as all that took place, no matter of what nature

it might be, concealed a certain meaning, indicated some internal relation: and such symbolic ceremonies again, for a moment, represented as living the old Empire of Germany, almost choked to death by so many parchments, papers, and books. But, on the other hand, I could not suppress a secret displeasure, when at home, I had, on behalf of my father, to transcribe the internal transactions, and at the same time to remark that here several powers, which balanced each other, stood in opposition, and only so far agreed, as they designed to limit the new ruler even more than the old one; that every one valued his influence only so far as he hoped to retain or enlarge his privileges, and better to secure his independence. Nay, on this occasion they were more attentive than usual, because they began to fear Joseph the Second, his vehemence, and probable plans.

With my grandfather and other members of the council, whose families I used to visit, this was no pleasant time, they had so much to do with meeting distinguished guests, complimenting, and the delivery of presents. No less had the magistrate, both in general and in particular, to defend himself, to resist, and to protest, as every one on such occasions desires to extort something from him, or burden him with something; and few of those to whom he appeals support him, or lend him their aid. In short, all that I had read in "Lersner's Chronicle" of similar incidents on similar occasions, with admiration of the patience and perseverance of those good old councilmen, came once more vividly before my eyes.

Many vexations arise also from this, that the city is gradually overrun with people, both useful and needless. In vain are the courts reminded, on the part of the city, of prescriptions of the Golden Bull, now, indeed, obsolete. Not only the deputies with their attendants, but many persons of rank, and others who come from curiosity or for private objects, stand under protection; and the question as to who is to be billeted out, and who is to hire his own lodging, is not always decided at once. The tumult constantly increases; and even those who have nothing to give, or to answer for, begin to feel uncomfortable.

Even we young people, who could quietly. contemplate it all, ever found something which did not quite satisfy our eyes. or our imagination. The Spanish mantles, the huge plumed hats of the ambassadors, and other objects here and there, had indeed a truly antique look; but there was a great deal, on the other hand, so half-new or entirely modern, that the affair assumed throughout a motley, unsatisfactory, often tasteless, appearance. We were, therefore, very happy to learn that great preparations were made on account of the journey to Frankfort of the emperor and future king; that the proceedings of the college of electors, which were based on the last electoral capitulation, were now going forward rapidly; and that the day of election had been appointed for the 27th of March. Now there was a thought of fetching the insignia of the empire from Nuremberg and Aix-la-Chapelle, and next we expected the entrance of the Elector of Mainz; while the disputes with his ambassadors about the quartering ever continued.

Meanwhile I pursued my clerical labours at home very actively, and perceived many little suggestions (*monita*) which came in from all sides, and were to be regarded in the new capitulation. Every rank desired to see its privileges guaranteed and its importance increased in this document. Very many such observations and desires were, however, put aside: much remained as it was, though the suggestors (*monentes*) received the most positive assurances that the neglect should in no wise ensue to their prejudice.

In the meantime the office of imperial marshal was

forced to undertake many dangerous affairs : the crowd of strangers increased, and it became more and more difficult to find lodgings for them. Nor was there unanimity as to the limits of the different precincts of the electors. The magistracy wished to keep from the citizens the burdens which they were not bound to bear ; and thus day and night there were hourly grievances, redresses, contests, and misunderstandings.

The entrance of the Elector of Mainz occurred on the 21st of May. Then began the cannonading, with which for a long time we were often to be deafened. This solemnity was important in the series of ceremonies; for all the men whom we had hitherto seen, high as they were in rank, were still only subordinates : but here appeared a sovereign, an independent prince, the first after the emperor, preceded and accompanied by a large retinue worthy of himself. Of the pomp which marked his entrance I should have much to tell, if I did not purpose returning to it hereafter, and on an occasion which no one could easily guess.

What I refer to is this : the same day Lavater, on his return home from Berlin, came through Frankfort, and saw the solemnity. Now, though such worldly formalities could not have the least value for him, this procession, with its display and all its accessories, might have been distinctly impressed on his very lively imagination; for many years afterward, when this eminent but singular man showed me a poetical paraphrase of, I believe, the Revelation of St. John, I discovered the entrance of Antichrist copied, step by step, figure by figure, circumstance by circumstance, from the entrance of the Elector of Mainz into Frankfort, in such a manner, too, that even the tassels on the heads of the dun-coloured horses were not wanting. More can be said on this point when I reach the epoch of that strange kind of poetry by which it was supposed that the myths of the Old and New Testaments were brought nearer to our view and feelings when they were completely travestied into the modern style, and clothed with the vestments of present life, whether gentle or simple. How this mode of treatment gradually obtained favour will be likewise discussed hereafter; yet I may here simply remark, that it could not well be carried farther than it was by Lavater and his emulators, one of these having described the three holy kings riding into Bethlehem in such modern form, that the princes and gentlemen whom Lavater used to visit were not to be mistaken as the persons.

We will, then, for the present, allow the Elector Emeric Joseph to enter the Compostello incognito, so to speak, and turn to Gretchen, whom, just as the crowd was dispersing, I spied in the crowd, accompanied by Pylades and his mistress, the three now seeming to be inseparable. We had scarcely come up to each other and exchanged greetings, than it was agreed that we should pass the evening together; and I kept the appointment punctually. The usual company had assembled; and each one had something to relate, to say, or to remark, — how one had been most struck by this thing, and another by that. "Your speeches," said Gretchen at last, "perplex me even more than the events of the time themselves. What I have seen I cannot make out, and should very much like to know what a great deal of it means." I replied that it was easy for me to render her this service. She had only to say what particularly interested her. This she did; and, as I was about to explain some points, it was found that it would be better to proceed in order. I not unskilfully compared these solemnities and functions to a play, in which the curtain was let down at will, while the actors played on, and was then raised again, so that the spectators could once more, to some extent, take part in the action. Being very talkative when I was allowed my own way, I related the whole, from the beginning down to the time present, in the best order, and, to make the subject of my discourse more apparent, did not fail to use the pencil and the large slate. Being only slightly interrupted by some questions and obstinate assertions of the others, I brought my discourse to a close, to the general satisfaction; while Gretchen, by her unbroken attention, had highly encouraged me. At last she thanked me, and envied, as she said, all who were informed of the affairs of this world, and knew how this and that came about and what it signified. She wished she were a boy, and managed to acknowledge, with much kindness, that she was indebted to me for a great deal of instruction. " If I were a boy," said she, " we would learn something good together at the university." The conversation continued in this strain: she definitively resolved to take instruction in French, of the absolute necessity of which she had become well aware in the milliner's shop. I asked her why she no longer went there; for during the latter times, not being able to go out much in the evening, I had often passed the shop during the day for her sake, merely to see her for a moment. She explained that she had not liked to expose herself there in these unsettled times. As soon as the city returned to its former condition, she intended to go there again.

Then the impending day of election was the topic of conversation. I contrived to tell, at length, what was going to happen, and how, and to support my demonstrations in detail by drawings on the tablet; for I had the place of conclave, with its altars, thrones, seats, and chairs, perfectly before my mind. We separated at the proper time, and in a particularly comfortable frame of mind.

For, with a young couple who are in any degree harmoniously formed by nature, nothing can conduce

to a more beautiful union than when the maiden is
anxious to learn, and the youth inclined to teach.
There arises from it a well-grounded and agreeable
relation. She sees in him the creator of her spiritual
existence ; and he sees in her a creature that ascribes
her perfection, not to nature, not to chance, not to any
one-sided inclination, but to a mutual will: and this
reciprocation is so sweet, that we cannot wonder, if,
from the days of the old and the new [1] Abelard, the
most violent passions, and as much happiness as unhappiness, have arisen from such an intercourse of two
beings.

With the next day began great commotion in the
city, on account of the visits paid and returned, which
now took place with the greatest ceremony. But what
particularly interested me, as a citizen of Frankfort,
and gave rise to a great many reflections, was the
taking of the oath of security (*Sicherheitseides*) by the
council, the military, and the body of citizens, not
through representatives, but personally and in mass ;
first, in the great hall of the Römer, by the magistracy
and staff-officers ; then in the great square (*Platz*), the
Römerberg, by all the citizens, according to their. re-
spective ranks, gradations, or quarterings ; and, lastly,
by the rest of the military. Here one could survey
at a single glance the entire commonwealth, assembled
for the honourable purpose of swearing security to the
head and members of the empire, and unbroken peace
during the great work now impending. The Electors
of Treves and of Cologne had now also arrived. On
the evening before the day of election, all strangers are
sent out of the city, the gates are closed, the Jews are
confined to their quarter, and the citizen of Frankfort
prides himself not a little that he alone may witness
so great a solemnity.

[1] The " *new* Abelard " is St. Preux, in the "Nouvelle Héloise "
of Rousseau. — TRANS.

All that had hitherto taken place was tolerably modern: the highest and high personages moved about only in coaches, but now we were going to see them in the primitive manner on horseback. The concourse and rush were extraordinary. I managed to squeeze myself into the Römer, which I knew as familiarly as a mouse does the private corn-loft, till I reached the main entrance, before which the electors and ambassadors, who had first arrived in their state coaches, and had assembled above, were now to mount their horses. The stately, well-trained steeds were covered with richly laced housings, and ornamented in every way. The Elector Emeric Joseph, a handsome, portly man, looked well on horseback. Of the other two I remember less, excepting that the red princes' mantles, trimmed with ermine, which we had been accustomed to see only in pictures before, seemed to us very romantic in the open air. The ambassadors of the absent temporal electors, with their Spanish dresses of gold brocade, embroidered over with gold, and trimmed with gold lace, likewise did our eyes good; and the large feathers particularly, that waved most splendidly from the hats, which were cocked in the antique style. But what did not please me were the short modern breeches, the white silk stockings, and the fashionable shoes. We should have liked half-boots, — gilded as much as they pleased, — sandals, or something of the kind, that we might have seen a more consistent costume.

In deportment the Ambassador von Plotho again distinguished himself from all the rest. He appeared lively and cheerful, and seemed to have no great respect for the whole ceremony. For when his frontman, an elderly gentleman, could not leap immediately on his horse, and he was therefore forced to wait some time in the grand entrance, he did not refrain from laughing, till his own horse was brought forward, upon

which he swung himself very dexterously, and was
again admired by us as a most worthy representative
of Frederick the Second.

Now the curtain was for us once more let down. I
had, indeed, tried to force my way into the church;
but that place was more inconvenient than agreeable.
The voters had withdrawn into the *sanctum*, where
prolix ceremonies usurped the place of a deliberate
consideration as to the election. After long delay,
pressure, and bustle, the people at last heard the name of
Joseph the Second, who was proclaimed King of Rome.

The thronging of strangers into the city became
greater and greater. Everybody went about in his
holiday clothes, so that at last none but dresses entirely of gold were found worthy of note. The
emperor and king had already arrived at Heusenstamm, a castle of the Counts of Schönborn, and were
there in the customary manner greeted and welcomed:
but the city celebrated this important epoch by spiritual festivals of all the religions, by high masses and
sermons; and, on the temporal side, by incessant firing
of cannon as an accompaniment to the " Te Deums."

If all these public solemnities, from the beginning
up to this point, had been regarded as a deliberate
work of art, not much to find fault with would have
been found. All was well prepared. The public
scenes opened gradually, and went on increasing in
importance; the men grew in number, the personages
in dignity, their appurtenances, as well as themselves,
in splendour, — and thus it advanced with every day,
till at last even a well-prepared and firm eye became
bewildered.

The entrance of the Elector of Mainz, which we
have refused to describe more completely, was magnificent and imposing enough to suggest to the imagination of an eminent man the advent of a great
prophesied world-ruler: even we were not a little

dazzled by it. But now our expectation was stretched to the utmost, as it was said that the emperor and the future king were approaching the city. At a little distance from Sachsenhausen, a tent had been erected in which the entire magistracy remained, to show the appropriate honour, and to proffer the keys of the city to the chief of the empire. Farther out, on a fair, spacious plain, stood another, a state pavilion, whither the whole body of electoral princes and ambassadors repaired; while their retinues extended along the whole way, that gradually, as their turns came, they might again move toward the city, and enter properly into the procession. By this time the emperor reached the tent, entered it; and the princes and ambassadors, after a most respectful reception, withdrew, to facilitate the passage of the chief ruler.

We who remained in the city, to admire this pomp within the walls and streets still more than could have been done in the open fields, were very well entertained for awhile by the barricade set up by the citizens in the lanes, by the throng of people, and by the various jests and improprieties which arose, till the ringing of bells and the thunder of cannon announced to us the immediate approach of majesty. What must have been particularly grateful to a Frankforter was, that on this occasion, in the presence of so many sovereigns and their representatives, the imperial city of Frankfort also appeared as a little sovereign: for her equerry opened the procession; chargers with armorial trappings, upon which the white eagle on a red field looked very fine, followed him; then came attendants and officials, drummers and trumpeters, and deputies of the council, accompanied by the clerks of the council, in the city livery, on foot. Immediately behind these were the three companies of citizen cavalry, very well mounted, — the same that we had seen from our youth, at the reception of the escort, and on other public occasions.

We rejoiced in our participation of the honour, and in our one hundred-thousandth part of a sovereignty which now appeared in its full brilliancy. The different trains of the hereditary imperial marshal, and of the envoys deputed by the six temporal electors, marched after these step by step. None of them consisted of less than twenty attendants and two state carriages, — some, even, of a greater number. The retinue of the spiritual electors was ever on the increase, — their servants and domestic officers seemed innumerable: the Elector of Cologne and the Elector of Treves had above twenty state carriages, and the Elector of Mainz quite as many alone. The servants, both on horseback and on foot, were clothed most splendidly throughout; the lords in the equipages, spiritual and temporal, had not omitted to appear richly and venerably dressed, and adorned with all the badges of their orders. The train of his imperial majesty now, as was fit, surpassed all the rest. The riding-masters, the led horses, the equipages, the shabracks and caparisons, attracted every eye; and the sixteen six-horse gala-wagons of the imperial chamberlains, privy councillors, high chamberlain, high stewards, and high equerry, closed, with great pomp, this division of the procession, which, in spite of its magnificence and extent, was still only to be the vanguard.

But now the line became concentrated more and more, while the dignity and parade kept on increasing. For in the midst of a chosen escort of their own domestic attendants, the most of them on foot, and a few on horseback, appeared the electoral ambassadors, as well as the electors in person, in ascending order, each one in a magnificent state carriage. Immediately behind the Elector of Mainz, ten imperial footmen, one and forty lackeys, and eight. *heyducks* [1] announced their

---

[1] A class of attendants dressed in Hungarian costume. — TRANS

majesties. The most magnificent state carriage, furnished even at the back part with an entire window of plate glass, ornamented with paintings, lacquer, carved work, and gilding, covered with red embroidered velvet on the top and inside, allowed us very conveniently to behold the emperor and king, the long-desired heads, in all their glory. The procession was led a long, circuitous route, partly from necessity, that it might be able to unfold itself, and partly to render it visible to the great multitude of people. It had passed through Sachsenhausen, over the bridge, up the Fahrgasse, then down the Zeile, and turned toward the inner city through the Katharinenpforte, formerly a gate, and, since the enlargement of the city, an open thoroughfare. Here it had been happily considered that, for a series of years, the external grandeur of the world had gone on expanding, both in height and breadth. Measure had been taken; and it was found that the present imperial state carriage could not, without striking its carved work and other outward decorations, get through this gateway, through which so many princes and emperors had gone backward and forward. They debated the matter, and, to avoid an inconvenient circuit, resolved to take up the pavements, and to contrive a gentle descent and ascent. With the same view, they had also removed all the projecting eaves from the shops and booths in the street, that neither crown nor eagle nor the genii should receive any shock or injury.

Eagerly as we directed our eyes to the high personages when this precious vessel with such precious contents approached us, we could not avoid turning our looks upon the noble horses, their harness, and its embroidery; but the strange coachmen and outriders, both sitting on the horses, particularly struck us. They looked as if they had come from some other nation, or even from another world, with their long black and yellow velvet coats, and their caps with large plumes of feathers, after the imperial court fashion. Now the crowd became so dense that it was impossible to distinguish much more. The Swiss guard on both sides of the carriage; the hereditary marshal holding the Saxon sword upwards in his right hand; the field-marshals, as leaders of the imperial guard, riding behind the carriage; the imperial pages in a body; and, finally, the imperial horse-guard (*Hatschiergarde*) itself, in black velvet frocks (*Flügelröck*), with all the seams edged with gold, under which were red coats and leather-coloured camisoles, likewise richly decked with gold. One scarcely recovered one's self from sheer seeing, pointing, and showing, so that the scarcely less splendidly clad body-guards of the electors were barely looked at; and we should, perhaps, have withdrawn from the windows, if we had not wished to take a view of our own magistracy, who closed the procession in their fifteen two-horse coaches; and particularly the clerk of the council, with the city keys on red velvet cushions. That our company of city grenadiers should cover the rear seemed to us honourable enough, and we felt doubly and highly edified as Germans and as Frankforters by this great day.

We had taken our place in a house which the procession had to pass again when it returned from the cathedral. Of religious services, of music, of rites and solemnities, of addresses and answers, of propositions and readings aloud, there was so much in church, choir, and conclave, before it came to the swearing of the electoral capitulation, that we had time enough to partake of an excellent collation, and to empty many bottles to the health of our old and young ruler. The conversation, meanwhile, as is usual on such occasions, reverted to the time past; and there were not wanting aged persons who preferred that to the present, — at least, with respect to a certain human interest and impassioned sympathy which then prevailed. At the

coronation of Francis the First all had not been so
settled as now; peace had not yet been concluded;
France and the Electors of Brandenburg and the Palatinate were opposed to the election; the troops of the
future emperor were stationed at Heidelberg, where he
had his headquarters; and the insignia of the empire,
coming from Aix, were almost carried off by the inhabitants of the Palatinate. Meanwhile, negotiations went
on; and on neither side was the affair conducted in
the strictest manner. Maria Theresa, though then pregnant, comes in person to see the coronation of her husband, which is at last carried into effect. She arrived
at Aschaffenburg, and went on board a yacht in order
to repair to Frankfort. Francis, coming from Heidelberg, thinks to meet his wife, but arrives too late: she
has already departed. Unknown, he jumps into a little
boat, hastens after her, reaches her ship; and the loving pair is delighted at this surprising meeting. The
story spreads immediately; and all the world sym-
pathises with this tender pair, so richly blessed with
children, who have been so inseparable since their
union, that once, on a journey from Vienna to Flor-
ence, they are forced to keep quarantine together on
the Venetian border. Maria Theresa is welcomed in the
city with rejoicings: she enters the Roman Emperor
Inn, while the great tent for the reception of her husband is erected on the Bornheim heath. There, of
the spiritual electors, only Mainz is found; and, of the
ambassadors of the temporal electors, only Saxony,
Bohemia, and Hanover. The entrance begins, and what
it may lack of completeness and splendour is richly
compensated by the presence of a beautiful lady. She
stands upon the balcony of the well-situated house,
and greets her husband with cries of " Vivat!" and
clapping of hands; the people joined, excited to the
highest enthusiasm. As the great are, after all, men,
the citizen deems them his equals when he wishes to

love them; and that he can best do when he can picture them to himself as loving husbands, tender parents, devoted brothers, and true friends. At that time all happiness had been wished and prophesied; and to-day it was seen fulfilled in the first-born son, to whom everybody was well inclined on account of his handsome, youthful form, and upon whom the world set the greatest hopes, on account of the great qualities that he showed.

We had become quite absorbed in the past and future, when some friends who came in recalled us to the present. They were of that class of people who know the value of novelty, and therefore hasten to announce it first. They were even able to tell of a fine humane trait in those exalted personages whom we had seen go by with the greatest pomp. It had been concerted that on the way, between Heusenstamm and the great tent, the emperor and king should find the Landgrave of Darmstadt in the forest. This old prince, now approaching the grave, wished to see once more the master to whom he had been devoted in former times. Both might remember the day when the landgrave brought over to Heidelberg the decree of the electors, choosing Francis as emperor, and replied to the valuable presents he received with protestations of unalterable devotion. These eminent persons stood in a grove of firs; and the landgrave, weak with old age, supported himself against a pine, to continue the conversation, which was not without emotion on both sides. The place was afterward marked in an innocent way, and we young people sometimes wandered to it.

Thus several hours had passed in remembrance of the old and consideration of the new, when the procession, though curtailed and more compact, again passed before our eyes; and we were enabled to observe and mark the detail more closely, and imprint it on our minds for the future.

From that moment the city was in uninterrupted motion; for until each and every one whom it behoved, and of whom it was required, had paid their respects to the highest dignities, and exhibited themselves one by one, there was no end to the marching to and fro: and the court of each one of the high persons present could be very conveniently repeated in detail.

Now, too, the insignia of the empire arrived. But, that no ancient usage might be omitted even in this respect, they had to remain half a day till late at night in the open field, on account of a dispute about territory and escort between the Elector of Mainz and the city. The latter yielded: the people of Mainz escorted the insignia as far as the barricade, and so the affair terminated for this time.

In these days I did not come to myself. At home I had to write and copy; everything had to be seen: and so ended the month of March, the second half of which had been so rich in festivals for us. I had promised Gretchen a faithful and complete account of what had lately happened, and of what was to be expected on the coronation-day. This great day approached; I thought more of how I should tell it to her than of what properly was to be told: all that came under my eyes and my pen I merely worked up rapidly for this sole and immediate use. At last I reached her residence somewhat late one evening, and was not a little proud to think how my discourse on this occasion would be much more successful than the first unprepared one. But a momentary incitement often brings us, and others through us, more joy than the most deliberate purpose can afford. I found, indeed, pretty nearly the same company; but there were some unknown persons among them. They sat down to play, all except Gretchen and her younger cousin, who remained with me at the slate. The dear girl expressed most gracefully her delight that she, though a stranger, had passed for a citizen on the election-day and had taken part in that unique spectacle. She thanked me most warmly for having managed to take care of her, and for having been so attentive as to procure her, through Pylades, all sorts of admissions by means of billets, directions, friends, and intercessions.

She liked to hear about the jewels of the empire. I promised her that we should, if possible, see these together. She made some jesting remarks when she learned that the garments and crown had been tried on the young king. I knew where she would be, to see the solemnities of the coronation-day, and directed her attention to everything that was impending, and particularly to what might be minutely inspected from her place of view.

Thus we forgot to think about time: it was already past midnight, and I found that I unfortunately had not the house-key with me. I could not enter the house without making the greatest disturbance. I communicated my embarrassment to her. "After all," said she, "it will be best for the company to remain together." The cousins and the strangers had already had this in mind, because it was not known where they would be lodged for the night. The matter was soon decided: Gretchen went to make some coffee, after bringing in and lighting a large brass lamp, furnished with oil and wick, because the candles threatened to burn out.

The coffee served to enliven us for several hours, but the game gradually slackened; conversation failed; the mother slept in the great chair; the strangers, weary from travelling, nodded here and there; and Pylades and his fair one sat in a corner. She had laid her head on his shoulder, and had gone to sleep; and he did not keep long awake. The younger cousin, sitting opposite to us by the slate, had crossed his arms before him, and slept with his face resting upon them. I sat in the window-corner, behind the table, and Gretchen by me. We talked in a low voice : but at last sleep overcame her also ; she leaned her head on my shoulder, and sank at once into a slumber. Thus I now sat, the only one awake, in a most singular position, in which the kind brother of death soon put me also to rest. I went to sleep; and, when I awoke, it was already bright day. Gretchen was standing before the mirror arranging her little cap : she was more lovely than ever, and, when I departed, cordially pressed my hands. I crept home by a roundabout way ; for, on the side toward the little Stag-ditch, my father had opened a sort of little peep-hole in the wall, not without the opposition of his neighbour. This side we avoided when we wanted not to be observed by him in coming home. My mother, whose mediation always came in well for us, had endeavoured to palliate my absence in the morning at breakfast, by the supposition that I had gone out early ; and I experienced no disagreeable effects from this innocent night.

Taken as a whole, this infinitely various world which surrounded me produced upon me but a very simple impression. I had no interest but to mark closely the outside of the objects, no business but that with which I had been charged by my father and Herr von Königsthal, by which, indeed, I perceived the inner course of things. I had no liking but for Gretchen, and no other view than to see and take in everything properly, that I might be able to repeat it with her, and explain it to her. Often when a train was going by, I described it half aloud to myself, to assure myself of all the particulars, and to be praised by my fair one for this attention and accuracy : the applause and acknowledgments of the others I regarded as a mere appendix.

I was indeed presented to many exalted and distinguished persons ; but partly, no one had time to trouble himself about others, and partly, older people do not know· at once how they should converse with a young man and try him. I, on my side, was likewise not particularly skilful in adapting myself to people. I generally won their favour, but not their approbation. Whatever occupied me was completely present to me, but I did not ask whether it might be also suitable to others. I was mostly too lively or too quiet, and appeared either importunate or sullen, just as persons attracted or repelled me; and thus I was considered to be indeed full of promise, but at the same time was declared eccentric.

The coronation-day dawned at last on the 3d of April, 1764: the weather was favourable, and everybody was in motion. I, with several of my relations and friends, had been provided with a good place in one of the upper stories of the Römer itself, where we might completely survey the whole. We betook ourselves to the spot very early in the morning, and from above, as in a bird's-eye view, contemplated the arrangements which we had inspected more closely the day before. There was the newly erected fountain, with two large tubs on the left and right, into which the double-eagle on the post was to pour from its two beaks white wine on this side, and red wine on that. There, gathered into a heap, lay the oats: here stood the large wooden hut, in which we had several days since seen the whole fat ox roasted and basted on a huge spit before a charcoal fire. All the avenues leading out from the Römer, and from other streets back to the Römer, were secured on both sides by barriers and guards. The great square was gradually filled; and the waving and pressure grew every moment stronger and more in motion, as the multitude always, if possible, endeavoured to reach the spot where some new scene arose, and something particular was announced.

All this time there reigned a tolerable stillness; and, when the alarm-bells were sounded, all the people seemed struck with terror and amazement. What first attracted the attention of all who could overlook the square from above, was the train in which the lords of Aix and Nuremberg brought the crown jewels to the cathedral. These, as palladia, had been assigned the first place in the carriage; and the deputies sat before them on the back seat with becoming reverence. Now the three electors betake themselves to the cathedral. After the presentation of the insignia to the Elector of Mainz, the crown and sword are immediately carried to the imperial quarters. The further arrangements and manifold ceremonies occupied, in the interim, the chief persons, as well as the spectators, in the church, as we other well-informed persons could well imagine.

In the meantime the ambassadors drove before our eyes up to the Römer, from which the canopy is carried by the under-officers into the imperial quarters. The hereditary marshal, Count von Pappenheim, instantly mounts his horse: he was a very handsome, slender gentleman, whom the Spanish costume, the rich doublet, the gold mantle, the high, feathered hat, and the loose, flying hair, became very well. He puts himself in motion; and, amid the sound of all the bells, the ambassadors follow him on horseback to the quarters of the emperor in still greater magnificence than on the day of election. One would have liked to be there too; as indeed, on this day, it would have been altogether desirable to multiply one's self. However, we told each other what was going on there. Now the emperor is putting on his domestic robes, we said, a new dress, made after the old Carolingian pattern. The hereditary officers receive the insignia, and with them get on horseback. The emperor in his robes, the Roman king in the Spanish habit, immediately mount their steeds; and, while this is done, the endless procession which precedes them has already announced them.

The eye was already wearied by the multitude

of richly dressed attendants and magistrates, and by the nobility, who, in stately fashion, were moving along; but when the electoral envoys, the hereditary officers, and at last, under the richly embroidered canopy, borne by twelve *Schöffen* and senators, the emperor, in romantic costume, and to the left, a little behind him, in the Spanish dress, his son, slowly floated along on magnificently adorned horses, the eye was no more sufficient for the sight. One would have liked to fix the scene, but for a moment, by a magic charm; but the glory passed on without stopping: and the space that was scarcely quitted was immediately filled again by the crowd, which poured in like billows.

But now a new pressure ensued; for another approach from the market to the Römer gate had to be opened, and a road of planks to be bridged over it, on which the train returning from the cathedral was to walk.

What passed within the cathedral, the endless ceremonies which precede and accompany the anointing, the crowning, the dubbing of knighthood, — all this we were glad to hear told afterward by those who had sacrificed much else to be present in the church.

The rest of us, in the interim, partook of a frugal repast; for in this festal day we had to be contented with cold meat. But, on the other hand, the best and oldest wine had been brought out of all the family cellars; so that, in this respect at least, we celebrated the ancient festival in ancient style.

In the square, the sight most worth seeing was now the bridge, which had been finished, and covered with orange and white cloth; and we who had stared at the emperor, first in his carriage and then on horseback, were now to admire him walking on foot. Singularly enough, the last pleased us the most; for we thought that in this way he exhibited himself both in the most natural and in the most dignified manner.

Older persons, who were present at the coronation of Francis the First, related that Maria Theresa, beautiful beyond measure, had looked on this solemnity from a balcony window of the Frauenstein house, close to the Römer. As her consort returned from the cathedral in his strange costume, and seemed to her, so to speak, like a ghost of Charlemagne, he had, as if in jest, raised both his hands, and shown her the imperial globe, the sceptre, and the curious gloves, at which she had broken out into immoderate laughter, which served for the great delight and edification of the crowd, which was thus honoured with a sight of the good and natural matrimonial understanding between the most exalted couple of Christendom. But when the empress, to greet her consort, waved her handkerchief, and even shouted a loud " vivat " to him, the enthusiasm and exultation of the people was raised to the highest, so that there was no end to the cheers of joy.

Now the sound of bells, and the van of the long train which gently made its way over the many-coloured bridge, announced that all was done. The attention was greater than ever, and the procession more distinct than before, particularly for us, since it now came directly up to us. We saw both, and the whole of the square, which was thronged with people, almost as if on a ground-plan. Only at the end the magnificence was too much crowded: for the envoys; the hereditary officers; the emperor and king, under the canopy (*Baldachin*); the three spiritual electors, who immediately followed; the *Schöffen* and senators, dressed in black; the gold-embroidered canopy (*Himmel*), — all seemed only one mass, which, moved by a single will, splendidly harmonious, and thus stepping from the temple amid the sound of the bells, beamed toward us as something holy.

A politico-religious ceremony possesses an infinite charm. We behold earthly majesty before our eyes, surrounded by all the symbols of its power; but, while it bends before that of heaven, it brings to our minds the communion of both. For even the individual can only prove his relationship with the Deity by subjecting himself and adoring.

The rejoicings which resounded from the market-place now spread likewise over the great square; and a boisterous "vivat" burst forth from thousands upon thousands of throats, and doubtless from as many hearts. For this grand festival was to be the pledge of a lasting peace, which indeed for many a long year actually blessed Germany.

Several days before, it had been made known by public proclamation, that neither the bridge nor the eagle over the fountain was to be exposed to the people, and they were therefore not, as at other times, to be touched. This was done to prevent the mischief inevitable with such a rush of persons. But, in order to sacrifice in some degree to the genius of the mob, persons expressly appointed went behind the procession, loosened the cloth from the bridge, wound it up like a flag, and threw it into the air. This gave rise to no disaster, but to a laughable mishap; for the cloth unrolled itself in the air, and, as it fell, covered a larger or smaller number of persons. Those now who took hold of the ends and drew them toward them, pulled all those in the middle to the ground, enveloped them and teased them till they tore or cut themselves through; and everybody, in his own way, had borne off a corner of the stuff made sacred by the footsteps of majesty.

I did not long contemplate this rough sport, but hastened from my high position through all sorts of little steps and passages, down to the great Römer-stairs, where the distinguished and majestic mass, which had been stared at from the distance, was to ascend in its undulating course. The crowd was not

great, because the entrances to the city hall were well
garrisoned ; and I fortunately reached at once the iron
balustrades above. Now the chief personages ascended
past me, while their followers remained behind in
the lower arched passages ; and I could observe them
on the thrice-broken stairs from all sides, and at last
quite close.

Finally both their majesties came up. Father and
son were altogether dressed like Menæchmi. The
emperor's domestic robes, of purple-coloured silk, richly
adorned with pearls and stones, as well as his crown,
sceptre, and imperial orb, struck the eye with good
effect. For all in them was new, and the imitation of
the antique was tasteful. He moved, too, quite easily
in his attire ; and his true-hearted, dignified face indicated at once the emperor and the father. The young
king, on the contrary, in his monstrous articles of
dress, with the crown jewels of Charlemagne, dragged
himself along as if he had been in a disguise ; so that
he himself, looking at his father from time to time,
could not refrain from laughing. The crown, which
it had been necessary to line a great deal, stood out
from his head like an overhanging roof. The dal-
matica, the stole, well as they had been fitted and
taken in by sewing, presented by no means an advantageous appearance. The sceptre and imperial orb
excited some admiration ; but one would, for the sake
of a more princely effect, rather have seen a strong
form, suited to the dress, invested and adorned with it.

Scarcely were the gates of the great hall closed
behind these figures, than I hurried to my former
place, which, being already occupied by others, I only
regained with some trouble.

It was precisely at the right time that I again took
possession of my window, for the most remarkable part
of all that was to be seen in public was just about to
take place. All the people had turned toward the

Römer; and a reiterated shout of "Vivat" gave us
to understand that the emperor and king, in their
vestments, were showing themselves to the populace
from the balcony of the great hall. But they were not
alone to serve as a spectacle, since another strange
spectacle occurred before their eyes. First of all, the
handsome, slender hereditary marshal flung himself
upon his steed: he had laid aside his sword; in
his right hand he held a silver-handled vessel, and
a tin spatula in his left. He rode within the barriers
to the great heap of oats, sprang in, filled the vessel to
overflow, smoothed it off, and carried it back again
with great dignity. The imperial stable was now provided for. The hereditary chamberlain then rode
likewise to the spot, and brought back a basin with
ewer and towel. But more entertaining for the spectators was the hereditary carver, who came to fetch
a piece of the roasted ox. He also rode, with a silver
dish, through the barriers, to the large wooden kitchen,
and came forth again with his portion covered, that he
might go back to the Römer. Now it was the turn of
the hereditary cup-bearer, who rode to the fountain
and fetched wine. Thus now was the imperial table
furnished; and every eye waited upon the hereditary
treasurer, who was to throw about the money. He,
too, mounted a fine steed, to the sides of whose saddle,
instead of holsters, a couple of splendid bags, embroidered with the arms of the Palatinate, were suspended.
Scarcely had he put himself in motion than he plunged
his hands into these pockets, and generously scattered,
right and left, gold and silver coins, which, on every
occasion, glittered merrily in the air like metallic rain.
A thousand hands waved instantly in the air to catch
the gifts; but hardly had the coins fallen when the
crowd tumbled over each other on the ground, and
struggled violently for the pieces which might have
reached the earth. As this agitation was constantly

repeated on both sides as the giver rode forwards, it afforded the spectators a very diverting sight. It was most lively at the close, when he threw out the bags themselves, and everybody tried to catch this highest prize.

Their Majesties had retired from the balcony; and another offering was to be made to the mob, who, on such occasions, would rather steal the gifts than receive them tranquilly and gratefully. The custom prevailed, in more rude and uncouth times, of giving up to the people on the spot the oats, as soon as the hereditary marshal had taken away his share; the fountain and the kitchen, after the cup-bearer and the carver had performed their offices. But this time, to guard against all mischief, order and moderation were preserved as far as possible. But the old malicious jokes, that when one filled a sack with oats another cut a hole in it, with sallies of the kind, were revived. About the roasted ox, a more serious battle was, as usual, waged on this occasion. This could only be contested en masse. Two guilds, the butchers and the wine-porters, had, according to ancient custom, again stationed themselves so that the monstrous roast must fall to one of the two. The butchers believed that they had the best right to an ox which they provided entire for the kitchen: the wine-porters, on the other hand, laid claim because the kitchen was built near the abode of their guild, and because they had gained the victory the last time, the horns of the captured steer still projecting from the latticed gable-window of their guild and meeting-house as a sign of victory. Both these companies had very strong and able members; but which of them conquered this time, I no longer remember.

But, as a festival of this kind must always close with something dangerous and frightful, it was really a terrible moment when the wooden kitchen itself was made a prize. The roof of it swarmed instantly with men, no one knowing how they got there: the boards were torn loose, and pitched down; so that one could not help supposing, particularly at a distance, that each would kill a few of those pressing to the spot. In a trice the hut was unroofed; and single individuals hung to the beams and rafters, in order to pull them also out of their joinings: nay, many floated above upon the posts which had been already sawn off below; and the whole skeleton, moving backwards and forwards, threatened to fall in. Sensitive persons turned their eyes away, and everybody expected a great calamity; but we did not hear of any mischief: and the whole affair, though impetuous and violent, had passed off happily.

Everybody knew now that the emperor and king would return from the cabinet, whither they had retired from the balcony, and feast in the great hall of the Römer. We had been able to admire the arrangements made for it, the day before; and my most anxious wish was, if possible, to look in to-day. I repaired, therefore, by the usual path, to the great staircase, which stands directly opposite the door of the hall. Here I gazed at the distinguished personages who this day acted as the servants of the head of the empire. Forty-four counts, all splendidly dressed, passed me, carrying the dishes from the kitchen; so that the contrast between their dignity and their occupation might well be bewildering to a boy. The crowd was not great, but, considering the little space, sufficiently perceptible. The hall-door was guarded, while those who were authorised went frequently in and out. I saw one of the Palatine domestic officials, whom I asked whether he could not take me in with him. He did not deliberate long, but gave me one of the silver vessels he just then bore, which he could do so much the more, as I was neatly clad; and thus I reached the sanctuary. The Palatine buffet stood to the left, directly by the door; and with some steps I placed myself on the elevation of it, behind the barriers.

At the other end of the hall, immediately by the windows, raised on the steps of the throne, and under canopies, sat the emperor and king in their robes; but the crown and sceptre lay at some distance behind them on gold cushions. The three spiritual electors, their buffets behind them, had taken their places on single elevations; the Elector of Mainz opposite their Majesties, the Elector of Treves at the right, and the Elector of Cologne at the left. This upper part of the hall was imposing and cheerful to behold, and excited the remark that the spiritual power likes to keep as long as possible with the ruler. On the contrary, the buffets and tables of all the temporal electors, which were, indeed, magnificently ornamented, but without occupants, made one think of the misunderstanding which had gradually arisen for centuries between them and the head of the empire. Their ambassadors had already withdrawn to eat in a side-chamber; and if the greater part of the hall assumed a sort of spectral appearance, by so many invisible guests being so magnificently attended, a large unfurnished table in the middle was still more sad to look upon; for there, also, many covers stood empty, because all those who had certainly a right to sit there had, for appearance' sake, kept away, that on the greatest day of honour they might not renounce any of their honour, if, indeed, they were then to be found in the city.

Neither my years nor the mass of present objects allowed me to make many reflections. I strove to see all as much as possible; and when the dessert was brought in, and the ambassadors reëntered to pay their court, I sought the open air, and contrived to refresh myself with good friends in the neighbourhood, after a day's half-fasting, and to prepare for the illumination in the evening.

This brilliant night I purposed celebrating in a right hearty way; for I had agreed with Gretchen, and Pylades and his mistress, that we should meet somewhere at nightfall. The city was already resplendent at every end and corner when I met my beloved. I offered Gretchen my arm: we went from one quarter to another, and found ourselves very happy in each other's society. The cousins at first were also of our party, but were afterward lost in the multitude of people. Before the houses of some of the ambassadors, where magnificent illuminations were exhibited, — those of the Elector Palatine were preëminently distinguished, — it was as clear as day. Lest I should be recognised, I had disguised myself to a certain extent; and Gretchen did not find it amiss. We admired the various brilliant representations and the fairy-like structures of flame by which each ambassador strove to outshine the others. But Prince Esterhazy's arrangements surpassed all the rest. Our little company were enraptured, both with the invention and the execution; and we were just about to enjoy this in detail, when the cousins again met us, and spoke to us of the glorious illumination with which the Brandenburg ambassador had adorned his quarters. We were not displeased at taking the long way from the Rossmarkt (Horse-market) to the Saalhof, but found that we had been villainously hoaxed.

The Saalhof is, toward the Main, a regular and handsome structure; but the part in the direction of the city is exceedingly old, irregular, and unsightly. Small windows, agreeing neither in form nor size, neither in a line nor placed at equal distances; gates and doors arranged without symmetry; a ground-floor mostly turned into shops, — it forms a confused outside, which is never observed by any one. Now, here this accidental, irregular, unconnected architecture had been followed; and every window, every door, every opening, was surrounded by lamps, — as indeed can be done with a well-built house; but here the most wretched and ill-formed of all facades was thus quite incredibly placed in the clearest light. Did one amuse one's self with this as with the jests of the *pagliasso*,[1] though not without scruple, since everybody must recognise something intentional in it, — just as people had before glossed on the previous external deportment of Von Plotho, so much prized in other respects, and, when once inclined toward him, had admired him as a wag, who, like his king, would place himself above all ceremonies, — one nevertheless gladly returned to the fairy kingdom of Esterhazy.

This eminent envoy, to honour the day, had quite passed over his own unfavourably situated quarters, and in their stead had caused the great esplanade of linden-trees in the Horse-market to be decorated in the front with a portal illuminated with colours, and at the back with a still more magnificent prospect. The entire enclosure was marked by lamps. Between the trees, stood pyramids and spheres of light upon transparent pedestals; from one tree to another were stretched glittering garlands, on which floated suspended lights. In several places bread and sausages were distributed among the people, and there was no want of wine.

Here now, four abreast, we walked very comfortably up and down; and I, by Gretchen's side, fancied that I really wandered in those happy Elysian fields where they pluck from the trees crystal cups that immediately fill themselves with the wine desired, and shake down fruits that change into every dish at will. At last we also felt such a necessity; and, conducted by Pylades, we found a neat, well-arranged eating-house.

[1] A sort of buffoon.

When we encountered no more guests, since everybody
was going about the streets, we were all the better
pleased, and passed the greatest part of the night most
happily and cheerfully, in the feeling of friendship,
love, and attachment.   When I had accompanied
Gretchen as far as her door, she kissed me on the
forehead.   It was the first and last time that she
granted me this favour; for, alas! I was not to see her
again.

The next morning, while I was yet in bed, my
mother entered, in trouble and anxiety. It was easy
to see when she was at all distressed. " Get up," she
said, " and prepare yourself for something unpleasant.
It has come out that you frequent very bad company,
and have involved yourself in very dangerous and bad
affairs.   Your father is beside himself; and we have
only been able to get thus much from him, that he
will investigate the affair by means of a third party.
Remain in your chamber, and await what may happen.
Councillor Schneider will come to you: he has the
commission both from your father and from the authorities; for the matter is already prosecuted, and may
take a very bad turn."

I saw that they took the affair for much worse than
it was; yet I felt myself not a little disquieted, even
if only the actual state of things should be detected.
My old " Messiah "-loving friend finally entered, with
the tears standing in his eyes : he took me by the arm,
and said, " I am heartily sorry to come to you on such
an affair.   I could not have supposed that you could
go astray so far. But what will not wicked companions and bad example do! Thus can a young,
inexperienced man be led step by step into crime!"
" I am conscious of no crime," I replied, " and as little
of having frequented bad company." " The question
now is not one of defence," said he, interrupting me,
" but of investigation, and on your part of an upright

confession." "What do you want to know?" retorted
I. He seated himself, drew out a paper, and began
to question me: "Have you not recommended N. N. to
your grandfather as a candidate for the . . . place?"
I answered, "Yes." "Where did you become acquainted with him?" "In my walks." "In what
company?" I hesitated, for I would not willingly
betray my friends. "Silence will not do now," he
continued, "for all is sufficiently known." "What is
known, then?" said I. "That this man has been
introduced to you by others like him—in fact,
by . . ." Here he named three persons whom I had
never seen nor known, which I immediately explained
to the questioner. "You pretend," he resumed, "not
to know these men, and have yet had frequent meetings with them." "Not in the least," I replied: "for,
as I have said, except the first, I do not know one of
them, and even him I have never seen in a house."
"Have you not often been in . . . street?" "Never,"
I replied. This was not entirely conformable to the
truth. I had once accompanied Pylades to his sweet-
heart, who lived in that street; but we had entered
by the back door, and remained in the summer-house.
I therefore supposed that I might permit myself the
subterfuge that I had not been in the street itself.

The good man put more questions, all of which I
could answer with a denial; for of all that he wished
to learn I knew nothing. At last he seemed to become vexed, and said, "You repay my confidence and
good will very badly: I come to save you. You cannot deny that you have composed letters for these
people themselves or for their accomplices, have furnished them writings, and have thus been accessory
to their evil acts; for the question is of nothing less
than of forged papers, false wills, counterfeit bonds,
and things of the sort. I have come, not only as
a friend of the family, I come in the name and by

order of the magistrates, who, in consideration of your connections and youth, would spare you and some other young persons, who, like you, have been lured into the net." I had thought it strange, that, among the persons he named, none of those with whom I had been intimate were found. The circumstances touched, without agreeing; and I could still hope to save my young friends. But the good man grew more and more urgent. I could not deny that I had come home late many nights, that I had contrived to have a house-key made, that I had been seen at public places more than once with persons of low rank and suspicious looks, that some girls were mixed up in the affair, — in short, everything seemed to be discovered but the names. This gave me courage to persist steadfastly in my silence. " Do not," said my excellent friend, " let me go away from you ; the affair admits of no delay ; immediately after me another will come, who will not grant you so much scope. Do not make the matter, which is bad enough, worse by your obstinacy."

I represented very vividly to myself the good cousins, and particularly Gretchen : I saw them arrested, tried, punished, disgraced ; and then it went through my soul like a flash of lightning, that the cousins, though they always observed integrity toward me, might have engaged in such bad affairs, at least the oldest, who never quite pleased me, who came home later and later, and had little to tell of a cheerful sort. Still I kept back my confession. " Personally," said I, " I am conscious of nothing evil, and can rest satisfied on that side ; but it is not impossible that those with whom I have associated may have been guilty of some daring or illegal act They may be sought, found, convicted, punished : I have hitherto nothing to reproach myself with, and will not do any wrong to those who have behaved well and kindly to me." He did not let me finish, but exclaimed, with some agitation, "Yes, they will be found out. These villains met in three houses. (He named the streets, he pointed out the houses, and, unfortunately, among them was the one I used to frequent.) The first nest is already broken up, and at this moment so are the two others. In a few hours the whole will be clear. Avoid, by a frank confession, a judicial inquiry, a confrontation, and all other disagreeable matters." The house was known and marked. Now I deemed silence useless; nay, considering the innocence of our meetings, I could hope to be still more useful to them than to myself. "Sit down!" I exclaimed, fetching him back from the door: "I will tell all, and at once lighten your heart and mine; only one thing I ask, — henceforth let there be no doubt of my veracity."

I soon told my friend the whole progress of the affair, and was at first calm and collected; but the more I brought to mind and pictured to myself the persons, objects, and events, so many innocent pleasures and charming enjoyments, and was forced to depose as before a criminal court, the more did the most painful feeling increase, so that at last I burst forth in tears, and gave myself up to unrestrained passion. The family friend, who hoped that now the real secret was coming to light (for he regarded my distress as a symptom that I was on the point of confessing with repugnance something monstrous), sought to pacify me; as with him the discovery was the all-important matter. In this he only partly succeeded; but so far, however, that I could eke out my story to the end. Though satisfied of the innocence of the proceedings, he was still doubtful to some extent, and put further questions to me, which excited me afresh, and transported me with pain and rage. I asserted, finally, that I had nothing more to say, and well knew that I need fear nothing, for I was innocent, of a good family, and well reputed; but that they might be just as guiltless without having it recognised, or being otherwise favoured. I declared at the same time, that if they were not spared like myself, that if their follies were not regarded with indulgence, and their faults pardoned, that if anything in the least harsh or unjust happened to them, I would do some violence to myself, and no one should prevent me. In this, too, my friend tried to pacify me; but I did not trust him, and was, when he quitted me at last, in a most terrible state. I now reproached myself for having told the affair, and brought all the positions to light. I foresaw that our childlike actions, our youthful inclinations and confidences, would be quite differently interpreted, and that I might perhaps involve the excellent Pylades in the matter, and render him very unhappy. All these images pressed vividly one after the other before my soul, sharpened and spurred my distress, so that I did not know what to do for sorrow. I cast myself at full length upon the floor, and moistened it with my tears.

I know not how long I may have lain, when my sister entered, was frightened at my gestures, and did all that she could to comfort me. She told me that a person connected with the magistracy had waited below with my father for the return of the family friend, and that, after they had been closeted together for some time, both the gentlemen had departed, had talked to each other with apparent satisfaction, and had even laughed. She believed that she had heard the words, "It is all right: the affair is of no consequence." "Indeed!" I broke out, "the affair is of no consequence for me, — for us: for I have committed no crime; and, if I had, they would contrive to help me through: but the others, the others," I cried, "who will stand by them?"

My sister tried to comfort me by circumstantially arguing that if those of higher rank were to be saved, a veil must also be cast over the faults of the more lowly. All this was of no avail. She had scarcely left than I again abandoned myself to my grief, and ever recalled alternately the images, both of my affection and passion, and of the present and possible misfortune. I repeated to myself tale after tale, saw only unhappiness following unhappiness, and did not fail in particular to make Gretchen and myself truly wretched.

The family friend had ordered me to remain in my room, and have nothing to do with any one but the family. This was just what I wanted, for I found myself best alone. My mother and sister came to see me from time to time, and did not fail to assist me vigorously with all sorts of good consolation; nay, even on the second day they came in the name of my father, who was now better informed, to offer me a perfect amnesty, which indeed I gratefully accepted: but the proposal that I should go out with him and look at the insignia of the empire, which were now exposed to the curious, I stubbornly rejected; and I asserted that I wanted to know nothing, either of the world or of the Roman Empire, till I was informed how that distressing affair, which for me could have no further consequences, had turned out for my poor acquaintance. They had nothing to say on this head, and left me alone. Yet the next day some further attempts were made to get me out of the house, and excite in me a sympathy for the public ceremonies. In vain! neither the great gala-day, nor what happened on the occasion of so many elevations of rank, nor the public table of the emperor and king, — in short, nothing could move me. The Elector of the Palatinate might come and wait on both their Majesties; these might visit the electors; the last electoral sitting might be attended for the despatch of business in arrear, and the renewal of the electoral union, — nothing could call me forth from my passionate solitude. I let the bells ring for the rejoicings, the emperor repair to the Capuchin Church, the electors and emperor depart, without on that account moving one step from my chamber. The final cannonading, immoderate as it might be, did not arouse me; and as the smoke of the powder dispersed, and the sound died away, so had all this glory vanished from my soul.

I now experienced no satisfaction except in ruminating on my misery, and in a thousandfold imaginary multiplication of it. My whole inventive faculty, my poetry and rhetoric, had pitched on this diseased spot, and threatened, precisely by means of this vitality, to involve body and soul into an incurable disorder. In this melancholy condition nothing more seemed to me worth a desire, nothing worth a wish. An infinite yearning, indeed, seized me at times to know how it had gone with my poor friends and my beloved, what had been the result of a stricter scrutiny, how far they were implicated in those crimes, or had been found guiltless. This also I circumstantially painted to myself in the most various ways, and did not fail to hold them as innocent and truly unfortunate. Sometimes I longed to see myself freed from this uncertainty, and wrote vehemently threatening letters to the family friend, insisting that he should not withhold from me the further progress of the affair. Sometimes I tore them up again, from the fear of learning my unhappiness quite distinctly, and of losing the principal consolation with which hitherto I had alternately tormented and supported myself.

Thus I passed both day and night in great disquiet, in raving and lassitude; so that I felt happy at last when a bodily illness seized me with considerable violence, when they had to call in the help of a physician, and think of every way to quiet me. They supposed that they could do it generally by the sacred assurance that all who were more or less involved in the guilt had been treated with the greatest forbearance; that my nearest friends, being as good as innocent, had been dismissed with a slight reprimand; and that Gretchen had retired from the city, and had returned to her own home. They lingered the most over this last point, and I did not take it in the best part; for I could discover in it, not a voluntary departure, but only a shameful banishment. My bodily and mental condition was not improved by this: my distress now only augmented; and I had time enough to torment myself by picturing the strangest romance of sad events, and an inevitably tragical catastrophe.

Part Two

Was man in der Jugend wünscht, hat man im Alter die Fülle.
What youth desires, old age brings it in abundance. — GOETHE

SIXTH BOOK.

THUS 1 felt urged alternately to promote and to retard my recovery; and a certain secret chagrin was now added to my other sensations, for I plainly perceived that I was watched, that they were loath to hand me any sealed paper without taking notice what effect it produced, whether I kept it secret, whether I laid it down open and the like. I therefore conjectured that Pylades, or one of the cousins, or even Gretchen herself, might have attempted to write to me, either to give or to obtain information. In addition to my sorrow, I was now more cross than hitherto, and had again fresh opportunities to exercise my conjectures, and to mislead myself into the strangest combinations.

It was not long before they gave me a special overseer. Fortunately it was a man whom I loved and valued. He had held the place of tutor in the family of one of our friends, and his former pupil had gone alone to the university. He often visited me in my sad condition; and they at last found nothing more natural than to give him a chamber next to mine, as he was then to provide me with employment, pacify me, and, as I was well aware, keep his eye on me. Still, as I esteemed him from my heart, and had already confided many things to him, though not my affection for Gretchen, I determined so much the more to be perfectly candid and straightforward with him; as it was intolerable to me to live in daily inter-

course with any one, and at the same time to stand on
an uncertain, constrained footing with him. It was
not long, then, before I spoke to him about the matter,
refreshed myself by the relation and repetition of the
minutest circumstances of my past happiness, and thus
gained so much, that he, like a sensible man, saw it
would be better to make me acquainted with the issue
of the story, and that, too, in its details and particulars, so that I might be clear as to the whole, and that,
with earnestness and zeal, I might be persuaded of the
necessity of composing myself, throwing the past
behind me, and beginning a new life. First he confided to me who the other young people of quality
were who had allowed themselves to be seduced, at the
outset, into daring hoaxes, then into sportive breaches
of police, afterward into frolicsome impositions on
others, and other such dangerous matters. Thus actually had arisen a little conspiracy, which unprincipled
men had joined, who, by forging papers and counter-
feiting signatures, had perpetrated many criminal
acts, and had still more criminal matters in preparation. The cousins, for whom I at last impatiently
inquired, had been found to be quite innocent, only
very generally acquainted with those others, and not
at all implicated with them. My client, owing to my
recommendation of whom I had been tracked, was one
of the worst, and had sued for that office chiefly that
he might undertake or conceal certain villainies. After
all this, I could at last contain myself no longer, and
asked what had become of Gretchen, for whom I, once
for all, confessed the strongest attachment. My friend
shook his head and smiled. "Make yourself easy,"
replied he: "this girl has passed her examination very
well, and has borne off honourable testimony to that
effect. They could discover nothing in her but what
was good and amiable: she even won the favour of
those who questioned her, and could not refuse her de-

sire of removing from the city. Even what she has confessed regarding you, my friend, does her honour : I have read her deposition in the secret reports myself, and seen her signature." "The signature !" exclaimed I, " which makes me so happy and so miserable. What has she confessed, then ? What has she signed ? " My friend delayed answering, but the cheerfulness of his face showed me that he concealed nothing dangerous. " If you must know, then," replied he at last, " when she was asked about you, and her intercourse with you, she said quite frankly, ' I cannot deny that I have seen him often and with pleasure ; but I have always treated him as a child, and my affection for him was truly that of a sister. In many cases I have given him good advice ; and, instead of instigating him to any equivocal action, I have hindered him from taking part in wanton tricks, which might have brought him into trouble.' "

My friend still went on making Gretchen speak like a governess ; but I had already for some time ceased to listen to him, for I was terribly affronted that she had set me down in the reports as a child, and believed myself at once cured of all passion for her. I even hastily assured my friend that all was now over. I also spoke no more of her, named her no more : but I could not leave off the bad habit of thinking about her, and of recalling her form, her air, her demeanour ; though now, in fact, all appeared to me in quite another light. I felt it intolerable that a girl, at the most only a couple of years older than me, should regard me as a child ; while I conceived I passed with her for a very sensible and clever youth. Her cold and repelling manner, which had before so charmed me, now seemed to me quite repugnant : the familiarities which she had allowed herself to take with me, but had not permitted me to return, were altogether odious. Yet all would have been well enough, if by signing that poetical love-letter, in which she had confessed a formal attachment to me, she had not given me a right to regard her as a sly and selfish coquette. Her masquerading it at the milliner's, too, no longer seemed to me so innocent; and I turned these annoying reflections over and over within myself until I had entirely stripped her of all her amiable qualities. My judgment was convinced, and I thought I must cast her away; but her image! — her image gave me the lie as often as it again hovered before me, which indeed happened often enough.

Nevertheless, this arrow with its barbed hooks was torn out of my heart: and the question then was, how the inward sanative power of youth could be brought to one's aid? I really put on the man; and the first thing instantly laid aside was the weeping and raving, which I now regarded as childish in the highest degree. A great stride for the better! For I had often, half the night through, given myself up to this grief with the greatest violence; so that at last, from my tears and sobbing, I came to such a point that I could scarcely swallow any longer; eating and drinking became painful to me; and my chest, which was so nearly concerned, seemed to suffer. The vexation I had constantly felt since the discovery made me banish every weakness. It seemed to me something frightful that I had sacrificed sleep, repose, and health for the sake of a girl who was pleased to consider me a babe, and to imagine herself, with respect to me, something very much like a nurse.

These depressing reflections, as I was soon convinced, were only to be banished by activity; but of what was I to take hold? I had, indeed, much to make up for in many things, and to prepare myself, in more than one sense, for the university, which I was now to attend; but I relished and accomplished nothing. Much appeared to me familiar and trivial:

for grounding myself, in several respects, I found neither strength within nor opportunity without; and I therefore suffered myself to be moved by the taste of my good room-neighbour, to a study which was altogether new and strange to me, and which for a long time offered me a wide field of information and thought. For my friend began to make me acquainted with the secrets of philosophy. He had studied in Jena, under Daries, and, possessing a well-regulated mind, had acutely seized the relations of that doctrine, which he now sought to impart to me. But, unfortunately, these things would not hang together in such a fashion in my brain. I put questions, which he promised to answer afterward: I made demands, which he promised to satisfy in future. But our most important difference was this: that I maintained a separate philosophy was not necessary, as the whole of it was already contained in religion and poetry. This he would by no means allow, but rather tried to prove to me that these must first be founded on philosophy; which I stubbornly denied, and, at every step in the progress of our discussions, found arguments for my opinion. For as in poetry a certain faith in the impossible, and as in religion a like faith in the inscrutable, must have a place, the philosophers appeared to me to be in a very false position who would demonstrate and explain both of them from their own field of vision. Besides, it was very quickly proved, from the history of philosophy, that one always sought a ground different from that of the other, and that the skeptic, in the end, pronounced everything groundless and useless.

However, this very history of philosophy, which my friend was compelled to go over with me, because I could learn nothing from dogmatical discourse, amused me very much, but only on this account, that one doctrine or opinion seemed to me as good as another, so far, at least, as I was capable of penetrating into it. With the most ancient men and schools I was best pleased, because poetry, religion, and philosophy were completely combined into one; and I only maintained that first opinion of mine with the more animation, when the book of Job and the Song and Proverbs of Solomon, as well as the lays of Orpheus and Hesiod, seemed to bear valid witness in its favour. My friend had taken the smaller work of Brucker as the foundation of his discourse; and, the farther we went on, the less I could make of it. I could not clearly see what the first Greek philosophers would have. Socrates I esteemed as an excellent, wise man, who in his life and death might well be compared with Christ. His disciples, on the other hand, seemed to me to bear a strong resemblance to the apostles, who disagreed immediately after their Master's death, when each manifestly recognised only a limited view as the right one. Neither the keenness of Aristotle nor the fulness of Plato produced the least fruit in me. For the Stoics, on the contrary, I had already conceived some affection, and even procured Epictetus, whom I studied with much interest. My friend unwillingly let me have my way in this one-sidedness, from which he could not draw me; for, in spite of his varied studies, he did not know how to bring the leading question into a narrow compass. He need only have said to me that in life action is everything, and that joy and sorrow come of themselves. However, youth should be allowed its own course: it does not stick to false maxims very long; life soon tears or charms it away again.

The season had become fine: we often went together into the open air, and visited the places of amusement which surrounded the city in great numbers. But it was precisely here that matters went worse with me; for I still saw the ghosts of the cousins everywhere, and feared, now here, now there, to see one of them step forward. Even the most indifferent glances of men annoyed me. I had lost that unconscious happiness of wandering about unknown and unblamed, and of thinking of no observer, even in the greatest crowds. Now hypochondriacal fancies began to torment me, as if I attracted the attention of the people, as if their eyes were turned on my demeanour, to fix it on their memories, to scàn and to find fault.

I therefore drew my friend into the woods; and, while I shunned the monotonous firs, I sought those fine, leafy groves, which do not indeed spread far in the district, but are yet of sufficient compass for a poor wounded heart to hide itself. In the remotest depths of the forest I sought out a solemn spot, where the oldest oaks and beeches formed a large, noble, shaded space. The ground was somewhat sloping, and made the worth of the old trunks only the more perceptible. Round this open circle closed the densest thickets, from which the mossy rocks mightily and venerably peered forth, and made a rapid fall for a copious brook.

Scarcely had I dragged hither my friend, who would rather have been in the open country by the stream, among men, when he playfully assured me that I showed myself a true German. He related to me circumstantially, out of Tacitus, how our ancestors found pleasure in the feelings which Nature so provides for us, in such solitudes, with her inartificial architecture. He had not been long discoursing of this, when I exclaimed, "Oh! why did not this precious spot lie in a deeper wilderness! why may we not train a hedge around it, to hallow and separate from the world both it and ourselves! Surely there is no more beautiful adoration of the Deity than that which needs no image, but which springs up in our bosom merely from the intercourse with nature!" What I then felt is still present to my mind: what I said I know not how to recall. Thus much, however, is certain, that the undetermined, widely expanding feelings of youth and of uncultivated nations are alone adapted to the sublime, which, if it is to be excited in us through external objects, formless, or moulded into incomprehensible forms, must surround us with a greatness to which we are not equal.

All men, more or less, have such a disposition, and seek to satisfy this noble want in various ways. But as the sublime is easily produced by twilight and night, when objects are blended, it is, on the other hand, scared away by the day, which separates and sunders everything; and so must it also be destroyed by every increase of cultivation, if it be not fortunate enough to take refuge with the beautiful, and unite itself closely with it, whereby both become equally undying and indestructible.

The brief moments of such enjoyments were still more shortened by my meditative friend: but, when I turned back into the world, it was altogether in vain that I sought, among the bright and barren objects around, again to arouse such feelings within me; nay, I could scarcely retain even the remembrance of them. My heart, however, was too far spoiled to be able to compose itself: it had loved, and the object was snatched away from it; it had lived, and life to it was embittered. A friend who makes it too perceptible that he designs to improve you, excites no feeling of comfort; while a woman who is forming you, while she seems to spoil you, is adored as a heavenly, joy-bringing being. But that form in which the idea of beauty manifested itself to me had vanished into distance; it often visited me under the shade of my oak-trees, but I could not hold it fast: and I felt a powerful impulse to seek something similar in the distance.

I had imperceptibly accustomed, nay, compelled, my friend and overseer to leave me alone; for, even in my sacred grove, those undefined, gigantic feelings were not sufficient for me. The eye was, above all others, the organ by which I seized the world. I had, from childhood, lived among painters, and had accustomed myself to look at objects, as they did, with reference to art. Now I was left to myself and to solitude, this gift, half natural, half acquired, made its appearance. Wherever I looked, I saw a picture; and whatever struck me, whatever gave me delight, I wished to fix, and began, in the most awkward manner, to draw after nature. To this end I lacked nothing less than everything; yet, though without any technical means, I obstinately persisted in trying to imitate the most magnificent things that offered themselves to my sight. Thus, to be sure, I acquired the faculty of paying a great attention to objects; but I only seized them as a whole, so far as they produced an effect: and, little as Nature had meant me for a descriptive poet, just as little would she grant me the capacity of a draughtsman for details. This, however, being the only way left me of uttering my thoughts, I stuck to it with so much stubborness, nay, even with melancholy, that I always continued my labours the more zealously the less I saw they produced.

But I will not deny that there was a certain mixture of roguery; for I had remarked, that if I chose for an irksome study a half-shaded old trunk, to the hugely curved roots of which clung well-lit fern, combined with twinkling maidenhair, my friend, who knew from experience that I should not be disengaged in less than an hour, commonly resolved to seek, with his books, some other pleasant little spot. Now nothing disturbed me in prosecuting my taste, which was so much the more active, as my paper was endeared to me by the circumstance that I had accustomed myself to see in it, not so much what stood upon it, as what I had been thinking of at any time and hour when I drew. Thus plants and flowers of the commonest kind may form a charming diary for us, because nothing that calls back the remembrance of a happy moment can be insignificant; and even now it would be hard for me to destroy as worthless many things of the kind that have remained to me from different epochs, because they transport me immediately to those times which I like to remember, although not without melancholy.

But, if such drawings may have had anything of interest in themselves, they were indebted for this advantage to the sympathy and attention of my father. He, informed by my overseer that I had become gradually reconciled to my condition, and, in particular, had applied myself passionately to drawing from nature, was very well satisfied, — partly because he himself set a high value on drawing and painting, partly because gossip Seekatz had once said to him, that it was a pity I was not destined for a painter. But here again the peculiarities of father and son came into conflict: for it was almost impossible for me to make use of a good, white, perfectly clean sheet of paper; gray old leaves, even if scribbled over on one side already, charmed me most, just as if my awkwardness had feared the touchstone of a white ground. Nor were any of my drawings quite finished; and how should I have executed a whole, which indeed I saw with my eyes, but did not comprehend, and how an individual object, which I had neither skill nor patience to follow out? My father's mode of training me in this respect was really to be admired. He kindly asked for my attempts, and drew lines round every imperfect sketch. He wished, by this means, to compel me to completeness and fulness of detail. The irregular leaves he cut straight, and thus made the beginning of a collection, in which he wished, at some future time, to rejoice at the progress of his son. It was, therefore, by no means disagreeable to him when my wild, restless disposition sent me roving about the country: he rather seemed pleased when I brought back a parcel of drawings on which he could exercise his patience, and in some measure strengthen his hopes.

They no longer said that I might relapse into my former attachments and connections: they left me by degrees perfect liberty. By accidental inducements and in accidental society I undertook many journeys to the mountain-range, which, from my childhood, had stood so distant and solemn before me. Thus we visited Homburg, Kroneburg, ascended the Feldberg, from which the prospect invited us still farther and farther into the distance. Königstein, too, was not left unvisited; Wiesbaden, Schwalbach, with its environs, occupied us many days; we reached the Rhine, which, from the heights, we had seen winding along far off. Mainz astonished us, but could not chain a youthful mind which was running into the open country; we were delighted with the situation of Biberich; and, contented and happy, we resumed our journey home.

This whole tour, from which my father had promised himself many a drawing, might have been almost without fruit; for what taste, what talent, what experience, does it not require to seize an extensive landscape as a picture! I was again imperceptibly drawn into a narrow compass, from which I derived some profit; for I met no ruined castle, no piece of wall which pointed to antiquity, that I did not think an object worthy of my pencil, and imitate as well as I could. Even the stone of Drusus, on the ramparts of Mainz, I copied at some risk, and with inconveniences which every one must experience who wishes to carry home with him some pictorial reminiscences of his travels. Unfortunately I had again brought with me nothing but the most miserable common paper, and had clumsily crowded several objects into one sheet. But my paternal teacher was not perplexed at this: he cut the sheets apart; had the parts which belonged to each other put together by the bookbinder; surrounded the single leaves with lines; and thus actually compelled me to draw the outline of different mountains up to the margin, and to fill up the foreground with some weeds and stones.

If his faithful endeavours could not increase my talent, nevertheless this mark of his love of order had upon me a secret influence, which afterward manifested itself vigorously in more ways than one.

From such rambling excursions, undertaken partly for pleasure, partly for art, and which could be performed in a short time, and often repeated, I was again drawn home, and that by a magnet which always acted upon me strongly: this was my sister. She, only a year younger than I, had lived the whole conscious period of my life with me, and was thus bound to me by the closest ties. To these natural causes was added a forcible motive, which proceeded from our domestic position: a father certainly affectionate and well-meaning, but grave, who, because he cherished within a very tender heart, externally, with incredible consistency, maintained a brazen sternness, that he might attain the end of giving his children the best education, and of building up, regulating, and preserving his well-founded house; a mother, on the other hand, as yet almost a child, who first grew up to consciousness with and in her two eldest children; these three, as they looked at the world with healthy eyes, capable of life, and desiring present enjoyment. This contradiction floating in the family increased with years. My father followed out his views unshaken and uninterrupted: the mother and children could not give up their feelings, their claims, their wishes.

Under these circumstances it was natural that brother and sister should attach themselves close to each other, and adhere to their mother, that they might singly snatch the pleasures forbidden as a whole. But since the hours of solitude and toil were very long compared with the moments of recreation and enjoyment, especially for my sister, who could never leave the house for so long a time as I could, the necessity she felt for entertaining herself with me was still sharpened by the sense of longing with which she accompanied me to a distance.

And as, in our first years, playing and learning, growth and education, had been quite common to both of us, so that we might well have been taken for twins, so did this community, this confidence, remain during the development of our physical and moral powers. That interest of youth; that amazement at the awakening of sensual impulses which clothe themselves in mental forms; of mental necessities which clothe themselves in sensual images; all the reflections upon these, which obscure rather than enlighten us, as the fog covers over and does not illumine the vale from which it is about to rise; the many errors and aberrations springing therefrom, — all these the brother and sister shared and endured hand in hand, and were the less enlightened as to their strange condition, as the nearer they wished to approach each other, to clear up their minds, the more forcibly did the sacred awe of their close relationship keep them apart.

Reluctantly do I mention, in a general way, what I undertook to set forth years ago, without being able to accomplish it. As I lost this beloved, incomprehensible being but too soon, I felt inducement enough to make her worth present to me: and thus arose in me the conception of a poetic whole, in which it might be possible to exhibit her individuality; but for this no other form could be devised than that of the Richardsonian novels. Only by the minutest detail, by endless particularities which bear vividly all the character of the whole, and, as they spring up from a wonderful depth, give some feeling of that depth, — only in such a manner would it have been in some degree possible to give a representation of this remarkable personality; for the spring can be apprehended only while it is flowing. But from this beautiful and pious design, as from so many others, the tumult of the world drew me away; and nothing now remains for me but to call up for a moment that blessed spirit, as if by the aid of a magic mirror.

She was tall, well and delicately formed, and had something naturally dignified in her demeanour, which melted away into a pleasing mildness. The lineaments of her face, neither striking nor beautiful, indicated a character which was not nor ever could be in union with itself. Her eyes were not the finest I have ever seen, but the deepest, behind which you expected the most; and when they expressed any affection, any love, their brilliancy was unequalled. And yet, properly speaking, this expression was not tender, like that which comes from the heart, and at the same time carries with it something of longing and desire: this expression came from the soul; it was full and rich; it seemed as if it would only give, without needing to receive.

But what in a manner quite peculiar disfigured her face, so that she would often appear positively ugly, was the fashion of those times, which not only bared the forehead, but, either accidentally or on purpose, did everything apparently or really to enlarge it. Now, as she had the most feminine, most perfect arched forehead, and, moreover, a pair of strong black eyebrows, and prominent eyes, these circumstances occasioned a contrast, which, if it did not repel every stranger at the first glance, at least did not attract him. She early felt it; and this feeling became constantly the more painful to her, the farther she advanced into the years when both sexes find an innocent pleasure in being mutually agreeable.

To nobody can his own form be repugnant; the ugliest, as well as the most beautiful, has a right to enjoy his own presence : and as favour beautifies, and every one regards himself in the looking-glass with favour, it may be asserted that every one must see himself with complacency, even if he would struggle against the feeling. Yet my sister had such a decided foundation of good sense, that she could not possibly be blind and silly in this respect; on the contrary, she perhaps knew more clearly than she ought,. that she stood far behind her female playfellows in external beauty, without feeling consoled by the fact that she infinitely surpassed them in internal advantages.

If a woman can find compensation for the want of beauty, she richly found it in the unbounded confidence, the regard and love, which all her female friends bore to her; whether they were older or younger, all cherished the same sentiments. A very pleasant society had collected around her : young men were not wanting who knew how to insinuate themselves; nearly every girl found an admirer; she alone had remained without a partner. While, indeed, her exterior was in some measure repulsive, the mind that gleamed through it was also more repelling than attractive; for the presence of any excellence throws others back upon themselves. She felt this sensibly : she did not conceal it from me, and her love was directed to me with so much the greater force. The case was singular enough. As confidants to whom one reveals a love-affair actually by genuine sympathy become lovers also, nay, grow into rivals, and at last, perchance, transfer the passion to themselves; so it was with us two: for, when my connection with Gretchen was torn asunder, my sister consoled me the more earnestly, because she secretly felt the satisfaction of having gotten rid of a rival; and I, too, could not but feel a quiet, half-mischievous pleasure, when she did me the justice to assure me that I was the only one who truly loved, understood, and esteemed her. If now, from time to time, my grief for the loss of Gretchen revived, and I suddenly began to weep, to lament, and to act in a disorderly manner, my despair for my lost one awakened in her likewise a similar despairing impatience as to the never-possessings, the failures, and miscarriages of such youthful attachments, that we both thought ourselves infinitely unhappy, and the more so, as, in this singular case, the confidants could not change themselves into lovers.

Fortunately, however, the capricious god of love, who needlessly does so much mischief, here for once interfered beneficially, to extricate us out of all perplexity. I had much intercourse with a young Englishman who was educated in Pfeil's boarding-school. He could give a good account of his own language : I practised it with him, and thus learned much concerning his country and people. He went in and out of our house long enough without my remarking in him a liking for my sister; yet he may have been nourishing it in secret, even to passion, for at last it declared itself unexpectedly and at once. She knew him, she esteemed him, and he deserved it. She had often made the third at our English conversations: we had both tried to catch from his mouth the irregularities of the English pronunciation, and thereby accustomed ourselves, not only to the peculiarities of its accent and sound, but even to what was most peculiar in the personal qualities of our teacher; so that at last it sounded strangely enough when we all seemed to speak as if out of one mouth. The pains he took to learn as much German from us in the like manner were to no purpose; and I think I have remarked that even this little love-affair was also, both orally and in writing, carried on in the English language. Both the young persons were very well suited to each other : he was tall and well built, as she was, only still more slender; his face, small and compact, might really have been pretty, had it not been too much disfigured by the smallpox; his manner was calm, precise, — one might often have called it dry and cold; but his heart was full of kindness and love, his soul full of generosity, and his attachments as lasting as they were decided and controlled. Now, this serious pair, who had but lately formed an attachment, were quite peculiarly distinguished among the others, who, being already better acquainted with each other, of more frivolous character, and careless as to the future, roved about with levity in these connections, which commonly pass away as the mere fruitless prelude to subsequent and more serious ties, and very seldom produce a lasting effect upon life.

The fine weather and the beautiful country did not remain unenjoyed by so lively a company : water-excursions were frequently arranged, because these are the most sociable of all parties of pleasure. Yet, whether we were going by water or by land, the individual attracting powers immediately showed themselves; each couple kept together : and for some men who were not engaged, of whom I was one, there remained either no conversation with the ladies at all, or only such as no one would have chosen for a day of pleasure. A friend who found himself in this situation, and who might have been in want of a partner chiefly for this reason, that, with the best humour, he lacked tenderness, and, with much intelligence, that delicate attention, without which connections of this kind are not to be thought of, — this man, after often humourously and wittily lamenting his condition, promised at the next meeting to make a proposal which would benefit himself and the whole company. Nor did he fail to perform his promise; for when, after a brilliant trip by water, and a very pleasant walk, reclining on the grass between shady knolls, or sitting on mossy rocks and roots of trees, we had cheerfully and happily consumed a rural meal, and our friend saw us all cheerful and in good spirits, he, with a waggish dignity, commanded us to sit close round him in a semicircle, before which he stepped, and began to make an emphatic peroration as follows :

"Most worthy friends of both sexes, paired and unpaired!" It was already evident from this address, how necessary it was that a preacher of repentance should arise, and sharpen the conscience of the company. "One part of my noble friends is paired, and they may find themselves quite happy; another unpaired, and these find themselves in the highest degree miserable, as I can assure you from my own experience : and although the loving couples are here in the majority, yet I would have them consider whether it is not a social duty to take thought for the whole. Why do we wish to assemble in such numbers, except to take a mutual interest in each other? and how can that be done when so many little secessions are to be seen in our circle? Far be it from me to insinuate anything against such sweet connections, or even to wish to disturb them; but 'there is a time for all things,' — an excellent great saying, of which, indeed, nobody thinks when his own amusement is sufficiently provided for."

He then went on with constantly increasing liveliness and gaiety to compare the social virtues with the tender sentiments. "The latter," said he, "can never fail us; we always carry them about with us, and every one becomes a master in them without practice: but we must go in quest of the former, we must take some trouble about them; and, though we progress in them as much as we will, we have never done learning them." Now he went into particulars. Many felt hit off, and they could not help casting glances at each other: yet our friend had this privilege, that nothing he did was taken ill; and so he could proceed without interruption.

"It is not enough to discover deficiencies: indeed, it is unjust to do so, if at the same time one cannot contrive to give the means for bettering the state of affairs. I will not, therefore, my friends, something like a preacher in Passion Week, exhort you in general terms to repentance and amendment: I rather wish all amiable couples the longest and most enduring happiness; and, to contribute to it myself in the surest manner, I propose to sever and abolish these most charming little segregations during our social hours. I have," he continued, "already provided for the execution of my project, if it should meet your approbation. Here is a bag in which are the names of the gentlemen: now draw, my fair ones, and be pleased to favour as your servant, for a week, him whom fate shall send you. This is binding only within our circle; as soon as that is broken up, these connections are also abolished, and the heart may decide who shall attend you home."

A great part of the company had been delighted with this address, and the manner in which he delivered it, and seemed to approve of the notion; yet some couples looked at each other as if they thought that it would not answer their purpose: he therefore cried with humourous vehemence:

"Truly! it surprises me that some one does not spring up, and, though others hesitate, extol my plan, explain its advantages, and spare me the pain of being my own encomiast. I am the oldest among you: may God forgive me for that! Already have I a bald pate, which is owing to my great meditation."

Here he took off his hat.

" But I should expose it to view with joy and honour if my lucubrations, which dry up my skin, and rob me of my finest adornment, could only be in some measure beneficial to myself and others. We are young, my friends, — that is good; we shall grow older, — that is bad; we take little offence at each other, — that is right, and in accordance with the season. But soon, my friends, the days will come when we shall have much to be displeased at in ourselves; then, let every one see that he makes all right with himself; but, at the same time, others will not take things ill of us, and on what account we shall not understand; for this we must prepare ourselves; this shall now be done."

He had delivered the whole speech, but especially the last part, with the tone and gesture of a Capuchin; for, as he was a Catholic, he might have had abundant opportunity to study the oratory of these fathers. He now appeared out of breath, wiped his youthful, bald head, which really gave him the look of a priest, and by these drolleries put the light-hearted company in such good humour that every one was eager to hear him longer. But, instead of proceeding, he drew open the bag, and turned to the nearest lady. " Now for a trial of it!" exclaimed he: " the work will do credit to the master. If in a week's time we do not like it, we will give it up, and stick to the old plan."

Half willingly, half on compulsion, the ladies drew their tickets; and it was easy to see that various passions were in play during this little affair. Fortunately it happened that the merry-minded were separated, while the more serious remained together, and so, too, my sister kept her Englishman; which, on both sides, they took very kindly of the god of love and luck.

The new chance-couples were immediately united by the *Antistes*, their healths were drank, and to all the more joy was wished, as its duration was to be but short. This was certainly the merriest moment that our company had enjoyed for a long time. The young men to whose share no lady had fallen, held, for this week, the office of providing for the mind, the soul, and the body, as our orator expressed himself, but especially, he hinted, for the soul, since both the others already knew how to help themselves.

These masters of ceremonies, who wished at once to do themselves credit, brought into play some very pretty new games, prepared at some distance a supper, which we had not reckoned on, and illuminated the yacht on our return at night, although there was no necessity for it in the bright moonlight; but they excused themselves by saying that it was quite conformable to the new social regulation to outshine the tender glances of the heavenly moon by earthly candles. The moment we touched the shore, our Solon cried, "*Ite, missa est!*" Each one now handed out of the vessel the lady who had fallen to him by lot, and then surrendered her to her proper partner, on receiving his own in exchange.

At our next meeting this weekly regulation was established for the summer, and the lots were drawn once more. There was no question but that this pleasantry gave a new and unexpected turn to the company; and every one was stimulated to display whatever of wit and grace was in him, and to pay court to his temporary fair one in the most obliging manner, since he might depend on having a sufficient store of complaisance for one week at least.

We had scarcely settled down, when, instead of thanking our orator, we reproached him for having kept to himself the best part of his speech, — the conclusion. He thereupon protested that the best part of a speech was persuasion, and that he who did not aim at persuasion should make no speech; for, as to conviction, that was a ticklish business. As, however, they gave him no peace, he began a Capuchinade on the spot, more comical than ever, perhaps, for the very reason that he took it into his head to speak on the most serious subjects. For with texts out of the Bible, which had nothing to do with the business; with similes which did not fit; with allusions which illustrated nothing, — he carried out the proposition, that whosoever does not know how to conceal his passions, inclinations, wishes, purposes, and plans, will come to no good in the world, but will be disturbed and made a butt in every end and corner; and that especially if one would be happy in love, one must take pains to keep it a most profound secret.

This thought ran through the whole, without, properly speaking, a single word of it being said. If you would form a conception of this singular man, let it be considered, that, being born with a good foundation, he had cultivated his talents, and especially his acuteness, in Jesuit schools, and had amassed an extensive knowledge of the world and of men, but only on the bad side. He was some two and twenty years old, and would gladly have made me a proselyte to his contempt for mankind; but this would not take with me, as I always had a great desire to be good myself, and to find good in others. Meanwhile, I was by him made attentive to many things.

To complete the *dramatis personæ* of every merry company, an actor is necessary who feels pleasure when the others, to enliven many an indifferent moment, point the arrows of their wit at him. If he is not merely a stuffed Saracen, like those on whom the knights used to practise their lances in mock battles, but understands himself how to skirmish, to rally, and to challenge, how to wound lightly, and recover himself again, and, while he seems to expose himself, to give others a thrust home, nothing more agreeable can be found. Such a man we possessed in our friend Horn, whose name, to begin with, gave occasion for all sorts of jokes, and who, on account of his small figure, was called nothing but Hörnchen (little Horn). He was, in fact, the smallest in the company, of a stout but pleasing form; a pug-nose, a mouth somewhat pouting, little sparkling eyes, made up a swarthy countenance which always seemed to invite laughter. His little compact skull was thickly covered with curly black hair: his beard was prematurely blue; and he would have liked to let it grow, that, as a comic mask, he might always keep the company laughing. For the rest, he was neat and nimble, but insisted that he had bandy legs, which everybody granted, since he was bent on having it so, but about which many a joke arose; for, since he was in request as a very good dancer, he reckoned it among the peculiarities of the fair sex, that they always liked to see bandy legs on the floor. His cheerfulness was indestructible, and his presence at every meeting indispensable. We two kept more together because he was to follow me to the university; and he well deserves that I should mention him with all honour, as he adhered to me for many years with infinite love, faithfulness, and patience.

By my ease in rhyming, and in winning from common objects a poetical side, he had allowed himself to be seduced into similar labours. Our little social excursions, parties of pleasure, and the contingencies that occurred in them, we decked out poetically; and thus, by the description of an event, a new event always arose. But as such social jests commonly degenerate into personal ridicule, and my friend Horn, with his burlesque representations, did not always keep within proper bounds, many a misunderstanding arose, which, however, could soon be softened down and effaced.

Thus, also, he tried his skill in a species of poetry which was then very much the order of the day, — the comic heroical poem. Pope's "Rape of the Lock" had called forth many imitations : Zachariä cultivated this branch of poetry on German soil; and it pleased every one, because the ordinary subject of it was some awkward fellow, of whom the genii made game, while they favoured the better one.

Although it is no wonder, yet it excites wonderment, when contemplating a literature, especially the German, one observes how a whole nation cannot get free from a subject which has been once given, and happily treated in a certain form, but will have it repeated in every manner, until, at last, the original itself is covered up, and stifled by the heaps of imitations.

The heroic poem of my friend was a voucher for this remark. At a great sledging-party, an awkward man has assigned to him a lady who does not like him : comically enough, there befalls him, one after another, every accident that can happen on such an occasion, until at last, as he is entreating for the sledge driver's right (a kiss), he falls from the back seat; for just then, as was natural, the Fates tripped him up. The fair one seizes the reins, and drives home alone, where a favoured friend receives her, and triumphs over his presumptuous rival. As to the rest, it was very prettily contrived that the four different kinds of spirits should worry him in turn, till at the end the gnomes hoist him completely out of the saddle. The poem, written in Alexandrines, and founded on a true story, highly delighted our little public; and we were convinced that it could well be compared with the "Walpurgisnight" of Löwen, or the "Renommist" of Zachariä.[1]

While, now, our social pleasures required but an

---

[1] This word, which signifies something like our "bully," is specially used to designate a fighting student. — TRANS.

evening, and the preparations for them only a few hours, I had enough time to read, and, as I thought, to study. To please my father, I diligently repeated the smaller work of Hopp, and could stand an examination in it forwards and backwards, by which means I made myself complete master of the chief contents of the institutes. But a restless eagerness for knowledge urged me farther: I lighted upon the history of ancient literature, and from that fell into an encyclopædism, in which I hastily read Gessner's " Isagoge " and Morhov's " Polyhistor," and thus gained a general notion of how many strange things might have happened in learning and life. By this persevering and rapid industry, continued day and night, I became more confused than instructed; but I lost myself in a still greater labyrinth when I found Bayle in my father's library, and plunged deeply into this work.

But a leading conviction, which was continually revived within me, was that of the importance of the ancient tongues; since from amidst this literary hurly-burly, thus much continually forced itself upon me, that in them were preserved all the models' of oratory, and at the same time everything else of worth that the world has ever possessed. Hebrew, together with Biblical studies, had retired into the background, and Greek likewise, since my acquaintance with it did not extend beyond the New Testament. I therefore the more zealously kept to Latin, the masterpieces in which lie nearer to us, and which, besides its splendid original productions, offers us the other wealth of all ages in translations, and the works of the greatest scholars. I consequently read much in this language, with great ease, and was bold enough to believe I understood the authors, because I missed nothing of the literal sense. Indeed, I was very indignant when I heard that Grotius had insolently declared, " he did not read Terence as boys do." Happy narrow-mindedness of youth! — nay, of men in general, that they can, at every moment of their existence, fancy themselves finished, and inquire after neither the true nor the false, after neither the high nor the deep, but merely after that which is suited to them.

I had thus learned Latin, like German, French, and English, merely by practice, without rules, and without comprehension. Whoever knows the then condition of scholastic instruction will not think it strange that I skipped grammar as well as rhetoric; all seemed to me to come together naturally: I retained the words, their forms and inflexions, in my ear and mind, and used the language with ease in writing and in chattering.

Michaelmas, the time fixed for my going to the university, was approaching; and my mind was excited quite as much about my life as about my learning. I grew more and more clearly conscious of an aversion to my native city. By Gretchen's removal, the heart had been broken out of the boyish and youthful plant: it needed time to bud forth again from its sides, and surmount the first injury by a new growth. My ramblings through the streets had ceased; I now, like others, only went such ways as were necessary. I never went again into Gretchen's quarter of the city, not even into its vicinity: and as my old walls and towers became gradually disagreeable to me, so also was I displeased at the constitution of the city; all that hitherto seemed so worthy of honour now appeared to me in distorted shapes. As grandson of the *Schultheiss* I had not remained unacquainted with the secret defects of such a republic; the less so, as children feel quite a peculiar surprise, and are excited to busy researches, as soon as something which they have hitherto implicitly revered becomes in any degree suspicious to them. The fruitless indignation of upright men, in opposition to those who are to be gained and even bribed by factions, had become but too plain to me: I hated every injustice beyond measure, for children are all moral rigourists. My father, who was concerned in the affairs of the city only as a private citizen, expressed himself with very lively indignation about much that had failed. And did I not see him, after so many studies, endeavours, pains, travels, and so much varied cultivation, between his four walls, leading a solitary life, such as I could never desire for myself? All this put together lay as a horrible load on my mind, from which I could only free myself by trying to contrive a plan of life altogether different from that which had been marked out for me. In thought I threw aside my legal studies, and devoted myself solely to the languages, to antiquities, to history, and to all that flows from them.

Indeed, at all times, the poetic imitation of what I had perceived in myself, in others, and in nature, afforded me the greatest pleasure. I did it with ever-increasing facility, because it came by instinct, and no criticism had led me astray; and, if I did not feel full confidence in my productions, I could certainly regard them as defective, but not such as to be utterly rejected. Although here and there they were censured, I still retained my silent conviction that I could not but gradually improve, and that sometime I might be honourably named along with Hagedorn, Gellert, and other such men. But such a distinction alone seemed to me too empty and inadequate; I wished to devote myself professionally and with zeal to those aforesaid fundamental studies, and, whilst I meant to advance more rapidly in my own works by a more thorough insight into antiquity, to qualify myself for a university professorship, which seemed to me the most desirable thing for a young man who strove for culture, and intended to contribute to that of others.

With these intentions I always had my eye upon Göttingen. My whole confidence rested upon men like Heyne, Michaelis, and so many others; my most ardent wish was to sit at their feet, and attend to their instructions. But my father remained inflexible. Howsoever some family friends, who were of my opinion, tried to influence him, he persisted that I must go to Leipzig. I was now resolved, contrary to his views and wishes, to choose a line of studies and of life for myself, by way of self-defence. The obstinacy of my father, who, without knowing it, opposed himself to my plans, strengthened me in my impiety; so that I made no scruple to listen to him by the hour, while he described and repeated to me the course of study and of life which I should pursue at the universities and in the world.

All hopes of Göttingen being cut off, I now turned my eyes toward Leipzig. There Ernesti appeared to me as a brilliant light: Morus, too, already awakened much confidence. I planned for myself in secret an opposition course, or rather I built a castle in the air, on a tolerably solid foundation; and it seemed to me quite romantically honourable to mark out my own path of life, which appeared the less visionary, as Griesbach had already made great progress in a similar way, and was commended for it by every one. The secret joy of a prisoner, when he has unbound the fetters, and rapidly filed through the bars of his jail-window, cannot be greater than was mine as I saw day after day disappear, and October draw nigh. The inclement season and the bad roads, of which everybody had something to tell, did not frighten me. The thought of making good my footing in a strange place, and in winter, did not make me sad; suffice it to say, that I only saw my present situation was gloomy, and represented to myself the other unknown world as light and cheerful. Thus I formed my dreams, to which I gave myself up exclusively, and promised myself nothing but happiness and content in the distance.

Closely as I kept these projects a secret from every one else, I could not hide them from my sister, who, after being very much alarmed about them at first, was finally consoled when I promised to send after her, so that she could enjoy with me the brilliant station I was to obtain, and share my comfort with me.

Michaelmas, so longingly expected, came at last, when I set out with delight, in company with the bookseller Fleischer and his wife (whose maiden name was Triller, and who was going to visit her father in Wittenberg); and I left behind me the worthy city in which I had been born and bred, with indifference, as if I wished never to set foot in it again.

Thus, at certain epochs, children part from parents, servants from masters, protégés from their patrons; and, whether it succeed or not, such an attempt to stand on one's own feet, to make one's self independent, to live for one's self, is always in accordance with the will of nature.

We had driven out through the Allerheiligen (All Saints) gate, and had soon left Hanau behind us, after which we reached scenes which aroused my attention by their novelty, if, at this season of the year, they offered little that was pleasing. A continual rain had completely spoiled the roads, which, generally speaking, were not then in such good order as we find them now; and our journey was thus neither pleasant nor happy. Yet I was indebted to this damp weather for the sight of a natural phenomenon which must be exceedingly rare, for I have seen nothing like it since, nor have I heard of its having been observed by others. It was this: namely, we were driving at night up a rising ground between Hanau and Gelhausen, and, although it was dark, we preferred walking to exposing ourselves to the danger and difficulty of that part of the road. All at once, in a ravine on the right-hand side of the way, I saw a sort of amphitheatre, wonderfully illuminated. In a funnel-shaped space there were innumerable little lights gleaming, ranged step-fashion over one another; and they shone so brilliantly that the eye was dazzled. But what still more confused the sight was, that they did not keep still, but jumped about here and there, as well downwards from above as vice versa, and in every direction. The greater part of them, however, remained stationary, and beamed on. It was only with the greatest reluctance that I suffered myself to be called away from this spectacle, which I could have wished to examine more closely. The postilion, when questioned, said that he knew nothing about such a phenomenon, but that there was in the neighbourhood an old stone-quarry, the excavation of which was filled with water. Now, whether this was a pandemonium of will-o'-the-wisps, or a company of luminous creatures, I will not decide.

The roads through Thuringia were yet worse; and unfortunately, at nightfall, our coach stuck fast in the vicinity of Auerstädt. We were far removed from all mankind, and did everything possible to work ourselves out. I failed not to exert myself zealously, and might thereby have overstrained the ligaments of my chest; for soon afterward I felt a pain, which went off and returned, and did not leave me entirely until after many years.

Yet on that same night, as if it had been destined for alternate good and bad luck, I was forced, after an unexpectedly fortunate incident, to experience a teasing vexation. We met, in Auerstädt, a genteel married couple, who had also just arrived, having been delayed by a similar accident; a pleasing, dignified man, in his best years, with a very handsome wife. They politely persuaded us to sup in their company, and I felt very happy when the excellent lady addressed a friendly word to me. But when I was sent out to hasten the soup which had been ordered, not having been accustomed to the loss of rest and the fatigues of travelling, such an unconquerable drowsiness overtook me, that actually I fell asleep while walking, returned into the room with my hat on my head, and, without remarking that the others were saying grace, placed myself with quiet unconsciousness behind the chair, and never dreamed that by my conduct I had come to disturb their devotions in a very droll way. Madame Fleischer, who lacked neither spirit nor wit nor tongue, entreated the strangers, before they had seated themselves, not to be surprised at anything they might see here; for that their young fellow traveller had in his nature much of the peculiarity of the Quakers, who believe that they cannot honour God and the king better than with covered heads. The handsome lady, who could not restrain her laughter, looked prettier than ever in consequence; and I would have given everything in the world not to have been the cause of a merriment which was so highly becoming to her countenance. I had, however, scarcely laid aside my hat, when these persons, in accordance with their polished manners, immediately dropped the joke, and, with the best wine from their bottle-case, completely extinguished sleep, chagrin, and the memory of all past troubles.

I arrived in Leipzig just at the time of the fair, from which I derived particular pleasure; for here I saw before me the continuation of a state of things belonging to my native city, familiar wares and traders, — only in other places, and in a different order. I rambled about the market and the booths with much interest; but my attention was particularly attracted by the inhabitants of the Eastern countries in their strange dresses, the Poles and Russians, and, above all, the Greeks, for the sake of whose handsome forms and dignified costume I often went to the spot.

But this animating bustle was soon over; and now the city itself appeared before me, with its handsome, high, and uniform houses. It made a very good impression upon me; and it cannot be denied, that in general, but especially in the silent moments of Sundays and holidays, it has something imposing; and when in the moonlight the streets were half in shadow, half-illuminated, they often invited me to nocturnal promenades.

In the meantime, as compared with that to which I had hitherto been accustomed, this new state of affairs was by no means satisfactory. Leipzig calls up before the spectator no antique time: it is a new, recently elapsed epoch, testifying commercial activity, comfort, and wealth, which announces itself to us in these monuments. Yet quite to my taste were the houses, which to me seemed immense, and which, fronting two streets, and embracing a citizen-world within their large courtyards, built round with lofty walls, are like large castles, nay, even half-cities. In one of these strange places I quartered myself; namely, in the Bombshell Tavern (*Feuerkugel*), between the Old and the New Newmarket (*Neumarkt*). A couple of pleasant rooms looking out upon a courtyard, which, on account of the thoroughfare, was not without animation, were occupied by the bookseller Fleischer during the fair, and by me taken for the rest of the time at a moderate price. As a fellow lodger I found a theological student, who was deeply learned in his professional studies, a sound thinker, but poor, and suffering much from his eyes, which caused him great anxiety for the future. He had brought this affliction upon himself by his inordinate reading till the latest dusk of the evening, and even by moonlight, to save a little oil. Our old hostess showed herself benevolent to him, always friendly to me, and careful for us both.

I now hastened with my letters of introduction to Hofrath Böhme, who, once a pupil of Maskow, and now his successor, was professor of history and public law. A little, thick-set, lively man received me kindly enough, and introduced me to his wife. Both of them, as well as the other persons whom I waited on, gave me the pleasantest hopes as to my future residence; but at first I let no one know of the design I entertained, although I could scarcely wait for the favourable moment when I should declare myself free from jurisprudence, and devoted to the study of the classics. I cautiously waited till the Fleischers had returned, that my purpose might not be too prematurely betrayed to my family. But I then went, without delay, to Hofrath Böhme, to whom, before all, I thought I must confide the matter, and with much self-importance and boldness of speech disclosed my views to him. However, I found by no means a good reception of my proposition. As professor of history and public law, he had a declared hatred for everything that savoured of the *belles-lettres*. Unfortunately, he did not stand on the best footing with those who cultivated them; and Gellert in particular, in whom I had, awkwardly enough, expressed much confidence, he could not even endure. To send a faithful student to those men, therefore, while he deprived himself of one, and especially under such circumstances, seemed to him altogether out of the question. He therefore gave me a severe lecture on the spot, in which he protested that he could not permit such a step without the permission of my parents, even if he approved of it himself, which was not the case in this instance. He then passionately inveighed against philology and the study of languages, but still more against poetical exercises, which I had indeed allowed to peep out in the background. He finally concluded, that, if I wished to enter more closely into the study of the ancients, it could be done much better by the way of jurisprudence. He brought to my recollection many elegant jurists, such as Eberhard, Otto, and Heineccius, promised me mountains of gold from Roman antiquities and the history of law, and showed me, clear as the sun, that I should here be taking no roundabout way, even if afterward, on more mature deliberation, and with the consent of my parents, I should determine to follow out my own plan. He begged me, in a friendly manner, to think the matter over once more, and to open my mind to him soon; as it would be necessary to come to a determination at once, on account of the impending commencement of the lectures.

It was, however, very polite of him not to press me on the spot. His arguments, and the weight with which he advanced them, had already convinced my pliant youth; and I now first saw the difficulties and doubtfulness of a matter which I had privately pictured to myself as so feasible. Frau Hofrath Böhme invited me shortly afterward. I found her alone. She was no longer young, and had very delicate health; was gentle and tender to an infinite degree; and formed a decided contrast to her husband, whose good nature was even blustering. She spoke of the conversation her husband had lately had with me, and once more placed the subject before me, in all its bearings, in so cordial a manner, so affectionately and sensibly, that I could not help yielding: the few reservations on which I insisted were also agreed upon by the other side.

Thereupon her husband regulated my hours; for I was to hear lectures on philosophy, the history of law, the Institutes, and some other matters. I was content with this; but I carried my point so as to attend Gellert's history of literature (with Stockhausen for a text-book), and his "Practicum" besides.

The reverence and love with which Gellert was regarded by all young people was extraordinary. I had already called on him, and had been kindly received by him. Not of tall stature; elegant without being lean; soft and rather pensive eyes; a very fine forehead; a nose aquiline, but not too much so; a delicate mouth; a face of an agreeable oval, — all made his presence pleasing and desirable. It cost some trouble to reach him. His two *Famuli* appeared like priests who guard a sanctuary, the access to which is not permitted to everybody, nor at every time : and such a precaution was very necessary; for he would have sacrificed his whole time, had he been willing to receive and satisfy all those who wished to become intimate with him.

At first I attended my lectures assiduously and faithfully, but the philosophy would not enlighten me at all. In the logic it seemed strange to me that I had so to tear asunder, isolate, and, as it were, destroy, those operations of the mind which I had performed with the greatest ease from my youth upward, and this in order to see into the right use of them. Of the thing itself, of the world, and of God, I thought I knew about as much as the professor himself; and, in more places than one, the affair seemed to me to come into a tremendous strait. Yet all went on in tolerable order till toward Shrovetide, when, in the neighbourhood of Professor Winkler's house on the Thomas Place, the most delicious fritters came hot out of the pan just at the hour of lecture: and these delayed us so long, that our note-books became disordered; and the conclusion of them, toward spring, melted away, together with the snow, and was lost.

The law-lectures very soon fared not any better, for I already knew just as much as the professor thought good to communicate to us. My stubborn industry in writing down the lectures at first, was paralysed by degrees; for I found it excessively tedious to pen down once more that which, partly by question, partly by answer, I had repeated with my father often enough to retain it for ever in my memory. The harm which is done when young people at school are advanced too far in many things was afterward manifested still more when time and attention were diverted from exercises in the languages, and a foundation in what are, properly speaking, preparatory studies, in order to be applied to what are called " Realities," which dissipate more than they cultivate, if they are not methodically and thoroughly taught.

I here mention, by the way, another evil by which students are much embarrassed. Professors, as well as other men in office, cannot all be of the same age: but when the younger ones teach, in fact, only that they may learn, and moreover, if they have talent, anticipate their age, they acquire their own cultivation altogether at the cost of their hearers; since these are not instructed in what they really need, but in that which the professor finds it necessary to elaborate for himself. Among the oldest professors, on the contrary, many are for a long time stationary: they deliver on the whole only fixed views, and, in the details, much that time has already condemned as useless and false. Between the two arises a sad conflict, in which young minds are dragged hither and thither, and which can scarcely be set right by the middle-aged professors, who, though possessed of sufficient learning and culture, always feel within themselves an active desire for knowledge and reflection.

Now, as in this way I learned to know much more than I could digest, whereby a constantly increasing uncomfortableness was forced upon me; so also from life I experienced many disagreeable trifles, — as, indeed, one must always pay one's footing when one changes one's place and comes into a new position.

The first thing the ladies blamed me for was my dress, for I had come from home to the university rather oddly equipped.

My father, who detested nothing so much as when something happened in vain, when any one did not know how to make use of his time, or found no opportunity for turning it to account, carried his economy of time and abilities so far, that nothing gave him greater pleasure than to kill two birds with one stone.[1] He had, therefore, never engaged a servant who could not be useful to the house in something else. Now, as he had always written everything with his own hand, and had, latterly, the convenience of dictating to the young inmate of the house, he found it most advantageous to have tailors for his domestics, who were obliged to make good use of their time, as they not only had to make their own liveries, but the clothes for my father and the children, besides doing all the mending. My father himself took pains to have the best materials and the best kind of cloth, by getting fine wares of the foreign merchants at the fair, and laying them up in store. I still remember well that he always visited the Herrn von Löwenicht, of Aix-la-Chapelle, and from my earliest youth made me acquainted with these and other eminent merchants.

Care was also taken for the fitness of the stuff. and there was a plentiful stock of different kinds of cloth, serge, and Götting stuff, besides the requisite lining; so that, as far as the materials were concerned, we might well venture to be seen. But the form spoiled almost everything. For, if one of our home-tailors was anything of a clever hand at sewing and making up a coat which had been cut out for him in masterly fashion, he was now obliged also to cut out the dress for himself, which did not always succeed to perfection. In addition to this, my father kept whatever belonged

---

[1] Literally, "to strike two flies with one flapper." — TRANS.

to his clothing in very good and neat order, and preserved more than used it for many years. Thus he had a predilection for certain old cuts and trimmings, by which our dress sometimes acquired a strange appearance.

In this same way had the wardrobe which I took with me to the university been furnished: it was very complete and handsome, and there was even a laced suit amongst the rest. Already accustomed to this kind of attire, I thought myself sufficiently well dressed; but it was not long before my female friends, first by gentle raillery, then by sensible remonstrances, convinced me that I looked as if I had dropped down out of another world. Much as I felt vexed at this, I did not see at first how I was to mend matters. But when Herr von Masuren, the favourite poetical country squire, once entered the theatre in a similar costume, and was heartily laughed at, more by reason of his external than his internal absurdity, I took courage, and ventured at once to exchange my whole wardrobe for a new-fashioned one, suited to the place, by which, however, it shrunk considerably.

When this trial was surmounted, a new one was to come up, which proved to be far more unpleasant, because it concerned a matter which one does not so easily put off and exchange.

I had been born and bred in the Upper-German dialect; and although my father always laboured to preserve a certain purity of language, and, from our youth upwards, had made us children attentive to what may be really called the defects of that idiom, and so prepared us for a better manner of speaking, I retained nevertheless many deeper-seated peculiarities, which, because they pleased me by their *naïveté*, I was fond of making conspicuous, and thus every time I used them incurred a severe reproof from my new fellow townsmen. The Upper-German, and perhaps chiefly he who lives by the Rhine and Main (for great rivers, like the seacoast, always have something animating about them), expresses himself much in similes and allusions, and makes use of proverbial sayings with a native common-sense aptness. In both cases he is often blunt: but, when one sees the drift of the expression, it is always appropriate; only something, to be sure, may often slip in, which proves offensive to a more delicate ear.

Every province loves its own dialect; for it is, properly speaking, the element in which the soul draws its breath. But every one knows with what obstinacy the Misnian dialect has contrived to domineer over the rest, and even, for a long time, to exclude them. We have suffered for many years under this pedantic tyranny, and only by reiterated struggles have all the provinces again established themselves in their ancient rights.

What a lively young man had to endure from this continual tutoring, may be easily inferred by any one who reflects that modes of thought, imagination, feeling, native character, must be sacrificed with the pronunciation which one at last consents to alter. And this intolerable demand was made by men and women of education, whose convictions I could not adopt, whose injustice I thought I felt, though I was unable to make it plain to myself. Allusions to the pithy Biblical texts were to be forbidden me, as well as the use of the honest-hearted expressions from the Chronicles. I had to forget that I had read the "Kaiser von Geisersberg," and eschew the use of proverbs, which nevertheless, instead of much fiddle-faddle, just hit the nail upon the head, — all this, which I had appropriated to myself with youthful ardour, I was now to do without: I felt paralysed to the core, and scarcely knew any more how I had to express myself on the commonest things. I was, moreover, told that one should speak as one writes, and write as one speaks; while to me, speaking and writing seemed once for all two different things, each of which might well maintain its own rights. And even in the Misniau dialect had I to hear many things which would have made no great figure on paper.

Every one who perceives in this the influence which men and women of education, the learned, and other persons who take pleasure in refined society, so decidedly exercised over a young student, would be immediately convinced that we were in Leipzig, even if it had not been mentioned. Each one of the German universities has a particular character; for, as no universal cultivation can pervade our fatherland, every place adheres to its own fashion, and carries out, even to the last, its own characteristic peculiarities: exactly the same thing holds good of the universities. In Jena and Halle roughness had been carried to the highest pitch: bodily strength, skill in fighting, the wildest self-help, was there the order of the day; and such a state of affairs can only be maintained and propagated by the most universal riot. The relations of the students to the inhabitants of those cities, various as they might be, nevertheless agreed in this, that the wild stranger had no regard for the citizen, and looked upon himself as a peculiar being, privileged to all sorts of freedom and insolence. In Leipzig, on the contrary, a student could scarcely be anything else than polite, as soon as he wished to stand on any footing at all with the rich, well-bred, and punctilious inhabitants.

All politeness, indeed, when it does not present itself as the flowering of a great and comprehensive mode of life, must appear restrained, stationary, and, from some points of view, perhaps, absurd; and so those wild huntsmen from the Saale[1] thought they had a great

---

[1] The river on which Halle is built. — TRANS.

superiority over the tame shepherds on the Pleisse.[1]
Zachariä's " Renommist" will always be a valuable
document, from which the manner of life and thought
at that time rises visibly forth ; as in general his
poems must be welcome to every one who wishes to
form for himself a conception of the then prevailing
state of social life and manners, which was indeed
feeble, but amiable on account of its innocence and
childlike simplicity.

All manners which result from the given relations
of a common existence are indestructible ; and, in my
time, many things still reminded us of Zachariä's epic
poem. Only one of our fellow academicians thought
himself rich and independent enough to snap his
fingers at public opinion. He drank acquaintance with
all the hackney-coachmen, whom he allowed to sit
inside the coach as if they were gentlemen, while he
drove them on the box; thought it a great joke to
upset them now and then, and contrived to satisfy
them for their smashed vehicles as well as for their
occasional bruises ; but otherwise he did no harm to
any one, seeming only to make a mock of the public
en masse. Once, on a most beautiful promenade-day,
he and a comrade of his seized upon the donkeys of
the miller in St. Thomas's Square : well-dressed, and in
their shoes and stockings, they rode around the city
with the greatest solemnity, stared at by all the
promenaders, with whom the glacis was swarming.
When some sensible persons remonstrated with him
on the subject, he assured them, quite unembarrassed,
that he only wanted to see how the Lord Christ might
have looked in a like case. Yet he found no imitators
and few companions.

For the student of any wealth and standing had
every reason to show himself attentive to the mercantile class, and to be the more solicitous about the

[1] The river near Leipzig. — TRANS.

proper external forms, as the colony[1] exhibited a
model of French manners. The professors, opulent
both from their private property and from their liberal
salaries, were not dependent upon their scholars; and
many subjects of the state, educated at the government
schools or other gymnasia, and hoping for preferment,
did not venture to throw off the traditional customs.
The neighbourhood of Dresden, the attention thence
paid to us, and the true piety of the superintendent of
the course of study, could not be without a moral, nay,
a religious influence.

At first this kind of life was not repugnant to me:
my letters of introduction had given me the *entrée* into
good families, whose circle of relatives also received
me well. But as I was soon forced to feel that the
company had much to find fault with in me, and that,
after dressing myself in their fashion, I must now talk
according to their tongue also: and as, moreover, I could
plainly see that I was, on the other hand, but little
benefited by the instruction and mental improvement
I had promised myself from my academical residence,
— I began to be lazy, and to neglect the social duties
of visiting, and other attentions; and indeed I should
have sooner withdrawn from all such connections,
had not fear and esteem attached me firmly to Hofrath
Böhme, and confidence and affection to his wife. The
husband, unfortunately, had not the happy gift of deal-
ing with young people, of winning their confidence,
and of guiding them, for the moment, as occasion
might require. When I visited him I never got any
good by it: his wife, on the contrary, showed a genuine
interest in me. Her ill health kept her constantly at
home. She often invited me to spend the evening

---

[1] Leipzig was so called, because a large and influential portion
of its citizens were sprung from a colony of Huguenots, who
settled there after the revocation of the edict of Nantes. — *American Note.*

with her, and knew how to direct and improve me in many little external particulars : for my manners were good, indeed; but I was not yet master of what is properly termed *étiquette.* Only one friend spent the evenings with her; but she was much more dictatorial and pedantic, for which reason she displeased me excessively : and, out of spite to her, I often resumed those unmannerly habits from which the other had already weaned me. Nevertheless she always had patience enough with me, taught me piquet, ombre, and similar games, the knowledge and practice of which is held indispensable in society.

But it was in the matter of taste that Madame Böhme had the greatest influence upon me, — in a negative way truly, yet one in which she agreed perfectly with the critics. The Gottsched waters[1] had inundated the German world with a true deluge, which threatened to rise up, even over the highest mountains. It takes a long time for such a flood to subside again, for the mire to dry away; and as in any epoch there are numberless aping poets, so the imitation of the flat and watery produced a chaos, of which now scarcely a notion remains. To find out that trash was trash was hence the greatest sport, yea, the triumph, of the critics of those days. Whoever had only a little common sense, was superficially acquainted with the ancients, and was somewhat more familiar with the moderns, thought himself provided with a standard scale which he could everywhere apply. Madame Böhme was an educated woman, who opposed the trivial, weak, and commonplace : she was, besides, the wife of a man who lived on bad terms with poetry in general, and would not even allow that of which she perhaps might have somewhat approved. She listened, indeed, for some time with patience, when I ventured to recite to

[1] That is to say, the influence of Gottsched on German literature, of which more is said in the next book. — TRANS.

her the verse or prose of famous poets who already stood in good repute, — for then, as always, I knew by heart everything that chanced in any degree to please me; but her complaisance was not of long duration. The first whom she outrageously abused were the poets of the Weisse school, who were just then often quoted with great applause, and had delighted me very particularly. If I looked more closely into the matter, I could not say she was wrong. I had sometimes even ventured to recite to her, though anonymously, some of my own poems; but these fared no better than the rest of the set. And thus, in a short time, the beautiful variegated meadows at the foot of the German Parnassus, where I was fond of luxuriating, were mercilessly mowed down; and I was even compelled to toss about the drying hay myself, and to ridicule that as lifeless which, a short time before, had given me such lively joy.

Without knowing it, Professor Morus came to strengthen her instructions. He was an uncommonly gentle and friendly man, with whom I became acquainted at the table of Hofrath Ludwig, and who received me very pleasantly when I begged the privilege of visiting him. Now, while making inquiries of him concerning antiquity, I did not conceal from him what delighted me among the moderns; when he spoke about such things with more calmness, but, what was still worse, with more profundity than Madame Böhme; and he thus opened my eyes, at first to my greatest chagrin, but afterward to my surprise, and at last to my edification.

Besides this, there came the Jeremiads, with which Gellert, in his course, was wont to warn us against poetry. He wished only for prose essays, and always criticised these first. Verses he treated as a sorry addition: and, what was the worst of all, even my prose found little favour in his eyes; for, after my old fashion, I used always to lay, as the foundation, a little romance, which I loved to work out in the epistolary form. The subjects were impassioned, the style went beyond ordinary prose, and the contents probably did not display any very deep knowledge of mankind in the author; and so I stood in very little favour with our professor, although he carefully looked over my labours as well as those of the others, corrected them with red ink, and here and there added a moral remark. Many leaves of this kind, which I kept for a long time with satisfaction, have unfortunately, in the course of years, at last disappeared from among my papers.

If elderly persons wish to play the pedagogue properly, they should neither prohibit nor render disagreeable to a young man anything which gives him pleasure, of whatever kind it may be, unless, at the same time, they have something else to put in its place, or can contrive a substitute. Everybody protested against my tastes and inclinations; and, on the other hand, what they commended to me lay either so far from me that I could not perceive its excellencies, or stood so near me that I thought it not a whit better than what they inveighed against. I thus became thoroughly perplexed on the subject, and promised myself the best results from a lecture of Ernesti's on " Cicero de Oratore." I learned something, indeed, from this lecture, but was not enlightened on the subject which particularly concerned me. What I demanded was a standard of opinion, and thought I perceived that nobody possessed it; for no one agreed with another, even when they brought forward examples: and where were we to get a settled judgment, when they managed to reckon up against a man like Wieland so many faults in his amiable writings, which so completely captivated us younger folks?

Amid this manifold distraction, this dismemberment of my existence and my studies, it happened that I took my dinners at Hofrath Ludwig's. He was a medical man, a botanist; and his company, with the exception of Morus, consisted of physicians just commencing or near the completion of their studies. Now, during these hours, I heard no other conversation than about medicine or natural history, and my imagination was drawn over into quite a new field. I heard the names of Haller, Linnæus, Buffon, mentioned with great respect; and, even if disputes often arose about mistakes into which it was said they had fallen, all agreed in the end to honour the acknowledged abundance of their merits. The subjects were entertaining and important, and enchained my attention. By degrees I became familiar with many names and a copious terminology, which I grasped more willingly as I was afraid to write down a rhyme, however spontaneously it presented itself, or to read a poem, for I was fearful that it might please me at the time, and that perhaps immediately afterward, like so much else, I should be forced to pronounce it bad.

This uncertainty of taste and judgment disquieted me more and more every day, so that at last I fell into despair. I had brought with me those of my youthful labours which I thought the best, partly because I hoped to get some credit by them, partly that I might be able to test my progress with greater certainty; but I found myself in the miserable situation in which one is placed when a complete change of mind is required, — a renunciation of all that one has hitherto loved and found good. However, after some time and many struggles, I conceived so great a contempt for my labours, begun and ended, that one day I burnt up poetry and prose, plans, sketches, and projects, all together on the kitchen hearth, and threw our good old landlady into no small fright and anxiety by the smoke which filled the whole house.

SEVENTH BOOK.

ABOUT the condition of German literature of those times so much has been written, and so exhaustively, that every one who takes any interest in it can be completely informed; in regard to it critics agree now pretty well; and what at present I intend to say piecemeal and disconnectedly concerning it, relates not so much to the way in which it was constituted in itself, as to its relation to me. I will therefore first speak of those things by which the public is particularly excited; of those two hereditary foes of all comfortable life, and of all cheerful, self-sufficient, living poetry, — I mean, satire and criticism.

In quiet times every one wants to live after his own fashion: the citizen will carry on his trade or his business, and enjoy the fruits of it afterward; thus will the author, too, willingly compose something, publish his labours, and, since he thinks he has done something good and useful, hope for praise, if not reward. In this tranquillity the citizen is disturbed by the satirist, the author by the critic; and peaceful society is thus put into a disagreeable agitation.

The literary epoch in which I was born was developed out of the preceding one by opposition. Germany, so long inundated by foreigners, interpenetrated by other nations, directed to foreign languages in learned and diplomatic transactions, could not possibly cultivate her own. Together with so many new ideas, innumerable foreign words were obtruded necessarily and unnecessarily upon her; and, even for objects already known, people were induced to make use of foreign expressions and turns of speech. The German, having run wild for nearly two hundred years in an unhappy tumultuary state, went to school with the French to learn manners, and with the Romans in order to express his thoughts with propriety. But this was to be done in the mother-tongue, when the literal application of those idioms, and their half-Germanisation, made both the social and business style ridiculous. Besides this, they adopted without moderation the similes of the southern languages, and employed them most extravagantly. In the same way they transferred the stately deportment of the prince-like citizens of Rome to the learned German small-town officers, and were at home nowhere, least of all with themselves.

But as in this epoch works of genius had already appeared, the German sense of freedom and joy also began to stir itself. This, accompanied by a genuine earnestness, insisted that men should write purely and naturally, without the intermixture of foreign words, and as common intelligible sense dictated. By these praiseworthy endeavours, however, the doors and gates were thrown open to an extended national insipidity, nay, — the dike was dug through by which the great deluge was shortly to rush in. Meanwhile, a stiff pedantry long stood its ground in all the four faculties, until at last, much later, it fled for refuge from one of them to another.

Men of parts, children of nature looking freely about them, had therefore two objects on which they could exercise themselves, against which they could labour, and, as the matter was of no great importance, give a vent to their petulance: these were, — a language disfigured by foreign words, forms, and turns of speech on the one hand, and the worthlessness of

such writings as had been careful to keep themselves
free from those faults on the other; though it occurred
to nobody, that, while they were battling against one
evil, the other was called on for assistance.

Liskow, a daring young man, first ventured to attack
by name a shallow, silly writer, whose awkward demeanour soon gave him an opportunity to proceed still
more severely. He then went farther, and constantly
aimed his scorn at particular persons and objects,
whom he despised and sought to render despicable, —
nay, even persecuted them with passionate hatred.
But his career was short; for he soon died, and was
gradually forgotten as a restless, irregular youth. The
talent and character shown in what he did, although
he had accomplished little, may have seemed valuable
to his countrymen; for the Germans have always
shown a peculiar pious kindliness to talents of good
promise, when prematurely cut off. Suffice it to say,
that Liskow was very soon praised and recommended
to us as an excellent satirist, who could have attained
a rank even above the universally beloved Rabener.
Here, indeed, we saw ourselves no better off than
before; for we could discover nothing in his writings
except that he had found the silly, silly, which seemed
to us quite a matter of course.

Rabener, well educated, grown up under good
scholastic instruction, of a cheerful, and by no means
passionate or malicious, disposition, took up general
satire. His censure of the so-called vices and follies
springs from the clear views of a quiet common sense,
and from a fixed moral conception of what the world
ought to be. His denunciation of faults and failings
is harmless and cheerful; and, in order to excuse even
the slight boldness of his writings, it is supposed that
the improving of fools by ridicule is no fruitless
undertaking.

Rabener's personal character will not easily appear

again. As an able, punctual man of business, he does his duty, and thus gains the good opinion of his fellow townsmen and the confidence of his superiors; along with which, he gives himself up to the enjoyment of a pleasant contempt for all that immediately surrounds him. Pedantic *literati*, vain youngsters, every sort of narrowness and conceit, he banters rather than satirises; and even his banter expresses no contempt. Just in the same way does he jest about his own condition, his misfortune, his life, and his death.

There is little of the æsthetic in the manner in which this writer treats his subjects. In external forms he is indeed varied enough, but throughout he makes too much use of direct irony; namely, in praising the blameworthy and blaming the praiseworthy, whereas this figure of speech should be used but extremely seldom; for, in the long run, it becomes annoying to clear-sighted men, perplexes the weak, while indeed it pleases the great middle class, who, without any special expense of mind, can fancy themselves more knowing than others. But whatever he brings before us, and however he does it, alike bears witness to his rectitude, cheerfulness, and equanimity; so that we always feel prepossessed in his favour. The unbounded applause of his own times was a consequence of such moral excellencies.

That people looked for originals to his general descriptions and found them, was natural; that individuals complained of him, followed from the above; his lengthy apologies that his satire is not personal, prove the spite it provoked. Some of his letters crown him at once as a man and an author. The confidential epistle in which he describes the siege of Dresden, and how he loses his house, his effects, his writings, and his wigs, without having his equanimity in the least shaken or his cheerfulness clouded, is highly valuable; although his contemporaries and fellow citizens could not forgive him his happy turn of mind. The letter where he speaks of the decay of his strength and of his approaching death is in the highest degree worthy of respect; and Rabener deserves to be honoured as a saint by all cheerful, intelligent men, who cheerfully resign themselves to earthly events.

I tear myself away from him reluctantly, yet I would make this remark: his satire refers throughout to the middle class; he lets us see here and there that he is also well acquainted with the higher ranks, but does not hold it advisable to come in contact with them. It may be said, that he has had no successor, that no one has been found who could consider himself equal or even similar to him.

Now for criticism! and first of all for the theoretic attempts. It is not going too far when we say that the ideal had, at that time, escaped out of the world into religion; it scarcely even made its appearance in moral philosophy; of a highest principle of art no one had a notion. They put Gottsched's "Critical Art of Poetry" into our hands; it was useful and instructive enough, for it gave us a historical information of all the kinds of poetry, as well as of rhythm and its different movements: the poetic genius was presupposed! But, besides that, the poet was to have acquirements and even learning: he should possess taste, and everything else of that kind. They directed us at last to Horace's "Art of Poetry:" we gazed at single golden maxims of this invaluable work, but did not know in the least what to do with it as a whole, or how we should use it.

The Swiss stepped forth as Gottsched's antagonists: they must take it into their heads to do something different, to accomplish something better; accordingly we heard that they were, in fact, superior. Breitinger's "Critical Art of Poetry" was taken in hand,

Here we reached a wider field, but, properly speaking, only a greater labyrinth, which was so much the more tiresome, as an able man, in whom we had confidence, was driving us about in it. Let a brief review justify these words.

For poetry in itself they had been able to find no fundamental axiom : it was too spiritual and too volatile. Painting, an art which one could hold fast with one's eyes and follow step by step with the external senses, seemed more favourable for such an end : the English and French had already theorised about plastic art; and, by a comparison drawn from this, it was thought that poetry might be grounded. The former presented images to the eye, the latter to the imagination : poetical images, therefore, were the first thing which was taken into consideration. People began with comparisons, descriptions followed, and only that was expressed which had always been apparent to the external senses.

Images, then! But where should these images be got except from nature ? The painter professedly imitated nature : why not the poet also ? But nature, as she lies before us, cannot be imitated : she contains so much that is insignificant and worthless, that one must make a selection; but what determines the choice ? one must select that which is important : but what is important ?

To answer this question, the Swiss may have taken a long time to consider; for they came to a notion, which is indeed singular, but clever, and even comical, inasmuch as they say, the new is always the most important : and after they have considered this for awhile, they discover that the marvellous is always newer than everything else.

They had now pretty well collected their poetical requisitions; but they had still to consider that the marvellous might also be empty, and without relation to man. But this relation, demanded as necessary, must be a moral one, from which the improvement of mankind should manifestly follow; and thus a poem had reached its utmost aim when, with everything else accomplished, it was useful besides. They now wished to test the different kinds of poetry according to all these requisites: those which imitated nature, besides being marvellous, and at the same time of a moral aim and use, were to rank as the first and highest. And, after much deliberation, this great preëminence was at last ascribed, with the highest degree of conviction, to Æsop's fables!

Strange as such a deduction may now appear, it had the most decided influence on the best minds. That Gellert and subsequently Lichtwer devoted themselves to this department, that even Lessing attempted to labour in it, that so many others turned their talents toward it, speaks for the confidence which this species of poetry had gained. Theory and practice always act upon each other: one can see from their works what is the men's opinion, and, from their opinions, predict what they will do.

Yet we must not dismiss our Swiss theory without doing it justice. Bodmer, with all the pains he took, remained theoretically and practically a child all his life. Breitinger was an able, learned, sagacious man, whom, when he looked rightly about him, the essentials of a poem did not all escape, — nay, it can be shown that he may have dimly felt the deficiencies of his system. Remarkable, for instance, is his query, "Whether a certain descriptive poem by König, on the 'Review-camp of Augustus the Second,' is properly a poem?" and the answer to it displays good sense. But it may serve for his complete justification that he, starting from a false point, on a circle almost run out already, still struck upon the main principle, and at the end of his book finds himself compelled to recommend as additions, so to speak, the representation of manners, character, passions, — in short, the whole inner man; to which, indeed, poetry preëminently belongs.

It may well be imagined into what perplexity young minds felt themselves thrown by such dislocated maxims, half-understood laws, and shivered-up dogmas. We adhered to examples, and there, too, were no better off; foreigners as well as the ancients stood too far from us; and from the best native poets always peeped out a decided individuality, to the good points of which we could not lay claim, and into the faults of which we could not but be afraid of falling. For him who felt anything productive in himself it was a desperate condition.

When one considers closely what was wanting in the German poetry, it was a material, and that, too, a national one: there was never a lack of talent. Here we make mention only of Günther, who may be called a poet in the full sense of the word. A decided talent, endowed with sensuousness, imagination, memory, the gifts of conception and representation, productive in the highest degree, ready at rhythm, ingenious, witty, and of varied information besides, — he possessed, in short, all the requisites for creating, by means of poetry, a second life within life, even within common real life. We admire the great facility with which, in his occasional poems, he elevates all circumstances by the feelings, and embellishes them with suitable sentiments, images, and historical and fabulous traditions. Their roughness and wildness belong to his time, his mode of life, and especially to his character, or, if one would have it so, his want of fixed character. He did not know how to curb himself; and so his life, like his poetry, melted away from him.

By his vacillating conduct, Günther had trifled away the good fortune of being appointed at the court of

Augustus the Second, where, in addition to every other species of ostentation, they were also looking about for a court-poet, who could give elevation and grace to their festivities, and immortalise a transitory pomp. Von König was more mannerly and more fortunate: he filled this post with dignity and applause.

In all sovereign states the material for poetry comes downwards from above; and "The Review-camp at Mühlberg" ("Das Lustlager bei Mühlberg") was, perhaps, the first worthy object, provincial, if not national, which presented itself to a poet. Two kings saluting one another in the presence of a great host, their whole courts and military state around them, well-appointed troops, a mock-fight, fêtes of all kinds, — this is business enough for the outward sense, and overflowing material for delineating and descriptive poetry.

This subject had, indeed, the internal defect, that it was only pomp and show, from which no real action could result. None except the very first distinguished themselves; and, even if they had done so, the poet could not render any one conspicuous lest he should offend the others. He had to consult the "Court and State Calender;" and the delineation of the persons therefore went off pretty dryly, — nay, even his contemporaries very strongly reproached him with having described the horses better than the men. But should not this redound to his credit, that he showed his art just where an object for it presented itself? The main difficulty, too, seems soon to have manifested itself to him, — since the poem never advanced beyond the first canto.

Amidst such studies and reflections, an unexpected event surprised me, and frustrated my laudable design of becoming acquainted with our new literature from the beginning. My countryman, John George Schlosser, after spending his academical years with industry and exertion, had repaired to Frankfort-on-the-Main, in the customary profession of an advocate; but his mind, aspiring and seeking after the universal, could not reconcile itself to this situation for many reasons. He accepted, without hesitation, an office as private secretary to the Duke Ludwig of Würtemberg, who resided in Treptow; for the prince was named among those great men who, in a noble and independent manner, purposed to enlighten themselves, their families, and the world, and to unite for higher aims. It was this Prince Ludwig who, to ask advice about the education of his children, had written to Rousseau, whose well-known answer began with the suspicious-looking phrase, " *Si j'avais le malheur d'être né prince.*"

Not only in the affairs of the prince, but also in the education of his children, Schlosser was now willingly to assist in word and deed, if not to superintend them. This noble young man, who harboured the best intentions and strove to attain a perfect purity of morals, would have easily kept men from him by a certain dry austerity, if his fine and rare literary cultivation, his knowledge of languages, and his facility at expressing himself by writing, both in verse and prose, had not attracted every one, and made living with him more agreeable. It had been announced to me that he would pass through Leipzig, and I expected him with longing. He came and put up at a little inn or wine-house that stood in the *Brühl* (Marsh), and the host of which was named Schönkopf. This man had a Frankfort woman for his wife; and although he entertained few persons during the rest of the year, and could lodge no guests in his little house, yet at fair-time he was visited by many Frankforters, who used to eat, and, in case of need, even take quarters, there also. Thither I hastened to find Schlosser, when he had sent to inform me of his arrival. I scarcely remembered having seen him before, and found a young, well-formed man, with a round, compressed face, without the features losing their sharpness on that account. The form of his rounded forehead, between black eyebrows and locks, indicated earnestness, sternness, and perhaps obstinacy. He was, in a certain measure, the opposite of myself; and this very thing doubtless laid the foundation of our lasting friendship. I had the greatest respect for his talents, the more so as I very well saw, that, in the certainty with which he acted and produced, he was completely my superior. The respect and the confidence which I showed him confirmed his affection, and increased the indulgence he was compelled to have for my lively, impetuous, and ever-excitable disposition, in such contrast with his own. He studied the English writers diligently : Pope, if not his model, was his aim ; and, in opposition to that author's "Essay on Man," he had written a poem in like form and measure, which was to give the Christian religion the triumph over the deism of the other work. From the great store of papers which he carried with him, he showed me poetical and prose compositions in all languages, which, as they challenged me to imitation, once more gave me infinite disquietude. Yet I contrived to get over it immediately by activity. I wrote German, French, English, and Italian poems, addressed to him, the subject-matter of which I took from our conversations, which were always important and instructive.

Schlosser did not wish to leave Leipzig without having seen face to face the men who had a name. I willingly took him to those I knew: with those whom I had not yet visited, I in this way became honourably acquainted; since he was received with distinction as a well-informed man of education, of already established character, and well knew how to pay for the outlay of conversation. I cannot pass over our visit we paid to Gottsched, as it exemplifies the character and manners of that man. He lived

very respectably in the first story of the Golden Bear,
where the elder Breitkopf, on account of the great
advantage which Gottsched's writings, translations, and
other aids had brought to the trade, had promised him
a lodging for life.

We were announced. The servant led us into a
large chamber, saying his master would come immediately. Now, whether we misunderstood a gesture
which he made, I cannot say: it is enough, we thought
he directed us into an adjoining room. We entered,
to witness a singular scene: for, on the instant, Gottsched, that tall, broad, gigantic man, came in at the
opposite door in a morning-gown of green damask
lined with red taffeta; but his monstrous head was
bald and uncovered. This, however, was to be immediately provided for: the servant rushed in at a side
door with a great full-bottomed wig in his hand (the
curls came down to the elbows), and handed the head-
ornament to his master with gestures of terror. Gottsched, without manifesting the least vexation, raised
the wig from the servant's arm with his left hand, and,
while he very dexterously swung it up on his head,
gave the poor fellow such a box on the ear with his
right paw, that the latter, as often happens in a comedy,
went spinning out at the door; whereupon the respectable old grandfather invited us quite gravely to be
seated, and kept up a pretty long discourse with good
grace.

As long as Schlosser remained in Leipzig, I dined
daily with him, and became acquainted with a very
pleasant set of boarders. Some Livonians, and the
son of Hermann (chief court-preacher in Dresden),
afterward burgomaster in Leipzig, and their tutor,
Hofrath Pfeil, author of the "Count von P.," a continuation of Gellert's "Swedish Countess;" Zachariä,
a brother of the poet; and Krebel, editor of geograph-
ical and genealogical manuals, — all these were polite,

cheerful, and friendly men. Zachariä was the most quiet; Pfeil, an elegant man, who had something almost diplomatic about him, yet without affectation, and with great good humour; Krebel, a genuine Falstaff, tall, corpulent, fair, with prominent, merry eyes, as bright as the sky, always happy and in good spirits. These persons all treated me in the most handsome manner, partly on Schlosser's account — partly, too, on account of my own frank good humour and obliging disposition; and it needed no great persuasion to make me partake of their table in future. In fact, I remained with them after Schlosser's departure, deserted Ludwig's table, and found myself so much the better off in this society, which was limited to a certain number, as I was very well pleased with the daughter of the family, a very neat, pretty girl, and had opportunities to exchange friendly glances with her, — a comfort which I had neither sought nor found by accident since the mischance with Gretchen. I spent the dinner-hours with my friends cheerfully and profitably. Krebel, indeed, loved me, and continued to tease me and stimulate me in moderation: Pfeil, on the contrary, showed his earnest affection for me by trying to guide and settle my judgment upon many points.

During this intercourse, I perceived through conversation, through examples, and through my own reflections, that the first step in delivering ourselves from the wishy-washy, long-winded, empty epoch, could be taken only by definiteness, precision, and brevity. In the style which had hitherto prevailed, one could not distinguish the commonplace from what was better; since all were brought down to a level with each other. Authors had already tried to escape from this wide-spread disease, with more or less success. Haller and Ramler were inclined to compression by nature: Lessing and Wieland were led to it by reflection. The former became by degrees quite epigrammatical in his poems, terse in " Minna," laconic in " Emilia Galotti," — it was not till afterward that he returned to that serene *naïveté* which becomes him so well in " Nathan." Wieland, who had been occasionally prolix in " Agathon," " Don Sylvio," and the " Comic Tales," becomes condensed and precise to a wonderful degree, as well as exceedingly graceful in " Musarion " and " Idris." Klopstock, in the first cantos of " The Messiah," is not without diffuseness : in his " Odes " and other minor poems he appears compressed, as also in his tragedies. By his emulation of the ancients, especially Tacitus, he sees himself constantly forced into narrower limits, by which he at last becomes obscure and unpalatable. Gerstenberg, a fine but eccentric talent, also distinguishes himself : his merit is appreciated, but on the whole he gives little pleasure. Gleim, diffuse and easy by nature, is scarcely once concise in his war-songs. Ramler is properly more a critic than a poet. He begins to collect what the Germans have accomplished in lyric poetry. He now finds, that scarcely one poem fully satisfies him : he must leave out, arrange, and alter, that the things may have some shape or other. By this means he makes himself almost as many enemies as there are poets and amateurs ; since every one, properly speaking, recognises himself only in his defects : and the public interests itself sooner for a faulty individuality than for that which is produced or amended according to a universal law of taste. Rhythm lay yet in the cradle, and no one knew of a method to shorten its childhood. Poetical prose came into the ascendant. Gessner and Klopstock excited many imitators : others, again, still demanded an intelligible metre, and translated this prose into rhythm. But even these gave nobody satisfaction, for they were obliged to omit and add ; and the prose originals always passed for the better of the two. But

While I now, like a shepherd on the Pleisse, was absorbed childishly enough in such tender subjects, and always chose only such as I could easily recall into my bosom, provision from a greater and more important side had long been made for German poets.

The first true and really vital material of the higher order came into German poetry through Frederick the Great and the deeds of the Seven Years' War. All national poetry must be shallow or become shallow which does not rest on that which is most universally human, — upon the events of nations and their shepherds, when both stand for one man. Kings are to be represented in war and danger, where, by that very means, they appear as the first, because they determine and share the fate of the very least, and thus become much more interesting than the gods themselves, who, when they have once determined the fates, withdraw from all participation in them. In this view of the subject, every nation, if it would be worth anything at all, must possess an epopee, to which the precise form of the epic poem is not necessary.

The war-songs started by Gleim maintain so high a rank among German poems, because they arose with and in the achievements which are their subject ; and because, moreover, their felicitous form, just as if a fellow combatant had produced them in the loftiest moments, makes us feel the most complete effectiveness.

Ramler sings the deeds of his king in a different and most noble manner. All his poems are full of matter, and occupy us with great, heart-elevating objects, and thus already maintain an indestructible value.

For the internal matter of the subject treated is the beginning and end of art. It will not, indeed, be denied that genius, that thoroughly cultivated artistical talent, can make everything out of everything by its method of treatment, and can subdue the most refractory material. But, when closely examined, the result is rather a trick of art than a work of art, which should rest upon a worthy object, that the treatment of it, by skill, pains, and industry, may present to us the dignity of the subject-matter only the more happily and splendidly.

The Prussians, and with them Protestant Germany, acquired thus for their literature a treasure which the opposite party lacked, and the want of which they have been able to supply by no subsequent endeavours. Upon the great idea which the Prussian writers might well entertain of their king, they first established themselves, and the more zealously as he, in whose name they did it all, wished once for all to know nothing about them. Already before this, through the French colony, afterward through the king's predilection for the literature of that nation and for their financial institutions, had a mass of French civilisation come into Prussia, which was highly advantageous to the Germans, since by it they were challenged to contradiction and resistance; thus the very aversion of Frederick from German was a fortunate thing for the formation of its literary character. They did everything to attract the king's attention, not indeed to be honoured, but only noticed, by him; yet they did it in German fashion, from an internal conviction; they did what they held to be right, and desired and wished that the king should recognise and prize this German uprightness. That did not and could not happen; for how can it be required of a king, who wishes to live and enjoy himself intellectually, that he shall lose his years in order to see what he thinks barbarous developed and rendered palatable too late? In matters of trade and manufacture, he might indeed force upon himself, but especially upon his people, very moderate substitutes instead of excellent foreign wares; but here everything comes to perfection more rapidly, and it needs not a man's lifetime to bring such things to maturity.

But I must here, first of all, make honourable mention of one work, the most genuine production of the Seven Years' War, and of perfect North German nationality: it is the first theatrical production caught from the important events of life, one of specific, temporary value, and one which therefore produced an incalculable effect, — "Minna von Barnhelm." Lessing, who, in opposition to Klopstock and Gleim, was fond of casting off his personal dignity, because he was confident that he could at any moment grasp and take it up again, delighted in a dissipated life in taverns and the world, as he always needed a strong counterpoise to his powerfully labouring interior; and for this reason, also, he had joined the suite of General Tauentzien. One easily discovers how the above-mentioned piece was generated betwixt war and peace, hatred and affection. It was this production which happily opened the view into a higher, more significant, world, from the literary and citizen world in which poetic art had hitherto moved.

The intense hatred in which the Prussians and Saxons stood toward each other during this war could not be removed by its termination. The Saxon now first felt, with true bitterness, the wounds which the upstart Prussian had inflicted upon him. Political peace could not immediately reëstablish a peace between their dispositions. But this was to be brought about symbolically by the above mentioned drama. The grace and amiability of the Saxon ladies conquer the worth, the dignity, and the stubbornness of the Prussians; and, in the principal as well as in the subordinate characters, a happy union of bizarre and contradictory elements is artistically represented.

If I have put my reader in some perplexity by these cursory and desultory remarks on German literature, I have succeeded in giving them a conception of that chaotic condition in which my poor brain found itself, when, in the conflict of two epochs so important for the literary fatherland, so much that was new crowded in upon me before I could come to terms with the old, so much that was old yet made me feel its right over me, when I believed I had already cause to venture on renouncing it altogether. I will at present try to impart, as well as possible, the way I entered on to extricate myself from this difficulty, if only step by step.

The period of prolixity into which my youth had fallen, I had laboured through with genuine industry, in company with so many worthy men. The numerous quarto volumes of manuscript which I left behind with my father might serve for sufficient witnesses of this; and what a mass of essays, rough draughts, and half - executed designs, had, more from despondency than conviction, gone up in smoke! Now, through conversation, through instruction in general, through so many conflicting opinions, but especially through my fellow-boarder Hofrath Pfeil, I learned to value more and more the importance of the subject-matter and the conciseness of the treatment; without, however, being able to make it clear to myself where the former was to be sought, or how the latter was to be attained. For, what with the great narrowness of my situation; what with the indifference of my companions, the reserve of the professors, the exclusiveness of the educated inhabitants; and what with the perfect insignificance of the natural objects, — I was compelled to seek for everything within myself. Whenever I desired a true basis in feeling or reflection for my poems, I was forced to grasp into my own bosom; whenever I required for my poetic representation an immediate intuition of an object or an event, I could not step outside the circle which was fitted to teach me, and inspire me with an interest. In this view I wrote at first certain little poems, in the form of songs or in a freer measure: they are founded on reflection, treat of the past, and for the most part take an epigrammatic turn.

And thus began that tendency from which I could not deviate my whole life through; namely, the tendency to turn into an image, into a poem, everything that delighted or troubled me, or otherwise occupied me, and to come to some certain understanding with myself upon it, that I might both rectify my conceptions of external things, and set my mind at rest about them. The faculty of doing this was necessary to no one more than to me, for my natural disposition whirled me constantly from one extreme to the other. All, therefore, that has been confessed by me, consists of fragments of a great confession; and this little book is an attempt which I have ventured on to render it complete.

My early affection for Gretchen I had now transferred to one Annette (*Aennchen*), of whom I can say nothing more than that she was young, handsome, sprightly, loving, and so agreeable that she well deserved to be set up for a time in the shrine of the heart as a little saint, that she might receive all that reverence which it often causes more pleasure to bestow than to receive. I saw her daily without hinderance; she helped to prepare the meals I enjoyed; she brought, in the evening at least, the wine I drank; and indeed our select club of noonday boarders was a warranty that the little house, which was visited by few guests except during the fair, well merited its good reputation. Opportunity and inclination were found for various kinds of amusement. But, as she neither could nor dared go much out of the house, the pastime was somewhat limited. We sang the songs of Zachariä; played the "Duke Michael" of Krüger, in which a knotted handkerchief had to take the place of the nightingale; and so, for awhile, it went on quite tolerably. But since such connections, the more innocent they are, afford the less variety in the long run, I was seized with that wicked distemper which seduces us to derive amusement from the torment of a beloved one, and to domineer over a girl's devotedness with wanton and tyrannical caprice. My ill humour at the failure of my poetical attempts, at the apparent impossibility of coming to a clear understanding about them, and at everything else that might pinch me here and there, I thought I might vent on her, because she truly loved me with all her heart, and did whatever she could to please me. By unfounded and absurd fits of jealousy, I destroyed our most delightful days, both for myself and her. She endured it for a time with incredible patience, which I was cruel enough to try to the uttermost. But, to my shame and despair, I was at last forced to remark that her heart was alienated from me, and that I might now have good ground for the madness in which I had indulged without necessity and without cause. There were also terrible scenes between us, in which I gained nothing; and I then first felt that I had truly loved her, and could not bear to lose her. My passion grew, and assumed all the forms of which it is capable under such circumstances: nay, at last I even took up the rôle which the girl had hitherto played. I sought everything possible in order to be agreeable to her, even to procure her pleasure by means of others; for I could not renounce the hope of winning her again. But it was too late! I had lost her really; and the frenzy with which I revenged my fault upon myself, by assaulting in various frantic ways my physical nature, in order to inflict some hurt on my moral nature, contributed very much to the bodily maladies under which I lost some of the best years of my life: indeed, I should perchance have been completely ruined by this loss, had not my poetic talent here shown itself particularly helpful with its healing power.

Already, at many intervals before, I had clearly enough perceived my ill conduct. I really pitied the poor child, when I saw her so thoroughly wounded by me, without necessity. I pictured to myself so often and so circumstantially her condition and my own, and, as a contrast, the contented state of another couple in our company, that at last I could not forbear treating this situation dramatically, as a painful and instructive penance. Hence arose the oldest of my extant dramatic labours, the little piece entitled, " Die Laune des Verliebten " (" The Lover's Caprice "), in the simple nature of which one may at the same time perceive the impetus of a boiling passion.

But, before this, a deep, significant, impulsive world had already interested me. Through my adventure with Gretchen and its consequences, I had early looked into the strange labyrinths by which civil society is undermined. Religion, morals, law, rank, connections, custom, all rule only the surface of city existence. The streets, bordered by splendid houses, are kept neat; and every one behaves himself there properly enough : but, indoors, it often seems only so much the more disordered ; and a smooth exterior, like a thin coat of mortar, plasters over many a rotten wall that tumbles together overnight, and produces an effect the more frightful, as it comes into the midst of a condition of repose. A great many families, far and near, I had seen already, either overwhelmed in ruin or kept miserably hanging on the brink of it, by means of bankruptcies, divorces, seduced daughters, murders, house-robberies, poisonings ; and, young as I was, I had often, in such cases, lent a hand for help and preservation. For as my frankness awakened confidence ; as my secrecy was proved ; as my activity feared no sacrifice, and loved best to exert itself in the most dangerous affairs, — I had often enough found opportunity to mediate, to hush up, to divert the lightning-flash, with every other assistance of the kind; in the course of which, as well in my own person as through others, I could not fail to come to the knowledge of many afflicting and humiliating facts. To relieve myself I designed several plays, and wrote the arguments [1] of most of them. But since the intrigues were always obliged to be painful, and almost all these pieces threatened a tragical conclusion, I let them drop one after another. " Die Mitschuldigen " (" The Accomplices ") is the only one that was finished, the cheerful and burlesque tone of which upon the gloomy family-ground appears as if accompanied by something causing anxiety ; so that, on the whole, it is painful in representation, although it pleases in detached passages. The illegal deeds, harshly expressed, wound the æsthetic and moral feeling, and the piece could therefore find no favour on the German stage ; although the imitations of it, which steered clear of those rocks, were received with applause.

Both the above-mentioned pieces were, however, written from a more elevated point of view, without my having been aware of it. They direct us to a considerate forbearance in casting moral imputations, and in somewhat harsh and coarse touches sportively express that most Christian maxim, *Let him who is without sin among you cast the first stone.*

Through this earnestness, which cast a gloom over my first pieces, I committed the mistake of neglecting very favourable materials which lay quite decidedly in my natural disposition. In the midst of these serious, and, for a young man, fearful, experiences, was developed in me a reckless humour, which feels

---

[1] " *Exposition,*" in a dramatic sense, properly means a statement of the events which take place before the action of the play commences. — TRANS.

itself superior to the moment, and not only fears no danger, but rather wantonly courts it. The reason of this lay in the exuberance of spirits in which the vigorous time of life so much delights, and which, if it manifests itself in a frolicsome way, causes much pleasure, both at the moment and in remembrance. These things are so usual, that, in the vocabulary of our young university friends, they are called *Suites*; and, on account of the close similarity of signification, to say "play *suites*," means just the same as to "play pranks."[1]

Such humourous acts of daring, brought on the theatre with wit and sense, are of the greatest effect. They are distinguished from intrigue, inasmuch as they are momentary, and that their aim, whenever they are to have one, must not be remote. Beaumarchais has seized their full value, and the effects of his "Figaro" spring preëminently from this. Whereas such good-humoured roguish and half-knavish pranks are practised with personal risk for noble ends, the situations which arise from them are æsthetically and morally considered of the greatest value for the theatre; as, for instance, the opera of "The Water-Carrier" treats perhaps the happiest subject which we have ever yet seen upon the stage.

To enliven the extreme tedium of daily life, I played off numberless tricks of the sort, partly without any aim at all, partly in the service of my friends, whom I liked to please. For myself, I could not say that I had once acted in this designedly, nor did I ever happen to consider a feat of the kind as a subject for art. Had I, however, seized upon and elaborated such materials, which were so close at hand, my earliest labours would have been more cheerful and available. Some incidents

---

[1] The real meaning of the passage is, that the idiom "*Possen reissen*" is used also with the university word "Suite," so that one can say "*Suiten reissen.*" — TRANS.

of this kind occur indeed later, but isolated and without design. For since the heart always lies nearer to us than the head, and gives us trouble, whereas the latter knows how to set matters to rights, the affairs of the heart had always appeared to me as the most important. I was never weary of reflecting upon the transient nature of attachments, the mutability of human character, moral sensuality, and all the heights and depths, the combination of which in our nature may be considered as the riddle of human life. Here, too, I sought to get rid of that which troubled me, in a song, an epigram, in some kind of rhyme; which, since they referred to the most private feelings and the most peculiar circumstances, could scarcely interest any one but myself. In the meantime, my external position had very much changed after the lapse of a short time. Madame Böhme, after a long and melancholy illness, had at last died: she had latterly ceased to admit me to her presence. Her husband could not be very much satisfied with me: I seemed to him not sufficiently industrious, and too frivolous. He especially took it very ill of me, when it was told him, that at the lectures on German Public Law, instead of taking proper notes, I had been drawing on the margin of my note-book the personages presented to our notice in them, such as the president of the chamber, the moderators and assessors, in strange wigs; and by this drollery had disturbed my attentive neighbours and set them laughing. After the loss of his wife he lived still more retired than before, and at last I shunned him in order to avoid his reproaches. But it was peculiarly unfortunate that Gellert would not use the power which he might have exercised over us. Indeed, he had not time to play the father-confessor, and to inquire after the character and faults of everybody: he therefore took the matter very much in the lump, and thought to curb us by means of the church forms. For this reason he commonly, when he admitted us to his presence, used to lower his little head, and, in his weeping, winning voice, to ask us whether we went regularly to church, who was our confessor, and whether we took the holy communion? If we came off badly at this examination, we were dismissed with lamentations: we were more vexed than edified, yet could not help loving the man heartily.

On this occasion I cannot forbear recalling somewhat of my earlier youth, in order to make it obvious that the great affairs of the ecclesiastical religion must be carried on with order and coherence, if they are to prove as fruitful as is expected. The Protestant service has too little fulness and consistency to be able to hold the congregation together; hence it easily happens that members secede from it, and either form little congregations of their own, or, without ecclesiastical connection, quietly carry on their citizen-life side by side. Thus for a considerable time complaints were made that churchgoers were diminishing from year to year, and, just in the same ratio, the persons who partook of the Lord's Supper. With respect to both, but especially the latter, the cause lies close at hand; but who dares to speak it out? We will make the attempt.

In moral and religious, as well as in physical and civil, matters, man does not like to do anything on the spur of the moment; he needs a sequence from which results habit; what he is to love and to perform, he cannot represent to himself as single or isolated; and, if he is to repeat anything willingly, it must not have become strange to him. If the Protestant worship lacks fulness in general, so let it be investigated in detail, and it will be found that the Protestant has too few sacraments, — nay, indeed, he has only one in which he is himself an actor, — the Lord's Supper; for baptism he sees only when it is performed on others,

and is not greatly edified by it. The sacraments are
the highest part of religion, the symbols to our senses
of an extraordinary divine favour and grace. In the
Lord's Supper earthly lips are to receive a divine
Being embodied, and partake of a heavenly under the
form of an earthly nourishment. This import is the
same in all kinds of Christian churches: whether
the sacrament is taken with more or less submission
to the mystery, with more or less accommodation as to
that which is intelligible, it always remains a great,
holy thing, which in reality takes the place of the
possible or the impossible, the place of that which
man can neither attain nor do without. But such
a sacrament should not stand alone: no Christian can
partake of it with the true joy for which it is given, if
the symbolical or sacramental sense is not fostered
within him. He must be accustomed to regard the
inner religion of the heart and that of the external
church as perfectly one, as the great universal sacrament, which again divides itself into so many others,
and communicates to these parts its holiness, inde-
structibleness, and eternity.

Here a youthful pair join hands, not for a passing
salutation or for the dance: the priest pronounces his
blessing upon them, and the bond is indissoluble. It
is not long before this wedded pair bring a likeness to
the threshold of the altar: it is purified with holy
water, and so incorporated into the Church that it cannot forfeit this benefit but through the most monstrous
apostasy. The child in the course of life goes on pro-
gressing in earthly things of his own accord, in heavenly things he must be instructed. Does it prove on
examination that this has been fully done, he is now
received into the bosom of the Church as an actual
citizen, as a true and voluntary professor, not without
outward tokens of the weightiness of this act. Now,
only, he is decidedly a Christian, now for the first time

he knows his advantages and also his duties. But, in the meantime, a great deal that is strange has happened to him as a man: through instruction and affliction he has come to know how critical appears the state of his inner self, and there will constantly be a question of doctrines and of transgressions; but punishment shall no longer take place. For here, in the infinite confusion in which he must entangle himself, amid the conflict of natural and religious claims, an admirable expedient is given him, in confiding his deeds and misdeeds, his infirmities and doubts, to a worthy man, appointed expressly for that purpose, who knows how to calm, to warn, to strengthen him, to chasten him likewise by symbolical punishments, and at last, by a complete washing away of his guilt, to render him happy, and to give him back, pure and cleansed, the tablet of his manhood. Thus prepared and purely set at rest by several sacramental acts, which on closer examination branch forth again into minuter sacramental traits, he kneels down to receive the host; and, that the mystery of this high act may be still enhanced, he sees the chalice only in the distance: it is no common eating and drinking that satisfies, it is a heavenly feast, which makes him thirst after heavenly drink.

Yet let not the youth believe that this is all he has to do! let not even the man believe it. In earthly relations we are at last accustomed to depend on ourselves; and, even there, knowledge, understanding, and character will not always suffice: in heavenly things, on the contrary, we have never finished learning. The higher feeling within us, which often finds itself not even truly at home, is, besides, oppressed by so much from without, that our own power hardly administers all that is necessary for counsel, consolation, and help. But, to this end, that remedy is instituted for our whole life; and an intelligent, pious man is continually waiting to show the right way to the wanderers, and to relieve the distressed.

And what has been so well tried through the whole life, is now to show forth all its healing power with tenfold activity at the gate of Death. According to a trustful custom, inculcated from youth upwards, the dying man receives with fervour those symbolical, significant assurances; and there, where every earthly warranty fails, he is assured, by a heavenly one, of a blessed existence for all eternity. He feels perfectly convinced that neither a hostile element nor a malignant spirit can hinder him from clothing himself with a glorified body, so that, in immediate relation with the Godhead, he may partake of the boundless happiness which flows forth from him.

Then, in conclusion, that the whole may be made holy, the feet also are anointed and blessed. They are to feel, even in the event of possible recovery, a repugnance to touching this earthly, hard, impenetrable soil. A wonderful elasticity is to be imparted to them, by which they spurn from under them the clod of earth which hitherto attracted them. And so, through a brilliant cycle of equally holy acts, the beauty of which we have only briefly hinted at, the cradle and the grave, however far asunder they may chance to be, are joined in one continuous circle.

But all these spiritual wonders spring not, like other fruits, from the natural soil, where they can neither be sown nor planted nor cherished. We must supplicate for them from another region, — a thing which cannot be done by all persons nor at all times. Here we meet the highest of these symbols, derived from pious tradition. We are told that one man may be more favoured, blessed, and sanctified from above than another. But, that this may not appear as a natural gift, this great boon, bound up with a heavy duty, must be communicated to others by one authorised person to another; and the greatest good that a man can attain, without his having to obtain it by his own wrestling or grasping, must be preserved and perpetuated on earth by spiritual inheritance. In the very ordination of the priest is comprehended all that is necessary for the effectual solemnising of those holy acts by which the multitude receive grace, without any other activity being needful on their part than that of faith and implicit confidence. And thus the priest joins the line of his predecessors and successors, in the circle of those anointed with him, representing the highest source of blessings, so much the more gloriously, as it is not he, the priest, whom we reverence, but his office; it is not his nod to which we bow the knee, but the blessing which he imparts, and which seems the more holy, and to come the more immediately from heaven, because the earthly instrument cannot at all weaken or invalidate it by its own sinful, nay, wicked, nature.

How is this truly spiritual connection shattered to pieces in Protestantism, by part of the above-mentioned symbols being declared apocryphal, and only a few canonical! and how, by their indifference to one of these, will they prepare us for the high dignity of the others?

In my time I had been confided to the religious instruction of a good old infirm clergyman, who had been confessor of the family for many years. The "Catechism," a "Paraphrase" of it, and the "Scheme of Salvation," I had at my fingers' ends. I lacked not one of the strongly proving Biblical texts, but from all this I reaped no fruit; for, as they assured me that the honest old man arranged his chief examination according to an old set form, I lost all pleasure and inclination for the business, spent the last week in all sorts of diversions, laid in my hat the loose leaves borrowed from an older friend, who had gotten them from the clergyman, and unfeelingly and senselessly read aloud all that I should have known how to utter with feeling and conviction.

But I found my good intention and my aspirations in this important matter still more paralysed by a dry, spiritless routine, when I was now to approach the confessional. I was indeed conscious of having many failings, but no great faults; and that very consciousness diminished them, since it directed me to the moral strength which lay within me, and which, with resolution and perseverance, was at last to become master over the old Adam. We were taught that we were much better than the Catholics for the very reason that we were not obliged to confess anything in particular in the confessional, — nay, that this would not be at all proper, even if we wished to do it. I did not like this at all; for I had the strangest religious doubts, which I would readily have had cleared up on such an occasion. Now, as this was not to be done, I composed a confession for myself, which, while it well expressed my state of mind, was to confess to an intelligent man, in general terms, that which I was forbidden to tell him in detail. But when I entered the old choir of the Barefoot Friars, when I approached the strange latticed closets in which the reverend gentlemen used to be found for that purpose, when the sexton opened the door for me, when I now saw myself shut up in the narrow place face to face with my spiritual grandsire, and he bade me welcome with his weak, nasal voice, all the light of my mind and heart was extinguished at once, the well-conned confession-speech would not cross my lips. In my embarrassment I opened the book in my hand, and read from it the first short form I saw, which was so general, that anybody might have spoken it with quite a safe conscience. I received absolution, and withdrew neither warm nor cold; went the next day with my parents to the table of the Lord, and for a few days behaved myself as was becoming after so holy an act.

In the sequel, however, there came over me that evil, which, from the fact of our religion being complicated by various dogmas, and founded on texts of Scripture which admit of several interpretations, attacks scrupulous men in such a manner that it brings on a hypochondriacal condition, and raises this to its highest point, to fixed ideas. I have known several men, who, though their manner of thinking and living was perfectly rational, could not free themselves from thinking about the sin against the Holy Ghost, and from the fear that they had committed it. A similar trouble threatened me on the subject of the communion; for the text, that one who unworthily partakes of the sacrament eateth and drinketh damnation to himself, had, very early, already made a monstrous impression upon me. Every fearful thing that I had read in the histories of the Middle Ages, of the judgments of God, of those most strange ordeals, by red-hot iron, flaming fire, swelling water, and even what the Bible tells us of the draught which agrees well with the innocent, but puffs up and bursts the guilty, — all this pictured itself to my imagination, and formed itself into the most frightful combinations; since false vows, hypocrisy, perjury, blasphemy, all seemed to weigh down the unworthy person at this most holy act, which was so much the more horrible, as no one could dare to pronounce himself worthy: and the forgiveness of sins, by which everything was to be at last done away, was found limited by so many conditions, that one could not with certainty dare appropriate it to one's self.

This gloomy scruple troubled me to such a degree, and the expedient which they would represent to me as sufficient seemed so bald and feeble, that it gave the bugbear only a more fearful aspect; and, as soon as I had reached Leipzig, I tried to free myself altogether from my connection with the Church. How oppressive, then, must have been to me the exhortations of Gellert, whom, considering the generally laconic style with which he was obliged to repel our obtrusiveness, I was unwilling to trouble with such singular questions, and the less so as in my more cheerful hours I was myself ashamed of them, and at last left completely behind me this strange anguish of conscience, together with church and altar.

Gellert, in accordance with his pious feelings, had composed for himself a course of ethics, which from time to time he publicly read, and thus in an honourable manner acquitted himself of his duty to the public. Gellert's writings had already, for a long time, been the foundation of German moral culture, and every one anxiously wished to see that work printed; but, as this was not to be done till after the good man's death, people thought themselves very fortunate to hear him deliver it himself in his lifetime. The philosophical auditorium [1] was at such times crowded, and the beautiful soul, the pure will, and the interest of the noble man in our welfare, his exhortations, warnings, and entreaties, uttered in a somewhat hollow and sorrowful tone, made indeed an impression for the moment; but this did not last long, the less so as there were many scoffers, who contrived to make us suspicious of this tender and, as they thought, enervating manner. I remember a Frenchman travelling through the town, who asked what were the maxims and opinions of the man who attracted such an immense concourse. When we had given him the necessary information, he shook his head, and said, smiling, " *Laissez le faire, il nous forme des dupes.*"

And thus also did good society, which cannot easily

---

[1] The lecture-room. The word is also used in university language to denote a professor's audience.

endure anything worthy near it, know how to spoil, on occasion, the moral influence which Gellert might have had upon us. Now it was taken ill of him that he instructed the Danes of distinction and wealth, who were particularly recommended to him, better than the other students, and had a marked solicitude for them; now he was charged with selfishness and nepotism for causing a *table d'hôte* to be established for these young men at his brother's house. This brother, a tall, good-looking, blunt, unceremonious, and somewhat coarse man, had, it was said, been a fencing-master; and, notwithstanding the too great lenity of his brother, the noble boarders were often treated harshly and roughly: hence the people thought they must again take the part of these young folks, and pulled about the good reputation of the excellent Gellert to such a degree, that, in order not to be mistaken about him, we became indifferent toward him, and visited him no more; yet we always saluted him in our best manner when he came riding along on his tame gray horse. This horse the elector had sent him, to oblige him to take an exercise so necessary for his health, — a distinction for which he was not easily to be forgiven.

And thus, by degrees, the epoch approached when all authority was to vanish from before me, and I was to become suspicious, — nay, to despair, even — of the greatest and best individuals, whom I had known or imagined.

Frederick the Second still stood at the head of all the distinguished men of the century in my thoughts; and it must therefore have appeared very surprising to me, that I could praise him as little before the inhabitants of Leipzig as formerly in my grandfather's house. They had felt the hand of war heavily, it is true; and therefore they were not to blame for not thinking the best of him who had begun and continued it. They, therefore, were willing to let him pass as a distinguished, but by no means as a great man. "There was no art," they said, "in performing something with great means; and, if one spares neither lands nor money nor blood, one may well accomplish one's purpose at last. Frederick had shown himself great in none of his plans, and in nothing that he had, properly speaking, undertaken. So long as it depended on himself, he had only gone on making blunders, and what was extraordinary in him had only come to light when he was compelled to make these blunders good again. It was purely from this that he had obtained his great reputation; since every man wishes for himself that same talent of making good, in a clever way, the blunders which he frequently commits. If one goes through the Seven Years' War, step by step, it will be found that the king quite uselessly sacrificed his fine army, and that it was his own fault that this ruinous feud had been protracted to so great a length. A truly great man and general would have got the better of his enemies much sooner." In support of these opinions they could cite infinite details, which I did not know how to deny; and I felt the unbounded reverence which I had devoted to this remarkable prince, from my youth upwards, gradually cooling away.

As the inhabitants of Leipzig had now destroyed for me the pleasant feeling of revering a great man; so did a new friend, whom I gained at the time, very much diminish the respect which I entertained for my present fellow citizens. This friend was one of the strangest fellows in the world. He was named Behrisch, and was tutor to the young Count Lindenau. Even his exterior was singular enough. Lean and well-built, far advanced in the thirties, a very large nose, and altogether marked features; he wore from morning till night a scratch which might well have been called a peruke, but dressed himself very neatly, and never went out but with his sword by his side and his hat under his arm. He was one of those men who have quite a peculiar gift of killing time, or, rather, who know how to make something out of nothing, in order to pass time away. Everything he did had to be done with slowness, and with a certain deportment which might have been called affected if Behrisch had not even by nature had something affected in his manner. He resembled an old Frenchman, and also spoke and wrote French very well and easily. His greatest delight was to busy himself seriously about drolleries, and to follow up without end any silly notion. Thus he was constantly dressed in gray; and as the different parts of his attire were of different material, and also of different shades, he could reflect for whole days as to how he should procure one gray more for his body, and was happy when he had succeeded in this, and could put to shame us who had doubted it, or had pronounced it impossible. He then gave us long, severe lectures about our lack of inventive power, and our want of faith in his talents.

For the rest, he had studied well, was particularly versed in the modern languages and their literature, and wrote an excellent hand. He was very well disposed toward me; and I, having been always accustomed and inclined to the society of older persons, soon attached myself to him. My intercourse served him, too, for a special amusement; since he took pleasure in taming my restlessness and impatience, with which, on the other hand, I gave him enough to do. In the art of poetry he had what is called taste, — a certain general opinion about the good and bad, the mediocre and tolerable; but his judgment was rather censorious, and he destroyed even the little faith in contemporary writers which I cherished within me, by unfeeling remarks, which he knew how to advance with wit and humour, about the writings and poems of this man and that. He received my productions with indulgence, and let me have my own way, but only on the condition that I should have nothing printed. He promised me, on the other hand, that he himself would copy those pieces which he thought good, and would present me with them in a handsome volume. This undertaking now afforded an opportunity for the greatest possible waste of time. For before he could find the right paper, before he could make up his mind as to the size, before he had settled the breadth of the margin and the form of handwriting, before the crow-quills were provided and cut into pens, and Indian ink was rubbed, whole weeks passed, without the least bit having been done. With just as much ado he always set about his writing, and really, by degrees, put together a most charming manuscript. The title of the poems was in German text; the verses themselves in a perpendicular Saxon hand; and at the end of every poem was an analogous vignette, which he had either selected somewhere or other, or had invented himself, and in which he contrived to imitate very neatly the hatching of the wood-cuts and tail-pieces which are used for such purposes. To show me these things as he went on, to celebrate beforehand in a comico-pathetical manner my good fortune in seeing myself immortalised in such exquisite handwriting, and that in a style which no printing-press could attain, gave another occasion for passing the most agreeable hours. In the meantime, his intercourse was always secretly instructive, by reason of his liberal acquirements, and, as he knew how to subdue my restless, impetuous disposition, was also quite wholesome for me in a moral sense. He had, too, quite a peculiar abhorrence of roughness; and his jests were always quaint without ever falling into the coarse or the trivial. He indulged himself in a distorted aversion from his countrymen, and described with ludicrous touches even what they were able to undertake. He was particularly inexhaustible in a comical representation of individual persons, as he found something to find fault with in the exterior of every one. Thus, when we lay together at the window, he could occupy himself for hours criticising the passers-by, and, when he had censured them long enough, in showing exactly and circumstantially how they ought to have dressed themselves, ought to have walked, and ought to have behaved, to look like orderly people. Such attempts, for the most part, ended in something improper and absurd; so that we did not so much laugh at how the man looked, but at how, perchance, he might have looked had he been mad enough to caricature himself. In all such matters, Behrisch went quite unmercifully to work, without being in the slightest degree malicious. On the other hand, we knew how to tease him, on our side, by assuring him that, to judge from his exterior, he must be taken, if not for a French dancing-master, at least for the academical teacher of the language. This reproval was usually the signal for dissertations an hour long, in which he used to set forth the difference, wide as the heavens, which there was between him and an old Frenchman. At the same time he commonly imputed to us all sorts of awkward attempts, that we might possibly have made for the alteration and modification of his wardrobe.

My poetical compositions, which I only carried on the more zealously as the transcript went on becoming more beautiful and more careful, now inclined altogether to the natural and the true; and if the subjects could not always be important, I nevertheless always endeavoured to express them clearly and pointedly, the more so as my friend often gave me to understand what a great thing it was to write down a verse on Dutch paper, with the crow-quill and Indian ink;

what time, talent, and exertion it required, which ought not to be squandered on anything empty and superfluous. He would, at the same time, open a finished parcel, and circumstantially to explain what ought not to stand in this or that place, or congratulate us that it actually did not stand there. He then spoke with great contempt of the art of printing, mimicked the compositor, ridiculed his gestures and his hurried picking out of letters here and there, and derived from this manœuvre all the calamities of literature. On the other hand, he extolled the grace and noble posture of a writer, and immediately sat down himself to exhibit it to us; while he rated us at the same time for not demeaning ourselves at the writing-table precisely after his example and model. He now reverted to the contrast with the compositor, turned a begun letter upside down, and showed how unseemly it would be to write anything from the bottom to the top, or from the right to the left, with other things of like kind with which whole volumes might have been filled.

With such harmless fooleries we squandered our precious time; while it could have occurred to none of us, that anything would chance to proceed out of our circle which would awaken a general sensation and bring us into not the best repute.

Gellert may have taken little pleasure in his " Practicum;" and if, perhaps, he took pleasure in giving some directions as to prose and poetical style, he did it most privately only to a few, among whom we could not number ourselves. Professor Clodius thought to fill the gap which thus arose in the public instruction. He had gained some renown in literature, criticism, and poetry, and, as a young, lively, obliging man, found many friends, both in the university and in the city. Gellert himself referred us to the lectures now commenced by him; and, as far as the principal matter was concerned, we remarked little difference. He, too, only criticised details, corrected likewise with red ink; and one found one's self in company with mere blunders, without a prospect as to where the right was to be sought. I had brought to him some of my little labours, which he did not treat harshly. But just at this time they wrote to me from home, that I must without fail furnish a poem for my uncle's wedding. I felt far removed from that light and frivolous period in which a similar thing would have given me pleasure; and, since I could get nothing out of the actual circumstance itself, I determined to trick out my work in the best manner with extraneous ornament. I therefore convened all Olympus to consult about the marriage of a Frankfort lawyer, and seriously enough, to be sure, as well became the festival of such an honourable man. Venus and Themis had quarrelled for his sake; but a roguish prank, which Amor played the latter, gained the suit for the former: and the gods decided in favour of the marriage.

My work by no means displeased me. I received from home a handsome letter in its praise, took the trouble to have another fair copy, and hoped to extort some applause from my professor also. But here I had missed my aim. He took the matter severely; and as he did not notice the tone of parody, which nevertheless lay in the notion, he declared the great expenditure of divine means for such an insignificant human end in the highest degree reprehensible; inveighed against the use and abuse of such mythological figures, as a false habit originating in pedantic times; found the expression now too high, now too low; and, in divers particulars, had indeed not spared the red ink, though he asserted that he had yet done too little.

Such pieces were read out and criticised anonymously, it is true; but we used to watch each other, and it remained no secret that this unfortunate assembly of the gods was my work : yet since his critique, when I took his point of view, seemed to be perfectly just, and those divinities more nearly inspected were in fact only hollow shadow-forms, I cursed all Olympus, flung the whole mythic Pantheon away ; and from that time Amor and Luna have been the only divinities which at all appear in my little poems.

Among the persons whom Behrisch had chosen as the butts of his wit, Clodius stood just at the head ; nor was it hard to find a comical side in him. Being of small stature, rather stout and thick-set, he was violent in his motions, somewhat impetuous in his utterances, and restless in his demeanour. In all this he differed from his fellow citizens, who, nevertheless, willingly put up with him on account of his good qualities, and the fine promise which he gave.

He was usually commissioned with the poems which had become necessary on festive occasions. In the so-called "Ode," he followed the manner employed by Ramler, whom, however, it alone suited. But Clodius, as an imitator, had especially marked the foreign words by means of which the poems of Ramler come forth with a majestic pomp, which because it is conformable to the greatness of his subject and the rest of his poetic treatment, produces a very good effect on the ear, feelings, and imagination. In Clodius, on the contrary, these expressions had a heterogeneous air ; since his poetry was in other respects not calculated to elevate the mind in any manner.

Now, we had often been obliged to see such poems printed and highly lauded in our presence ; and we found it highly offensive, that he who had sequestered the heathen gods from us, now wished to hammer together another ladder to Parnassus out of Greek and Roman word-rungs. These oft-recurring expressions stamped themselves firmly on our memory ; and in a merry hour, when we were eating some most excellent cakes in the kitchen-gardens (*Kohlgärten*), it all at once struck me to put together these words of might and power, in a poem on the cake-baker Hendel. No sooner thought than done! And let it stand here too, as it was written on the wall of the house with a lead-pencil.

"O Hendel, dessen Ruhm vom *Süd* zum *Norden* reicht,
Vernimm den *Päan* der zu deinen Ohren steigt.
Du bäckst was *Gallien* und *Britten* emsig suchen,
Mit *schöpfrischen Genie, originelle* Kuchen.
Des Kaffee's *Ocean*, der sich vor dir ergiesst,
Ist süsser als der Saft der vom *Hymettus* fliesst.
Dein Haus ein *Monument*, wie wir den Künsten lohnen
Umhangen mit *Trophän*, erzählt den *Nationen:*
Auch ohne *Diadem* fand Hendel hier sein Glück
Und raubte dem *Cothurn* gar manch Achtgroschenstück.
Glänzt deine *Urn* dereinst in majestäts'chen *Pompe*,
Dann weint der *Patriot* an deinem *Katacombe.*
Doch leb! dein *Torus* sey von edler Brut ein *Nest*,
Steh' hoch wie der *Olymp*, wie der *Parnassus* fest!
Kein *Phalanx* Griechenland mit römischen *Ballisten*
Vermög *Germanien* und Hendel zu verwüsten.
Dein *Wohl* is unser *Stolz*, dein *Leiden* unser *Schmerz*,
Und Hendel's *Tempel ist der Musensöhne Herz.*" [1]

[1] The humour of the above consists, not in the thoughts, but in the particular words employed. These have no remarkable effect in English, as to us the words of Latin origin are often as familiar as those which have Teutonic roots; and these form the chief peculiarity of the style. We have therefore given the poem in the original language, with the peculiar words (as indicated by Goethe) in italics, and subjoined a literal translation. It will be observed that we have said that the peculiarity consists *chiefly*, not *solely*, in the use of the foreign words; for there are two or three instances of unquestionably German words, which are italicised on account of their high-sounding pomp.
"O Hendel, whose fame extends from *south* to *north*, hear the *pæan* which ascends to thine ears! Thou bakest that which *Gauls* and *Britons* industriously seek, (thou bakest) with *creative genius original* cakes. The *ocean* of coffee which pours itself out before thee is sweeter than the juice which flows from *Hymettus*. Thy house, a *monument*, how we reward the arts, hung round with *trophies*, tells the *nations:* 'Even without a *diadem*, Hendel formed his fortune here, and robbed the *Cothurnus* of many an eight-groschen-piece.' When thy *urn* shines hereafter in majestic

This poem had its place for a long time among many others which disfigured the walls of that room, without being noticed; and we, who had sufficiently amused ourselves with it, forgot it altogether amongst other things. A long time afterward, Clodius came out with his "Medon," whose wisdom, magnanimity, and virtue we found infinitely ridiculous, much as the first representation of the piece was applauded. That evening, when we met together in the wine-house, I made a prologue in doggerel verse, in which Harlequin steps out with two great sacks, places them on each side of the *proscenium*, and, after various preliminary jokes, tells the spectators in confidence, that in the two sacks moral æsthetic dust is to be found, which the actors will very frequently throw into their eyes. One, to wit, was filled with good deeds, that cost nothing; and the other with splendidly expressed opinions, that had no meaning behind them. He reluctantly withdrew, and sometimes came back, earnestly exhorted the spectators to attend to his warning and shut their eyes, reminded them that he had always been their friend, and meant well with them, with many more things of the kind. This prologue was acted in the room, on the spot, by friend Horn: but the jest remained quite among ourselves, not even a copy had been taken; and the paper was soon lost. However, Horn, who had performed the Harlequin very prettily, took it into his head to enlarge my poem to Hendel by several verses, and then to make it refer to "Medon." He read it to us: but we could not take any pleasure in it, for we did not find the additions even ingenious: while the first poem, being written for

pomp, then will the *patriot* weep at thy *catacomb*. But live! let thy bed (*torus*) be the *nest* of a noble brood, stand high as *Olympus*, and firm as *Parnassus*. May no *phalanx* of Greece with Roman *ballistæ* be able to destroy *Germania* and Hendel. Thy *weal* is our *pride*, thy *woe* our *pain*, and Hendel's *temple* is the *heart* of the *sons of the Muses*." — TRANS.

quite a different purpose, seemed to us disfigured. Our friend, displeased with our indifference, or rather censure, may have shown it to others, who found it new and amusing. Copies were now made of it, to which the reputation of Clodius's "Medon" gave at once a rapid publicity. Universal disapproval was the consequence, and the originators (it was soon found out that the poem had proceeded from our clique) were severely censured; for nothing of the sort had been seen since Cronegk's and Rost's attacks upon Gottsched. We had besides already secluded ourselves, and now found ourselves quite in the case of the owl with respect to the other birds. In Dresden, too, they did not like the affair; and it had for us serious, if not unpleasant, consequences. For some time, already, Count Lindenau had not been quite satisfied with his son's tutor. For although the young man was by no means neglected, and Behrisch kept himself either in the chamber of the young count, or at least close to it, when the instructors gave their daily lessons, regularly frequented the lectures with him, never went out in the daytime without him, and accompanied him in all his walks, yet the rest of us were always to be found in Apel's house, and joined them whenever they went on a pleasure ramble: this already excited some attention. Behrisch, too, accustomed himself to our society, and at last, toward nine o'clock in the evenings, generally transferred his pupil into the hands of the *valet de chambre*, and went in quest of us to the wine-house, whither, however, he never used to come but in shoes and stockings, with his sword by his side, and commonly his hat under his arm. The jokes and fooleries, which he generally started, went on *ad infinitum*. Thus, for instance, one of our friends had a habit of going away precisely at ten, because he had a connection with a pretty girl, with whom he could converse only at that hour. We did not like to lose him; and one evening, when we sat very happily together, Behrisch secretly determined that he would not let him off this time. At the stroke of ten, the other arose and took leave. Behrisch called after him, and begged him to wait a moment, as he was just going with him. He now began, in the most amusing manner, first to look after his sword, which stood just before his eyes, and in buckling it on behaved awkwardly, so that he could never accomplish it. He did this, too, so naturally, that no one took offence at it. But when, to vary the theme, he at last went farther, so that the sword came now on the right side, now between his legs, an universal laughter arose, in which the man in a hurry, who was likewise a merry fellow, chimed in, and let Behrisch have his own way till the happy hour was past, when, for the first time, there followed general pleasure and agreeable conversation till deep into the night.

Unfortunately Behrisch, and we through him, had a certain other propensity for some girls who were better than their reputation, — by which our own reputation could not be improved. We had often been seen in their garden ; and we directed our walks thither, even when the young count was with us. All this may have been treasured up, and at last communicated to his father : enough, he sought, in a gentlemanly manner, to get rid of the tutor, to whom the event proved fortunate. His good exterior, his knowledge and talents, his integrity, which no one could call in question, had won him the affection and esteem of distinguished persons, on whose recommendation he was appointed tutor to the hereditary Prince of Dessau, and at the court of a prince, excellent in every respect, found a solid happiness.

The loss of a friend like Behrisch was of the greatest consequence to me. He had spoiled while he cultivated me ; and his presence was necessary, if the pains he had thought good to spend upon me were in any degree to bring forth fruit for society. He knew how to engage me in all kinds of pretty and agreeable things, in whatever was just appropriate, and to bring out my social talents. But as I had gained no self-dependence in such things, so when I was alone again I immediately relapsed into my confused and crabbed disposition, which always increased, the more discontented I was with those about me, since I fancied that they were not contented with me. With the most arbitrary caprice, I took offence at what I might have considered an advantage; thus alienated many with whom I had hitherto been on a tolerable footing; and on account of the many disagreeable consequences which I had drawn on myself and others, whether by doing or leaving undone, by doing too much or too little, was obliged to hear the remark from my well-wishers, that I lacked experience. The same thing was told me by every person of sound sense who saw my productions, especially when these referred to the external world. I observed this as well as I could, but found in it little that was edifying, and was still forced to add enough of my own to make it only tolerable. I had often pressed my friend Behrisch, too, that he would make plain to me what was meant by experience? But, because he was full of nonsense, he put me off with fair words from one day to another, and at last, after great preparations, disclosed to me, that true experience was properly when one experiences how an experienced man must experience in experiencing his experience. Now, when we scolded him outrageously, and called him to account for this, he assured us that a great mystery lay hidden behind these words, which we could not comprehend until we had experienced . . . and so on without end, — for it cost him nothing to talk on in that way by the quarter of an hour, — since the experience would always become more experienced and at last come to true experience.

When we were about to despair at such fooleries, he protested that he had learned this way of making himself intelligible and impressive from the latest and greatest authors, who had made us observe how one can rest a restful rest, and how silence, in being silent, can constantly become more silent.

By chance an officer, who came among us on furlough, was praised in good company as a remarkable, sound-minded, and experienced man, who had fought through the Seven Years' War, and had gained universal confidence. It was not difficult for me to approach him, and we often went walking with each other. The idea of experience had almost become fixed in my brain, and the craving to make it clear to me passionate. Being of a frank disposition, I disclosed to him the uneasiness in which I found myself. He smiled, and was kind enough to tell me, as an answer to my question, something of his own life, and generally of the world immediately about us; from which, indeed, little better was to be gathered than that experience convinces us that our best thoughts, wishes, and designs are unattainable, and that he who fosters such vagaries, and advances them with eagerness, is especially held to be an experienced man.

Yet, as he was a gallant, good fellow, he assured me that he had himself not quite given up these vagaries, and felt himself tolerably well off with the little faith, love, and hope which remained. He then felt obliged to tell me a great deal about war, about the sort of life in the field, about skirmishes and battles, especially so far as he had taken part in them; when these vast events, by being considered in relation to a single individual, gained a very marvellous aspect. I then led him on to an open narration of the late situation of the court, which seemed to me quite like a tale. I heard of the bodily strength of Augustus the Second, of his many children and his vast expenses, then of his successor's love of art and of making collections; of Count Brühl and his boundless love of magnificence, which in detail appeared almost absurd, of his numerous banquets and gorgeous amusements, which were all cut off by Frederick's invasion of Saxony. The royal castles now lay in ruins, Brühl's splendours were annihilated, and, of the whole, a glorious land, much injured, alone remained.

When he saw me astonished at that mad enjoyment of fortune, and then grieved by the calamity that followed, and informed me that one expects from an experienced man exactly this, that he shall be astonished at neither the one nor the other, nor take too lively an interest in them, I felt a great desire still to remain awhile in the same inexperience as hitherto; in which desire he strengthened me, and very urgently entreated me, for the present at least, always to cling to agreeable experiences, and to try to avoid those that were disagreeable as much as possible, if they should intrude themselves upon me. But once, when the discussion was again about experience in general, and I related to him those ludicrous phrases of my friend Behrisch, he shook his head, smiling, and said, "There, one sees how it is with words which are only once uttered! These sound so comical, nay, so silly, that it would seem almost impossible to put a rational meaning into them; and yet, perhaps, the attempt might be made."

And, when I pressed him, he replied in his intelligent, cheerful manner, "If you will allow me, while commenting on and completing your friend's observations, to go on after his fashion, I think he meant to say, that experience is nothing else than that one experiences what one does not wish to experience; which is what it amounts to for the most part, at least in this world."

EIGHTH BOOK.

ANOTHER man, although infinitely different from Behrisch in every respect, might yet be compared with him in a certain sense: I mean Oeser, who was also one of those men who dream away their lives in a comfortable state of being busy. His friends themselves secretly acknowledged, that, with very fine natural powers, he had not spent his younger years in sufficient activity; for which reason he never went so far as to practise his art with perfect technicality. Yet a certain diligence appeared to be reserved for his old age; and, during the many years which I knew him, he never lacked invention or laboriousness. From the very first moment he had attracted me very much: even his residence, strange and portentous, was highly charming to me. In the old castle Pleissenburg, at the right-hand corner, one ascended a repaired, cheerful, winding staircase. The saloons of the Academy of Design, of which he was director, were found to the left, and were light and roomy; but he himself could only be reached through a narrow, dark passage, at the end of which one first sought the entrance into his apartments, having just passed between the whole suite of them and an extensive granary. The first apartment was adorned with pictures from the later Italian school, by masters whose grace he used highly to commend. As I, with some noblemen, had taken private lessons of him, we were permitted to draw here; and we often penetrated into his adjoining private cabinet, which contained at the same time his few books, collections of art and natural curiosities, and whatever else might have most interested him. Everything was arranged with taste, simply, and in such a manner that the little space held a great deal. The furniture, presses, and portfolios were elegant, without affectation or superfluity. Thus also the first thing which he recommended to us, and to which he always recurred, was simplicity in everything that art and manual labour united are called upon to produce. Being a sworn foe to the scroll-and-shell style, and of the whole taste for quaintness, he showed us in copperplates and drawings old patterns of the sort, contrasted with better decorations and simpler forms of furniture, as well as with other appurtenances of a room; and, because everything about him corresponded with these maxims, his words and instructions made a good and lasting impression on us. Besides this, he had an opportunity to let us see his opinions in practice; since he stood in good consideration, both with private and with official persons, and was asked for advice when there were new buildings and alterations. He seemed in general to be more fond of preparing things on occasion, for a certain end and use, than of undertaking and completing such as exist for themselves and require a greater perfection; he was therefore always ready and at hand when the publishers needed larger and smaller copperplates for any work; thus the vignettes to Winckelmann's first writings were etched by him. But he often made only very sketchy drawings, to which Geyser knew very well how to adapt himself. His figures had throughout something general, not to say ideal. His women were pleasing and agreeable, his children *naïve* enough; only he could not succeed with the men, who, in his spirited but always clouded, and at the same time foreshortening, manner, had for the most part the look of Lazzaroni. Since he designed his composition less with regard to

form than to light, shade, and masses, the general
effect was good; as indeed all that he did and produced
was attended by a peculiar grace. As he at the same
time neither could nor would control a deep-rooted
propensity to the significant and the allegorical — to
that which excites a secondary thought, so his works
always furnished something to reflect upon, and were
complete through a conception, even where they could
not be so from art and execution. This bias, which is
always dangerous, frequently led him to the very
bounds of good taste, if not beyond them. He often
sought to attain his views by the oddest notions and
by whimsical jests; nay, his best works always have a
touch of humour. If the public were not always satisfied with such things, he revenged himself by a new
and even stranger drollery. Thus he afterward exhibited, in the anteroom of the great concert-hall, an ideal
female figure, in his own style, who was raising a pair
of snuffers to a taper; and he was extraordinarily
delighted when he was able to cause a dispute on the
question, whether this singular muse meant to snuff
the light or to extinguish it? when he roguishly allowed
all sorts of bantering by-thoughts to peep forth.

But the building of the new theatre, in my time,
made the greatest noise; in which his curtain, when it
was still quite new, had certainly an uncommonly
charming effect. Oeser had taken the Muses out of
the clouds, upon which they usually hover on such
occasions, and set them upon the earth. The statues
of Sophocles and Aristophanes, around whom all the
modern dramatic writers were assembled, adorned a
vestibule to the Temple of Fame. Here, too, the goddesses of the arts were likewise present; and all was
dignified and beautiful. But now comes the oddity!
Through the open centre was seen the portal of the
distant temple: and a man in a light jerkin was passing between the two above-mentioned groups, and,

without troubling himself about them, directly up to the temple; he was seen from behind, and was not particularly distinguished. Now, this man was to represent Shakespeare, who without predecessors or followers, without concerning himself about models, went to meet immortality in his own way. This work was executed on the great floor over the new theatre. We often assembled around him there, and in that place I read aloud to him the proof-sheets of " Musarion."

As to myself, I by no means advanced in the practice of the art. His instructions worked upon our mind and our taste; but his own drawing was too undefined to guide me, who had only glimmered along by the objects of art and of nature, to a severe and decided practice. Of the faces and bodies he gave us rather the aspect than the forms, rather the postures than the proportions. He gave us the conceptions of the figures, and desired that we should impress them vividly upon our minds. That might have been beautifully and properly done, if he had not had mere beginners before him. If, on this account, a preëminent talent for instruction may be well denied him, it must, on the other hand, be acknowledged that he was very discreet and politic, and that a happy adroitness of mind qualified him very peculiarly for a teacher in a higher sense. The deficiencies under which each one laboured he clearly saw; but he disdained to reprove them directly, and rather hinted his praise and censure indirectly and very laconically. One was now compelled to think over the matter, and soon came to a far deeper insight. Thus, for instance, I had very carefully executed, after a pattern, a nosegay on blue paper, with white and black crayon, and partly with the stump, partly by hatching it up, had tried to give effect to the little picture. After I had been long labouring in this way, he once came behind me, and said, " More paper!" upon which he immediately withdrew. My neighbour and I puzzled our heads as to what this could mean; for my bouquet, on a large half-sheet, had plenty of space around it. After we had reflected a long while, we thought, at last, that we had hit his meaning, when we remarked, that, by working together the black and the white, I had quite covered up the blue ground, had destroyed the middle tint, and, in fact, with great industry, had produced a disagreeable drawing. As to the rest, he did not fail to instruct us in perspective, and in light and shade, sufficiently indeed, but always so that we had to exert and torment ourselves to find the application of the principles communicated. Probably his view with regard to us who did not intend to become artists, was only to form the judgment and taste, and to make us acquainted with the requisites of a work of art, without precisely requiring that we should produce one. Since, moreover, patient industry was not my talent, for nothing gave me pleasure except what came to me at once, so by degrees I became discouraged, if not lazy; and, as knowledge is more comfortable than doing, I was quite content to follow wherever he chose, after his own fashion, to lead us.

At this time the "Lives of the Painters," by D'Argenville, was translated into German: I obtained it quite fresh, and studied it assiduously enough. This seemed to please Oeser; and he procured us an opportunity of seeing many a portfolio out of the great Leipzig collections, and thus introduced us to the history of the art. But even these exercises produced in me an effect different from that which he probably had in mind. The manifold subjects which I saw treated by artists awakened the poetic talent in me: and, as one easily makes an engraving for a poem; so did I now make poems to the engravings and drawings, by contriving to present to myself the personages introduced in them in this their previous and subsequent condition, and sometimes to compose a little song which might have suited them; and thus accustomed myself to consider the arts in connection with each other. Even the mistakes which I made, so that my poems were often descriptive, were useful to me in the sequel, when I came to more reflection, by making me attentive to the differences between the arts. Of such little things many were in the collection which Behrisch had arranged, but there is nothing left of them now.

The atmosphere of art and taste in which Oeser lived, and into which one was drawn, provided one visited him frequently, was the more and more worthy and delightful, because he was fond of remembering departed or absent persons, with whom he had been, or still continued to be, on good terms; for, if he had once given any one his esteem, he remained unalterable in his conduct toward him, and always showed himself equally friendly.

After we had heard Caylus preëminently extolled among the French, he made us also acquainted with Germans of activity in this department. Thus we learned that Professor Christ, as an amateur, a collector, a connoisseur, a fellow labourer, had done good service for art, and had applied his learning to its true improvement. Heinecken, on the contrary, could not be honourably mentioned, partly because he devoted himself too assiduously to the ever-childish beginnings of German art, which Oeser little valued, partly because he had once treated Winckelmann shabbily, which could never be forgiven him. Our attention, however, was strongly drawn to the labours of Lippert, since our instructor knew how to set forth his merits sufficiently. " For," he said, " although single statues and larger groups of sculpture remain the foundation and the summit of all knowledge of art, yet, either as originals or as casts, they are seldom to be seen; on the contrary, by Lippert, a little world of gems is made known, in which the more comprehensible merit of the ancients, their happy invention, judicious composition, tasteful treatment, are made more striking and intelligible, while, from the great number of them, comparison is much more possible." While now we were busying ourselves with these as much as was allowed, Winckelmann's lofty life of art in Italy was pointed out, and we took his first writings in hand with devotion; for Oeser had a passionate reverence for him which he was able easily to instil into us. The problematical part of those little treatises, which are, besides, confused even from their irony, and from their referring to opinions and events altogether peculiar, we were, indeed, unable to decipher; but as Oeser had great influence over us, and incessantly gave them out to us as the gospel of the beautiful, and still more of the tasteful and the pleasing, we found out the general sense, and fancied, that, with such interpretations, we should go on the more securely, as we regarded it no small happiness to draw from the same fountain from which Winckelmann had allayed his earliest thirst.

No greater good fortune can befall a city, than when several educated men, like-minded in what is good and right, live together in it. Leipzig had this advantage, and enjoyed it the more peacefully, as so many differences of judgment had not yet manifested themselves. Huber, a print collector and well-experienced connoisseur, had furthermore the gratefully acknowledged merit of having determined to make the work of German literature known to the French; Kreuchauf, an amateur with a practised eye, who, as the friend of the whole society of art, might regard all collections as his own; Winkler, who much loved to share with others the intelligent delight he cherished for his treasures; many more who were added to the list,—all lived and laboured with one feeling; and, often as I was permitted to be present when they examined works of art, I do not remember that a dispute ever arose. The school from which the artist had proceeded, the time in which he lived, the peculiar talent which nature had bestowed on him, and the degree of excellence to which he had brought it in his performances, were always fairly considered. There was no predilection for spiritual or temporal subjects, for landscape or for city views, for animate or inanimate : the question was always about accordance with art.

Now, although from their situation, mode of thought, abilities, and opportunities, these amateurs and collectors inclined more to the Dutch school, yet, while the eye was practised on the endless merits of the northwestern artist, a look of reverential longing was always turned toward the southeast.

And so the university, where I neglected the ends of both my family and myself, was to ground me in that in which I afterward found the greatest satisfaction of my life : the impression of those localities, too, in which I received such important incitements, has always remained to me most dear and precious. The old Pleissenburg; the rooms of the Academy; but, above all, the abode of Oeser ; and no less the collections of Winkler and Richter, — I have always vividly present before me.

But a young man, who, while older persons are conversing with each other on subjects already familiar to them, is instructed only incidentally, and for whom the most difficult part of the business — that of rightly arranging all — yet remains, must find himself in a very painful situation. I therefore, as well as others, looked about with longing for some new light, which was indeed to come to us from a man to whom we owed so much already.

The mind can be highly delighted in two ways, — by perception and conception. But the former demands a worthy object, which is not always at hand, and a proportionate culture, which one does not immediately attain. Conception, on the other hand, requires only susceptibility: it brings its subject-matter with it, and is itself the instrument of culture. Hence that beam of light was most welcome to us which that most excellent thinker brought down to us through dark clouds. One must be a young man to render present to one's self the effect which Lessing's "Laocoön" produced upon us, by transporting us out of the region of scanty perceptions into the open fields of thought. The *ut pictura poesis,* so long misunderstood, was at once laid aside: the difference between plastic and speaking art [1] was made clear; the summits of the two now appeared sundered, however near their bases might border on each other. The plastic artist was to keep himself within the bounds of the beautiful, if the artist of language, who cannot dispense with the significant in any kind, is permitted to ramble abroad beyond them. The former labours for the outer sense, which is satisfied only by the beautiful; the latter for the imagination, which may even reconcile itself to the ugly. All the consequences of this splendid thought were illumined to us as by a lightning-flash: all the criticism which had hitherto guided and judged was thrown away like a worn-out coat. We considered ourselves freed from all evil, and fancied we might venture to look down with some compassion upon the otherwise so splendid sixteenth century, when, in German sculptures and poems, they knew how to represent life only under the form of a fool hung with bells, death under the misformed shape of a rattling skeleton, and the necessary and accidental evils of the world under the image of the caricatured Devil.

What enchanted us most was the beauty of that

---

[1] "*Bildende und Rendende Kunst.*" The expression "speaking art" is used to produce a corresponding antithesis, though "*belles-lettres*" would be the ordinary rendering. — TRANS.

thought, that the ancients had recognised death as the brother of sleep, and had represented them similar, even to confusion, as becomes Menæchmi. Here we could first do high honour to the triumph of the beautiful, and banish the ugly of every kind into the low sphere of the ridiculous within the realm of art, since it could not be utterly driven out of the world.

The splendour of such leading and fundamental conceptions appears only to the mind upon which they exercise their infinite activity, — appears only to the age in which, after being longed for, they come forth at the right moment. Then do those at whose disposal such nourishment is placed fondly occupy whole periods of their lives with it, and rejoice in a superabundant growth ; while men are not wanting, meanwhile, who resist such an effect on the spot, nor others who afterward haggle and cavil at its high meaning.

But, as conception and perception mutually require each other, I could not long work up these new thoughts without an infinite desire arising within me to see important works of art, once and away, in great number. I therefore determined to visit Dresden without delay. I was not in want of the necessary cash : but there were other difficulties to overcome, which I needlessly increased still further, through my whimsical disposition ; for I kept my purpose a secret from every one, because I wished to contemplate the treasures of art there quite after my own way, and, as I thought, to allow no one to perplex me. Besides this, so simple a matter became more complicated by still another eccentricity.

We have weaknesses, both by birth and by education ; and it may be questioned which of the two gives us the most trouble. Willingly as I made myself familiar with all sorts of conditions, and many as had been my inducements to do so, an excessive aversion from all inns had nevertheless been instilled into me by my

father. This feeling had taken firm root in him on
his travels through Italy, France, and Germany. Although he seldom spoke in images, and only called
them to his aid when he was very cheerful, yet he
used often to repeat that he always fancied he saw
a great cobweb spun across the gate of an inn, so
ingeniously that the insects could indeed fly in, but
that even the privileged wasps could not fly out again
unplucked. It seemed to him something horrible that
one should be obliged to pay immoderately for renouncing one's habits and all that was dear to one in life,
and living after the manner of publicans and waiters.
He praised the hospitality of the olden time; and,
reluctantly as he otherwise endured even anything
unusual in the house, he yet practised hospitality, especially toward artists and virtuosi. Thus gossip Seekatz
always had his quarters with us; and Abel, the last
musician who handled the *viol di gamba* with success
and applause, was well received and entertained. With
such youthful impressions, which nothing had as yet
rubbed off, how could I have resolved to set foot in an
inn in a strange city? Nothing would have been
easier than to find quarters with good friends. Hofrath
Krebel, Assessor Hermann, and others, had often
spoken to me about it already; but even to these my
trip was to remain a secret, and I hit upon a most
singular notion. My next-room neighbour, the industrious theologian, whose eyes unfortunately constantly
grew weaker and weaker, had a relation in Dresden,
a shoemaker, with whom from time to time he corresponded. For a long while already this man had
been highly remarkable to me on account of his expressions, and the arrival of one of his letters was
always celebrated by us as a holiday. The mode in
which he replied to the complaints of his cousin, who
feared blindness, was quite peculiar: for he did not
trouble himself about grounds of consolation, which are

always hard to find ; but the cheerful way in which he looked upoᴀ his own narrow, poor, toilsome life, the merriment which he drew, even from evils and inconveniences, the indestructible conviction that life is in itself and on its own account a blessing, communicated itself to him who read the letter, and, for the moment at least, transposed him into a like mood. Enthusiastic as I was, I had often sent my compliments to this man, extolled his happy natural gift, and expressed the wish to become acquainted with him. All this being premised, nothing seemed to me more natural than to seek him out, to converse with him, — nay, to lodge with him, and to learn to know him intimately. My good candidate, after some opposition, gave me a letter, written with difficulty, to carry with me; and, full of longing, I went to Dresden in the yellow coach, with my matriculation in my pocket.

I went in search of my shoemaker, and soon found him in the suburb (*Vorstadt*). He received me in a friendly manner, sitting upon his stool, and said, smiling, after he had read the letter, "I see from this, young sir, that you are a whimsical Christian." "How so, master?" I replied. "No offence meant by '*whimsical*'," he continued : "one calls every one so who is not consistent with himself; and I call you a whimsical Christian because you acknowledge yourself a follower of our Lord in one thing, but not in another." On my requesting him to enlighten me, he said further, "It seems that your view is, to announce glad tidings to the poor and lowly; that is good, and this imitation of the Lord is praiseworthy : but you should reflect, besides, that he rather sat down to table with prosperous rich folks, where there was good fare, and that he himself did not despise the sweet scent of the ointment, of which you will find the opposite in my house."

This pleasant beginning put me at once in good

humour, and we rallied each other for some time. His wife stood doubting how she should board and lodge such a guest. On this point, too, he had notions which referred, not only to the Bible, but also to "Gottfried's Chronicle;" and when we were agreed that I was to stay, I gave my purse, such as it was, into the charge of my hostess, and requested her to furnish herself from it, if anything should be necessary. When he would have declined it, and somewhat waggishly gave me to understand that he was not so burned out as he might appear, I disarmed him by saying, "Even if it were only to change water into wine, such a well-tried domestic resource would not be out of place, since there are no more miracles nowadays." The hostess seemed to find my conduct less and less strange: we had soon accommodated ourselves to each other, and spent a very merry evening. He remained always the same, because all flowed from one source. His peculiarity was an apt common sense, which rested upon a cheerful disposition, and took delight in uniform habitual activity. That he should labour incessantly was his first and most necessary care; that he regarded everything else as secondary, — this kept up his comfortable state of mind; and I must reckon him before many others in the class of those who are called practical unconscious philosophers.[1]

The hour when the gallery was to be opened appeared, after having been expected with impatience. I entered into this sanctuary, and my astonishment surpassed every conception which I had formed. This room, returning into itself, in which splendour and neatness reigned together with the deepest stillness; the dazzling frames, all nearer to the time in which

---

[1] "*Pratische Philosophen, bewusstlose Weltweisen.*" It is impossible to give two substantives, as in the original, since this is effected by using first the word of Greek, then the word of German origin, whereas we have but one. — TRANS.

they had been gilded; the floor polished with beeswax; the spaces more trodden by spectators than used
by copyists, — imparted a feeling of solemnity, unique
of its kind, which so much the more resembled the sensation with which one treads a church, as the adorn-
ments of so many a temple, the objects of so much
adoration, seemed here again set up only for the sacred
purposes of art. I readily put up with the cursory
description of my guide, only I requested that I might
be allowed to remain in the outer gallery. Here, to
my comfort, I felt really at home. I had already seen
the works of several artists, others I knew from engravings, others by name. I did not conceal this, and
I thus inspired my conductor with some confidence:
nay, the rapture which I expressed at pieces where the
pencil had gained the victory over nature delighted
him; for such were the things which principally
attracted me, where the comparison with known nature
must necessarily enhance the value of art.

When I again entered my shoemaker's house for
dinner, I scarcely believed my eyes; for I fancied I
saw before me a picture by Ostade, so perfect that all
it needed was to be hung up in the gallery. The position of the objects, the light, the shadow, the brownish
tint of the whole, the magical harmony, — everything
that one admires in those pictures, I here saw in reality.
It was the first time that I perceived, in so high a
degree, the faculty which I afterward exercised with
more consciousness; namely, that of seeing nature with
the eyes of this or that artist, to whose works I had
devoted a particular attention. This faculty has afforded
me much enjoyment, but has also increased the desire
zealously to abandon myself, from time to time, to the
exercise of a talent which nature seemed to have
denied me.

I visited the gallery at all permitted hours, and continued to express too loudly the ecstasy with which I

beheld many precious works. I thus frustrated my laudable purpose of remaining unknown and unnoticed; and whereas only one of the underkeepers had hitherto had intercourse with me, the gallery-inspector, Counsellor Riedel, now also took notice of me, and called my attention to many things which seemed chiefly to lie within my sphere. I found this excellent man just as active and obliging then, as when I afterward saw him during many years, and as he shows himself to this day. His image has, for me, interwoven itself so closely with those treasures of art, that I can never regard the two apart: the remembrance of him has even accompanied me to Italy, where, in many large and rich collections, his presence would have been very desirable.

Since, even with strangers and unknown persons, one cannot gaze on such works silently and without mutual sympathy, — nay, since the first sight of them is rather adapted, in the highest degree, to open hearts toward each other, I there got into conversation with a young man who seemed to be residing at Dresden, and to belong to some embassy. He invited me to come in the evening to an inn where a lively company met, and where, by each one's paying a moderate reckoning, one could pass some very pleasant hours.

I repaired thither, but did not find the company; and the waiter somewhat surprised me when he delivered the compliments of the gentleman who made the appointment with me, by which the latter sent an excuse for coming somewhat later, with the addition that I must not take offence at anything that might occur; also, that I should have nothing to pay beyond my own score. I knew not what to make of these words: my father's cobwebs came into my head, and I composed myself to await whatever might befall. The company assembled; my acquaintance introduced me; and I could not be attentive long, without discovering that they were aiming at the mystification of a young man, who showed himself a novice by an obstreperous, assuming deportment : I therefore kept very much on my guard, so that they might not find delight in selecting me as his fellow. At table this intention became more apparent to everybody, except to himself. They drank more and more deeply : and, when a vivat in honour of sweethearts was started every one solemnly swore that there should never be another out of those glasses ; they flung them behind them, and this was the signal for far greater follies. At last I withdrew very quietly ; and the waiter, while demanding quite a moderate amount, requested me to come again, as they did not go on so wildly every evening. I was far from my lodgings, and it was near midnight when I reached them. I found the doors unlocked ; everybody was in bed ; and one lamp illuminated the narrow domestic household, where my eye, more and more practised, immediately perceived the finest picture by Schalken, from which I could not tear myself away, so that it banished from me all sleep.

The few days of my residence in Dresden were solely devoted to the picture-gallery. The antiquities still stood in the pavilion of the great garden ; but I declined seeing them, as well as all the other precious things which Dresden contained, being but too full of the conviction, that, even in and about the collection of paintings, much must yet remain hidden from me. Thus I took the excellence of the Italian masters more on trust and in faith, than by pretending to any insight into them. What I could not look upon as nature, put in the place of nature, and compare with a known object, was without effect upon me. It is the material impression which makes the beginning even to every more elevated taste.

With my shoemaker I lived on very good terms. He was witty and varied enough, and we often outvied each other in merry conceits: nevertheless, a man who thinks himself happy, and desires others to do the same, makes us discontented; indeed, the repetition of such sentiments produces weariness. I found myself well occupied, entertained, excited, but by no means happy; and the shoes from his last would not fit me. We parted, however, as the best friends; and even my hostess, on my departure, was not dissatisfied with me.

Shortly before my departure, something else very pleasant was to happen. By the mediation of that young man, who wished to somewhat regain his credit with me, I was introduced to the Director von Hagedorn, who, with great kindness, showed me his collection, and was highly delighted with the enthusiasm of the young lover of art. He himself, as becomes a connoisseur, was quite peculiarly in love with the pictures which he possessed, and therefore seldom found in others an interest such as he wished. It gave him particular satisfaction that I was so excessively pleased with a picture by Schwanefeld, and that I was not tired of praising and extolling it in every single part; for landscapes, which again reminded me of the beautiful clear sky under which I had grown up, of the vegetable luxuriance of those spots, and of whatever other favours a warmer climate offers to man, were just the things that most affected me in the imitation, while they awakened in me a longing remembrance.

These delightful experiences, preparing both mind and sense for true art, were nevertheless interrupted and damped by one of the most melancholy sights, — by the destroyed and desolate condition of so many of the streets of Dresden through which I took my way. The Mohrenstrasse in ruins, and the Church (*Kreuzkirche*) of the Cross, with its shattered tower, impressed themselves deeply upon me, and still stand like a gloomy spot in my imagination. From the cupola of the Lady Church (*Frauenkirche*) I saw these pitiable ruins scattered about amid the beautiful order of the city. Here the clerk commended to me the art of the architect, who had already fitted up church and cupola for so undesirable an event, and had built them bomb-proof. The good sacristan then pointed out to me the ruins on all sides, and said doubtfully and laconically, "The enemy hath done this!"

At last, though very loath, I returned to Leipzig, and found my friends, who were not used to such digressions in me, in great astonishment, busied with all sorts of conjectures as to what might be the import of my mysterious journey. When, upon this, I told them my story quite in order, they declared it was only a made-up tale, and sagaciously tried to get at the bottom of the riddle which I had been waggish enough to conceal under my shoemaker-lodgings.

But, could they have looked into my heart, they would have discovered no waggery there; for the truth of that old proverb, "He that increaseth knowledge increaseth sorrow," had struck me with all its force: and the more I struggled to arrange and appropriate to myself what I had seen, the less I succeeded. I had at last to content myself with a silent after-operation. Ordinary life carried me away again; and I at last felt myself quite comfortable when a friendly intercourse, improvement in branches of knowledge which were suitable for me, and a certain practice of the hand, engaged me in a manner less important, but more in accordance with my strength.

Very pleasant and wholesome for me was the connection I formed with the Breitkopf family. Bernhard Christoph Breitkopf, the proper founder of the family, who had come to Leipzig as a poor journeyman printer, was yet living, and occupied the Golden Bear, a respectable house in the New Newmarket, with Gottsched as an inmate. The son, Johann Gottlob Immanuel, had already been long married, and was the father of many children. They thought they could not spend a part of their considerable wealth better than in putting up, opposite the first house, a large new one, the Silver Bear, which they built higher and more extensive than the original house itself. Just at the time of the building I became acquainted with the family. The eldest son, who might have been some years older than I, was a well-formed young man, devoted to music, and practised to play skilfully on both the piano and the violin. The second, a true, good soul, likewise musical, enlivened the concerts which were often got up, no less than his elder brother. They were both kindly disposed toward me, as well as their parents and sisters. I lent them a helping hand during the building up and the finishing, the furnishing and the moving in, and thus formed a conception of much that belongs to such an affair: I also had an opportunity of seeing Oeser's instructions put in practice. In the new house, which I had thus seen erected, I was often a visitor. We had many pursuits in common; and the eldest son set some of my songs to music, which, when printed, bore his name, but not mine, and have been little known. I have selected the best, and inserted them among my other little poems. The father had invented or perfected musical type. He granted me the use of a fine library, which related principally to the origin and progress of printing; and thus I gained some knowledge in that department. I found there, moreover, good copper-plates, which exhibited antiquity, and advanced on this side also my studies, which were still further promoted by the circumstance that a considerable collection of casts had fallen into disorder in moving. I set them right again as well as I could, and in doing so was compelled to search Lippert and other authorities. A physician, Doctor Reichel, likewise an inmate of the house, I consulted from time to time when I felt, if not sick, yet unwell; and thus we led together a quiet, pleasant life.

I was now to enter into another sort of connection in this house; for the copper-plate engraver, Stock, had moved into the attic. He was a native of Nuremberg, a very industrious man, and, in his labours, precise and methodical. He also, like Geyser, engraved, after Oeser's designs, larger and smaller plates, which came more and more into vogue for novels and poems. He etched very neatly, so that his work came out of the aquafortis almost finished; and but little touching-up remained to be done with the graver, which he handled very well. He made an exact calculation how long a plate would occupy him, and nothing could call him off from his work if he had not completed the daily task he had set himself. Thus he sat working by a broad table, by the great gable-window, in a very neat and orderly chamber, where his wife and two daughters afforded him a domestic society. Of these last, one is happily married, and the other is an excellent artist: they have continued my friends all my life long. I now divided my time between the upper and lower stories, and attached myself much to the man, who, together with his persevering industry, possessed an excellent humour, and was good nature itself.

The technical neatness of this branch of art charmed me, and I associated myself with him to execute something of the kind. My predilection was again directed toward landscape, which, while it amused me in my solitary walks, seemed in itself more attainable and more comprehensible for works of art than the human figure, which discouraged me. Under his directions, therefore, I etched, after Thiele and others, various landscapes, which, although executed by an unpractised hand, produced some effect, and were well received. The grounding (varnishing) of the plates, the putting in the high lights, the etching, and at last the biting with aquafortis, gave me variety of occupation; and I soon got so far that I could assist my master in many things. I did not lack the attention necessary for the biting, and I seldom failed in anything; but I had not care enough in guarding against the deleterious vapours which are generated on such occasions, and these may have contributed to the maladies which afterward troubled me for a long time. Amidst such labours, lest anything should be left untried, I often made woodcuts also. I prepared various little printing-blocks after French patterns, and many of them were found fit for use.

Let me here make mention of some other men who resided in Leipzig, or tarried there for a short time. Weisse, the custom-house collector of the district, in his best years, cheerful, friendly, and obliging, was loved and esteemed by us. We would not, indeed, allow his theatrical pieces to be models throughout, but we suffered ourselves to be carried away by them; and his operas, set to music by Hiller in an easy style, gave us much pleasure. Schiebler, of Hamburg, pursued the same track; and his "Lisuard and Dariolette" was likewise favoured by us. Eschenburg, a handsome young man, but little older than we were, distinguished himself advantageously among the students. Zachariä was pleased to spend some weeks with us, and, being introduced by his brother, dined every day with us at the same table. We rightly deemed it an honour to gratify our guest in return, by a few extra dishes, a richer dessert, and choicer wine; for, as a tall, well-formed, comfortable man, he did not conceal his love of good eating. Lessing came at a time when we had I know not what in our heads: it was our good pleasure to go nowhere on his account, — nay, even to avoid the places to which he came, probably because we thought ourselves too good to stand at a distance, and could make no pretension to obtain a closer intimacy with him. This momentary absurdity, which, however, is nothing rare in presuming and freakish youth, proved, indeed, its own punishment in the sequel; for I have never set eyes on that eminent man, who was most highly esteemed by me.

Notwithstanding all our efforts relative to art and antiquity, we each of us always had Winckelmann before our eyes, whose ability was acknowledged in his country with enthusiasm. We read his writings diligently, and tried to make ourselves acquainted with the circumstances under which he had written the first of them. We found in them many views which seemed to have originated with Oeser, even jests and whims after his fashion: and we did not rest until we had formed some general conception of the occasion on which these remarkable and sometimes so enigmatical writings had arisen, though we were not very accurate: for youth likes better to be excited than instructed, and it was not the last time that I was to be indebted to Sibylline leaves for an important step in cultivation.

It was then a fine period in literature, when eminent men were yet treated with respect; although the disputes of Klotz and Lessing's controversies already indicated that this epoch would soon close. Winckelmann enjoyed an universal, unassailed reverence; and it is known how sensitive he was with regard to anything public which did not seem commensurate with his deeply felt dignity. All the periodical publications joined in his praise, the better class of tourists came back from him instructed and enraptured, and the new views which he gave extended themselves over science and life. The Prince of Dessau had raised himself up to a similar degree of respect. Young, well and nobly minded, he had on his travels and at other times shown himself truly desirable. Winckelmann was in

the highest degree delighted with him, and, whenever
he mentioned him, loaded him with the handsomest
epithets. The laying out of a park, then unique, the
taste for architecture, which Von Erdmannsdorf supported by his activity, everything spoke in favour of a
prince, who, while he was a shining example for the
rest, gave promise of a golden age for his servants and
subjects. We young people now learned with rejoicings that Winckelmann would return back from Italy,
visit his princely friend, call on Oeser by the way, and
so come within our sphere of vision. We made no
pretensions to speaking with him, but we hoped to see
him; and, as at that time of life one willingly changes
every occasion into a party of pleasure, we had already
agreed upon a journey to Dessau, where in a beautiful
spot, made glorious by art, in a land well governed and
at the same time externally adorned, we thought to lie
in wait, now here, now there, in order to see with our
own eyes these men so highly exalted above us walking about. Oeser himself was quite elated if he only
thought of it, and the news of Winckelmann's death
fell down into the midst of us like a thunderbolt from
a clear sky. I still remember the place where I first
heard it; it was in the court of the Pleissenburg, not
far from the little gate through which one used to go
up to Oeser's residence. One of my fellow pupils met
me, and told me that Oeser was not to be seen, with
the reason why. This monstrous event[1] produced a
monstrous effect: there was an universal mourning
and lamentation, and Winckelmann's untimely death
sharpened the attention paid to the value of his life.
Perhaps, indeed, the effect of his activity, if he had
continued it to a more advanced age, would probably
not have been so great as it now necessarily became,
when, like many other extraordinary men, he was distinguished by fate through a strange and calamitous end.

[1] Winckelmann was assassinated. — TRANS.

Now, while I was infinitely lamenting the death of Winckelmann, I did not think that I should soon find myself in the case of being apprehensive about my own life; since, during all these events, my bodily condition had not taken the most favourable turn. I had already brought with me from home a certain touch of hypochondria, which, in this new sedentary and lounging life, was rather increased than diminished. The pain in my chest, which I had felt from time to time ever since the accident at Auerstädt, and which after a fall from horseback had perceptibly increased, made me dejected. By an unfortunate diet I destroyed my powers of digestion; the heavy Merseburg beer clouded my brain; coffee, which gave me a peculiarly melancholy tone, especially when taken with milk after dinner, paralysed my bowels, and seemed completely to suspend their functions, so that I experienced great uneasiness on this account, yet without being able to embrace a resolution for a more rational mode of life. My natural disposition, supported by the sufficient strength of youth, fluctuated between the extremes of unrestrained gaiety and melancholy discomfort. Moreover, the epoch of cold-water bathing, which was unconditionally recommended, had then begun. One was to sleep on a hard bed, only slightly covered, by which all the usual perspiration was suppressed. These and other follies, in consequence of some misunderstood suggestions of Rousseau, would, it was promised, bring us nearer to nature, and deliver us from the corruption of morals. Now, all the above, without discrimination, applied with injudicious alternation, were felt by many most injuriously; and I irritated my happy organisation to such a degree, that the particular systems contained within it necessarily broke out at last into a conspiracy and revolution, in order to save the whole.

One night I awoke with a violent hemorrhage, and

had just strength and presence of mind enough to waken my next-room neighbour. Doctor Reichel was called in, who assisted me in the most friendly manner; and thus for many days I wavered betwixt life and death : and even the joy of a subsequent improvement was embittered by the circumstance that, during that eruption, a tumour had formed on the left side of the neck, which, after the danger was past, they now first found time to notice. Recovery is, however, always pleasing and delightful, even though it takes place slowly and painfully : and, since nature had helped herself with me, I appeared now to have become another man; for I had gained a greater cheerfulness of mind than I had known for a long time, and I was rejoiced to feel my inner self at liberty, although externally a wearisome affliction threatened me.

But what particularly set me up at this time was, to see how many eminent men had, undeservedly, given me their affection. Undeservedly, I say; for there was not one among them to whom I had not been troublesome through contradictory humours, not one whom I had not more than once wounded by morbid absurdity, — nay, whom I had not stubbornly avoided for a long time, from a feeling of my own injustice. All this was forgotten : they treated me in the most affectionate manner, and sought, partly in my chamber, partly as soon as I could leave it, to amuse and divert me. They drove out with me, entertained me at their country houses, and I seemed soon to recover.

Among these friends I name first of all Doctor Hermann, then senator, afterward burgomaster at Leipzig. He was among those boarders with whom I had become acquainted through Schlosser, the one with whom an always equable and enduring connection was maintained. One might well reckon him the most industrious of his academical fellow citizens. He attended his lectures with the greatest regularity, and his private industry remained always the same. Step by step, without the slightest deviation, I saw him attain his doctor's degree, and then raise himself to the assessorship, without anything of all this appearing arduous to him, or his having in the least hurried or been too late with anything. The gentleness of his character attracted me, his instructive conversation held me fast; indeed, I really believe that I took delight in his methodical industry especially for this reason, because I thought, by acknowledgments and high esteem, to appropriate to myself at least a part of a merit of which I could by no means boast.

He was just as regular in the exercise of his talents and the enjoyment of his pleasures as in his business. He played the harpsichord with great skill, drew from nature with feeling, and stimulated me to do the same; when, in his manner, on gray paper and with black and white chalk, I used to copy many a willow-plot on the Pleisse, and many a lovely nook of those still waters, and at the same time longingly to indulge in my fancies. He knew how to meet my sometimes comical disposition with merry jests; and I remember many pleasant hours which we spent together when he invited me, with mock solemnity, to a *tête-à-tête* supper, where with some dignity, by the light of waxen candles, we ate what they call a council-hare, which had run into his kitchen as a perquisite of his place, and, with many jokes in the manner of Behrisch, were pleased to season the meat and heighten the spirit of the wine. That this excellent man, who is still constantly labouring in his respectable office, rendered me the most faithful assistance during a disease, of which there was indeed a foreboding, but which had not been foreseen in its full extent; that he bestowed every leisure hour upon me, and, by remembrances of former happy times, contrived to brighten the gloomy moment, — I still acknowledge with the sincerest thanks, and rejoice that after so long a time I can give them publicly.

Besides this worthy friend, Groening of Bremen particularly interested himself in me. I had made his acquaintance only a short time before, and first discovered his good feeling toward me during my misfortune: I felt the value of this favour the more warmly, as no one is apt to seek a closer connection with invalids. He spared nothing to give me pleasure, to draw me away from musing on my situation, to hold up to my view and promise me recovery and a wholesome activity in the nearest future. How often have I been delighted, in the progress of life, to hear how this excellent man has in the weightiest affairs shown himself useful, and indeed a blessing to his native city.

Here, too, it was that friend Horn uninterruptedly brought into action his love and attention. The whole Breitkopf household, the Stock family, and many others, treated me like a near relative; and thus, through the good will of so many friendly persons, the feeling of my situation was soothed in the tenderest manner.

I must here, therefore, make particular mention of a man with whom I first became acquainted at this time, and whose instructive conversation so far blinded me to the miserable state in which I was, that I actually forgot it. This was Langer, afterward librarian at Wolfenbüttel. Eminently learned and instructed, he was delighted at my voracious hunger after knowledge, which, with the irritability of sickness, now broke out into a perfect fever. He tried to calm me by perspicuous summaries; and I have been very much indebted to his acquaintance, short as it was, since he understood how to guide me in various ways, and made me attentive whither I had to direct myself at the present moment. I felt all the more obliged to this important man, as my intercourse exposed him to some danger; for when, after Behrisch, he got the situation of tutor to the young Count Lindenau, the father made it an express condition with the new Mentor that he should have no intercourse with me. Curious to become acquainted with such a dangerous subject, he frequently found means of meeting me indirectly. I soon gained his affection; and he, more prudent than Behrisch, called for me by night: we went walking together, conversed on interesting things, and at last I accompanied him to the very door of his mistress; for even this externally severe, earnest, scientific man had not kept free from the toils of a very amiable lady.

German literature, and with it my own poetical undertakings, had already for some time become strange to me; and, as is usually the result in such an autodidactic circular course, I turned back toward the beloved ancients who still constantly, like distant blue mountains, distinct in their outlines and masses, but indiscernible in their parts and internal relations, bounded the horizon of my intellectual wishes. I made an exchange with Langer, in which I at last played the part of Glaucus and Diomedes: I gave up to him whole baskets of German poets and critics, and received in return a number of Greek authors, the reading of whom was to give me recreation, even during the most tedious convalescence.

The confidence which new friends repose in each other usually develops itself by degrees. Common occupation and tastes are the first things in which a mutual harmony shows itself; then the mutual communication generally extends over past and present passions, especially over love-affairs: but it is a lower depth which opens itself, if the connection is to be perfected; the religious sentiments, the affairs of the heart which relate to the imperishable, are the things which both establish the foundation and adorn the summit of a friendship.

The Christian religion was fluctuating between its own historically positive base and a pure deism, which, grounded on morality, was in its turn to lay the foundation of ethics. The diversity of characters and modes of thought here showed itself in infinite gradations, especially when a leading difference was brought into play by the question arising as to how great a share reason, and how great a share the feelings, could and should have in such convictions. The most lively and ingenious men showed themselves, in this instance, like butterflies, who, quite regardless of their caterpillar state, throw away the chrysalis veil in which they have grown up to their organic perfection. Others, more honestly and modestly minded, might be compared to the flowers, which, although they unfold themselves to the most beautiful bloom, yet do not tear themselves from the root, from the mother stalk, nay, — rather through this family connection first bring the desired fruit to maturity. Of this latter class was Langer; for although a learned man, and eminently versed in books, he would yet give the Bible a peculiar preëminence over the other writings which have come down to us, and regard it as a document from which alone we could prove our moral and spiritual pedigree. He belonged to those who cannot conceive an immediate connection with the great God of the universe: a mediation, therefore, was necessary for him, an analogy to which he thought he could find everywhere in earthly and heavenly things. His discourse, which was pleasing and consistent, easily found a hearing with a young man, who, separated from worldly things by an annoying illness, found it highly desirable to turn the activity of his mind toward the heavenly. Grounded as I was in the Bible, all that was wanted

was merely the faith to explain as divine that which
I had hitherto esteemed in human fashion, — a belief
the easier for me, since I had made my first acquaintance with that book as a divine one. To a sufferer,
to one who felt himself delicate, nay, weak, the gospel
was therefore welcome; and even though Langer, with
all his faith, was at the same time a very sensible
man, and firmly maintained that one should not let
the feelings prevail, should not let one's self be led
astray into mysticism, I could not have managed to
occupy myself with the New Testament without feeling and enthusiasm.

In such conversations we spent much time; and he
grew so fond of me as an honest and well-prepared
proselyte, that he did not scruple to sacrifice to me
many of the hours destined for his fair one, and even
to run the risk of being betrayed and looked upon
unfavourably by his patron, like Behrisch. I returned
his affection in the most grateful manner; and, if what
he did for me would have been of value at any time,
I could not but regard it, in my present condition, as
worthy of the highest honour.

But as when the concert of our souls is most
spiritually attuned, the rude, shrieking tones of the
world usually break in most violently and boister-
ously, and the contrast which has gone on exercising
a secret control affects us so much the more sensibly
when it comes forward all at once: thus was I not
to be dismissed from the peripatetic school of my
Langer without having first witnessed an event, strange
at least for Leipzig; namely, a tumult which the
students excited, and that on the following pretence.
Some young people had quarrelled with the city
soldiers, and the affair had not gone off without violence. Many of the students combined to revenge
the injuries inflicted. The soldiers resisted stubbornly,
and the advantage was not on the side of the very

discontented academical citizens. It was now said that respectable persons had commended and rewarded the conquerors for their valiant resistance; and, by this, the youthful feeling of honour and revenge was mightily excited. It was publicly said, that, on the next evening, windows would be broken in: and some friends who brought me word that this was actually taking place, were obliged to carry me there; for youth and the multitude are always attracted by danger and tumult. There really began a strange spectacle. The otherwise open street was lined on one side with men who, quite quiet, without noise or movement, were waiting to see what would happen. About a dozen young fellows were walking singly up and down the empty sidewalk, with the greatest apparent composure; but, as soon as they came opposite the marked house, they threw stones at the windows as they passed by, and this repeatedly as they returned backward and forward, as long as the panes would rattle. Just as quietly as this was done, all at last dispersed; and the affair had no further consequences.

With such a ringing echo of university exploits, I left Leipzig in the September of 1768, in a comfortable hired coach, and in the company of some respectable persons of my acquaintance. In the neighbourhood of Auerstädt I thought of that previous accident; but I could not forebode that which many years afterward would threaten me from thence with still greater danger, just as little as in Gotha, where we had the castle shown to us, I could think in the great hall adorned with stucco figures, that so much favour and affection would befall me on that very spot.

The nearer I approached my native city, the more I recalled to myself doubtingly the circumstances, prospects, and hopes with which I had left home; and it was with a very disheartening feeling that I now returned, as it were, like one shipwrecked. Yet, since

I had not very much with which to reproach myself, I contrived to compose myself tolerably well : however, the welcome was not without emotion. The great vivacity of my nature, excited and heightened by sickness, caused an impassioned scene. I might have looked worse than I myself knew, since for a long time I had not consulted a looking-glass; and who does not become used to himself? Suffice it to say, they silently resolved to communicate many things to me only by degrees, and before all things to let me have some repose, both bodily and mental.

My sister immediately associated herself with me, and as previously, from her letters, so I could now more in detail and accurately understand the circumstances and situation of the family. My father had, after my departure, applied all his didactic taste to my sister; and in a house completely shut up, rendered secure by peace, and even cleared of lodgers, he had cut off from her almost every means of looking about and finding some recreation abroad. She had by turns to pursue and work at French, Italian, and English; besides which he compelled her to practise a great part of the day on the harpsichord. Nor was her writing to be neglected; and I had already remarked that he had directed her correspondence with me, and had let his doctrines come to me through her pen. My sister was and still continued to be an undefinable being, the most singular mixture of strength and weakness, of stubbornness and pliability, which qualities operated now united, now isolated by will and inclination. Thus she had, in a manner which seemed to me fearful, turned the hardness of her character against her father, whom she did not forgive for having, in these three years, hindered, or embittered to her, so many innocent joys; and of his good and excellent qualities she would not acknowledge even one. She did all he commanded and arranged, but in the most unamiable manner in the world. She did it in the established routine, but nothing more and nothing less. Not from love or a desire to please did she accommodate herself to anything, so that this was one of the first things about which my mother complained to me in private. But, since love was as essential to my sister as to any human being, she turned her affection wholly on me. Her care in nursing and entertaining me absorbed all her time: her female companions, who were swayed by her without her intending it, had likewise to contrive all sorts of things to be pleasing and consolatory to me. She was inventive in cheering me up, and even developed some germs of comical humour which I had never known in her, and which became her very well. There soon arose between us a coterie-language, by which we could converse before all people without their understanding us; and she often used this gibberish with great pertness in the presence of our parents.

My father was personally tolerably comfortable. He was in good health, spent a great part of the day in the instruction of my sister, went on with the description of his travels, and was longer in tuning his lute than in playing on it. He concealed at the same time, as well as he could, his vexation at finding, instead of a vigorous, active son, who ought now to take his degree and run through the prescribed course of life, an invalid who seemed to suffer still more in soul than in body. He did not conceal his wish that they would be expeditious with my cure; but one was forced to be specially on one's guard in his presence against hypochondriacal expressions, because he could then become passionate and bitter.

My mother, by nature very lively and cheerful, spent under these circumstances very tedious days. Her little housekeeping was soon provided for. The good woman's mind, inwardly never unoccupied, wished to find an interest in something; and that which was nearest at hand was religion, which she embraced the more fondly as her most eminent female friends were cultivated and hearty worshippers of God. At the head of these stood Fräulein von Klettenberg. She is the same person from whose conversations and letters arose the "Confessions of a Beautiful Soul," which are found inserted in "Wilhelm Meister." She was slenderly formed, of the middle size: a hearty natural demeanour had been made still more pleasing by the manners of the world and the court. Her very neat attire reminded of the dress of the Herrnhut women. Her serenity and peace of mind never left her; she looked upon her sickness as a necessary element of her transient earthly existence; she suffered with the greatest patience, and, in painless intervals, was lively and talkative. Her favourite, nay, indeed, perhaps her only, conversation, was on the moral experiences which a man who observes himself can form in himself; to which was added the religious views which, in a very graceful manner, nay, with genius, came under her consideration as natural and supernatural. It scarcely needs more to recall back to the friends of such representations, that complete delineation composed from the very depths of her soul. Owing to the very peculiar course she had taken from her youth upwards, the distinguished rank in which she had been born and educated, and the liveliness and originality of her mind, she did not agree very well with the other ladies who had set out on the same road to salvation. Frau Griesbach, the chief of them, seemed too severe, too dry, too learned: she knew, thought, comprehended, more than the others, who contented themselves with the development of their feelings; and she was therefore burdensome to them, because every one neither could nor would carry with her so great an apparatus on the road to bliss. But for this reason most of

them were indeed somewhat monotonous, since they
confined themselves to a certain terminology which
might well have been compared to that of the later
sentimentalists. Fräulein von Klettenberg guided her
way between both extremes, and seemed, with some
self-complacency, to see her own reflections in the
image of Count Zinzendorf, whose opinions and actions
bore witness to a higher birth and more distinguished
rank. Now she found in me what she needed, a lively
young creature, striving after an unknown happiness,
who, although he could not think himself an extraordinary sinner, yet found himself in no comfortable
condition, and was perfectly healthy neither in body
nor soul. She was delighted with what nature had
given me, as well as with much which I had gained
for myself. And, if she conceded to me many advantages, this was by no means humiliating to her: for, in
the first place, she never thought of emulating one of
the male sex; and, secondly, she believed, that, in
regard to religious culture, she was very much in
advance of me. My disquiet, my impatience, my
striving, my seeking, investigating, musing, and wavering, she interpreted in her own way, and did not
conceal from me her conviction, but assured me in
plain terms that all this proceeded from my having
no reconciled God. Now, I had believed from my
youth upwards that I stood on very good terms with
my God, — nay, I even fancied to myself, according to
various experiences, that he might even be in arrears
to me; and I was daring enough to think that I had
something to forgive him. This presumption was
grounded on my infinite good will, to which, as it
seemed to me, he should have given better assistance.
It may be imagined how often I got into disputes on
this subject with my friend, which, however, always
terminated in the friendliest way, and often, like my
conversations with the old rector, with the remark,

"that I was a foolish fellow, for whom many allowances must be made."

I was much troubled with the tumour in my neck, as the physician and surgeon wished first to disperse this excrescence, afterward, as they said, to draw it to a head, and at last thought it best to open it; so for a long time I had to suffer more from inconvenience than pain, although toward the end of the cure the continual touching with lunar caustic and other corrosive substances could not but give me very disagreeable prospects for every fresh day. The physician and surgeon both belonged to the Pious Separatists, although both were of highly different natural characters. The surgeon, a slender, well-built man, of easy and skilful hand, was unfortunately somewhat hectic, but endured his condition with truly Christian patience, and did not suffer his disease to perplex him in his profession. The physician was an inexplicable, sly-looking, fair-spoken, and, besides, an abstruse, man, who had quite won the confidence of the pious circle. Being active and attentive, he was consoling to the sick ; but, more than by all this, he extended his practice by the gift of showing in the background some mysterious medicines prepared by himself, of which no one could speak, since with us the physicians were strictly prohibited from making up their own prescriptions. With certain powders, which may have been some kind of digestive, he was not so reserved, but that powerful salt, which could only be applied in the greatest danger, was only mentioned among believers ; although no one had yet seen it or traced its effects. To excite and strengthen our faith in the possibility of such an universal remedy, the physician, wherever he found any susceptibility, had recommended certain chemico-alchemical books to his patients, and given them to understand, that, by one's own study of them, one could well attain this treasure for one's self, which was the more necessary, as the mode of its preparation, both for physical, and especially for moral, reasons, could not be well communicated; nay, that in order to comprehend, produce, and use this great work, one must know the secrets of nature in connection, since it was not a particular, but an universal remedy, and could indeed be produced under different forms and shapes. My friend had listened to these enticing words. The health of the body was too nearly allied to the health of the soul: and could a greater benefit, a greater mercy, be shown toward others than by appropriating to one's self a remedy by which so many sufferings could be assuaged, so many a danger averted? She had already secretly studied Welling's "Opus Mago-cabalisticum," for which, however, as the author himself immediately darkens and removes the light he imparts, she was looking about for a friend, who, in this alternation of glare and gloom, might bear her company. It needed small incitement to inoculate me also with this disease. I procured the work, which, like all writings of this kind, could trace its pedigree in a direct line up to the Neo-Platonic school. My chief labour in this book was most accurately to notice the obscure hints by which the author refers from one passage to another, and thus promises to reveal what he conceals, and to mark down on the margin the number of the page where such passages as should explain each other were to be found. But even thus the book still remained dark and unintelligible enough, except that one at last studied one's self into a certain terminology, and, by using it according to one's own fancy, believed that one was, at any rate, saying, if not understanding, something. The work mentioned before makes very honourable mention of its predecessors, and we were incited to investigate those original sources themselves. We turned to the works of Theophrastus, Paracelsus, and Basilius Valentinus, as well as to those of Helmont,

Starkey, and others, whose doctrines and directions, resting more or less on nature and imagination, we endeavoured to see into and follow out. I was particularly pleased with the "Aurea Catena Homeri," in which nature, though perhaps in fantastical fashion, is represented in a beautiful combination; and thus sometimes by ourselves, sometimes together, we employed much time on these singularities, and spent the evenings of a long winter — during which I was compelled to keep my chamber — very agreeably, since we three (my mother being included) were more delighted with these secrets than we could have been at their elucidation.

In the meantime, a very severe trial was preparing for me: for a disturbed, and, one might even say, for certain moments, destroyed digestion, excited such symptoms, that, in great tribulation, I thought I should lose my life; and none of the remedies applied would produce any further effect. In this last extremity my distressed mother constrained the embarrassed physician with the greatest vehemence to come out with his universal medicine. After a long refusal, he hastened home at the dead of night, and returned with a little glass of crystallised dry salt, which was dissolved in water, and swallowed by the patient. It had a decidedly alkaline taste. The salt was scarcely taken than my situation appeared relieved; and from that moment the disease took a turn which, by degrees, led to my recovery. I need not say how much this strengthened and heightened our faith in our physician, and our industry to share in such a treasure.

My friend, who, without parents or brothers and sisters, lived in a large, well-situated house, had already before this begun to purchase herself a little air-furnace, alembics, and retorts of moderate size, and, in accordance with the hints of Welling, and the significant signs of our physician and master, operated principally on iron, in which the most healing powers were said to be concealed, if one only knew how to open it. And as the volatile salt which must be produced made a great figure in all the writings with which we were acquainted ; so, for these operations, alkalies also were required, which, while they flowed away into the air, were to unite with these superterrestrial things, and at last produce, *per se*, a mysterious and excellent neutral salt.

No sooner was I in some measure restored, and, favoured by the change in the season, once more able to occupy my old gable chamber, then I also began to provide myself with a little apparatus. A small air-furnace with a sand-bath was prepared ; and I very soon learned to change the glass alembics, with a piece of burning match-cord, into vessels in which the different mixtures were to be evaporated. Now were the strange ingredients of the macrocosm and microcosm handled in an odd, mysterious manner ; and, before all, I attempted to produce neutral salts in an unheard-of way. But what, for a long time, kept me busy most, was the so-called *Liquor Silicum* (flint juice), which is made by melting down pure quartz flint with a proper proportion of alkali, whence results a transparent glass, which melts away on exposure to the air, and exhibits a beautiful clear fluidity. Whoever has once prepared this himself, and seen it with his own eyes, will not blame those who believe in a maiden earth, and in the possibility of producing further effects upon it by means of it. I had become quite skilful in preparing this *Liquor Silicum ;* the fine white flints which are found in the Main furnished a perfect material for it : and I was not wanting in the other requisites, nor in diligence. But I wearied at last, because I could not but remark that the flinty substance was by no means so closely combined with the salt as I had philosophically imagined, for it very easily separated itself again ; and this most beautiful mineral fluidity, which, to my greatest astonishment, had sometimes appeared in the form of an animal jelly, always deposited a powder, which I was forced to pronounce the finest flint dust, but which gave not the least sign of anything productive in its nature from which one could have hoped to see this maiden earth pass into the maternal state.

Strange and unconnected as these operations were, I yet learned many things from them. I paid strict attention to all the crystallisations that might occur, and became acquainted with the external forms of many natural things: and, inasmuch as I well knew that in modern times chemical subjects were treated more methodically, I wished to get a general conception of them; although, as a half adept, I had very little respect for the apothecaries and all those who operated with common fire. However, the chemical "Compendium" of Boerhaave attracted me powerfully, and led me on to read several of his writings, in which (since, moreover, my tedious illness had inclined me toward medical subjects) I found an inducement to study also the "Aphorisms" of this excellent man, which I was glad to stamp upon my mind and in my memory.

Another employment, somewhat more human, and by far more useful for my cultivation at the moment, was reading through the letters which I had written home from Leipzig. Nothing reveals more with respect to ourselves, than when we again see before us that which has proceeded from us years before, so that we can now consider ourselves as an object of contemplation. But, of course, I was as yet too young, and the epoch which was represented by those papers was still too near. As in our younger years we do not in general easily cast off a certain self-complacent conceit, this especially shows itself in despising what we have been but a little time before; for while, indeed, we perceive, as we advance from step to step, that those things which we regard as good and excellent in ourselves and others do not stand their ground, we think we can best extricate ourselves from this dilemma by ourselves throwing away what we cannot preserve. So it was with me also. For as in Leipzig I had gradually learned to set little value on my childish labours, so now my academical course seemed to me likewise of small account; and I did not understand, that, for this very reason, it must be of great value to me, as it elevated me to a higher degree of observation and insight. My father had carefully collected and sewed together the letters I had written to him, as well as those to my sister; nay, he had even corrected them with attention, and improved the mistakes, both in writing and in grammar.

What first struck me in these letters was their exterior: I was shocked at an incredible carelessness in the handwriting, which extended from October, 1765, to the middle of the following January. But, in the middle of March, there appeared all at once a quite compressed, orderly hand, such as I used formerly to employ in writing for a prize. My astonishment resolved itself into gratitude toward good Gellert, who, as I now well remembered, whenever we handed in our essays to him, represented to us, in his hearty tone of voice, that it was our sacred duty to practise our hand as much, nay, more, than our style. He repeated this as often as he caught sight of any scrawled, careless writing, on which occasion he often said that he would much like to make a good hand of his pupils the principal end in his instructions; the more so as he had often remarked that a good hand led the way to a good style.

I could further notice that the French and English passages in my letters, although not free from blunders, were nevertheless written with facility and freedom.

These languages I had likewise continued to practise in my correspondence with George Schlosser, who was still at Treptow; and I had remained in constant communication with him, by which I was instructed in many secular affairs (for things did not always turn out with him quite as he had hoped), and acquired an ever increasing confidence in his earnest, noble way of thinking.

Another consideration which could not escape me in going over these letters, was that my good father, with the best intentions, had done me a special mischief. and had led me into that odd way of life into which I had fallen at last. He had repeatedly warned me against card-playing; but Frau Hofrath Böhme, as long as she lived, contrived to persuade me, after her own fashion, by declaring that my father's warnings were only against the abuse. Now, as I likewise saw the advantages of it in society, I readily submitted to being led by her. I had indeed the sense of play, but not the spirit of play: I learned all games easily and rapidly, but I could never keep up the proper attention for a whole evening. Therefore, however good a beginning I would make, I invariably failed at the end, and made myself and others lose; through which I went off, always out of humour, either to the supper-table or out of the company. Scarcely had Madame Böhme died, who, moreover, had no longer kept me in practice during her tedious illness, when my father's doctrine gained force: I at first begged to be excused from joining the card-tables; and, as they now did not know what else to do with me, I became even more of a burden to myself than to others, and declined the invitations, which then became more rare, and at last ceased altogether. Play, which is much to be recommended to young people, especially to those who incline to be practical, and wish to look about in the world for themselves, could never, indeed, become a passion with me; for I never got any farther, no matter how long I might have been playing. Had any one given me a general view of the subject, and made me observe how here certain signs and more or less of chance form a kind of material, at which judgment and activity can exercise themselves; had any one made me see several games at once, — I might sooner have become reconciled. With all this, at the time of which I am now speaking, I had, from the above considerations, come to the conviction, that one should not avoid social games, but should rather strive after a certain skill in them. Time is infinitely long; and each day is a vessel into which a great deal may be poured, if one would actually fill it up.

Thus variously was I occupied in my solitude; the more so, as the departed spirits of the different tastes to which I had from time to time devoted myself had an opportunity to reappear. I then again took up drawing: and as I always wished to labour directly from nature, or rather from reality, I made a picture of my chamber, with its furniture, and the persons who were in it; and, when this no more amused me, I represented all sorts of town tales, which were told at the time, and in which interest was taken. All this was not without character and a certain taste; but unfortunately the figures lacked proportion and the proper vigour, besides which the execution was extremely misty. My father, who continued to take pleasure in these things, wished to have them more distinct, wanting everything to be finished and properly completed. He therefore had them mounted and surrounded with ruled lines; nay, the painter Morgenstern, his domestic artist, — the same who afterward made himself known, and indeed famous, by his church-views, — had to insert the perspective lines of the rooms and chambers, which then, indeed, stood in pretty harsh contrast with those cloudy looking figures. In this manner he thought he would make me gain greater accuracy; and, to please him, I drew various objects of still life, in which, since the originals stood as patterns before me, I could work with more distinctness and precision. At last I took it into my head to etch once more. I had composed a tolerably interesting landscape, and felt myself very happy when I could look out for the old receipts given me by Stock, and could, at my work, call to mind those pleasant times. I soon bit the plate and had a proof taken. Unluckily the composition was without light and shade, and I now tormented myself to bring in both; but, as it was not quite clear to me what was really the essential point, I could not finish. Up to this time I had been quite well, after my own fashion; but now a disease attacked me which had never troubled me before. My throat, namely, had become completely sore, and particularly what is called the "uvula" very much inflamed: I could only swallow with great pain, and the physicians did not know what to make of it. They tormented me with gargles and hair pencils, but could not free me from my misery. At last it struck me that I had not been careful enough in the biting of my plates, and that, by often and passionately repeating it, I had contracted this disease, and always revived and increased it. To the physicians this cause was plausible, and very soon certain on my leaving my etching and biting, and that so much the more readily as the attempt had by no means turned out well, and I had more reason to conceal than to exhibit my labours; for which I consoled myself the more easily, as I very soon saw myself free from the troublesome disease. Upon this I could not refrain from the reflection, that my similar occupations at Leipzig might have greatly contributed to those diseases from which I had suffered so much. It is, indeed, a tedious, and withal a melancholy, business to take too much care of ourselves, and of what injures and benefits us; but there is no question but that, with the wonderful idiosyncrasy of human nature on the one side, and the infinite variety in the mode of life and pleasure on the other, it is a wonder that the human race has not worn itself out long ago. Human nature appears to possess a peculiar kind of toughness and many-sidedness, since it subdues everything which approaches it, or which it takes into itself, and, if it cannot assimilate, at least makes it indifferent. In case of any great excess, indeed, it must yield to the elements in spite of all resistance, as the many endemic diseases and the effects of brandy convince us. Could we, without being morbidly anxious, keep watch over ourselves as to what operates favourably or unfavourably upon us in our complicated civil and social life, and would we leave off what is actually pleasant to us as an enjoyment, for the sake of the evil consequences, we should thus know how to remove with ease many an inconvenience which, with a constitution otherwise sound, often troubles us more than even a disease. Unfortunately, it is in dietetics as in morals, — we cannot see into a fault till we have got rid of it; by which nothing is gained, for the next fault is not like the preceding one, and therefore cannot be recognised under the same form.

While I was reading over the letters which had been written to my sister from Leipzig, this remark, among others, could not escape me, — that, from the very beginning of my academical course, I had esteemed myself very clever and wise, since, as soon as I had learned anything, I put myself in the place of the professor, and so became didactic on the spot. I was amused to see how I had immediately applied to my sister whatever Gellert had imparted or advised in his lectures, without seeing, that, both in life and in books, a thing may be proper for a young man without being suitable for a young lady; and we both together made

merry over these mimicries. The poems also which I
had composed in Leipzig were already too poor for me ;
and they seemed to me cold, dry, and, in respect of all
that was meant to express the state of the human
heart or mind, too superficial. This induced me, now
that I was to leave my father's house once more, and
go to a second university, again to decree a great high
auto-da-fé against my labours. Several commenced
plays, some of which had reached the third or the
fourth act, while others had only the plot fully made
out, together with many other poems, letters, and papers, were given over to the fire : and scarcely anything was spared except the manuscript by Behrisch,
" Die Laune des Verliebten " and " Die Mitschuldigen,"
which latter play I constantly went on improving with
peculiar affection ; and, as the piece was already complete, I again worked over the plot, to make it more
bustling and intelligible. Lessing, in the first two acts
of his " Minna," had set up an unattainable model of
the way in which a drama should be developed ; and
nothing was to me of greater importance than to
thoroughly enter into his meaning and views.

The recital of whatever moved, excited, and occupied
me at this time, is already circumstantial enough ; but
I must nevertheless recur to that interest with which
supersensuous things had inspired me, of which I,
once for all, so far as might be possible, undertook to
form some notion.

I experienced a great influence from an important
work that fell into my hands : it was Arnold's " History
of the Church and of Heretics." This man is not
merely a reflective historian, but at the same time
pious and feeling. His sentiments chimed in very
well with mine ; and what particularly delighted me
in his work was, that I received a more favourable
notion of many heretics, who had been hitherto represented to me as mad or impious. The spirit of con-

tradiction and the love of paradoxes are inherent in us all. I diligently studied the different opinions: and as I had often enough heard it said that every man has his own religion at last, so nothing seemed more natural to me than that I should form mine too; and this I did with much satisfaction. The Neo-Platonism lay at the foundation; the hermetical, the mystical, the cabalistic, also contributed their share; and thus I built for myself a world that looked strange enough.

I could well represent to myself a Godhead which has gone on producing itself from all eternity; but, as production cannot be conceived without multiplicity, so it must of necessity have immediately appeared to itself as a Second, which we recognise under the name of the Son; now, these two must continue the act of producing, and again appear to themselves in a Third, which was just as substantial, living, and eternal as the Whole. With these, however, the circle of the Godhead was complete; and it would not have been possible for them to produce another perfectly equal to them. But, since the work of production always proceeded, they created a fourth, which already fostered in himself a contradiction, inasmuch as it was, like them, unlimited, and yet at the same time was to be contained in them and bounded by them. Now, this was Lucifer, to whom the whole power of creation was committed from this time, and from whom all other beings were to proceed. He immediately displayed his infinite activity by creating the whole body of angels, — all, again, after his own likeness, unlimited, but contained in him and bounded by him. Surrounded by such a glory, he forgot his higher origin, and believed that he could find himself in himself; and from this first ingratitude sprang all that does not seem to us in accordance with the will and purposes of the Godhead. Now, the more he concentrated himself within himself, the more painful must it have become to him, as well as to all the spirits whose sweet uprising to their origin he had embittered. And so that happened which is intimated to us under the form of the Fall of the Angels. One part of them concentrated itself with Lucifer, the other turned itself again to its origin. From this concentration of the whole creation — for it had proceeded out of Lucifer, and was forced to follow him — sprang all that we perceive under the form of matter, which we figure to ourselves as heavy, solid, and dark, but which, since it is descended, if not even immediately, yet by filiation, from the Divine Being, is just as unlimited, powerful, and eternal as its sire and grandsire. Now, the whole mischief, if we may call it so, having arisen merely through the one-sided direction of Lucifer, the better half was indeed wanting to this creation; for it possessed all that is gained by concentration, while it lacked all that can be effected by expansion alone: and so the entire creation might have been destroyed by everlasting concentration, become annihilated with its father Lucifer, and have lost all its claims to an equal eternity with the Godhead. This condition the Elohim contemplated for a time: and they had their choice, to wait for those eons, in which the field would again have become clear, and space would be left them for a new creation; or, if they would, to seize upon that which existed already, and supply the want, according to their own eternity. Now, they chose the latter, and by their mere will supplied in an instant the whole want which the consequence of Lucifer's undertaking drew after it. They gave to the Eternal Being the faculty of expansion, of moving toward them: the peculiar pulse of life was again restored, and Lucifer himself could not avoid its effects. This is the epoch when that appeared which we know as light, and when that began which we are accustomed to designate by the word creation. However much this multiplied itself by progressive degrees,

through the continually working vital power of the
Elohim, still a being was wanting who might be able
to restore the original connection with the Godhead:
and thus man was produced, who in all things was to be
similar, yea, equal to the Godhead, but thereby, in
effect, found himself once more in the situation of
Lucifer, that of being at once unlimited and limited;
and since this contradiction was to manifest itself in
him through all the categories of existence, and a perfect consciousness, as well as a decided will, was to
accompany his various conditions, it was to be foreseen that he must be at the same time the most perfect and the most imperfect, the most happy and the
most unhappy, creature. It was not long before he,
too, completely acted the part of Lucifer. True ingratitude is the separation from the benefactor; and
thus that fall was manifest for the second time, although
the whole creation is nothing and was nothing but a
falling from and returning to the original.

One easily sees how the Redemption is not only
decreed from eternity, but is considered as eternally
necessary, — nay, that it must ever renew itself through
the whole time of generation [1] and existence. In this
view of the subject, nothing is more natural than for
the Divinity himself to take the form of man, which
had already prepared itself as a veil, and to share his
fate for a short time, in order, by this assimilation,
to enhance his joys and alleviate his sorrows. The
history of all religions and philosophies teaches us,
that this great truth, indispensable to man, has been
handed down by different nations, in different times,
in various ways, and even in strange fables and images,
in accordance with their limited knowledge: enough,
if it only be acknowledged that we find ourselves in a

[1] " Das Werden," the state of becoming, as distinguished from
that of being. The word, which is most useful to the Germans,
can never be rendered properly in English. — TRANS.

condition which, even if it seems to drag us down and oppress us, yet gives us opportunity, nay, even makes it our duty, to raise ourselves up, and to fulfil the purposes of the Godhead in this manner, that, while we are compelled on the one hand to concentrate ourselves (*uns zu verselbsten*), we, on the other hand, do not omit to expand ourselves (*uns zu entselbstigen*) in regular pulsation.[1]

---

[1] If we could make use of some such verbs as " inself " and " unself," we should more accurately render this passage. — TRANS.

NINTH BOOK.

"THE heart is often affected, moreover, to the advantage of different, but especially of social and refined, virtues; and the more tender sentiments are excited and unfolded in it. Many touches, in particular, will impress themselves, which give the young reader an insight into the more hidden corner of the human heart and its passions, — a knowledge which is more worth than all Latin and Greek, and of which Ovid was a very excellent master. But yet it is not on this account that the classic poets, and therefore Ovid, are placed in the hands of youth. We have received from a kind Creator a variety of mental powers, to which we must not neglect giving their proper culture in our earliest years, and which cannot be cultivated, either by logic or metaphysics, Latin or Greek. We have an imagination, before which, since it should not seize upon the very first conceptions that chance to present themselves, we ought to place the fittest and most beautiful images, and thus accustom and practise the mind to recognise and love the beautiful everywhere, and in nature itself, under its determined, true, and also in its finer, features. A multitude of conceptions and general knowledge is necessary to us, as well for the sciences as for daily life, which can be learned out of no compendium. Our feelings, affections, and passions should be advantageously developed and purified."

This significant passage, which is found in "The Universal German Library," was not the only one of its kind. Similar principles and similar views manifested

384

themselves in many directions. They made upon us lively youths a very great impression, which had the more decided effect, as it was strengthened besides by Wieland's example; for the works of his second brilliant period clearly showed that he had formed himself according to such maxims. And what more could we desire? Philosophy, with its abstruse questions, was set aside; the classic languages, the acquisition of which is accompanied by so much drudgery, one saw thrust into the background; the compendiums, about the sufficiency of which Hamlet had already whispered a word of caution into our ears, came more and more into suspicion. We were directed to the contemplation of an active life, which we were so fond of leading; and to the knowledge of the passions, which we partly felt, partly anticipated, in our own bosoms, and which, if though they had been rebuked formerly, now appeared to us as something important and dignified, because they were to be the chief object of our studies; and the knowledge of them was extolled as the most excellent means of cultivating our mental powers. Besides, such a mode of thought was quite in accordance with my own conviction, — nay, with my poetical mode of treatment. I therefore, without opposition, after I had thwarted so many good designs, and seen so many fair hopes vanish, reconciled myself to my father's intention of sending me to Strasburg, where I was promised a cheerful, gay life, while I should prosecute my studies, and at last take my degree.

In spring I felt my health, but still more my youthful spirits, restored, and once more longed to be out of my father's house, though with reasons far different from those on the first time. The pretty chambers and spots where I had suffered so much had become disagreeable to me, and with my father himself there could be no pleasant relation. I could not quite pardon him for having manifested more impatience than was reasonable at the relapse of my disease, and at my tedious recovery; nay, for having, instead of comforting me by forbearance, frequently expressed himself in a cruel manner, about that which lay in no man's hand, as if it depended only on the will. And he, too, was in various ways hurt and offended by me.

For young people bring back from the university general ideas, which, indeed, is quite right and good; but, because they fancy themselves very wise in this, they apply them as a standard to the objects that occur, which must then, for the most part, lose by the comparison. Thus I had gained a general notion of architecture, and of the arrangement and decoration of houses, and imprudently, in conversation, had applied this to our own house. My father had designed the whole arrangement of it, and carried out its construction with great perseverance; and, considering that it was to be exclusively a residence for himself and his family, nothing could be objected to it: in this taste, also, very many of the houses in Frankfort were built. An open staircase ran up through the house, and touched upon large anterooms, which might very well have been chambers themselves, as, indeed, we always passed the fine season in them. But this pleasant, cheerful existence for a single family — this communication from above to below — became the greatest inconvenience as soon as several parties occupied the house, as we had but too well experienced on the occasion of the French quartering. For that painful scene with the king's lieutenant would not have happened, nay, my father would even have felt all those disagreeable matters less, if, after the Leipzig fashion, our staircase had run close along the side of the house, and a separate door had been given to each story. This style of building I once praised highly for its advantages, and showed my father the possibility of altering his staircase also; whereat he got into an incredible passion, which was the more violent as, a short time before, I had found fault with some scrolled looking-glass frames, and rejected certain Chinese hangings A scene ensued, which, indeed, was again hushed up and smothered; but it hastened my journey to the beautiful Alsace, which I accomplished in a newly contrived comfortable diligence, without delay, and in a short time.

I had alighted at the Ghost (*Geist*) tavern, and hastened at once to satisfy my most earnest desire and to approach the minster, which had long since been pointed out to me by fellow travellers, and had been before my eyes for a great distance. When I first perceived this colossus through the narrow lanes, and then stood too near before it, in the truly confined little square, it made upon me an impression quite of its own kind, which I, being unable to analyse on the spot, carried with me only indistinctly for this time, as I hastily ascended the building, so as not to neglect the beautiful moment of a high and cheerful sun, which was to disclose to me at once the broad, rich land.

And now, from the platform, I saw before me the beautiful country in which I should for a long time live and reside: the handsome city; the wide-spreading meadows around it, thickly set and interwoven with magnificent trees; that striking richness of vegetation which follows in the windings of the Rhine, marks its banks, islands, and aits. Nor is the level ground, stretching down from the south, and watered by the Iller, less adorned with varied green. Even westward, toward the mountains, there are many low grounds, which afford quite as charming a view of wood and meadow-growth, just as the northern and more hilly part is intersected by innumerable little brooks, which promote a rapid vegetation everywhere. If one imagines, between these luxuriantly outstretched meads, between these joyously scattered groves, all land adapted for tillage, excellently prepared, verdant, and ripening, and the best and richest spots marked by hamlets and farmhouses, and this great and immeasurable plain, prepared for man, like a new paradise, bounded far and near by mountains partly cultivated, partly overgrown with woods, he will then conceive the rapture with which I blessed my fate, that it had destined me, for some time, so beautiful a dwelling-place.

Such a fresh glance into a new land in which we are to abide for a time has still the peculiarity, both pleasant and foreboding, that the whole lies before us like an unwritten tablet. As yet no sorrows and joys which relate to ourselves are recorded upon it; this cheerful, varied, animated plain is still mute for us; the eye is only fixed on the objects so far as they are intrinsically important, and neither affection nor passion has especially to render prominent this or that spot. But a presentiment of the future already disquiets the young heart; and an unsatisfied craving secretly demands that which is to come and may come, and which at all events, whether for good or ill, will imperceptibly assume the character of the spot in which we find ourselves.

Having descended the height, I still tarried awhile before the face of the venerable pile; but what I could not quite clearly make out, either the first or the following time, was, that I regarded this miracle as a monster, which must have terrified me, if it had not, at the same time, appeared to me comprehensible by its regularity, and even pleasing in its finish. Yet I by no means busied myself with meditating on this contradiction, but suffered a monument so astonishing quietly to work upon me by its presence.

I took small, but well-situated and pleasant, lodgings, on the north side of the Fish-market, a fine, long street, where the everlasting motion came to the assistance of every unoccupied moment. I then delivered my letters of introduction, and found among my patrons a merchant, who, with his family, was devoted to those pious opinions sufficiently known to me, although, as far as regarded external worship, he had not separated from the Church. He was a man of intelligence withal, and by no means hypocritical in his conduct. The company of boarders which was recommended to me, and, indeed, I to it, was very agreeable and entertaining. A couple of old maids had long kept up this boarding-house with regularity and good success: there might have been about ten persons, older and younger. Of these latter, one named Meyer, a native of Lindau, is most vividly present to my mind. From his form and face he might have been considered one of the handsomest of men, if, at the same time, he had not had something of the sloven in his whole appearance. In like manner his splendid natural talents were marred by an incredible levity, and his excellent temper by an unbounded dissoluteness. He had an open, jovial face, rather more round than oval: the organs of the senses, the eyes, nose, mouth, and ears, could be called rich; they showed a decided fulness, without being too large. His mouth was particularly charming, owing to his curling lips; and his whole physiognomy had the peculiar expression of a rake, from the circumstance that his eyebrows met across his nose, which, in a handsome face, always produces a pleasant expression of sensuality. By his jovialness, sincerity, and good nature, he made himself beloved by all. His memory was incredible; attention at the lectures was no effort for him; he retained all he heard, and was intellectual enough to take an interest in everything, and this the more easily, as he was studying medicine. All his impressions remained vivid; and his waggery in repeating the lectures and mimicking the professors often went so far, that, when he had heard three different lectures in one morning, he would, at the dinner-table, interchange the professors with each other, paragraph-wise, and often even more abruptly, which motley lecture frequently entertained us, but often, too, became troublesome.

The rest were more or less polite, steady, serious people. A pensioned knight of the order of St. Louis was one of these; but the majority were students, all really good and well-disposed; only they were not allowed to go beyond their usual allowance of wine. That this should not be easily done was the care of our president, one Doctor Salzmann. Already in the sixties and unmarried, he had attended this dinner-table for many years, and maintained its good order and respectability. He possessed a handsome property, kept himself close and neat in his exterior, even belonging to those who always go in shoes and stockings, and with their hat under their arm. To put on the hat was with him an extraordinary action. He commonly carried an umbrella, wisely reflecting that the finest summer days often bring thunder-storms and passing showers over the country.

With this man I talked over my design of continuing to study jurisprudence at Strasburg, so as to be able to take my degree as soon as possible. Since he was exactly informed of everything, I asked him about the lectures I should have to hear, and what he generally thought of the matter. To this he replied, that it was not in Strasburg as in the German universities, where they try to educate jurists in the large and learned sense of the term. Here, in conformity with the relation toward France, all was really directed to the practical, and managed in accordance with the opinions of the French, who readily stop at what is given. They tried to impart to every one certain general principles and preliminary knowledge, they compressed as much as possible, and communicated only what was most necessary. Hereupon he made me acquainted with a man, in whom, as a *repetent*,[1] great confidence was entertained; which he very soon managed to gain from me also. By way of introduction, I began to speak with him on subjects of jurisprudence; and he wondered not a little at my swaggering: for, during my residence at Leipzig, I had gained more of an insight into the requisites for the law than I have hitherto taken occasion to state in my narrative, though all I had acquired could only be reckoned as a general encyclopedical survey, and not as proper definite knowledge. University life, even if in the course of it we may not exactly have to boast of industry, nevertheless affords endless advantages in every kind of cultivation, because we are always surrounded by men who either possess or are seeking science, so that, even if unconsciously, we are constantly drawing some nourishment from such an atmosphere.

My repetent, after he had had patience with my rambling discourse for some time, gave me at last to understand that I must first of all keep my immediate object in view, which was, to be examined, to take my degree, and then, perchance, to commence practice. "Regarding the former," said he, "the subject is by no means investigated at large. It is inquired how and when a law arose, and what gave the internal or external occasion for it: there is no inquiry as to how it has been altered by time and custom, or how far it has perhaps been perverted by false interpretation

[1] A repetent is one of a class of persons to be found in the German universities, and who assist students in their studies. They are somewhat analogous to the English tutors, but not precisely: for the latter render their aid *before* the recitation; while the repetent *repeats* with the student, in private, the lectures he has previously heard from the professor. Hence his name, which might be rendered *repeater*, had we any corresponding class of men in England or America, which would justify an English word. — *American Note.*

or the perverted usage of the courts. It is in such
investigations that learned men quite peculiarly spend
their lives, whereas we inquire into that which exists
at present · this we stamp firmly on our memory, that
it may always be ready when we wish to employ it
for the use and defence of our clients. Thus we
qualify our young people for their future life, and the
rest follows in proportion to their talents and activity." Hereupon he handed me his pamphlets, which
were written in question and answer, and in which I
could have stood a pretty good examination at once;
for Hopp's smaller law-catechism was yet perfectly in
my memory: the rest I supplied with some diligence,
and, against my will, qualified myself in the easiest
manner as a candidate.

But since in this way all my own activity in the
study was cut off, — for I had no sense for anything
positive, but wished to have everything explained historically, if not intelligibly, — I found for my powers
a wider field, which I employed in the most singular
manner by devoting myself to a matter of interest
which was accidentally presented to me from without.

Most of my fellow boarders were medical students.
These, as is well known, are the only students who
zealously converse about their science and profession,
even out of the hours of study. This lies in the
nature of the case. The objects of their endeavours
are those most obvious to the senses, and at the same
time the highest, the most simple, and the most complicated. Medicine employs the whole man, for it
occupies itself with man as a whole. All that the
young man learns refers directly to an important, dangerous indeed, but yet in many respects lucrative, practice. He therefore devotes himself passionately to
whatever is to be known and to be done, partly
because it is interesting in itself, partly because it

opens to him the joyous prospect of independence and wealth.

At table, then, I heard nothing but medical conversations, just as formerly in the boarding-house of Hofrath Ludwig. In our walks and in our pleasure-parties likewise not much else was talked about: for my fellow boarders, like good fellows, had also become my companions at other times; and they were always joined on all sides by persons of like minds and like studies. The medical faculty in general shone above the others, with respect both to the celebrity of the professors and the number of the students; and I was the more easily borne along by the stream, as I had just so much knowledge of all these things that my desire for science could soon be increased and inflamed. At the commencement of the second half-year, therefore, I attended Spielmann's course on chemistry, another on anatomy by Lobstein, and proposed to be right industrious, because, by my singular preliminary or rather extra knowledge, I had already gained some respect and confidence in our society.

Yet this trifling and piecemeal way of study was even to be once more seriously disturbed; for a remarkable political event set everything in motion, and procured us a tolerable succession of holidays. Marie Antoinette, Archduchess of Austria and Queen of France, was to pass through Strasburg on her road to Paris. The solemnities by which the people are made to take notice that there is greatness in the world were busily and abundantly prepared; and especially remarkable to me was the building which stood on an island in the Rhine between the two bridges, erected for her reception and for surrendering her into the hands of her husband's ambassadors. It was but slightly raised above the ground; had in the centre a grand saloon, on each side smaller ones; then followed other chambers, which extended somewhat backward. In short, had it been more durably built, it might have answered very well as a pleasure-house for persons of rank. But that which particularly interested me, and for which I did not grudge many a *Büsel* (a little silver coin then current) in order to procure a repeated entrance from the porter, was the embroidered tapestry with which they had lined the whole interior. Here, for the first time, I saw a specimen of those tapestries worked after Raffaelle's cartoons; and this sight was for me of very decided influence, as I became acquainted with the true and the perfect on a large scale, though only in copies. I went and came, and came and went, and could not satiate myself with looking; nay, a vain endeavour troubled me, because I would willingly have comprehended what interested me in so extraordinary a manner. I found these side-chambers highly delightful and refreshing, but the chief saloon so much the more shocking. This had been hung with many larger, more brilliant and richer, hangings, which were surrounded with crowded ornaments, worked after pictures by the modern French.

Now, I might perhaps have become reconciled to this style also, as my feelings, like my judgment, did not readily reject anything entirely; but the subject was excessively revolting to me. These pictures contained the history of Jason, Medea, and Creusa, and therefore an example of the most unhappy marriage. To the left of the throne was seen the bride struggling with the most horrible death, surrounded by persons full of sympathising woe; to the right was the father, horrified at the murdered babes before his feet; whilst the Fury, in her dragon-car, drove along into the air. And, that the horrible and atrocious should not lack something absurd, the white tail of that magic bull flourished out on the right hand from behind the red velvet of the gold-embroidered back of the throne;

while the fire-spitting beast himself and the Jason who was fighting with him, were completely covered by the sumptuous drapery.

Here all the maxims which I had made my own in Oeser's school were stirring within my bosom. It was without proper selection and judgment, to begin with, that Christ and the apostles were brought into the side-halls of a nuptial building; and doubtless the size of the chambers had guided the royal tapestry-keeper. This, however, I willingly forgave, because it had turned out so much to my advantage; but a blunder like that in the grand saloon put me altogether out of my self-possession, and with animation and vehemence I called on my comrades to witness such a crime against taste and feeling. "What!" cried I, without regarding the bystanders, "is it permitted so thoughtlessly to place before the eyes of a young queen, at her first setting foot in her dominions, the representation of the most horrible marriage that perhaps ever was consummated? Is there among the French architects, decorators, upholsterers, not a single man who understands that pictures represent something, that pictures work upon the mind and feelings, that they make impressions, that they excite forebodings? It is just the same as if they had sent the most ghastly spectre to meet this beauteous and pleasure-loving lady at the very frontiers!" I know not what I said besides: enough, my comrades tried to quiet me and to remove me out of the house, that there might be no offence. They then assured me that it was not everybody's concern to look for significance in pictures; that to themselves, at least, nothing of the sort would have occurred; while the whole population of Strasburg and the vicinity, which was to throng thither, would no more take such crotchets into their heads than the queen herself and her court.

I well yet remember the beauteous and lofty mien,

as cheerful as it was imposing, of this youthful lady. Perfectly visible to us all in her glass carriage, she seemed to be jesting with her female attendants, in familiar conversation, about the throng that poured forth to meet her train. In the evening we roamed through the streets to look at the various illuminated buildings, but especially the glowing spire of the minster, with which, both near and in the distance, we could not sufficiently feast our eyes.

The queen pursued her way: the country people dispersed, and the city was soon quiet as ever. Before the queen's arrival, the very reasonable regulation had been made, that no deformed persons, no cripples nor disgusting invalids, should show themselves on her route. People joked about this; and I made a little French poem in which I compared the advent of Christ, who seemed to wander upon earth particularly on account of the sick and the lame, with the arrival of the queen, who scared these unfortunates away. My friends let it pass: a Frenchman, on the contrary, who lived with us, criticised the language and metre very unmercifully, although, as it seemed, with too much foundation; and I do not remember that I ever made a French poem afterward.

No sooner had the news of the queen's happy arrival rung from the capital, than it was followed by the horrible intelligence, that, owing to an oversight of the police during the festal fireworks, an infinite number of persons, with horses and carriages, had been destroyed in a street obstructed by building materials, and that the city, in the midst of the nuptial solemnities, had been plunged into mourning and sorrow. They attempted to conceal the extent of the misfortune, both from the young royal pair and from the world, by burying the dead in secret; so that many families were convinced only by the ceaseless absence of their members that they, too, had been swept off by this awful event. That, on this occasion, those ghastly figures in the grand saloon again came vividly before my mind, I need scarcely mention; for every one knows how powerful certain moral impressions are when they embody themselves, as it were, in those of the senses.

This occurrence was, however, destined moreover to place my friends in anxiety and trouble by means of a prank in which I indulged. Among us young people who had been at Leipzig, there had been maintained ever afterward a certain itch for imposing on and in some way mystifying one another. With this wanton love of mischief I wrote to a friend in Frankfort (he was the one who had amplified my poem on the cake-baker Hendel, applied it to *Medon,* and caused its general circulation) a letter dated from Versailles, in which I informed him of my happy arrival there, my participation in the solemnities, and other things of the kind, but at the same time enjoined the strictest secrecy. I must here remark, that, from the time of that trick which had caused us so much annoyance, our little Leipzig society had accustomed itself to persecute him from time to time with mystifications, and this especially as he was the drollest man in the world, and was never more amiable than when he was discovering the cheat into which he had deliberately been led. Shortly after I had written this letter, I went on a little journey, and remained absent about a fortnight. Meanwhile the news of that disaster had reached Frankfort: my friend believed me in Paris, and his affection led him to apprehend that I might have been involved in the calamity. He inquired of my parents and other persons to whom I was accustomed to write, whether any letters had arrived; and, as it was just the time when my journey kept me from sending any, they were altogether wanting. He went about in the greatest uneasiness, and at last told the matter in confidence to our nearest friends, who were now in equal anxiety. Fortunately this conjecture did not reach my parents until a letter had arrived announcing my return to Strasburg. My young friends were satisfied to learn that I was alive, but remained firmly convinced that I had been at Paris in the interim. The affectionate intelligence of the solicitude they had felt on my account affected me so much that I vowed to leave off such tricks for ever; but, unfortunately, I have often since allowed myself to be guilty of something similar. Real life frequently loses its brilliancy to such a degree, that one is many a time forced to polish it up again with the varnish of fiction.

This mighty stream of courtly magnificence had now flowed by, and had left in me no other longing than after those tapestries of Raffaelle, which I would willingly have gazed at, revered, nay, adored, every day and every hour. Fortunately, my passionate endeavours succeeded in interesting several persons of consequence in them, so that they were taken down and packed up as late as possible. We now gave ourselves up again to our quiet, easy routine of the university and society; and in the latter the Actuary Salzmann, president of our table, continued to be the general pedagogue. His intelligence, complaisance, and dignity, which he always contrived to maintain amid all the jests, and often even in the little extravagances which he allowed us, made him beloved and respected by the whole company; and I could mention but few instances where he showed his serious displeasure, or interposed with authority in little quarrels and disputes. Yet among them all I was the one who most attached myself to him; and he was not less inclined to converse with me, as he found me more variously accomplished than the others, and not so one-sided in judgment. I also followed his directions in external matters; so that he could, without hesitation, publicly acknowledge me as his companion and comrade: for, although he only filled an office which seems to be of little influence, he administered it in a manner which redounded to his highest honour. He was actuary to the Court of Wards (*Pupillen-Collegium*); and there, indeed, like the perpetual secretary of a university, he had, properly speaking, the management of affairs in his own hands. Now, as he had performed the duties of this office with the greatest exactness for many years, there was no family, from the first to the last, which did not owe him its gratitude; as indeed scarcely any one in the whole administration of government can earn more blessings or more curses than one who takes charge of the orphans, or, on the contrary, squanders or suffers to be squandered their property and goods.

The Strasburgers are passionate walkers, and they have a good right to be so. Let one turn his steps as he will, he will find pleasure-grounds, partly natural, partly adorned by art in ancient and modern times, all of them visited and enjoyed by a cheerful, merry little people. But what made the sight of a great number of pedestrians still more agreeable here than in other places, was the various costume of the fair sex. The middle class of city girls yet retained the hair twisted up and secured by a large pin, as well as a certain close style of dress, in which anything like a train would have been unbecoming: and the pleasant part of it was, that this costume did not differ violently according to the rank of the wearer; for there were still some families of opulence and distinction who would not permit their daughters to deviate from this costume. The rest followed the French fashion, and this party made some proselytes every year. Salzmann had many acquaintances and an entrance everywhere: a very pleasant circumstance for his companion, especially in summer, for good company and refreshment were found in all the public gardens far and near, and more than one invitation for this or that pleasant day was received. On one such occasion I found an opportunity to recommend myself very rapidly to a family which I was visiting for only the second time. We were invited, and arrived at the appointed hour. The company was not large : some played and some walked as usual. Afterward, when they were to go to supper, I saw our hostess and her sister speaking to each other with animation, and as if in a peculiar embarrassment. I accosted them, and said, " I have indeed no right, ladies, to force myself into your secrets; but perhaps I may be able to give you good counsel, or even to serve you." Upon this they disclosed to me their painful dilemma ; namely, that they had invited twelve persons to table, and that just at that moment a relation had returned from a journey, who now, as the thirteenth, would be a fatal *memento mori*, if not for himself, yet certainly for some of the guests. " The case is very easily mended," replied I : " permit me to take my leave, and stipulate for indemnification." As they were persons of consequence and good breeding, they would by no means allow this, but sent about in the neighbourhood to find a fourteenth. I suffered them to do so ; yet when I saw the servant coming in at the garden-gate without having effected his errand, I stole away and spent my evening pleasantly under the old linden-trees of the Wanzenau. That this self-denial was richly repaid me was a very natural consequence.

A certain kind of general society is not to be thought of without card-playing. Salzmann renewed the good instructions of Madame Böhme ; and I was the more docile as I had really seen, that by this little sacrifice, if it be one, one may procure one's self much pleasure, and even a greater freedom in society than one would otherwise enjoy. The old piquet, which had gone to sleep, was again looked out; I learned whist; I made myself, according to the directions of my Mentor, a card-purse, which was to remain untouched under all circumstances; and I now found opportunity to spend most of my evenings with my friend in the best circles, where, for the most part, they wished me well, and pardoned many a little irregularity, to which, nevertheless, my friend, though kindly enough, used to call my attention.

But that I might experience symbolically how much one, even in externals, has to adapt one's self to society, and direct one's self according to it, I was compelled to something which seemed to me the most disagreeable thing in the world. I had really very fine hair; but my Strasburg hair-dresser at once assured me that it was cut much too short behind, and that it would be impossible to make a *frizure* of it in which I could show myself, since nothing but a few short curls in front were decreed lawful; and all the rest, from the crown, must be tied up in a cue or a hair-bag. Nothing was left but to put up with false hair till the natural growth was again restored according to the demands of the time. He promised me that nobody should ever remark this innocent deception (against which I objected at first very earnestly), if I could resolve upon it immediately. He kept his word, and I was always looked upon as the young man who had the best and the best-dressed head of hair. But as I was obliged to remain thus propped up and powdered from early morning, and at the same time to take care not to betray my false ornament by heating myself or by violent motions, this restraint in fact contributed much to my behaving for a time more quietly and politely, and accustomed me to going with my hat under my arm, and consequently in shoes and stockings also; however I did not venture to neglect wearing understockings of fine leather, as a defence against the Rhine gnats, which, on the fine summer evenings, generally spread themselves over the meadows and gardens. Under these circumstances, violent bodily motion being denied me, our social conversations grew more and more animated and impassioned; indeed, they were the most interesting in which I had hitherto ever borne part.

With my way of feeling and thinking, it cost me nothing to let every one pass for what he was, — nay, for that which he wished to pass for; and thus the frankness of a fresh, youthful heart, which manifested itself almost for the first time in its full bloom, made me many friends and adherents. Our company of boarders increased to about twenty persons; and, as Salzmann kept up his accustomed order, everything continued in its old routine, — nay, the conversation was almost more decorous, as every one had to be on his guard before several. Among the newcomers was a man who particularly interested me: his name was Jung, the same who afterward became known under the name of Stilling. In spite of an antiquated dress, his form had something delicate about it, with a certain sturdiness. A bag-wig did not disfigure his significant and pleasing countenance. His voice was mild, without being soft and weak: it became even melodious and powerful as soon as his ardour was roused, which was very easily done. On becoming better acquainted with him, one found in him a sound common sense, which rested on feeling, and therefore took its tone from the affections and passions; and from this very feeling sprang an enthusiasm for the good, the true, and the just, in the greatest possible purity. For the course of this man's life had been very simple, and yet crowded with events and with manifold activity. The element of his energy was indestructible faith in God, and in an assistance flowing immediately from him, which evidently manifested

itself in an uninterrupted providence, and in an unfail-
ing deliverance out of all troubles and from every evil.
Jung had made many such experiences in his life, and
they had often been repeated of late in Strasburg: so
that, with the greatest cheerfulness, he led a life frugal
indeed, but free from care, and devoted himself most
earnestly to his studies; although he could not reckon
upon any certain subsistence from one quarter to
another. In his youth, when on a fair way to become a charcoal-burner, he took up the trade of a
tailor; and after he had instructed himself, at the
same time, in higher matters, his knowledge-loving mind
drove him to the occupation of schoolmaster. This
attempt failed; and he returned to his trade, from
which, however, since every one felt for him confidence and affection, he was repeatedly called away,
again to take a place as private tutor. But for his
most internal and peculiar training he had to thank
that wide-spread class of men who sought out their
salvation on their own responsibility, and who, while
they strove to edify themselves by reading the Scriptures and good books, and by mutual exhortation and
confession, thereby attained a degree of cultivation
which must excite surprise. For while the interest
which always accompanied them and which maintained them in fellowship rested on the simplest foundation of morality, well-wishing and well-doing, the
deviations which could take place with men of such
limited circumstances were of little importance; and
hence their consciences, for the most part, remained
clear, and their minds commonly cheerful: so there
arose no artificial, but a truly natural, culture, which
had yet this advantage over others, that it was suitable
to all ages and ranks, and was generally social by its
nature. For this reason, too, these persons were, in
their own circle, truly eloquent, and capable of expressing themselves appropriately and pleasingly on all the

tenderest and best concerns of the heart. Now, good Jung was in this very case. Among a few persons, who, if not exactly like-minded with himself, did not declare themselves averse from his mode of thought, he was found, not only talkative but eloquent: in particular, he related the history of his life in the most delightful manner, and knew how to make all the circumstances plainly and vividly present to his listeners. I persuaded him to write them down, and he promised to do so. But because, in his way of expressing himself, he was like a somnambulist, who must not be called by name lest he should fall from his elevation, or like a gentle stream, to which one dare oppose nothing lest it should foam, he was often constrained to feel uncomfortable in a more numerous company. His faith tolerated no doubt, and his conviction no jest. While in friendly communication he was inexhaustible, everything came to a standstill with him when he met with contradiction. I usually helped him through on such occasions, for which he repaid me with honest affection. Since his mode of thought was nothing strange to me, but on the contrary I had already become accurately acquainted with it in my very best friends of both sexes; and since, moreover, it generally interested me with its naturalness and *naïveté*, — he found himself on the very best terms with me. The bent of his intellect was pleasing to me; nor did I meddle with his faith in miracles, which was so useful to him. Salzmann likewise behaved toward him with forbearance, — I say with forbearance, for Salzmann, in conformity with his character, his natural disposition, his age and circumstances, could not but stand and continue on the side of the rational, or rather the common-sense, Christians, whose religion properly rested on the rectitude of their characters, and a manly independence, and who therefore did not like to meddle or have anything to do with feelings which might easily have led them into gloom, or with mysticism, which might easily have led them into the dark. This class, too, was respectable and numerous: all men of honour and capacity understood each other, and were of the like persuasion, as well as of the same mode of life.

Lerse, likewise our fellow boarder, also belonged to this number: a perfectly upright young man, and, with limited gifts of fortune, frugal and exact. His manner of life and housekeeping was the closest I ever knew among students. He was, of us all, the most neatly dressed, and yet always appeared in the same clothes; but he managed his wardrobe with the greatest care, kept everything about him clean, and required all things in ordinary life to go according to his example. He never happened to lean anywhere, or to prop his elbow on the table; he never forgot to mark his table-napkin; and the maid always had a bad time of it when the chairs were not found perfectly clean. With all this, he had nothing stiff in his exterior. He spoke cordially, with precise and dry liveliness, in which a light ironical joke was very becoming. In figure he was well built, slender, and of fair height: his face was pock-pitted and homely, his little blue eyes cheerful and penetrating. As he had cause to tutor us in so many respects, we let him be our fencing-master besides, for he drew a very fine rapier; and it seemed to give him sport to play off upon us, on this occasion, all the pedantry of this profession. Moreover, we really profited by him, and had to thank him for many sociable hours, which he induced us to spend in good exercise and practice.

By all these peculiarities, Lerse completely qualified himself for the office of arbitrator and umpire in all the small and great quarrels which happened, though but rarely, in our circle, and which Salzmann could not hush up in his fatherly way. Without the external forms, which do so much mischief in universities, we represented a society bound together by circumstances and good feeling, which others might occasionally touch, but into which they could not intrude. Now, in his judgment of internal piques, Lerse always showed the greatest impartiality ; and, when the affair could no longer be settled by words and explanations, he knew how to conduct the desired satisfaction, in an honourable way, to a harmless issue. In this no man was more clever than he : indeed, he often used to say, that since heaven had destined him for a hero neither in war nor in love, he would be content, both in romances and fighting, with the part of second. Since he remained the same throughout, and might be regarded as a true model of a good and steady disposition, the conception of him stamped itself as deeply as amiably upon me ; and, when I wrote " Götz von Berlichingen," I felt myself induced to set up a memorial of our friendship, and to give the gallant fellow, who knew how to subordinate himself in so dignified a manner, the name of Franz Lerse.

While, by his constant humourous dryness, he continued ever to remind us of what one owed to one's self and to others, and how one ought to behave in order to live at peace with men as long as possible, and thus gain a certain position toward them, I had to fight, both inwardly and outwardly, with quite different circumstances and adversaries, being at strife with myself, with the objects around me, and even with the elements. I was then in a state of health which furthered me sufficiently in all that I would and should undertake; only there was a certain irritability left behind, which did not always let me be in equilibrium. A loud sound was disagreeable to me, diseased objects awakened in me loathing and horror. But I was especially troubled with a giddiness which came over me every time I looked down from a height. All these

infirmities I tried to remedy, and, indeed, as I wished
to lose no time, in a somewhat violent way. In the
evening, when they beat the tattoo, I went near the
multitude of drums, the powerful rolling and beating
of which might have made one's heart burst in one's
bosom. All alone I ascended the highest pinnacle of
the minster spire, and sat in what is called the neck,
under the nob or crown, for a quarter of an hour, before I would venture to step out again into the open
air, where, standing upon a platform scarce an ell
square, without any particular holding, one sees the
boundless prospect before; while the nearest objects
and ornaments conceal the church, and everything upon
and above which one stands. It is exactly as if one
saw one's self carried up into the air in a balloon.
Such troublesome and painful sensations I repeated
until the impression became quite indifferent to me;
and I have since then derived great advantage from
this training, in mountain travels and geological studies,
and on great buildings, where I have vied with the
carpenters in running over the bare beams and the
cornices of the edifice, and even in Rome, where one
must run similar risks to obtain a nearer view of important works of art. Anatomy, also, was of double
value to me, as it taught me to endure the most repulsive sights, while I satisfied my thirst for knowledge.
And thus I also attended the clinical course of the
elder Doctor Ehrmann, as well as the lectures of his
son on obstetrics, with the double view of becoming
acquainted with all conditions, and of freeing myself
from all apprehension as to repulsive things. And I
have actually succeeded so far, that nothing of this
kind could ever put me out of my self-possession. But
I endeavoured to harden myself, not only against these
impressions on the senses, but also against the infec-
tions of the imagination. The awful and shuddering
impressions of the darkness in churchyards, solitary

places, churches, and chapels by night, and whatever may be connected with them, I contrived to render likewise indifferent ; and in this, also, I went so far that day and night, and every locality, were quite the same to me : so that even when, in later times, a desire came over me once more to feel in such scenes the pleasing shudder of youth, I could hardly compel this, in any degree, by calling up the strangest and most fearful images.

In my efforts to free myself from the pressure of the too gloomy and powerful, which continued to rule within me, and seemed to me sometimes as strength, sometimes as weakness, I was thoroughly assisted by that open, social, stirring manner of life, which attracted me more and more, to which I accustomed myself, and which I at last learned to enjoy with perfect freedom. It is not difficult to remark in the world, that man feels himself most freely and most perfectly rid of his own feelings when he represents to himself the faults of others, and expatiates upon them with complacent censoriousness. It is a tolerably pleasant sensation even to set ourselves above our equals by disapprobation and misrepresentation ; for which reason good society, whether it consists of few or many, is most delighted with it. But nothing equals the comfortable self-complacency, when we erect ourselves into judges of our superiors, and of those who are set over us, — of princes and statesmen, — when we find public institutions unfit and injudicious, only consider the possible and actual obstacles, and recognise neither the greatness of the invention, nor the coöperation which is to be expected from time and circumstances in every undertaking.

Whoever remembers the condition of the French kingdom, and is accurately and circumstantially acquainted with it from later writings, will easily figure to himself how, at that time, in the Alsatian semi-France, people used to talk about the king and his ministers, about the court and court favourites. These were new subjects for my love of instructing myself, and very welcome ones to my pertness and youthful conceit. I observed everything accurately, noted it down industriously ; and I now see, from the little that is left, that such accounts, although only put together on the moment, out of fables and uncertain general rumours, always have a certain value in after times, because they serve to confront and compare the secret made known at last with what was then already discovered and public, and the judgments of contemporaries, true or false, with the convictions of posterity.

Striking, and daily before the eyes of us street-loungers, was the project for beautifying the city ; the execution of which, according to draughts and plans, began in the strangest fashion to pass from sketches and plans into reality. Intendant Gayot had undertaken to new-model the angular and uneven lanes of Strasburg, and to lay the foundations of a respectable, handsome city, regulated by line and level. Upon this, Blondel, a Parisian architect, drew a plan, by which a hundred and forty householders gained in room, eighty lost, and the rest remained in their former condition. This plan accepted, but not to be put into execution at once, now, should in course of time have been approaching completion ; and, meanwhile, the city oddly enough wavered between form and formlessness. If, for instance, a crooked side of a street was to be straightened, the first man who felt disposed to build moved forward to the appointed line, perhaps, too, his next neighbour, but perhaps, also, the third or fourth resident from him ; by which projections the most awkward recesses were left, like front courtyards, before the houses in the background. They would not use force, yet without compulsion they would never have got on : on which account no man, when his house was once condemned, ventured to improve or replace anything that related to the street. All these strange accidental inconveniences gave to us rambling idlers the most welcome opportunity of practising our ridicule; of making proposals, in the manner of Behrisch, for accelerating the completion, and of constantly doubting the possibility of it, although many a newly erected handsome building should have brought us to other thoughts. How far that project was advanced by the length of time, I cannot say.

Another subject on which the Protestant Strasburgers liked to converse was the expulsion of the Jesuits. These fathers, as soon as the city had fallen to the share of the French, had made their appearance and sought a *domicilium*. But they soon extended themselves and built a magnificent college, which bordered so closely on the minster that the back of the church covered a third part of its front. It was to be a complete quadrangle, and have a garden in the middle: three sides of it were finished. It is of stone, and solid, like all the buildings of these fathers. That the Protestants were pushed hard, if not oppressed by them, lay in the plan of the society which made it a duty to restore the old religion in its whole compass. Their fall, therefore, awakened the greatest satisfaction in the opposite party; and people saw, not without pleasure, how they sold their wines, carried away their books: and the building was assigned to another, perhaps less active, order. How glad are men when they get rid of an opponent, or only of a guardian! and the herd does not reflect, that, where there is no dog, it is exposed to wolves.

Now, since every city must have its tragedy, at which children and children's children shudder; so in Strasburg frequent mention was made of the unfortunate Prætor Klingling, who, after he had mounted the highest step of earthly felicity, ruled city and country with almost absolute power, and enjoyed all that

wealth, rank, and influence could afford, had at last
lost the favour of the court, and was dragged up to
answer for all in which he had been indulged hitherto,
— nay, was even thrown into prison, where, more than
seventy years old, he died an ambiguous death.

This and other tales, that knight of St. Louis, our
fellow boarder, knew how to tell with passion and animation; for which reason I was fond of accompanying
him in his walks, unlike the others, who avoided such
invitations, and left me alone with him. As with new
acquaintances I generally took my ease for a long time
without thinking much about them or the effect which
they were exercising upon me, so I only remarked
gradually that his stories and opinions rather unsettled
and confused than instructed and enlightened me. I
never knew what to make of him, although the riddle
might easily have been solved. He belonged to the
many to whom life offers no results, and who, therefore, from first to last, exert themselves on individual
objects. Unfortunately he had with this a decided
desire, nay, even passion, for meditating, without having any capacity for thinking; and in such men a
particular notion easily fixes itself fast, which may be
regarded as a mental disease. To such a fixed view
he always came back again, and was thus in the long
run excessively tiresome. He would bitterly complain
of the decline of his memory, especially with regard to
the latest events, and maintained, by a logic of his own,
that all virtue springs from a good memory, and all
vice, on the contrary, from forgetfulness. This doctrine
he contrived to carry out with much acuteness; as, indeed, anything may be maintained when one has no
compunction to use words altogether vaguely, and to
employ and apply them in a sense now wider, now
narrower, now closer, now more remote.

At first it was amusing to hear him; nay, his per-
suasiveness even astonished us. We fancied we were

standing before a rhetorical sophist, who for jest and practice knew how to give a fair appearance to the strangest things. Unfortunately this first impression became blunted but too soon; for at the end of every discourse, manage the thing as I would, the man came back again to the same theme. He was not to be held fast to older events, although they interested him, — although he had them present to his mind with their minutest circumstances. Indeed, he was often, by a small circumstance, snatched out of the middle of a wild historical narrative, and thrust into his detestable favourite thought.

One of our afternoon walks was particularly unfortunate in this respect: the account of it may stand here instead of similar cases, which might weary if not vex the reader.

On the way through the city we were met by an old female mendicant, who, by her beggings and importunities, disturbed him in his story. "Pack yourself off, old witch!" said he, and walked by. She shouted after him the well-known retort, — only somewhat changed, since she saw well that the unfriendly man was old himself, — "If you did not wish to be old, you should have had yourself hanged in your youth!" He turned round violently, and I feared a scene. "Hanged," cried he, "have myself hanged! No: that could not have been, — I was too honest a fellow for that; but hang myself — hang up my own self — that is true — that I should have done: I should have turned a charge of powder against myself, that I might not live to see that I am not even worth that any more." The woman stood as if petrified; but he continued, "You have said a great truth, witch-mother; and, as they have neither drowned nor burned you yet, you shall be paid for your proverb." He handed her a *Büsel*, a coin not usually given to a beggar.

We had crossed over the first Rhine-bridge, and

were going to the inn where we meant to stop; and I was trying to lead him back to our previous conversation, when, unexpectedly, a very pretty girl met us on the pleasant foot-path, remained standing before us, bowed prettily, and cried, " Eh, eh, captain, where are you going?" and whatever else is usually said on such an occasion. " Mademoiselle," replied he, somewhat embarrassed, " I know not — " " How?" said she, with graceful astonishment, " do you forget your friends so soon?" The word " forget" fretted him: he shook his head and replied, peevishly enough, " Truly, mademoiselle, I did not know — " She now retorted with some humour, yet very temperately, " Take care, captain: I may mistake you another time!" And so she hurried past, taking huge strides, without looking round. At once my fellow traveller struck his forehead with both his fists: " Oh, what an ass I am!" exclaimed he, " what an old ass I am! Now, you see whether I am right or not." And then, in a very violent manner, he went on with his usual sayings and opinions, in which this case still more confirmed him. I cannot and would not repeat what a philippic discourse he held against himself. At last he turned to me, and said, " I call you to witness! You remember that small-ware woman at the corner, who is neither young nor pretty? I salute her every time we pass, and often exchange a couple of friendly words with her; and yet it is thirty years ago since she was gracious to me. But now I swear it is not four weeks since this young lady showed herself more complaisant to me than was reasonable; and yet I will not recognise her, but insult her in return for her favours! Do I not always say, that ingratitude is the greatest of vices, and no man would be ungrateful if he were not forgetful?"

We went into the inn; and nothing but the tippling, swarming crowd in the anterooms stopped the invectives which he rattled off against himself and his contemporaries. He was silent, and I hoped pacified, when we stepped into an upper chamber, where we found a young man pacing up and down alone, whom the captain saluted by name. I was pleased to become acquainted with him; for the old fellow had said much good of him to me, and had told me that this young man, being employed in the war-bureau, had often disinterestedly done him very good service when the pensions were stopped. I was glad that the conversation took a general turn; and, while we were carrying it on, we drank a bottle of wine. But here, unluckily, another infirmity which my knight had in common with obstinate men developed itself. For as, on the whole, he could not get rid of that fixed notion; so did he stick fast to a disagreeable impression of the moment, and suffer his feelings to run on without moderation. His last vexation about himself had not yet died away; and now was added something new, although of quite a different kind. He had not long cast his eyes here and there before he noticed on the table a double portion of coffee, and two cups, and might besides, being a man of gallantry, have traced some other indication that the young man had not been so solitary all the time. And scarcely had the conjecture arisen in his mind, and ripened into a probability that the pretty girl had been paying a visit here, than the most outrageous jealousy added itself to that first vexation, so as completely to perplex him.

Now, before I could suspect anything, — for I had hitherto been conversing quite harmlessly with the young man, — the captain, in an unpleasant tone, which I well knew, began to be satirical about the pair of cups, and about this and that. The young man, surprised, tried to turn it off pleasantly and sensibly, as is the custom among men of good breeding: but the old fellow continued to be unmercifully rude; so that there was nothing left for the other to do but to seize his

hat and cane, and at his departure to leave behind him
a pretty unequivocal challenge. The fury of the captain now burst out the more vehemently, as he had
in the interim drunk another bottle of wine almost
by himself. He struck the table with his fist, and
cried more than once, "I will strike him dead!" It
was not, however, meant quite so badly as it sounded;
for he often used this phrase when any one opposed or
otherwise displeased him. Just as unexpectedly the
business grew worse on our return; for I had the want
of foresight to represent to him his ingratitude toward
the young man, and to remind him how strongly he
had praised to me the ready obligingness of this official person. No! such rage of a man against himself
I never saw again: it was the most passionate conclusion to that beginning to which the pretty girl had
given occasion. Here I saw sorrow and repentance
carried into caricature, and, as all passion supplies the
place of genius, to a point really genius-like. He then
went over all the incidents of our afternoon ramble
again, employed them rhetorically for his own self-
reproach, brought up the old witch at last before him
once more, and perplexed himself to such a degree, that
I could not help fearing he would throw himself into
the Rhine. Could I have been sure of fishing him
out again quickly, like Mentor his Telemachus, he
might have made the leap; and I should have brought
him home cooled down for this occasion.

I immediately confided the affair to Lerse; and we
went the next morning to the young man, whom my
friend in his dry way set laughing. We agreed to
bring about an accidental meeting, where a reconciliation should take place of itself. The drollest thing
about it was, that this time the captain, too, had
slept off his rudeness, and found himself ready to
apologise to the young man, to whom petty quarrels
were of some consequence. All was arranged in one

morning; and, as the affair had not been kept quite secret, I did not escape the jokes of my friends, who might have foretold me, from their own experience, how troublesome the friendship of the captain could become upon occasion.

But now, while I am thinking what should be imparted next, there comes again into my thoughts, by a strange play of memory, that reverend minsterbuilding, to which in those days I devoted particular attention, and which, in general, constantly presents itself to the eye, both in the city and in the country.

The more I considered the façade, the more was that first impression strengthened and developed, that here the sublime has entered into alliance with the pleasing. If the vast, when it appears as a mass before us, is not to terrify; if it is not to confuse, when we seek to investigate its details, — it must enter into an unnatural, apparently impossible, connection, it must associate to itself the pleasing. But now, since it will be impossible for us to speak of the impression of the minster except by considering both these incompatible qualities as united, so do we already see, from this, in what high value we must hold this ancient monument; and we begin in earnest to describe how such contradictory elements could peaceably interpenetrate and unite themselves.

First of all, without thinking of the towers, we devote our considerations to the façade alone, which powerfully strikes the eye as an upright, oblong parallelogram. If we approach it at twilight, in the moonshine, on a starlight night, when the parts appear more or less indistinct and at last disappear, we see only a colossal wall, the height of which bears an advantageous proportion to the breadth. If we view it by day, and by the power of the mind abstract from the details, we recognise the front of a building which not only encloses the space within, but also covers much in its vicinity. The openings of this monstrous surface point to internal necessities, and according to these we can at once divide it into nine compartments. The great middle door, which opens into the nave of the church, first meets the eye. On both sides of it lie two smaller ones, belonging to the cross-ways. Over the chief door our glance falls upon the wheel-shaped window, which is to spread an awe-inspiring light within the church and its vaulted arches. At its sides appear two large, perpendicular, oblong openings, which form a striking contrast with the middle one, and indicate that they belong to the base of the rising towers. In the third story are three openings in a row, which are designed for belfries and other church necessities. Above them one sees the whole horizontally closed by the balustrade of the gallery, instead of a cornice. These nine spaces described are supported, enclosed, and separated into three great perpendicular divisions by four pillars rising up from the ground.

Now, as it cannot be denied that there is in the whole mass a fine proportion of height to breadth, so also in the details it maintains a somewhat uniform lightness by means of these pillars and the narrow compartments between them.

But if we adhere to our abstraction, and imagine to ourselves this immense wall without ornaments, with firm buttresses, with the necessary openings in it, but only so far as necessity requires them, we even then must allow that these chief divisions are in good proportion : thus the whole will appear solemn and noble indeed, but always heavily unpleasant, and, being without ornament, unartistical. For a work of art, the whole of which is conceived in great, simple, harmonious parts, makes indeed a noble and dignified impression ; but the peculiar enjoyment which the pleasing produces can only find place in the consonance of all developed details.

And it is precisely here that the building we are examining satisfies us in the highest degree, for we see all the ornaments fully suited to every part which they adorn : they are subordinate to it, they seem to have grown out of it. Such a manifoldness always gives great pleasure, since it flows of its own accord from the suitable, and therefore at the same time awakens the feeling of unity. It is only in such cases that the execution is prized as the summit of art.

By such means, now, was a solid piece of masonry, an impenetrable wall, which had moreover to announce itself as the base of two heaven-high towers, made to appear to the eye as if resting on itself, consisting in itself, but at the same time light and adorned, and, though pierced through in a thousand places, to give the idea of indestructible firmness.

This riddle is solved in the happiest manner. The openings in the wall, its solid parts, the pillars, everything has its peculiar character, which proceeds from its particular destination : this communicates itself by degrees to the subdivisions ; hence everything is adorned in proportionate taste, the great as well as the small is in the right place, and can be easily comprehended, and thus the pleasing presents itself in the vast. I would refer only to the doors sinking in perspective into the thickness of the wall, and adorned without end in their columns and pointed arches ; to the window with its rose springing out of the round form ; to the outline of its framework, as well as to the slender reed-like pillars of the perpendicular compartments. Let one represent to himself the pillars retreating step by step, accompanied by little, slender, light-pillared, pointed structures, likewise striving upward, and furnished with canopies to shelter the images of the saints, and how at last every rib, every boss, seems like a flower-head and row of leaves, or some other natural object transformed into stone. ' One may compare, if not the building itself, yet representations of the whole and of its parts, for the purpose of reviewing and giving life to what I have said. It may seem exaggerated to many; for I myself, though transported into love for this work at first sight, required a long time to make myself intimately acquainted with its value.

Having grown up among those who found fault with Gothic architecture, I cherished my aversion from the abundantly overloaded, complicated ornaments which, by their capriciousness, made a religious, gloomy character highly adverse. I strengthened myself in this repugnance, since I had only met with spiritless works of this kind, in which one could perceive neither good proportions nor a pure consistency. But here I thought I saw a new revelation of it, since what was objectionable by no means appeared, but the contrary opinion rather forced itself upon my mind.

But the longer I looked and considered, I all the while thought I discovered yet greater merits beyond that which I have already mentioned. The right proportion of the larger divisions, the ornamental, as judicious as rich, even to the minutest, were found out; but now I recognised the connection of these manifold ornaments amongst each other, the transition from one leading part to another, the enclosing of details, homogeneous indeed, but yet greatly varying in form, from the saint to the monster, from the leaf to the dental. The more I investigated, the more I was astonished; the more I amused and wearied myself with measuring and drawing, so much the more did my attachment increase, so that I spent much time, partly in studying what actually existed, partly in restoring, in my mind and on paper, what was wanting and unfinished, especially in the towers.

Finding that this building had been based on old German ground, and grown thus far in genuine German times, and that the name of the master, on his modest gravestone, was likewise of native sound and origin, I ventured, being incited by the worth of this work of art, to change the hitherto decried appellation of " Gothic architecture," and to claim it for our nation as "German architecture;" nor did I fail to bring my patriotic views to light, first orally, and afterward in a little treatise dedicated to the memory of Ervinus a Steinbach.

If my biographical narrative should come down to the epoch when the said sheet appeared in print, which Herder afterward inserted in his pamphlet, "Von Deutscher Art und Kunst" ("Of German Manner and Art"), much more will be said on this weighty subject. But, before I turn from it this time, I will take the opportunity to vindicate the motto prefixed to the present volume with those who may have entertained some doubt about it. I know indeed very well, that in opposition to this honest, hopeful old German saying, " Of whatever one wishes in youth, he has abundance in old age," many would quote contrary experience, and many trifling comments might be made; but much, also, is to be said in its favour: and I will explain how I understand it.

Our wishes are presentiments of the capabilities which lie within us, and harbingers of that which we shall be in a condition to perform. Whatever we are able and would like to do, presents itself to our imagination, as without us and in the future. We feel a longing after that which we already possess in secret. Thus a passionate anticipating grasp changes the truly possible into a dreamed reality. Now, if such a bias lies decidedly in our nature, then, with every step of our development will a part of the first wish be fulfilled, — under favourable circumstances in the direct way, under unfavourable in the circuitous way, from which we always come back again to the other. Thus we see men by perseverance attain to earthly wealth. They surround themselves with riches, splendour, and external honour. Others strive yet more certainly after intellectual advantages, acquire for themselves a clear survey of things, a peacefulness of mind, and a certainty for the present and the future.

But now there is a third direction, which is compounded of both, and the issue of which must be the most surely successful. When a man's youth falls into a pregnant time ; when production overweighs destruction, and a presentiment is early awakened within him as to what such an epoch demands and promises, — he will then, being forced by outward inducements into an active interest, take hold now here, now there, and the wish to be active on many sides will be lively within him. But so many accidental hinderances are associated with human limitation, that here a thing, once begun, remains unfinished : there that which is already grasped falls out of the hand, and one wish after another is dissipated. But had these wishes sprung out of a pure heart, and in conformity with the necessities of the times, one might composedly let them lie and fall right and left, and be assured that these must not only be found out and picked up again, but that also many kindred things, which one has never touched and never even thought of, will come to light. If, now, during our own lifetime, we see that performed by others, for which we ourselves felt an earlier call, but had been obliged to give it up, with much besides, then the beautiful feeling enters the mind that only mankind combined is the true man, and that the individual can only be joyous and happy when he has the courage to feel himself in the whole.

This contemplation is here in the right place; for when I reflect on the affection which drew me to these antique edifices, when I reckon up the time which I devoted to the Strasburg minster alone, the attention

with which I afterward examined the cathedral at
Cologne, and that at Freiburg, and more and more felt
the value of these buildings, I could even blame myself
for having afterward lost sight of them altogether, —
nay, for having left them completely in the background,
being attracted by a more developed art. But when
now, in the latest times, I see attention again turned to
those objects; when I see affection, and even passion,
for them appearing and flourishing; when I see able
young persons seized with this passion, recklessly devoting powers, time, care, and property to these memo-
rials of a past world, — then am I reminded with
pleasure that what I formerly would and wished had a
value. With satisfaction I see that they not only
know how to prize what was done by our forefathers,
but that, from existing unfinished beginnings, they try
to represent, in pictures at least, the original design, so
as thus to make us acquainted with the thought, which
is ever the beginning and end of all undertakings; and
that they strive with considerate zeal to clear up and
vivify what seems to be a confused past. Here I especially applaud the brave Sulpiz Boisserée, who is
indefatigably employed in a magnificent series of
copperplates to exhibit the cathedral of Cologne as the
model of those vast conceptions, the spirit of which,
like that of Babel, strove up to heaven, and which were
so out of proportion to earthly means that they were
necessarily stopped fast in their execution. If we have
been hitherto astonished that such buildings proceeded
only so far, we shall learn with the greatest admiration
what was really designed to be done.

Would that literary-artistical undertakings of this
kind were duly patronised by all who have power,
wealth, and influence; that the great and gigantic
views of our forefathers may be presented to our contemplation; and that we may be able to form a
conception of what they dared to desire. The insight

resulting from this will not remain fruitless ; and the judgment will, for once at least, be in a condition to exercise itself on these works with justice. Nay, this will be done most thoroughly if our active young friend, besides the monograph devoted to the cathedral of Cologne, follows out in detail the history of our mediæval architecture. When whatever is to be known about the practical exercise of this art is further brought to light, when the art is represented in all its fundamental features by a comparison with the Græco-Roman and the Oriental Egyptian, little can remain to be done in this department. And I, when the results of such patriotic labours lie before the world, as they are now known in friendly private communications, shall be able, with true content, to repeat that motto in its best sense, " Of whatever one wishes in youth, he will have enough in old age."

But if, in operations like these, which belong to centuries, one can trust one's self to time, and wait for opportunity, there are, on the contrary, other things which in youth must be enjoyed at once, fresh, like ripe fruits. Let me be permitted, with this sudden turn, to mention dancing, of which the ear is reminded, as the eye is of the minster, every day and every hour in Strasburg and all Alsace. From early youth my father himself had given my sister and me instruction in dancing, a task which must have comported strangely enough with so stern a man. But he did not suffer his composure to be put out by it : he drilled us in the positions and steps in a manner the most precise ; and, when he had brought us far enough to dance a minuet, he played for us something easily intelligible in three-four time, on a *flute-douce*, and we moved to it as well as we could. On the French theatre, likewise, I had seen from my youth upwards, if not ballets, yet *pas seuls* and *pas de deux*, and had noticed in them various strange motions of the feet, and all sorts of springs.

When we had had enough of the minuet, I requested
my father to play some other dance-music, of which
our music-books, in their jigs and murkies,[1] offered us
a rich supply; and I immediately found out, of myself,
the steps and other motions for them, the time being
quite suitable to my limbs, and, as it were, born with
them. This pleased my father to a certain degree;
indeed, he often, by way of joke for himself and us, let
the "monkies" dance in this way. After my misfortune with Gretchen, and during the whole of my residence in Leipzig, I did not make my appearance again
on the floor: on the contrary, I still remember, that
when, at a ball, they forced me into a minuet, both
measure and motion seemed to have abandoned my
limbs, and I could no longer remember either the steps
or the figures; so that I should have been put to disgrace and shame if the greater part of the spectators
had not maintained that my awkward behaviour was
pure obstinacy, assumed with the view of depriving the
ladies of all desire to invite me and draw me into their
circle against my will.

During my residence in Frankfort I was quite cut
off from such pleasures; but in Strasburg, with other
enjoyments of life, there soon arose in my limbs the
faculty of keeping time. On Sundays and week-days
one sauntered by no pleasure-ground without finding
there a joyous crowd assembled for the dance, and for
the most part revolving in the circle. Moreover, there
were private balls in the country houses; and people
were already talking of the brilliant masquerades of
the coming winter. Here, indeed, I should have been
out of my place, and useless to the company, when a
friend, who waltzed very well, advised me to practise
myself first in parties of a lower rank, so that afterward

[1] A "murki" is defined as an old species of short composition
for the harpsichord, with a lively murmuring accompaniment in
the bass. — TRANS.

I might be worth something in the highest. He took me to a dancing-master, who was well known for his skill. This man promised me, that, when I had in some degree repeated the first elements and made myself master of them, he would then lead me farther. He was one of your dry, ready French characters, and received me in a friendly manner. I paid him a month in advance, and received twelve tickets, for which he agreed to give me certain hours' instruction. The man was strict and precise, but not pedantic; and, as I already had some previous practice, I soon gave him satisfaction, and received his commendation.

One circumstance, however, greatly facilitated the instruction of this teacher: he had two daughters, both pretty, and both not yet twenty. Having been instructed in this art from their youth upward, they showed themselves very skilful, and might have been able, as partners, soon to help even the most clumsy scholars into some cultivation. They were both very polite, spoke nothing but French; and I, on my part, did my best, that I might not appear awkward or ridiculous before them. I had the good fortune that they likewise praised me, and were always willing to dance a minuet to their father's little violin, and, what indeed was more difficult for them, to initiate me by degrees into waltzing and whirling. Their father did not seem to have many customers, and they led a lonely life. For this reason they often asked me to remain with them after my hour, and to chat away the time a little, which I the more willingly did, as the younger one pleased me well; and generally they both altogether behaved very becomingly. I often read aloud something from a novel, and they did the same. The elder, who was as handsome as, perhaps even handsomer than, the second, but who did not correspond with my taste so well as the latter, always conducted herself toward me more obligingly, and more kindly in every respect. She was always at hand during the lesson, and often protracted it: hence I sometimes thought myself bound to offer back a couple of tickets to her father, which, however, he did not accept. The younger, on the contrary, although never showing me any ill will, was more reserved, and waited till she was called by her father before she relieved the elder.

The cause of this became manifest to me one evening; for when, after the dance was done, I was about to go into the sitting-room with the elder, she held me back, and said, "Let us remain here a little longer; for I will confess to you that my sister has with her a woman who tells fortunes from cards, and who is to reveal to her how matters stand with an absent lover, on whom her whole heart hangs, and upon whom she has placed all her hope. Mine is free," she continued, "and I must accustom myself to see it despised." I thereupon said sundry pretty things to her, replying that she could at once convince herself on that point by consulting the wise woman likewise; that I would do so myself, for I had long wished to learn something of the kind, but lacked faith. She blamed me for this, and assured me that nothing in the world was surer than the responses of this oracle; only it must be consulted, not out of sport and mischief, but solely in real affairs. However, I at last compelled her to go with me into that room, as soon as she had ascertained that the consultation was over. We found her sister in a very cheerful humour: and even toward me she was kinder than usual, sportive, and almost witty; for, since she seemed to be secure of an absent friend, she may have thought it no treachery to be a little gracious with a present friend of her sister's, which she thought me to be. The old woman was now flattered, and good payment was promised her if she would tell the truth to the elder sister and to me. With the usual preparations and ceremonies she began her business, in order to tell the fair one's fortune first. She carefully considered the situation of the cards, but seemed to hesitate, and would not speak out what she had to say. " I see now," said the younger, who was already better acquainted with the interpretation of such a magic tablet, " you hesitate, and do not wish to disclose anything disagreeable to my sister; but that is a cursed card!" The elder one turned pale, but composed herself, and said, " Only speak out: it will not cost one's head!" The old woman, after a deep sigh, showed her that she was in love; that she was not beloved; that another person stood in the way; and other things of like import. We saw the good girl's embarrassment. The old woman thought somewhat to improve the affair by giving hopes of letters and money. " Letters," said the lovely child, " I do not expect; and money I do not desire. If it is true, as you say, that I love, I deserve a heart that loves me in return." " Let us see if it will not be better," replied the old woman, as she shuffled the cards and laid them out a second time; but before the eyes of all of us it had only become still worse. The fair one stood, not only more lonely, but surrounded with many sorrows. Her lover had moved somewhat farther, and the intervening figures nearer. The old woman wished to try it a third time, in hopes of a better prospect; but the beautiful girl could restrain herself no longer, — she broke out into uncontrollable weeping, her lovely bosom heaved violently, she turned round, and rushed out of the room. I knew not what to do. Inclination kept me with the one present: compassion drove me to the other. My situation was painful enough. " Comfort Lucinda," said the younger: " go after her." I hesitated. How could I comfort her without at least assuring her of some sort of affection? and could I do that at such a

moment in a cool, moderate manner? "Let us go together," said I to Emilia. "I know not whether my
presence will do her good," replied she. Yet we went,
but found the door bolted. Lucinda made no answer,
we might knock, shout, entreat, as we would. "We
must let her have her own way," said Emilia: "she
will not have it otherwise now." And, indeed, when
I called to my mind her manner from our very first
acquaintance, she always had something violent and
unequal about her, and chiefly showed her affection
for me by not behaving to me with rudeness. What
was I to do? I paid the old woman richly for the
mischief she had caused, and was about to go, when
Emilia said, "I stipulate that the cards shall now be
cut for you too." The old woman was ready. "Do
not let me be present," cried I, and hastened down-
stairs.

The next day I had not courage to go there. The
third day, early in the morning, Emilia sent me word
by a boy, — who had already brought me many a mes-
sage from the sisters, and had carried back flowers and
fruits to them in return, — that I should not fail that
day. I came at the usual hour, and found the father
alone, who, in many respects, improved my paces and
steps, my goings and comings, my bearing and behaviour, and, moreover, seemed to be satisfied with
me. The younger daughter came in toward the end
of the hour, and danced with me a very graceful
minuet, in which her movements were extraordinarily
pleasing, and her father declared that he had rarely
seen a prettier and more nimble pair upon his floor.
After the lesson, I went as usual into the sitting-room;
the father left us alone; I missed Lucinda. "She is
in bed," said Emilia, "and I am glad of it: do not
be concerned about it. Her mental illness is first
alleviated when she fancies herself bodily sick: she
does not like to die, and therefore she then does what

we wish. We have certain family medicines which she takes, and reposes; and thus, by degrees, the swelling waves subside. She is indeed too good and amiable in such an imaginary sickness; and as she is in reality very well, and is only attacked by passion, she imagines various kinds of romantic deaths, with which she frightens herself in a pleasant manner, like children when we tell them ghost-stories. Thus, only last night, she announced to me with great vehemence, that this time she should certainly die; and that only when she was really near death, they should bring again before her the ungrateful, false friend, who had at first acted so handsomely to her, and now treated her so ill; she would reproach him bitterly, and then give up the ghost." "I know not that I am guilty," exclaimed I, "of having expressed any sort of affection for her. I know somebody who can best bear me witness in this respect." Emilia smiled, and rejoined, "I understand you; and, if we are not discreet and determined, we shall all find ourselves in a bad plight together. What will you say if I entreat you not to continue your lessons? You have, I believe, four tickets yet of the last month: and my father has already declared that he finds it inexcusable to take your money any longer, unless you wish to devote yourself to the art of dancing in a more serious manner; what is required by a young man of the world you possess already." "And do you, Emilia, give me this advice, to avoid your house?" replied I. "Yes, I do," said she, "but not of myself. Only listen! When you hastened away, the day before yesterday, I had the cards cut for you; and the same response was repeated thrice, and each time more emphatically. You were surrounded by everything good and pleasing, by friends and great lords; and there was no lack of money. The ladies kept themselves at some distance. My poor sister in particular stood always the farthest off: one other advanced constantly nearer to you, but never came up to your side; for a third person, of the male sex, always came between. I will confess to you that I thought that I myself was meant by the second lady, and after this confession you will best comprehend my well-meant counsel. To an absent friend I have promised my heart and my hand; and, until now, I loved him above all: yet it might be possible for your presence to become more important to me than hitherto; and what kind of a situation would you have between two sisters, one of whom you had made unhappy by your affection, and the other by your coldness, and all this ado about nothing and only for a short time? For, if we had not known already who you are and what are your expectations, the cards would have placed it before my eyes in the clearest manner. Fare you well!" said she, and gave me her hand. I hesitated. "Now," said she, leading me toward the door, "that it may really be the last time that we shall speak to each other, take what I would otherwise have denied you." She fell upon my neck, and kissed me most tenderly. I embraced her, and pressed her to my bosom.

At this moment the side-door flew open; and her sister, in a light but becoming night-dress, rushed out and cried, "You shall not be the only one to take leave of him!" Emilia let me go; and Lucinda seized me, clung close to my heart, pressed her black locks upon my cheeks, and remained in this position for some time. And thus I found myself between the two sisters, in the dilemma Emilia had prophesied to me a moment before. Lucinda let me loose, and looked earnestly into my face. I was about to grasp her hand and say something friendly to her; but she turned herself away, walked with violent steps up and down the room for some time, and then threw herself into a corner of the sofa. Emilia went to her, but was immediately repulsed; and here began a scene which is yet painful to me in the recollection, and which, although really it had nothing theatrical about it, but was quite suitable to a lively young Frenchwoman, could only be properly repeated in the theatre by a good and feeling actress.

Lucinda overwhelmed her sister with a thousand reproaches. "This is not the first heart," she cried, "that was inclining itself to me, and that you have turned away. Was it not just so with him who is absent, and who at last betrothed himself to you under my very eyes? I was compelled to look on; I endured it; but I know how many thousand tears it has cost me. This one, too, you have now taken away from me, without letting the other go; and how many do you not manage to keep at once? I am frank and good-natured; and every one thinks he knows me soon, and may neglect me. You are secret and quiet, and people think wonders of what may be concealed behind you. Yet there is nothing behind but a cold, selfish heart that can sacrifice everything to itself; this nobody learns so easily, because it lies deeply hidden in your breast: and just as little do they know of my warm, true heart, which I carry about with me as open as my face."

Emilia was silent, and had sat down by her sister, who became constantly more and more excited in her discourse, and let certain private matters slip out, which it was not exactly proper for me to know. Emilia, on the other hand, who was trying to pacify her sister, made me a sign from behind that I should withdraw; but, as jealousy and suspicion see with a thousand eyes, Lucinda seemed to have noticed this also. She sprang up and advanced to me, but not with vehemence. She stood before me, and seemed to be thinking of something. Then she said, "I know that I have lost you: I make no further pretensions to you. But neither shall you have him, sister!" So saying, she took a thorough hold of my head, thrusting both her hands into my locks and pressing my face to hers, and kissed me repeatedly on the mouth. "Now," cried she, "fear my curse! Woe upon woe, for ever and ever, to her who kisses these lips for the first time after me! Dare to have anything more to do with him! I know Heaven hears me this time. And you, sir, hasten now, hasten away as fast as you can!"

I flew down the stairs, with the firm determination never again to enter the house.

END OF VOLUME I.

X2902X

71

041